Death So Noble

Jonathan F. Vance

Death So Noble:

Memory, Meaning, and the First World War

UBCPress / Vancouver

Printed in Canada on acid-free paper ∞

ISBN 0-7748-0601-X (hardcover)
ISBN 0-7748-0600-1 (paperback)

Canadian Cataloguing in Publication Data

Vance, Jonathan Franklin William, 1963-
    Death so noble

    Includes bibliographical references and index.
    ISBN 0-7748-0601-X (bound)
    ISBN 0-7748-0600-1 (pbk)

    1. World War, 1914-1918 – Canada. 2. World
War, 1914-1918 – Canada – Public opinion. 3. World
War, 1914-1918 – Participation, Canadian – Public
opinion. 4. Public opinion – Canada. I. Title.

D547.C2V36 1997   940.3'71   C96-910768-4

This book has been published with the help of a
grant from the Humanities and Social Sciences
Federation of Canada, using funds provided by the
Social Sciences and Humanities Research Council of
Canada.

UBC Press gratefully acknowledges the ongoing
support to its publishing program from the Canada
Council, the Province of British Columbia Cultural
Services Branch, and the Department of Communi-
cations of the Government of Canada.

UBC Press
University of British Columbia
2029 West Mall
Vancouver, BC v6t 1z2
(604) 822-3259
Fax: 1-800-668-0821
E-mail: info@ubcpress.ubc.ca
http://www.ubcpress.ubc.ca

Dedicated to

William Thomas Starr

Lance Corporal

Canadian Field Artillery

1892-1985

He came through the Great War

with body and soul intact.

Contents

Illustrations

Burning.' (William H. Wiley)

Acknowledgments

Even when I was a child growing up in the 1960s, the First World War surrounded me. Every Sunday, we would visit my grandfather, who had spent some of the best years of his life in Flanders with the Canadian Field Artillery. Above the desk in his study was a long sepia photograph of his unit, taken in Toronto in 1915 before the battery left for France. Beside it, on the bookshelf, sat a small portrait of my grandfather, looking every inch a soldier in his immaculate uniform, a swagger stick across his lap and the slightest suggestion of a satisfied smile on his face.

Had I been a less typical child, I would have realized that, even on the drive to my grandfather's house in Hamilton, the First World War was an inescapable presence in the landscape. Memorial Park and the Memorial Hall, Memorial School, the cenotaph in Gore Park, the huge German howitzer squatting sullenly in Dundurn Park, the club rooms of the Canadian Corps Association, the Cross of Sacrifice in Hamilton Cemetery – we must have passed a dozen reminders of the Great War, all in the course of a thirty-minute drive. On subsequent travels while researching this book, I came to learn that Hamilton was little different from countless other Canadian communities in this respect.

If the Sunday drives of my childhood provided the earliest inspiration for this study, many other factors have allowed it to come to fruition. The Social Sciences and Humanities Research Council provided the funding that made the research and writing possible, while the Laurier Centre for Military, Strategic, and Disarmament Studies at Wilfrid Laurier University gave me a most hospitable home through the life of the project.

At the same time, I must thank the many archivists who smoothed the way for my research, especially Charles Armour (Dalhousie University), Cheryl Avery (University of Saskatchewan), Ron Berntson (Nutana

Collegiate Institute), K.V. Bligh (House of Lords Record Office), Elise Brunet (Law Society of Upper Canada Archives), Barry Cahill (Public Archives of Nova Scotia), Colleen Dempsey (National Archives of Canada), Burt Glendenning (Public Archives of New Brunswick), George Henderson (Queen's University), Percy Johnson (McGill University), Michael Moody (Imperial War Museum), Debora Prokopchuk (University of Manitoba), Cameron Pulsifer (Canadian War Museum), Nancy Sadek (University of Guelph), Carl Spadoni (McMaster University), and Pat Townsend (Acadia University). Amy Menary and Karen Scott of Wilfrid Laurier University's library went above and beyond the call of duty in searching out obscure published sources for me. My thanks also go out to the many people who responded to my requests for assistance by sending photographs and transcriptions of their church and community war memorials and by digging into their local archives on my behalf.

I must also thank a number of friends and colleagues who have been kind enough to read and comment upon parts of this manuscript: Canon Richard Berryman, Kelly Boyd, Terry Copp, J.L. Granatstein, Norman Knowles, David Lenarcic, David Marshall, Robert Rutherdale, William H. Wiley, and Suzanne Zeller. Their suggestions and advice have made this a better book than it would have been without their assistance. At UBC Press, I received sterling guidance from Camilla Jenkins and Laura Macleod, expert editing from Barbara Tessman, and warm encouragement from Jean Wilson.

Finally, many other relatives and friends provided all forms of assistance and hospitality at various stages of the research: Raymond and Wanda Blake, Val and Ralph Carpenter, Kate and Bill Donkin, Laura Duncan, Graham Rawlinson, Daniel Robinson, Judy and Vern Shute, John Starr and Susan Markham. My parents, too, have supported this work in every conceivable manner, not the least of which has been my father's single-minded quest to photograph Canadian war memorials. At the same time, my debt to my wife, Cheryl, and my children, Gordon and Julia, goes beyond expression. They must have wondered many times why the Great War has exercised such a hold over me. I hope this book provides a partial answer.

Permission Notes

An honest attempt has been made to secure permission for all material used, and if there are errors or omissions, these are wholly unintentional and the Publisher will be grateful to learn of them.

The work of Duncan Campbell Scott is reproduced with the permission of John G. Aylen, Ottawa, Canada.

An excerpt from Alden Nowlan's 'Ypres: 1915,' in *The Mysterious Naked Man* (Toronto: Clarke, Irwin 1969) appears courtesy of Irwin Publishing.

Photography for the Canadian War Museum is by William Kent.

Excerpts from *Rilla of Ingleside* by L.M. Montgomery are reprinted with the authorization of David Macdonald and Ruth Macdonald, who are the hiers of L.M. Montgomery. *Rilla of Ingleside* is a trademark and a Canadian official mark of the Anne of Green Gables Licensing Authority, which is owned by the heirs of L.M. Montgomery and the Province of Prince Edward Island and located in Charlottetown, Prince Edward Island.

Death So Noble

Nothing is here for tears, nothing to wail
Or knock the breast; no weakness, no contempt,
Dispraise, or blame; nothing but well and fair,
And what may quiet us in a death so noble.

John Milton,
'Samson Agonistes'

Introduction

O<small>NE OF THE</small> most favourably reviewed books of 1937 was Philip Child's *God's Sparrows,* the tale of Dan Thatcher's trying journey towards self-understanding. It was also one of the last Canadian novels about the Great War to appear before the country went to battle for the second time in a generation. Child, born in Hamilton, Ontario, in 1898, had enlisted from the University of Toronto in 1917 and eventually reached the front lines as an artillery subaltern. Looking back from the late 1930s, he had this to say about the war he survived: 'The thousands went into battle not ignobly, not as driven sheep or hired murderers – in many moods doubtless – but as free men with a corporate if vague feeling of brotherhood because of a tradition they shared and an honest belief that they were doing their duty in a necessary task. He who says otherwise lies, or has forgotten.'[1] For Philip Child, the only valid memory of the war was his own. Anything else was the product of deceit or amnesia.

This book is about memory. It is about constructing a mythic version of the events of 1914-18 from a complex mixture of fact, wishful thinking, half-truth, and outright invention, and expressing that version in novel and play, in bronze and stone, in reunion and commemoration, in song and advertisement. These diverse media were used to convey the myth to those people who had not experienced the events themselves and to ensure that a certain version of the war became the intellectual property of all Canadians, not simply those who had lived through 1914-18. In this way, the myth both shaped, and was shaped by, Canadian society in the interwar years; to use Lynn Hunt's terms, the text of the myth configured the context as much as the context created the text.[2]

Readers who look to this book for new insights into specific incidents of those four years will be disappointed, because I have relatively little to say about the war itself. For this I make no apologies. Much has been written about the events of the war and their political, economic, and social dimensions, but very little on how contemporaries conceived of the war, how they represented it, and how they accommodated it into their collective consciousness in the 1920s and 1930s. In turning my attention to these matters, I began with the same assumption that Mary Louise Roberts made about postwar France: that perceptions, whether or not they are grounded in fact, have a cultural and intellectual reality that warrants attention. So, rather than focusing on the objective realities of 1914-18, I have endeavoured to convey contemporaries' *sense* of the past, which, as Raphael Samuel reminds us, is as much a subject for historical enquiry as what transpired in the past.[3] In the case of the Great War, the latter did not necessarily determine the former; Canadians remembered their first world war in terms that sometimes bore little resemblance to its actualities.

Nevertheless, many observers still construct arguments without reference to the dichotomy emphasized by Roberts and Samuel. They continue to work from the assumption that the objective reality of the war was identical to the way contemporaries conceived of it. A recent historian of pacifism, for example, suggested that the broad mass of Canadian society must have been sympathetic to pacifism (or at least must have shared a sense of revulsion about the prospect of future war) because 'the appalling slaughter of mechanized trench warfare left an indelible scar on the Canadian psyche.'[4] To make such an argument is to misconstrue the past. It is to assume that, simply because we judge the First World War to have been an appalling slaughter, people who lived through it must also have judged it in this way. This is clearly an assumption that the historian cannot make. As this book will show, the subjects of historical study tend to view their past in terms that do not always correspond to our own images of it. When we assume that they perceived events as we have reconstructed them, we deduce at our peril.

This is not to suggest that we should give up as pointless the attempt to describe accurately the events of 1914-18. However, if we are to come to any conclusions about the Great War's legacy, in political, social, psychological, or any other terms, we must be careful to discuss it in the language of its contemporaries. We must realize that those people who lived under the shadow of the war may have had a very different understanding of it than we have expected them to. If we are to speak of 'the ghosts of the Great War,' as some historians have done, we must be clear about what those ghosts looked like.[5] Until we are, any efforts to understand the war's impact on interwar Canada will be in vain. Can we appreciate, for example, the place of pacifism in the 1920s and 1930s without first appreciating how Canadians comprehended the meaning of 1914-18? Can we sketch the shape of English-Canadian nationalism, indebted as it was to the events of the war years, without a grasp of how contemporaries interpreted those events? Can we analyze the attitudes of September 1939 without first understanding how the thousands of men who flocked to enlist that autumn, not to mention their loved ones, conceived of the previous war? Surely we cannot. If we wish to understand anything about the impact of the war on Canada, we must begin with the social memory of the Great War, that hopeful, emotional, and occasionally inconsistent vision of events that developed in the two decades after the Armistice. And we cannot stop at simply describing that memory and declaring it to be misleading.[6] If we are really to understand how the First World War imprinted itself upon the consciousness of Canadians, we must first understand the form it took in their minds and why that form evolved.

An attempt to understand how the Great War changed the outlook of the Western world lay behind the first seminal work on the intellectual legacy of 1914-18, Paul Fussell's *The Great War and Modern Memory*. A triumph of cultural history, Fussell's book interpreted the First World War as a watershed that dramatically altered the western conception of war. After 1918, according to Fussell, it was no longer possible to think of human conflict in traditional terms. Flanders had put to rest the tired old formulas; Passchendaele and the Somme had dragged the Western world into modernism. Fussell's work has been very influential and has inspired a legion of followers to carry his ideas into a variety of national case studies. Yet he has not been without his detractors. The American literary theorist Lynne Hanley, for example, has criticized Fussell for constructing the memory of the war almost exclusively from the ruminations of white Anglo-American males of literary inclination who served on the Western Front. By the same token, recent scholars such as Rosa Maria Bracco and David Englander have begun to re-examine the cultural and philosophical legacy of the war, painting very different pictures than those sketched by Fussell and his intellectual heirs.[7] They find conservatism and tradition persisting deep within interwar societies as a sort of bedrock of stability. Where Fussell identified the forces of change, they have emphasized continuity; in opposition to the shock of the new, they have found an old order that is much more resilient than *The Great War and Modern Memory* allowed. Furthermore, implicit in their work (and in my own) is the suggestion that such findings are not exceptional but might well be replicated elsewhere by adopting a methodology that treats all sources, regardless of their literary quality, on an equal footing.

This returns us to the criticism of Lynne Hanley, that Fussell's sources were so very unrepresentative. No one can deny that he drew on the best of Great War literature to reach his conclusions, but what of the countless other people whose writing shaped the memory of the war? By using aesthetic quality as a criterion for selecting sources, Fussell shut himself off from a much larger canon of work, that of the inept novelist, the bad versifier, and the talentless essayist. Very few people can write superb poetry; very many of us can write deplorable verse. By looking at the ways in which amateur writers captured the war, our eyes are opened to a new and more representative range of interpretation. 'In every literature a society contemplates its own image,' wrote Marc Bloch. If we are to comprehend that image, we cannot use aesthetic standards to decide which pieces of literature deserve consideration.[8]

The same argument can be made for including a broader range of opinions expressed by people outside the ranks of the literati. Escott Reid, O.D. Skelton, and Arthur Lower were among the most articulate commentators on Canadian affairs in the interwar era, and their impassioned pleas against repeating the folly of 1914-18 have impressed generations of historians. Yet it is unwise, in analyzing perceptions of the war, to give such people undue weight. For every Frank Underhill, there were countless Canadians who aired conflicting views just as passionately in the rather less august fora of the small-town newspaper, the smoky Canadian Legion hall, and the IODE meeting. Few of them had the perspicacity or intellect of a Reid or a Skelton, but all were capable of making their own judgments of the Great War's significance for Canada. Just because such visions were not articulated in flawless prose does not negate their validity as evidence in reconstructing Canada's memory of the war.

But we cannot stop with the views of the armchair poet and politician. We cannot appreciate how a society remembered an event simply through a narrow band of traditional sources, for these forms of expression alone cannot tell us all we need to know. Instead, we must venture further afield, into areas that have been fruitfully mined by socio-anthropologists such as Victor Turner, theologians such as Owen Chadwick, and art historians such as Marina Warner. What do the inscriptions on memorial tablets reveal about a community's view of the fallen? Why were the same hymns used again and again at Armistice Day ceremonies? What rituals did ex-soldiers perform at their reunions? Why did Canadians name their children after battles? We can glean as much about the memory of the war from observing where the mothers of the dead sat at war memorial unveilings as from the finest poem or the most insightful commentary on international affairs. Indeed, to look for the war's impact only in these latter places is to look for versions that would have touched the lives of average Canadians the least.

In the final reckoning, it was average Canadians who were responsible for the myth. The memory of the war was not simply a creation of Anglo-Canadian intellectuals, political leaders, social elites, and renowned members of the literati. Though these groups undoubtedly played a significant role in the propagation of the myth, it would never have caught on without active and enthusiastic support elsewhere in the Canadian mosaic. It is this diversity of authorship that makes the memory of the war so fascinating. It crossed boundaries of gender, class, religion, ethnicity, and region; few groups or individuals failed to accept it, at least in part. Indeed, one is struck by similarities in the response to the war among varied groups. In the arcane field of welcome-home medals, the images and inscriptions on medals chosen by the Brotherhood of Railroad Trainmen or the International Brotherhood of Blacksmiths, Drop Forgers, and Helpers were not very different from those chosen by the conservative farming community of Fulbeck, Alberta, or the middle-class school trustees of Fraser Valley, British Columbia. War memorial inscriptions, Armistice Day sermons, letters to the editor, veterans' reunions – in each case, even significant ethno-cultural or socio-economic discrepancies seem to have had little impact on how the war was remembered.

I do not wish to suggest, however, that the mythic version of the war was accepted unanimously. Throughout the interwar era, and particularly in the mid-1930s, a revisionist interpretation did emerge, most strongly in the universities and the Protestant churches. This view, which described the war as a futile slaughter whose main root was economic, pointed to the tragedy of 1914-18 as the prime reason why war had to be avoided at all costs. For these revisionists, peace was threatened as much by this mythic version of the war as by any dictator's aggression. Yet even as they criticized it, the revisionists themselves helped shape the myth. Not surprisingly, their critique of the war raised the hackles of the myth's proponents, who were moved to restate their memory in ever stronger terms. Just as significantly, revisionists often implicitly accepted the terms of the myth even as they were trying to condemn it. In this way, this small but vocal minority also contributed significantly to the process wherein the myth was constantly reshaped in its own image.

IN THIS BOOK I use terms like memory, myth, and nostalgia advisedly, in the full knowledge that some readers will disapprove of the connotations I put on them. They may well raise objections to my use of the term 'myth,' especially as I make little reference to the considerable body of literature on precisely what constitutes a myth. While admitting the value of this work, I have no desire to add to it; it is not my intention to enter into a prolonged debate on semantics, a debate that other scholars have carried on for some time. Instead, I hope that readers will be satisfied with a brief discussion of these notions as I understand them for the purposes of this study.

I have employed 'myth' to refer simply to the particular conception of the Great War that is my central concern. I do so, not because that conception conforms strictly to any of the definitions of myth that have been proposed by scholars working in the field, but because the word seems to capture the combination of invention, truth, and half-truth that characterizes Canada's memory of the war. In this respect, I have worked from Roland Barthes's assumption that a myth is a system of communication. In itself, it is not an idea but rather a conveyer of ideas or, to use his phrase, a mode of signification. But this characteristic is less important for my purposes than Barthes's identification of the properties of myth. 'Myth does not deny things,' he writes:

> it purifies them, it makes them innocent, it gives them a natural and eternal justification, it gives them a clarity which is not that of an explanation but that of a statement of fact ... it abolishes the complexity of human acts, it gives them the simplicity of essence ... it organizes a world which is without contradictions because it is without depth, a world wide open and wallowing in the evident, it establishes a blissful clarity: things appear to mean something by themselves.[9]

Barthes's remarks capture the essence of Canada's myth of the war: it evolved into a discourse that communicated the past in a pure, unambiguous, and simple fashion.

One of the tools that the myth employed was nostalgia, perhaps the least contentious of the terms used in this book. It might best be defined as the tendency to look back upon past events with a certain yearning, as if the past were somehow preferable to the present. In this sense, nostalgia is most likely to thrive when current realities are less than ideal. Dissatisfied with the present, we may recall an earlier era and transform that time into something of a golden age. This is not done on the basis of historical facts that tell us that wages were higher or unemployment lower in the good old days, but on inferences made from a series of opposites.[10] If society appears to be drifting aimlessly, there must have been a time when life had direction and meaning; if human existence appears confusing and senseless, there must have been a time when it was clear and purposeful. In short, if things are bad now, there must have been a time when they were good. In this way, nostalgia is entirely non-specific. It does not identify precisely what made a century or a decade ago the best time to be alive; it merely asserts that life was better then.

Nostalgia was an important element in Canada's memory of the war, as it is in any society's conception of its past. Social memory has recently become very much in vogue as a subject for study. A shared memory is one of the cornerstones of a society as we understand it. Individuals who constitute any social order share a common vision of history that locates the community in time and space, giving it an appreciation of its own past as well as a sense of its future. The dominant or collective memory of a society is not always (perhaps, even, not often) based on historical fact, but on a set of assumptions about what the past was like.[11]

Much of the literature on social memory turns on the contrast between the dominant or civic memory and the popular or private memory.[12] The dominant memory emerges after a struggle between conflicting interpretations of historical events and comes to act as a bulwark for the establishment. The past becomes an excuse for the present, justifying the social or political order on the grounds that it was ordained by history. The dominant memory claims that the status quo exists because the past wills it. In doing so, it sets out what should be remembered (as well as how it should be remembered) and what should be forgotten. Individuals who do not subscribe to the dominant memory, who refuse to forget or remember what it prescribes, become subversives. Their private memories are driven underground, to exist as a potentially threatening undercurrent to the social order.

Yet I do not wish to overemphasize the notion that the myth of Canada's war existed to bolster the social order. It may indeed have been put to this purpose by some individuals, but that is not the primary reason why it was embraced so widely. I will argue that the memory of the war was so appealing because it filled needs. For some people, it was consolatory; for others, it was explanatory. It could also be didactic, inspirational, and even entertaining. It may have had the coincidental side effect of channelling potentially threatening discontent into benign outlets, but that was not its primary motive. In this respect, we might return to Marc Bloch. 'Through the very fact of their respect for the past,' he wrote, 'people came to reconstruct it as they considered it ought to have been.'[13] In remembering the war, Canadians were concerned first and foremost with utility: those four years had to have been of some use. The war had to be recalled in such a way that positive outcomes, beyond the defeat of German aggression, were clear. In short, the mythic version existed to fashion a usable past out of the Great War.

Historians have been only too happy to aid and abet this process by articulating a vision of the war as a nation-building experience of signal importance. Canada's progress from colony to nation by way of Flanders, an interpretation born in the earliest days of the war, has become the standard method of judging the impact of 1914-18. Pierre Berton adopted it as the theme for his popular history of the Battle of Vimy Ridge, which described the success of the Canadian Corps in capturing the ridge in April 1917 after attacks by French armies had failed, while C.P. Stacey saw the First World War as the most important event in Canadian history. Writing in the centennial year, he suggested that the creation of the Canadian Corps was 'perhaps the greatest thing she [Canada] has done to this day' and cited the capture of Vimy as the one milestone 'to mark progress on the road to national maturity.' In the conventional wisdom, the Great War has become, to borrow Desmond Morton and J.L. Granatstein's phrase, Canada's war of independence.[14]

On a political level and in the realm of international recognition, there is no denying the validity of the idea. Resolution 9, pressed on Britain's Imperial War Cabinet by Robert Borden in 1917, was the thin edge of the wedge, which eventually culminated in the Statute of Westminster. Canada's seat at the Paris Peace Conference and its independent signature of international treaties were also consequences of the victories won by Canadian troops on the Western Front. Yet on a domestic level, historians have had to admit that the Great War was as divisive as it was unifying. Four years of battle, both in the trenches and at home, did not create a single nationalism, but instead strengthened the two nationalisms of French and English Canada; both societies gained a greater appreciation of their separate identities from the experience of war. Even the ever-optimistic Stacey had to concede that the war was profoundly negative in its impact on French-English relations in Canada.[15]

In the three decades since Stacey's address, our vision of war has become decidedly more jaundiced. To Auschwitz and Hiroshima have been added Vietnam, Somalia, and Bosnia – these are the lenses through which today's generation now views the human activity of war. The calculated barbarism that has characterized post-1939 conflicts has made us loath to admit that there can be anything positive about war. Even Canada's social memory of the Second World War, as just a war as the modern world has seen, is dominated by overtones of negativity. Notions of individual heroism, self-sacrifice, and fighting in a good cause have been pushed to the background by a dominant memory that has come to emphasize mismanagement, injustice, failure, and cupidity. When the McKenna brothers produced their now notorious documentary on Canada's war effort, they chose to focus on the disastrous defence of Hong Kong, the disastrous raid on Nuremberg, and the disastrous battles for Verrières Ridge. They were strongly criticized for their choices, but the McKennas were simply articulating Canada's social memory of the war, a memory characterized by a marked reluctance to celebrate success.[16] Many Canadians know of the failed raid on Dieppe. How many know of the success of Canadian soldiers at Ortona or in Operation Wellhit?

Canada's memory of the First World War was very different. Dominated by the successful defence of Ypres in 1915, the capture of Vimy Ridge in 1917, and the triumphant Hundred Days that preceded the Armistice of 1918, it gave short shrift to the failures and disappointments of the war. Determined to see 1914-18 as the progenitor of good, it refused to countenance a preoccupation with the horrors of battle or with the grief of loss and was unwilling even to make Stacey's concession regarding the war's divisiveness. Instead, in the 1920s and 1930s, the war evolved into the tool that could weld together the nation. If new Canadians, members of the First Nations, English, and French could simply focus on the positive aspects of the war and agree to forget the negative, then the country was destined for greatness. Provincial jealousies, ethnic antipathies, even the mutual resentments harboured by Canada's founding races – all would crumble to dust under the unifying influence of the myth of the war. Confederation had established the administrative framework for a Canadian nation but had created nothing more than an arid and sometimes ineffectual edifice. Only the memory of the Great War could breathe life into Canada, giving birth to a national consciousness that would carry the country to the heights of achievement.

In hindsight, such hopes might seem a little naive. How could a war that saw the deaths of 60,000 Canadians and the wounding of 170,000 others become a constructive force in the nation's history? How could an era that witnessed conscription riots, political gerrymandering such as the Military Voters Act, and singular displays of spite on the part of otherwise reasonable Canadians be the basis on which the nation could be united at last? How could intelligent and rational citizens seriously hope that a pan-Canadian nationalism could be borne of such divisive times? This book is an attempt to answer those questions.

CHAPTER I

The Just War

DAYBREAK on 11 November 1918 found the units of the Canadian Corps clustered around the Belgian city of Mons. Previously the scene of the war's first important skirmish between troops of Germany and the British Empire, Mons had been captured hours earlier by elements of the Royal Canadian Regiment and the 42nd Battalion of Montreal. At about 6:30 AM, Canadian Corps headquarters received a message that an armistice had been signed and that hostilities should cease at 11:00 AM. Over the next few hours, the news was transmitted down through the units of the Corps, and by 9:00 AM most of the soldiers had been informed. The war was over.

The troops reacted to the news with anything from stoic resignation to mild jubilation. Vincent Goodman, a New Brunswicker in the 2nd Canadian Motor Machine Gun Brigade, recalled that the men in his unit 'took the news calmly, almost passively.' Artillery officer H.C. Pullen wrote to his sister from his battery's billets at Marly that 'the troops let a yell out of themselves and then turned in to clean harness as usual.'[1] Private Pat Wyld of the Canadian Forestry Corps celebrated with his mates by bouncing flares down the cobbled streets of Valenciennes. Will Bird related a different but perhaps more characteristic response to news of the Armistice. An officer had been dispatched to an isolated outpost to convey the cheering news that the war was over, but the sergeant who commanded the post was unmoved. 'Beg pardon, sir,' he said after a slight pause, 'but 'oo's won?'[2]

Bird's sergeant may have had his doubts, but there was no such scepticism in Canada's collective memory of the war. That vision affirmed November 1918 as a clear and unequivocal victory for the Allied cause. The Hun had been vanquished, and civilization had been saved from the threat of barbarism. Still, there was no guarantee that the salvation was permanent, and the memory of the war accepted that such a struggle might well have to be waged again. In this way, it acted as a powerful antidote to pacifism, for it assumed that the truest lovers of peace were those people who were willing to fight for it. Because the country had gone to war to preserve peace, Canada could look back with pride at its first world war. The nation had fought a good fight; it had been a just war.

I

WHILE THE MEN of the Canadian Corps reacted to news of the Armistice with restraint, their friends and families at home erupted into spontaneous celebrations. 'Never again to most of us will come the exaltation of the morning of November 11,' predicted a Fredericton newspaper. Students at Acadia University started a huge bonfire on campus and then paraded through Wolfville, Nova Scotia, to rouse any residents who lingered in their beds. In Brandon, Manitoba, jubilant townspeople in various states of undress jammed the streets, singing, dancing, and waving flaming torches. The quiet of St. George, New Brunswick, was shattered by the ringing of church and school bells and the blowing of whistles, a cacophony that continued for the rest of the day. In the small town of Burford, Ontario, four-year-old Mel Robertson and his sister were awakened before dawn by the sound of church bells, a factory whistle, and a babble of voices in the street: 'When we called out our hired girl came in with a lamp and told us the War had ended. She then brought us tin dish pans and we beat on them with curling tongs until our parents got up. Then we were dressed and went outside where we found people everywhere – some with coats over their night-clothes. On the main corner a woman with an accordion was playing "Praise God from whom all blessings flow."'[3]

H. Léonard, *Hip! Hip! Hip! Hurrah!* The Canadian entry into Mons, 11 November 1918. Canadian soldiers may have reacted more with relief or resignation than with the joy suggested in this sketch. (NAC PA6217)

Once relative calm had been restored, Canadians gathered in a more orderly fashion to give thanks for the nation's deliverance. A service held at Toronto's St. James Cathedral was entirely typical of celebrations convened across the country. 'O God Our Help in Ages Past' and 'A Hymn of Victory (Now Praise the Lord of Glory)' rang through the nave as worshippers expressed their gratitude in song. For the lesson, the minister chose a reading from the First Book of Chronicles, in which the people of David offer thanks to God for their deliverance. In a combination of misconception and wishful thinking, the order of service proclaimed 'the signing of the Armistice by Germany Signifying her Unconditional Surrender.'[4]

Of course, there had been no unconditional surrender, and even the Treaty of Versailles, which officially ended the war in Europe, would not be signed for another eight months. That event gave Canadians an excuse to repeat the revelries in celebration of Peace Day on 19 July 1919. In Guelph, Ontario, a civic procession ended at a huge bonfire and fireworks display, while in Revelstoke, British Columbia, as many as 25,000 people gathered to watch an evening peace pageant staged by local women. One source estimated that three-quarters of Vancouver's population turned out for the peace celebration in that city. In Saskatoon, a two-mile-long parade of veterans, schoolchildren, local service clubs, and police and firemen wound its way through the streets; at the parade's conclusion, thirty white doves were released as emblems of peace.[5]

The most striking characteristic of Peace Day, however, was its similarity to Armistice Day. Indeed, many Canadians evidently looked upon

The townspeople of Oshawa, Ontario, parade through the city streets to celebrate the announcement of the Armistice on 11 November 1918. The banner to the right reads 'The Beast of Berlin Is Gone.' (The Thomas Bouckley Collection 2125, The Robert McLaughlin Gallery, Oshawa, Ontario)

Peace Day as another opportunity to celebrate victory. In one British Columbia newspaper, most of the advertisements marking Peace Day were titled 'Victory and Peace.' An advertisement for Woodward Department Stores depicts a woman holding a shield that lists Canadian victories on the battlefield, while the Hudson's Bay Company used St. George standing triumphant over a dragon wrapped in a banner marked 'Militarism.' In more than one city, municipal officials borrowed captured German field guns from the Department of Militia and Defence to tow through the streets as part of Peace Day parades.[6] It was perhaps the last time that Canadians copied the ancient practice of parading with the trophies of war, a practice that had more to do with proclaiming triumph over the enemy than celebrating the return to peace. Residents of Saskatoon had their own reminder that German military might had been vanquished. After watching the doves of peace flutter into the afternoon sky, they could adjourn to the Thélus Theatre (formerly the Strand, it had been renamed in honour of a village near Vimy Ridge that had been captured by Prairie battalions in 1917) for a seven-reel war film entitled *Crashing through to Berlin,* a chronicle of Germany's defeat at the hands of 'the "Treat 'Em Rough" Boys.'

The desire to mark the defeat of imperial Germany, then, was central to the celebrations of both Armistice Day and Peace Day. The spontaneous outbursts of 11 November 1918 reflected the joy of a society's recognition that the years of sacrifice had paid off in victory. The events of 19 July 1919 were more carefully contrived and orchestrated yet were underpinned by the same assumption. Despite attempts by planners to focus on the symbols

To mark Peace Day on 19 July 1919, the women of Fenelon Falls, Ontario, dressed in costumes that represented the Allied nations and performed a pageant entitled 'Hands across the Border.' (Fenelon Falls Museum)

of peace, notions of military victory were so prevalent that they overshadowed everything else. The sincere thanks tendered to God for the triumph in battle, the advertisements that placed victory ahead of peace, the constant reminders of the defeat of imperial Germany – all indicated a broad acceptance of the idea that Canadians were really celebrating not the return to peace, but a victory of arms over the enemy.

Indeed, it was victory that dominated the discourse about the end of the war. Rather than graciously accepting victory and celebrating instead the return to peace, Canadians were determined to enjoy their day in the sun by trumpeting their triumph at every occasion. After four years of tragedy, it was difficult to resist the temptation to gloat. 'Victory is ours,' crowed the principal of Queen's University in 1918, 'victory far more complete than we had dared to hope for.' Even the historian, poet, and ex-soldier Edgar McInnis, generally one of the more moderate commentators on the war, came close to gloating in his 1920 collection *The Road to Arras*:

> They have not passed! Their scornful, sneering lies,
> Their senseless hate and blind brutality,
> Their ranting boasts and unctuous blasphemies
> Have naught availed – to us the victory![9]

In the postwar years, every conceivable aspect of the war was interpreted as a symbol of victory. The fallen became 'the morning stars that herald the day of Victory – of the victory of good over evil, kindness over cruelty, jus-

Parading with the trophies of victory. In honour of Peace Day, the citizens of Owen Sound, Ontario, towed captured German artillery pieces through the streets. The sign indicates that the gun was captured by the 4th Canadian Mounted Rifles. The boy in the clown suit was killed in Canada's next war. (Grey County Historical Society)

tice over tyranny.' They were not simply casualties of war; they were signs of triumph over 'the boasting war-lord's might.'[8] William Rothenstein's *The Watch on the Rhine,* a Canadian War Memorials Fund painting of a huge artillery piece louring silently over the river, did not symbolize the ascendency of technology or the fact that the guns had been stilled. For observers such as Hector Charlesworth, the critic and associate editor of *Saturday Night,* it was 'singularly suggestive of conquest.' By the same token, Alfred Bastien's *Canadians Passing in Front of the Arc de Triomphe* was in no way allegorical; its only message was 'the thrill of victory.'[9]

William Rothenstein, *The Watch on the Rhine (The Last Phase).* The fact that the human figure is dwarfed by the gun and the pile of shells made little impact on contemporary observers. (Canadian War Museum, 8740)

It would be a mistake to ascribe the emphasis on victory simply to the enthusiasm of the immediate postwar years. Throughout the 1920s and 1930s, the language of commemoration was dominated by the figures of Winged Victory and the rejoicing soldier, symbols of earthly triumph that constituted the single most important theme in war memorials erected by Canadians. While there may have been some spiritual side to these elements as symbolizing a victory over death, the temporal significance should not be understated. Both the artistic context and the contemporary views of these memorials confirm that they marked, more than anything else, an earthly triumph.

The figure of Winged Victory had been thrust firmly into twentieth-century iconography in 1863, when a statue of the goddess Nike was discovered by French archaeologists at Samothrace, in the Aegean Sea. Scholars concluded that it had been erected to mark a Rhodian naval triumph over the Syrians in the second century BC. With its beauty, grace, and dynamism, the Nike of Samothrace quickly captured the public imagination, and the winged female figure as a symbol of earthly victory immediately re-entered the artistic vocabulary. North Americans of the early twentieth century would most likely have been familiar with the image from Augustus St. Gaudens's statue of Winged Victory leading General William T. Sherman, unveiled in New York City in 1903.[10]

Because the figure was such a fresh motif in 1914, it is hardly surprising that Canadians took it into their language of commemoration. In doing so, they commissioned many memorials that strongly echoed the Sherman statue. A bronze relief in the Montreal suburb of Notre-Dame-de-Grâce shows the figure of Victory exhorting a rank of soldiers, while G.W. Hill's Westmount memorial features a winged figure pointing the way to a marching infantryman. In Beamsville, Ontario, the Angel of Victory urges on a soldier, while in Sherbrooke, a winged female stands above three soldiers, spurring them to victory with the laurel wreath she holds. In each case, the artistic context clarifies the meaning: the winged figure is not an angel shepherding the fallen into heaven but a personification of victory showing warriors the way to triumph on the battlefield.

Another image of victory that proliferates in memorial sculpture is the soldier holding his hat or rifle aloft in jubilation. There has been a tendency to interpret this too as symbolizing a spiritual victory, but a different meaning emerges when the context is taken into account. One of the most well-known images to come out of Canada's participation in the Boer War was Richard Caton Woodville's *The Dawn of Majuba Day,* which depicts members of the Royal Canadian Regiment celebrating their victory at Paardeberg in February 1900. In the middle ground are visible the surrendering Boer soldiers, but attention is drawn most forcefully to the Canadian soldiers, the most prominent of whom holds his helmet aloft and raises a cry of triumph at the defeat of the enemy. The image was adapted for Ottawa's Boer War memorial and, in 1915, was echoed by Bernard Partridge's famous illustration in *Punch* to commemorate the Canadian defence of Ypres. One of the most reproduced illustrations of the war, the Partridge etching shows a soldier clutching the Red Ensign and holding his hat aloft on the muzzle of his rifle; his head is

On G.W. Hill's memorial in Westmount, Montreal, the Angel of Victory directs a marching soldier towards triumph on the battlefield. (*Monuments commémoratifs de la province de Québec* [Quebec City: Commission des Monuments Historiques 1923], 1:355)

bandaged and a cry of exultation is on his lips. Like Caton Woodville's painting, Partridge's etching was a very human expression of joy for a victory over the enemy.

When it came time to commemorate the dead of the Great War, many Canadian communities turned to this popular image of temporal victory, and the celebrating soldier became as prominent as the Winged Victory in the language of commemoration. He graced the welcome-home medal presented to soldiers from Shawinigan Falls, Québec, and was immortalized in stained glass in Kingston's Memorial Hall. G.W. Hill adapted the figure for the war memorial in Lachute, Québec, described by the Commission des Monuments Historiques as 'un soldat d'infanterie tenant sa carabine dans sa main gauche et acclamant la victoire des Alliés.'[11] Memorials in Longueuil, Québec, and Kingston, Shelburne, and Chatham, Ontario, feature variations on the theme: the soldier, arm raised triumphantly, gazes upwards to raise a cry of victory or utter thanks for the enemy's defeat.

Richard Caton Woodville, *The Dawn of Majuba Day*. The surrendering Boer soldiers are almost invisible in the centre ground, overshadowed by the celebrating Canadians to the left and in the foreground. (Royal Canadian Regiment / Royal Canadian Military Institute)

Bernard Partridge's illustration in honour of the defence of Ypres by Canadian troops following the German gas attacks of April 1915. Note all of the conventions of Victorian battle painting: the silent artillery piece, the spent shells, the bomb burst overhead, and the clutched flag. (*Punch*, 5 May 1915)

Just as striking as the degree to which metaphors for victory dominated the language of commemoration was the lack of any meaningful challenge to this practice. In 1925 H.W. Hart of Victoria, disturbed by memorials that glorified victory instead of pointing to the evils of war or the blessings of peace, suggested raising a different sort of monument, one that would have had more in common with the later Vietnam Memorial in Washington. It would consist of a panel listing the number of dead, wounded, widows, and orphans from all nations, accompanied by the simple inscription, 'Wherein is the glory of war?' Despite assiduous efforts, Hart had to admit that his scheme failed to generate any interest whatsoever; Canadians evidently had no taste for such gloomy commemorations.[12] The glow of victory was no time to raise awkward questions about whether the triumph had been a pyrrhic one. Dwelling on the cost of the war merely diverted attention from what had been won or, just as importantly, from what might have been lost.

II

VICTORY REMAINED such a precious possession simply because of the consequences of defeat. As Canadians remembered it, the war had been a struggle between civilization and barbarism in which the Allied armies held the ramparts against the spread of brutality and ruthlessness. It was for good reason that 'Hun' remained the most popular epithet for the enemy: a German victory would have meant nothing less than the descent into a new Dark Age. For this reason, the losses that concerned Hart were irrelevant, for they were a small price to pay for the survival of the free world. In Canada's memory, the war had not destroyed 'the happy equation between civilization and victory,' as A.J.P. Taylor suggested.[13] On the contrary, civilization had been preserved by the victory over imperial Germany.

Of course, a few Canadians insisted on muddying the waters by looking for villains in all the wrong places. Some pinned blame on 'the avaricious financier, and none too honest politician.' Equally loathsome were Stephen Leacock's Mr. Spugg, who selflessly sent to war his chauffeur, his gardener, and finally his valet, and Mr. Grunch, who complained that the government's war income tax was unfair because it let off the man without an income.[14] 'Were we on God's side then? was God on our side?' wondered the prolific Maritime writer Theodore Goodridge Roberts. 'My dear duffers, we were working for fat tradesmen who had shells and bacon and hot air to sell.' Leslie Roberts, an ex-soldier like his New Brunswick namesake, was just as cynical in marvelling 'that countless lives might be snuffed in the name of the Prince of Peace, so that the politician, profiteer, man of

The celebrating soldier in bronze: the memorial to the men of the 21st Battalion in Kingston, Ontario. Note the stylized sunrise on the plinth, another significant motif in memorial imagery that pointed to the resurrection of the dead. (J. Peter Vance)

wealth and sometime even the rector himself, may sip tea or whiskey in patriotic ease.'[15]

As insightful as they seem to modern minds, these conclusions found little room in Canada's memory of the war. In 1925, the Reverend Charles W. Gordon, better known to the world as the novelist Ralph Connor, affirmed that a war between civilized people was wicked but inferred that this rule of thumb did not apply to the late conflict, because only the Allied side could call itself civilized.[16] Germany, on the other hand, represented all that was opposed to civilization: Prussianism, Junkerdom, militarism, or any other pejorative term that came to mind. There was no point in search-ing the nineteenth-century alliance structure, imperial expansion, or the rise of industrial competition for the causes of the war. It 'had its founda-tion in German autocracy,' proclaimed an Ottawa cleric matter of factly; any other theory about the war's causes merely diverted attention from this self-evident truth.[17]

The myth of the war, then, placed the enemy in precisely the same place it had been in 1914. Furthermore, despite the popular notion that there was no desire to be 'beastly to the Boche,' only a few Canadians openly expressed a willingness to be conciliatory towards Germany for its wartime conduct. The poet Norah Holland asked her readers to 'Cheer if you will the brave deed done, with laurels the victor crown, / But keep one leaf of your wreath of bay for the men who are lost and down.'[18] Holland called for forbearance and forgiveness; few Canadians were as generous.

Indeed, there was little abatement of interest in the atrocity tales that had so chilled the blood of readers during the war. Terms like Hunnishness and *schrecklichkeit* (frightfulness) lost little of their potency in the postwar years and were repeated to confirm the real nature of the enemy that the Allies had faced. Though tales of a crucified Canadian soldier were dis-credited, writers were not shy about reminding their readers of other war crimes committed by the Central Powers.[19] German abuse of prisoners of war remained a sore point with Canadians, and the memoirs of former cap-tives sold well in the years immediately following the war. Far from scold-ing such works for perpetuating wartime hatreds, Canadians reviewers often praised them for doing just that. The tale of one private who escaped from captivity, for example, was lauded for leaving the reader 'in no doubt of the basic brutality of German militarism.'[20] Some of the more notori-ous misdeeds remained popular fodder for writers, and the execution of British nurse Edith Cavell and the torpedoing of the British passenger liner *Lusitania* were staples of poetry collections through the 1920s and 1930s. In Saint John, hundreds of people braved the cold of February 1920 to line up

for a film about wartime atrocities called *Auction of Souls,* while Frank
Carrel, the editor of the Québec *Daily Telegraph,* devoted an entire chapter
of his book *Impressions of War* to 'Hun Heinousness.' Other chapters were lib-
erally sprinkled with horrors like a crucified kitten wired into a booby trap
and the rape of Belgian nuns.[21]

Even the physical damage of the war was taken as proof of German
evil. Photographs of ruined Belgian and French cities were common in postwar illustrated volumes, including some published by the government; the
1918 report of the Overseas Military Forces of Canada, for example,
includes photographs captioned 'An Abiding Record of the Enemy's Wanton
Destruction' and 'The Hand of the Hun in Cambrai.' Poetry, too, often
dwelt on these tangible signs of German evil. 'Rheims,' written by the poet
and Bishop's University language professor Frank Oliver Call, was
addressed to the shattered cathedral in that city: 'Do thy mute bells to all
the world proclaim / Thy martyred glory and thy foeman's shame?' The
destruction of the city of Ypres, though a legitimate target for German
artillery, was also taken as a sign of German wantonness. Commenting on
the rebuilding of the city, the editor of the *Globe* expressed hope that the

THE HAND OF THE HUN IN CAMBRAI.

'A little party of Canadians entering the Ruins of Cambrai. A picture typical of the havoc
wrought by German mines.' Captions like these left little doubt as to the villains of the war.
When such pictures were published, the captions usually reminded readers that the destruction was not caused in battle, but by the retreating German army. (Overseas Military Forces
of Canada, *Report of the Ministry, Overseas Military Forces of Canada, 1918* [London, 1918], 169)

James Kerr-Lawson, *The Cloth Hall, Ypres.*
The size of the horses and riders accentuates the magnitude of the destruction.
(Canadian War Museum 8352)

new Ypres would have a better fate than the old one, which fell victim to 'frightfulness.'[22] James Kerr-Lawson's canvas of the ruined Cloth Hall in Ypres was occasionally exhibited under the title *The Footprint of the Hun*. The word 'cloven' was implicit.

Most of these accounts date from the years immediately after the war, but such enmity was not confined to the period of postwar hysteria. Indeed, Canadians demonstrated a long memory when it came to the war's excesses. Despite later Allied experiments with poison gas, Canadians never forgot that the Germans had used it first. In 1928, Vancouver poet Kate Colquhoun decried the 'foul methods' that Germany resorted to at Ypres in 1915 when they could not win by fighting fairly. The following year, Kim Beattie, a regimental historian and writer of popular trench doggerel, published 'The First Gas,' an even more bitter commentary on the battle:

> The cowardly bastard! He done this job;
> They're strangled an' choked wi' gas;
> An' they had no chance to croak
> Like a fightin' sojer bloke
> – God'll never let this pass![23]

Nor were Canadians willing to forget the murders of women and children in occupied France and Belgium. The 1926 history of the Canadian Grenadier Guards cited 'definite and authentic information' that the Germans had slaughtered Belgian civilians, and in a 1936 piece by a Nova Scotia playwright, the dramatic action turns on the murder of Belgian women and children.[24] German attacks on hospitals and hospital ships, the destruction of French cities in the summer of 1918, the adoption of unrestricted submarine warfare – all continued to enrage Canadians well into the 1930s. Even Canada's 'official' war film was generously dosed with references to northern France being 'ruthlessly violated' and 'defenceless vessels sinking on the desolate wastes of the ocean.' On the eve of the next war, journalist Pierre van Paassen, who had been shamed into enlisting while a divinity student in Toronto in 1914, lamented the continuing credulity of Canadians when it came to wartime atrocity tales: 'hundreds of thousands of easy-going citizens of the Dominion are firmly persuaded that ... Belgian babies were currently carried on the point of German bayonets, that Bavarian yodelers took a particular delight in cutting off the breasts of Flemish nuns, that the Huns boiled enemy corpses in order to extract grease for the soap in the Kaiser's bath.'[25]

Most Canadians knew full well where to lay blame for these excesses – not upon war as a social act or on the darkness in the human heart, but squarely on the shoulders of Germany, and often on the head of Kaiser Wilhelm himself. As a consequence, representations of the kaiser came to be characterized by extreme bitterness. An amateur poet in rural Ontario envisioned the Devil giving up his dominion over hell to his rival from imperial Germany: 'It breaks my heart to leave a job that I love so well, / But the kaiser knows better how to run a real hell.'[26] A disgruntled Nova Scotian had a different fate in mind for Wilhelm Hohenzollern:

> For a man of any nation
> > Guilty of this conflagration
> How much lenience would you deem the proper scope?
> > Viewed aright from any angle,
> In your vision he will dangle
> > From a tough and solid piece of hempen rope.

Even on Peace Day 1919, when Canadians might have taken the opportunity to exercise a spirit of forgiveness, many people were in no mood to be charitable. The venerable journalist and caricaturist J.W. Bengough, in his 'Lines for the Peace Day Celebration,' gloated that 'the Teuton despot, panting with dismay, / Lies helpless in the dust his vileness stains.'[27] At the festivities in Hamilton, Mayor Charles Booker, still grieving the death of his only son at the front in October 1918, demanded that the kaiser and his warlords face justice for their crimes. 'I have come to believe,' he confided to the cheering crowd, 'that the only good German is a dead German.' The people of Guelph, Ontario, would have applauded the mayor's comments. The Peace Day parade in that city included a mannequin of the kaiser, complete with a rope around his neck; the crowd roared as the effigy was consigned to the bonfire.[28]

Not everyone felt this degree of antipathy towards Wilhelm on a personal level. It was more common to indict Germany in a more general sense, often by objectifying the enemy in ways that perpetuated propagandized wartime stereotypes. Every conceivable term of opprobrium was repeated in the interwar years, from 'the horrible Hun and the unspeakable Turk' to 'Germany, like an unchained beast, plung[ing] across defenceless Belgium to devour France.'[29] The German armies continued to be referred to as 'Hun hordes' or fiends 'mad with the lust of conquest and dead to every sense of honour,' and the Reverend Wellington Bridgeman was certainly not alone in declaring that 'the Austro-Hun has forfeited the right to dwell among decent people.'[30]

Even those Canadians who were dubious about atrocity tales and reluctant to fasten blame upon the Germans, individually or collectively, still had little doubt that the war had been justified. Shortly after the Armistice, a Methodist minister in Ontario predicted that veterans would need 'time to analyze and relate their experiences ... [before they] are able to present the inner truth and meaning of it [the war].'[31] Many Canadians had no need of such reflection; for them, the truth and meaning of the war had always been manifest, and remained so after the victory had been won. In the view of the *Globe*'s editor, a decade of peace gave no reason to look any deeper into the meaning of November 1918 and the war it ended: 'Twelve years have elapsed since the world conflict armistice was announced, and during this period of retrospection there has been no alteration of view in regard to the justness of the war. Rather, the conviction has grown that, while the years of battle presented the tragedy of the ages, it was all necessary to the prevention of a still greater and more lasting tragedy.'[32] On the eve of the war, British Foreign Secretary Sir Edward Grey stood in his Foreign Office window and watched the lights being extinguished as a precaution against air raids. 'The lamps are going out all over Europe,' he is reputed to have said in a remark that has become part of the iconography of 1914. As far as Canadians were concerned, there remained little doubt that the war had been necessary to prevent the tragedy of eternal darkness.

Some Canadians continued to insist through the 1920s and 1930s that the country had gone to war to avoid German domination. If Britain fell, wrote Colonel George Nasmith, 'Canada would be next ... [The soldiers] were fighting for their own homes.' A Toronto veteran agreed, maintaining that the volunteers of 1914 had enlisted because they visualized German troops reaching Calais, from where they would embark for Canada. As an ex-soldier in Guelph, Ontario, put it, 'there would now be a German flag flying over our "Old Canadian Home" instead of the Union Jack,' if not for the sacrifice of 60,000 Canadian lives.[33] For this reason, many war memorials suggested that the country had narrowly escaped German occupation. The deaths of Canadian soldiers 'helped under God to save their country,' proclaimed the memorial in Bedford, Nova Scotia. 'The men were very good unto us and we were not hurt,' stated a number of other memorials. 'They were a wall against us born by night and day.'

The image of German *uhlans* trotting up Dorchester Street or Yonge Street was less common than the contention that certain fundamental principles had to be defended. There were, in the words of an Ontario cleric, 'principles that we / Have on the field of conflict seen well tried, / For which our loved ones spent themselves and died.'[34] In some cases, these principles were given no more specific identity than Right or Good. 'I will go forth to battle for the right,' declared a character representing the youth of Acadia University going to war, and few Canadians would have disagreed with him.[35] An Armistice Day supplement to Canadian newspapers in 1928 asked Canadians to feel 'thankfulness that our cause was a righteous one,' and even ten years later, a Prairie divinity student was able to interpret the war in simple terms of right and wrong: 'They gave their all in the belief that thus / Must human rights be saved, and states yet rife / With wrong be raised to nobler planes of life.' This was the simple reason, according to the chancellor of Toronto's Victoria University, why the lives of Canadians had not been wasted: the Allies were right, and Germany was wrong.[36]

Other Canadians preferred to interpret the war not just as a defence of good or right, but as a defence of humanity and civilization. 'They left their homes to safeguard humanity and to add a bright band to the chaplet of history,' declared Chancellor A.L. McCrimmon of McMaster University. 'Young and full of promise! What an offering at the Altar of Liberty!' This notion, that the fallen had given their lives 'in defence of those principles which all good citizens regard as worth preserving in the best interests of humanity,' was one of the most common refrains in Canada's memory of the war.[37] Listeners tuning in to the General Motors of Canada radio program in 1931 heard it, and ex-soldiers in the Brotherhood of Railroad Trainmen found it on the welcome-home medals presented to them by their union.[38] The sacrifice of Canada's sons and daughters had helped to save humanity from barbarism.

This theme also dominated the language of commemoration, often through the use of a figure representing Humanity or Civilization. This affirmed what had been at stake during the war and, in transforming humanity into a ward of the Allied governments, also confirmed that Germany was inhuman and uncivilized. This is especially evident in the work of sculptor Walter Allward. *Saturday Night* described his war memorial in Peterborough, Ontario, as representing the collapse of barbarism in the face of civilization: 'civilization stands in a commanding position, with outstretched hand, the idle shield worn on the back of the figure and an idle sword expressing the idea that there can be no further conflict ... the figure of strife or barbarism, beaten and retreating before the strength of civilization, the sword has fallen to the ground and the flambou [*sic*] has been extinguished.' His sketch for the Bank of Commerce memorial was similar, depicting a male figure who 'plants his strong foot upon the neck of a recumbent and still struggling brute beast of wilful war waged by a misguided nation.'[39] The victory of civilization over Hunnishness was thus validated in bronze.

It was also validated by the inscriptions that hundreds of Canadian communities chose for their monuments. They frequently affirm that the war had been fought for civilization, humanity, or ideals like Liberty, Truth, Justice, Honour, Mercy, or Freedom. Such inscriptions, which list the specific principles at stake and confirm the value of fighting for those principles, proliferate in every Canadian province. Often listed as a trinity, there is apparently little logic in the values that any given community chose to list. A plaque in St. Paul's Church in Charlottetown recorded that Lieutenant Frederic John Longworth, killed in action a day before the Armistice, died 'For Liberty, for Honour, for Righteousness.' The fallen of Mahone Bay, Nova Scotia, gave their lives for truth, justice, and liberty; in Orangeville, Ontario, it was freedom, truth, and righteousness. Only occa-

Walter Allward's war memorial in Stratford, Ontario. He used the same allegorical figures, Civilization standing triumphant over Barbarism, in other war memorials. (J. Peter Vance)

sionally is an inscription more revealing of local sensibilities. On the bilingual memorial in Lac-Mégantic, Québec, the French text notes that the soldiers had died 'pour la défense de la liberté et de la civilisation,' two concepts nearer to the Gallic heart than the 'freedom and righteousness' listed in the English text.

It went without saying that any sacrifice, including the supreme sacrifice, was more than justified in defence of these eternal principles. In this regard, virtually every Canadian war memorial can be considered a patriotic memorial (to use Antoine Prost's phrase), one whose inscription renders a value judgment on the sacrifice.[40] Such monuments affirm the nobility and rectitude of the struggle waged by Canadian soldiers and honour those people who were willing to lay down their lives to check the spread of militarism and barbarism. By their service, they had helped to banish the darkness into which the world had been plunged in 1914.

III

IN THE FACE of this inspiring vision of the Great War, a few faint voices tried to shape an alternate vision. Neutralists, non-interventionists, and isolationists, many of them intellectuals like Frank Underhill, Arthur Lower, and Escott Reid, railed against involvement in wars that, in their view, little concerned Canada directly. Because they conducted their campaign in the rarefied atmosphere of *Canadian Forum,* university campuses, and the Canadian Institute of International Affairs, however, these elites posed little real threat to the just war theory. More dangerous was the very vocal pacifist lobby, which carried a critique of war into the streets, churches, and public schools. The poet Wilson Macdonald, whose patriotic verse, such as 'The Girl behind the Man behind the Gun,' had given way to impassioned and slightly overdone pacifist poetry, painted the war not as a righteous defender of civilization but as a hideous beast:

> His feet are rotting
> > From a slow gangrene;
> His tusks are yellow
> > And his eyes are green.
> But the church of god
> > Calls him sweet and clean.[41]

In Saskatoon, Violet McNaughton eschewed Macdonald's poetic excesses and developed instead a more rational critique of the war, using the women's page of the *Western Producer* to disseminate a mixture of traditional pacifism and western cooperative ideals. The Women's International League for Peace and Freedom (WIL), headquartered in Vancouver and led by Laura Jamieson, Lucy Woodsworth, and Agnes Macphail, organized lectures, festivals, and a range of other activities intended to 'make peace as interesting as war.' WIL peace conferences, often held to coincide with Armistice Day, featured addresses by prominent pacifists such as J.S. Woodsworth and Rabbi Maurice Eisendrath, as well as the obligatory poetry reading by Macdonald. The lectures were often complemented by church services, discussion groups, and ceremonies to decorate the graves of nurses, firefighters, and other 'heroes of peace.'[42]

Despite such efforts, adherents to the pacifist movement remained a small minority in Canadian society. The leading organizations never had a large membership, and their communitarian ventures were pitifully small. Even the movement's peak, when it brought together a rough coalition of pacifists, social gospellers, and liberal internationalists, lasted only a few years, from the late 1920s to the mid-1930s. With the rise of fascism in Europe, allied groups melted away, many under the pressure of having to choose between preserving democracy and social justice and holding to the ideals of non-violence.

But if fascism stood in the way of a strong Canadian pacifist movement, so too did the memory of the Great War. According to that memory, August 1914 had given the civilized world (in other words, the Allies) a choice: either fight to preserve the values that were deemed to underlie society, or sacrifice those values in the interests of preserving peace. By opting to fight in 1914, Canada had made the only possible choice. The slaughter of the next four years did little to shake the nation's faith that the choice had been right. It would temper their public displays of enthusiasm when the choice had to be made again in 1939, but it would serve as no brake on enlistment, unity, or less obvious shows of patriotism.

That the war had been a necessary evil was accepted by most veterans. E.L.M. Burns, who would command Canadian troops in the field during the Second World War, quoted approvingly a line from Ernst Jünger, the ex-soldier and reluctant darling of the German political right: 'There are ideals in comparison with which the life of an individual or even of a people has no weight.'[43] In 1934, a former nursing sister agreed: 'Our only choice in the last resort is to be prepared to defend ourselves, or accept slavery and extinction ... Is it to be our creed that *nothing* is worth dying for?' Vancouver veteran F.W. Bagnall, a former YMCA worker and a very devout man, abhorred war but admitted its necessity if greater evils were to be avoided; he did not understand how others failed to grasp this fundamental reality.[44]

It was not simply that old soldiers wanted to justify a war in which they suffered and that took the lives of so many of their comrades. On the contrary, the belief that Canada had been right to fight to defend a set of principles was widespread in society. When the Woman's Christian Temperance Union suggested in 1925 that the Anglican Church reconsider its support for cadet training in public schools and Anglican universities, a synod committee disagreed. Military training was imperative, concluded the committee, because it was the duty of every Christian to be ready to defend sacred principles like freedom, justice, and truth. It was not enough to avoid an aggressor and hope the threat would pass. 'War is a bad thing,' wrote a Toronto cleric, 'but when a mad dog runs amuck [sic] it must be met with proper methods.'[45] At a Montreal Armistice Day service in 1933, Sir Andrew Macphail concurred, declaring that 'peace and war is not the antithesis. The antithesis of a slothful peace is not war but massacre. That has always been the fate of every docile, passive and submissive people.' War was an evil, but it was not the supreme evil; it was infinitely preferable to a peace purchased by the abandonment of a society's most treasured values and principles. In response to Neville Chamberlain's 'Peace in our Time' speech on the signing of the Munich agreement, Sir Charles G.D. Roberts read his poem 'Peace with Dishonour' to the University of Guelph's 1938 Armistice Day service. In it, Roberts held that he did not shrink from the 'red flame of war, the anguish of women, / The dropped bomb, the gas-choked breath,' because all of these eventually passed. His soul, however, cringed from the 'long dishonour, brief cowed peace. / For freedom stripped and cast to the loud pack. / *This* stain endures.'[46] For Sir Charles 'God Damn,' pacifism was flawed simply because it asked Canadians to jettison every philosophy they valued most highly rather than take up arms against another nation.

Roberts was not the only Canadian to believe this. On Armistice Day, the Canadian Youth Congress (CYC) made a practice of soliciting messages in support of world peace from prominent Canadians. The responses received in 1937 are revealing. Certainly many politicians, clerics, and educators expressed wholehearted support for the efforts of the CYC, but a number of individuals pointed out the inherent weakness of pacifism, its refusal to recognize the existence of a just war. Derwyn T. Owen, the archbishop of Toronto, stressed that 'in all our efforts to promote peace we should remember the claims of justice,' while Adele Plumptre, the Toronto politician, educator, and philanthropist, noted that 'there can be no peace without a foundation of justice in international relations.' General Alex Ross, president of the Canadian Legion, responded at greater length: 'I am convinced of the fact that we who took up arms under similar circumstances [in 1914] played our part in a manner which history will proclaim as adequate ... [W]e fought no war of conquest but we fought sincerely and honestly to secure the peace of the world. But we failed in that purpose and therefore it is with this sense of failure and in a spirit of humility I speak and say that it is futile and hopeless to simply proclaim our desire for peace.' Pacifism was not enough, maintained Ross. People had to be willing to fight to defend what they valued.[47]

The widespread acceptance of the just war thesis through the 1920s and 1930s was, as much as Nazism, the rock upon which the ship of pacifism came to grief. For Armistice Day 1935, *Saturday Night* printed a thoughtful reflection on the relationship between memory, pacifism, and the Great War. The editor decided that there was little honour to those who served or died 'by the constant reiteration of the thought that their sacrifice was vain and mistaken, and that no such sacrifice should ever have to be repeated.' The contention that all war was futile was irritating at the best of times, but especially so on the anniversary of the Armistice 'which marked the saving of Europe from the possibility – at any rate for a generation or so – of complete domination by one of the least humane, least tolerant, and least freedom-loving of its races.' Furthermore, pacifists achieved nothing with their protests against war: 'If those who hate war – and its hatefulness we have no wish to deny – would content themselves with making every effort that lies in their power to ensure that the behaviour of their nation shall be so wise, so just and so humane that no other nation can possibly make war on it without gross injustice and inhumanity, we should have no word to say against them. Unfortunately, we see little sign of any such effort on their part.'[48] In short, even Canada had not yet reached that level of spirituality that freed people from the need to go to war. For this reason, the pacifist position was entirely too simplistic. No one could deny that universal cooperation and love were the ultimate goals of the human race. However, it was folly to suggest that this state of grace could be achieved without sacrifice.

That the Great War represented one of the sacrifices along the road to universal amity is evident in Canada's memory of the war. Allward's sketch for the Bank of Commerce memorial, the male figure with its foot upon the neck of the beast of war, was intended to be constructive, not destructive. It stressed 'the ameliorating forces of re-creation, which by the power of benevolent ideas in evolution will tend to make the savagery of war impossible.'[49] In this interpretation, the war waged by the Allies had been a force for good, because its only goal was the prevention of future conflict. The sculptor's memorial on Vimy Ridge carried the same message, according to *Saturday Night*: 'There is in the symbolism of this monument no suggestion of that characteristic element of the shallower popular philosophy of our post-war day, the emotional rebellion against all forms of human strife, the strident clamour for the immediate establishment of the millennium on the basis of the present division of the world's surface among the existing sovereign states.' Allward's figures demonstrated that the pacifist position was untenable, for in the 1930s the most it could realistically hope for was an artificial peace that was legalistic and treaty-based. Instead, the true goal should be a peace that was spiritual in nature. That peace 'will be brought nearer only as we each and every one learn ... to be actuated by a much livelier sense of the universal brotherhood of man and the relative unimportance of racial and national divisions.'[50]

The mythicized version of the war, then, proved that pacifism was a bankrupt philosophy, because only those people who were willing to fight for peace and freedom would be able to secure it. With this, the soldier became the foremost advocate of peace; as someone who was willing to fight and die to secure peace, he was the ultimate pacifist. Criticism of Armistice Day or war memorials on the grounds that they perpetuated wartime hatreds missed the point, for such commemorations marked not a war, but a quest for peace. As the Canadian Legion put it, 'all the living sacrifices made upon the fields of battle, and commemorated on all our War Memorials were made in the truer interest of Peace, and not in those of war.'[51] The decorated hero had no 'passion for war'; the men who enlisted in 1914 were not warmongers who joined up 'because they enjoyed the prospect of slaughtering foreign men who had nothing to do with war being declared.' On the contrary, 'it was through his love of peace that he shouldered the burden of kit and accoutrements and went forth to do battle – a struggle that should have been made lighter and shorter by the assistance of those professed so-called pacifists who are decrying him today.'[52]

What was true of the soldier was even more true of the veteran; he was not 'pugnacious and anxious for war' but rather was 'the greatest and sincerest pacifist extant.' Only the veteran, who had experienced first-hand the horror of war, could fully appreciate the need for a true pacifism. 'We know war and its aftermath,' said former Canadian Corps commander Sir Arthur Currie at the unveiling of the Peterborough memorial in 1929. 'We speak of peace with the authority of service.' Veterans were men who 'deplored war, its military discipline, its hardships, its trail of suffering, but who to-morrow, if their country needed their services, would immediately respond to the call, would make any sacrifice to ensure a more lasting peace.'[53] The pacifist-soldier, then, was not a contradiction in terms. The veteran of the Great War was a truer pacifist than Wilson Macdonald or any WIL member, for only the veteran had been willing to risk death on the battlefield in defence of peace.

WHEN H.G. WELLS coined the phrase 'the war that will end war,' he intended 'war' as a euphemism for Prussianism or militarism.[54] In this sense, he was entirely correct, and Canadians never lost sight of the fact that November 1918 marked a victory over the forces of barbarism. Yet Wells's phrase was also interpreted in a literal sense: the Great War would put an end to the human activity of war. The fact that this assertion proved optimistic in no way compromised its basic validity within the context of the myth. It was unfortunate that the Great War had not marked the dawn of eternal peace, yet there was no reason to believe that this dawn would not eventually come. The war only verified what many people already knew, that the road to peace might well lead humanity through conflict. If aggressors were met on that road, they had to be faced and defeated. Only by fighting for the principles that Canadians valued could they one day enjoy a state of peace founded on universal love and cooperation.

That did not mean, of course, that the nation should leap at every chance to go to war. Were the majority of Canadians willing to fight for the League of Nations over Manchuria and Ethiopia? Probably not. Did they support Neville Chamberlain, the self-proclaimed 'go-getter for peace,' in his efforts to appease Nazi Germany? Almost certainly. Yet when appeasement had been tried and had failed, they accepted war as a last resort, an unfortunate but necessary evil. They did so for a number of reasons, not the least of which was the fact that the notion of a just war against an intransigent and dangerous aggressor had been nurtured in the public consciousness in the two decades after 1918.

Clearly, the journey to everlasting peace would take humanity through a number of just wars. The true pacifist, then, was not the publicist who railed from a soapbox against every form of war, but the soldier who was prepared to stand in the vanguard. One could never achieve peace simply by talking about it; one had to be willing to sacrifice more than a few well chosen words and the odd poem for something so precious. The only way to demonstrate a real commitment to peace was to be willing to fight and die for it. In Canada's vision of the war, the soldier was the twentieth-century version of the Prince of Peace.

CHAPTER 2

Christit in Flanders

THERE WERE FEW stauncher supporters of the war than Canada's clergy. For them, the atrocities committed by the enemy demanded that the Allied nations become agents of divine retribution, cleansing the earth of those who defiled Christendom with their crimes. The Great War became a crusade, a holy war that pitted Christians against the pagans of Europe. At stake was not the territorial integrity of Belgium or the holdings of some farmers in Picardy, but the very values upon which Christianity was founded. This was a war for righteousness, the best kind of war that could be fought.

Caught up in the excitement of August 1914, Canadian church leaders threw themselves solidly behind the crusade. Within the Methodist Church, general superintendent Samuel D. Chown and Dr. W.B. Creighton, the editor of the *Christian Guardian,* nailed the king's colours to the church's mast and girded themselves to lead their flock against the German Antichrist. 'A war in defence of weakness against strength, a war for truth and plighted pledge, for freedom against oppression, is God's war wherever waged,' thundered the *Presbyterian Record* in October 1914.[1] From St. Stephen's Church in Winnipeg, the Reverend Charles W. Gordon (soon to go overseas as a military chaplain) told Canadians that 'the gage of the German Kaiser and of his Prussian Junkerdom, [has been] hurled in the teeth of Christian civilization.' Summoning the God of Righteousness and Truth to the aid of the Allies, he called upon the men of his congregation to take up the challenge.[2] No true Christian could remain aloof from the fight. Patriotism could be no mere sentiment, heard the congregation of St. Mary's Cathedral in Hamilton: 'It is a duty of conscience, of religion.' From pulpit and pen came an endless stream of exhortations to the faithful to rally in defence of the faith. Khaki, insisted Chown, had become a sacred colour.[3]

The white heat of religious fervour that surrounded the declaration of war and the first accounts of German atrocities could not be sustained, however. The slaughters of the Somme and Passchendaele made it increasingly difficult to reconcile the war with a benign, omnipotent Creator. Grieving families might well have wondered if Gordon's God of Righteousness really sanctioned the maiming and killing of millions of his children. Were all events really part of God's plan, as the tenets of historical theology suggested? And what of the men at the front? Were they fighting to preserve an orthodox Christianity that sought, in the interests of social reform and moral improvement, to curb the drinking, gambling, and other pastimes that provided temporary diversions from the hell surrounding them? For Canadians who reflected upon the relationship of religion to war, these were troubling questions.

Yet there was a solution to the problem of maintaining the relevance of Christianity in the face of the war: a return to the very root of the faith, Jesus himself. By emphasizing Christ's journey through suffering and sacrifice to redemption and salvation, the tragedy of Flanders could be explicated. Just as Jesus had given his life so humanity could survive, so too did the soldiers offer their lives for humanity. In this theology, each death was an atonement, each wound a demonstration of God's love, and each soldier a fellow sufferer with Christ. Only this brand of preaching appealed to the imagination of the troops, whose folk religion mixed superstition and mysticism with a marked ignorance of liturgy and doctrine. Only this could console bereaved relatives who found cold comfort in the churches' historical theology.[4]

The war's end only served to strengthen this view, and the seed that had been planted took root in the public consciousness as a simple way to comprehend the war. For the legless veteran, there seemed no way to explain his disability in light of historical theology; surely God's eternal plan did not demand that he be crippled and unable to support his family. The same dilemma hounded the desolate widow and the parents of the neurasthenic son. Did the progress of the human race towards perfection demand that their lives be ruined? The figure of Jesus Christ and the notion of redemption through sacrifice, in contrast, offered real solace. By drawing a parallel between the sacrifice of Christ and the sacrifices of 1914-18, the war took on a sense of purpose. The soldier gave his leg, the woman her husband, and the parents their son's mind, all to save the world. By offering what was most precious to them, these people had partaken of Christ's sacrifice. Jesus became a metaphor for the tragedy of the war; through the 1920s and 1930s, Christ, rather than the practice and teachings of the Christian churches, became the spiritual centrepiece of Canada's memory of the war.

SOLDIERS PASSING THROUGH the battle zones of France and Belgium could not help but be struck by the frequency of roadside shrines. On their travels, they constantly passed these rustic calvaries, in villages, on verges, or at isolated crossroads. Some were intact, but others had inevitably fallen prey to bomb or shell. The sight of a shattered crucifix, the body of Christ pierced by a bullet or shrapnel fragment, could be a powerful lesson to a marching infantryman. It reminded him of one who suffered 2,000 years earlier, and in whose footsteps he followed. It may also have offered the comforting thought that he did not suffer alone, but in the company of Jesus.

A shattered roadside shrine near Quéant, October 1918. Has some irreverent soldier placed Christ's arm on the block of stone as a salute to passing comrades? (NAC PA3367)

These thoughts, often no more than hinted at in the letters and diaries of soldiers, were expanded into an entire theology in the memory of the war. When the chancellor of Victoria University declared that 'all fine and good things which lie in the heart of Christianity were at stake,' he knew full well that Jesus was at the heart of Christianity and that the values at stake were not those of the twentieth-century Christian churches, but of Christ himself. As one soldier put it, Jesus had been the first to fall in Flanders because 'the very principles for which Christ gave His life are identically those principles for which Britain is to-day giving her life-blood.'[5]

In defending those principles, the men of the Canadian Expeditionary Force (CEF) became more than simply soldiers of the king; they were soldiers of Christ. Contrary to what pacifists might believe, said a Toronto cleric, 'soldier of Jesus Christ' was not a contradiction in terms. The Bible commended soldierly virtues and praised the piety of the centurions of Capernaum, Jerusalem, and Caesarea, and the Great War proved that this praise had been entirely appropriate. 'Soldier' and 'Jesus Christ' had been 'gloriously reconciled' by the experience of the trenches, he wrote.[6] Many congregations evidently agreed. A verse from Paul's second letter to Timothy

('Thou therefore endure hardness as a good soldier of Jesus Christ') appears frequently on church war memorials, and parishioners would have known the verse that follows, 'No man that warreth entangleth himself with the affairs of *this* life.' By his service, the soldier of Christ had elevated himself above the temporal; by fighting spiritual battles, he had entered the spiritual realm.

Indeed, he had joined the great Christian warriors of history. Of that company, a number of illustrious names became popular metaphors, each bringing slightly different shadings to the motif. David was a potent image to describe Canada, for it suggested the young Canadian army's victory over Teutonic might. Grace Blackburn, in her enigmatic novel *The Man Child,* likened Canada to David facing the German Goliath, and many churches found the comparison entirely apt.[7] The boy soldier appears twice in the memorial windows of St. Paul's Church in Toronto, and the 42nd Battalion window in the Church of St. Andrew and St. Paul in Montreal depicts David holding the head of Goliath.

The Knights of the Round Table constituted another popular spiritual metaphor that had the advantage of combining a righteous quest with the fellowship of comrades in a common cause. It could, of course, be a powerful source of irony. When Philip Child transformed the battered table of Dan Thatcher's mess into a Round Table, with 'the Major sitting in the role of King Arthur at the end,' he also described the rest of the surroundings: a shell hole in the wall that had been covered by an old newspaper, an oil-drum stove, a wealth of age-old wine stains.[8] It is a depressing scene, and one that highlights how little the soldiers have in common with the shining knights of yore. But more frequently, the metaphor was chosen to reveal the true nature of the soldiers. The veteran who remembered his comrades as members of 'a New Round Table' or the Charlottetown poet who called Canada's war dead 'God's white knights ... / Who pledged their service to restore the Grail' were being entirely literal in their use of the image.[9] By defeating the German armies, the nation's fallen had followed in the footsteps of King Arthur and his knights; with their quest, they had returned righteousness to the earth and made it safe for the faithful again.

A more powerful symbol for the soldier, more potent even than David or the Round Table, was the crusader, the man who responded to the church's call and quit his home to help vanquish the infidel. Indeed, the crusading knight is the most common motif in stained-glass windows erected as war memorials. In the Zion Tabernacle in Hamilton, a knight kneels before Christ, the shape of his sword echoing the symbol of the ideals he defends. A window to Captain Thomas George Bragley in the Church of the Ascension in Montreal shows a Christian knight kneeling at an altar, and in

Central United Church in Port Colborne, Ontario, the memorial window shows a medieval knight bearing a flag away from the figure of Christ. He looks back at Jesus, who stands in front of a shining cross and holds his hands towards the warrior. Through such imagery, the exhausted and mud-spattered soldiers were transformed into crusaders in gleaming armour; they were no longer the Poor Bloody In-fantry, but rather 'knights upon a holy quest.'[10] 'It seems to me that I knew Lancelot and Tristrim in Flanders,' mused Theodore Goodridge Roberts. 'Knightly vision was theirs.' That vision took in not a cratered ribbon of mud winding through shattered fields, but the shining path that led to the promised land. 'I never came away from listening posts on the front line,' recalled former divisional commander Sir Archibald Macdonell, 'without feeling that the men in the ranks were like knights of old.' They were the stuff of legend, figures who would be spoken of in reverential tones.[11]

The memorial window to Captain T.G. Bragley in the former Church of the Ascension in Montreal. (Peter Harper)

These crusaders, however, were more than just soldiers *for* Christ. When Marjorie Pickthall wrote of the continuance of Canada's harvest being purchased by the thorns and agony of the men at the front, she had more in mind than the soldier as a modern-day crusader.[12] Through his death in battle, the individual soldier sacrificed his life to atone for the sins of the world. In attributing the symbols of Christ's crucifixion to the lowly infantryman, Pickthall, like so many other observers, transformed him into the universal victim suffering for humanity. The soldier *was* Christ.

More recent critics have dismissed what Stanley Cooperman has called the Jesus-in-Khaki image for its 'obscene religiosity.'[13] Given explicit expression in John Oxenham's poem 'Christs All' and the patriotic song 'Christ in Flanders,' the image may seem unpalatable to modern readers, who see in it the worst sort of pseudo-religious sanction for slaughter.[14] Obscene or not, its persistence in postwar Canada is remarkable. It crossed the boundaries of region, class, religion, and generation, and was enunciated by supporters and critics of the war myth alike. It was central to Canada's memory of the Great War.

Canada's fallen soldiers were not simply labourers, clerks, and farmers who had died in battle; they were saviours whose suffering and sacrifice were one and the same with Christ's. 'Who are we that we should pretend to stand before these saviours?' queried the speaker at a Nova Scotia memorial dedication. 'Verily, these whom we reverence, our soldier-dead, are greater than us ... They had suddenly become as gods ... [At] calvary places in France, Flanders and England, [they] gave up their mortal lives, and are amongst the great saviours of mankind.'[15] When the relatives of Captain Allan Gray selected the verses for a memorial window in Holy Trinity Church in Burford, Ontario, they had good reason to choose 'This is my beloved son in whom I am well pleased' and 'Behold the lamb of God.'

The Great Sacrifice
'I am the Resurrection and the Life'

James Clark's *The Great Sacrifice,* with its focus on the unity between soldier and Christ, became a popular motif in the language of commemoration. (Collection unknown)

Churchgoers, of course, would have known that this last verse concluded, 'that taketh away the sins of the world.' The window drew a direct parallel between the soldier and Christ: by using the agony of Jesus to symbolize the agony of the soldier, it admitted of the inverse relationship. The soldier's suffering represented Christ's; the sacrifice of the infantryman became one with the sacrifice of the lamb of God in atoning for the sins of the world.

In few places was this connection more explicit than in *The Great Sacrifice,* by British artist Sir James Clark. Clark's rendering of a soldier lying dead at the feet of Christ is a powerful evocation of the religious interpretation of the war. Peace and composure are reflected on the face of the soldier. His hand covers the wound on Christ's foot, affirming the link between his own suffering and that of the Saviour. Above the soldier is the crucified Christ, who gazes down at the infantryman as if to recognize in the soldier's wounds and death a community of sacrifice.[16] This very potent image was copied frequently across Canada. A 1928 Armistice Day newspaper supplement featured an engraving of the work, and the Toronto Centennial Committee chose it as the frontispiece to its 1934 souvenir booklet. St. Philip's Roman Catholic Church in Hamilton used a version of the image on its memorial plaque, and in St. John's Cathedral in Winnipeg, the image was embellished with the figure of an angel, who holds the Crown of Life and a palm frond. Just as fronds were strewn along Christ's path into Jerusalem, so too are they intended to line the soldier's path into the Kingdom of Heaven.

If James Clark offered the most evocative visual expression of the union between Christ and soldier, the most poignant literary enunciations of this unity came from three very different writers: Marjorie Pickthall, Canon Frederick George Scott, and George Godwin. Products of different generations and different regions, the three experienced the war in very different ways. Yet for each of them, the Christ-in-Flanders image resonated strongly.

Marjorie Pickthall, the daughter of an Anglican cleric, came to Canada from England in 1889 while still a infant. At the tender age of seventeen, she began her literary career with a prize poem in the Toronto *Mail & Empire,* and from then until her untimely death in 1922, she produced a steady stream of poems, novels, short stories, and essays. Pickthall spent the war years in England, where a valiant (and ultimately vain) quest to perform useful warwork kept her from devoting all of her talents to capturing the war in verse. She did, however, write a handful of war poems, one of which she entitled 'Marching Men':

> Under the level winter sky
> I saw a thousand Christs go by.
> They sang an idle song and free
> As they went up to calvary.
>
> Careless of eye and coarse of lip,
> They marched in holiest fellowship.
> That heaven might heal the world, they gave
> Their earth-born dreams to deck the grave.
>
> With souls unpurged and steadfast breath
> They supped the sacrament of death.
> And for each one, far off, apart,
> Seven swords have rent a woman's heart.[17]

The metaphor is significant. Pickthall, though the product of an orthodox Protestant upbringing, displayed a broad heterodoxy in her work; paganism,

Christianity, classicism, and mysticism all find their way into her writing. Yet it was the figure of Christ, an image that had long fascinated her, that seemed to offer the best hope of comprehending the sacrifices of the soldiers. For Pickthall, characterized by her biographer as a Christian *wandervogel,* only the figure of Jesus could give a spiritual meaning to the war.[18]

If Pickthall was an adventurer in religious thought, Frederick George Scott was a very orthodox high Anglican who saw no need to venture outside his own faith for answers. Born in 1861, Scott was of the same generation as Pickthall's father and served as rector of St. Matthew's Church in Quebec City for forty-five years. When war came, he dropped everything to offer his services to the cause. Despite being well over fifty, Scott smuggled himself onto a troopship and sailed for Europe with the First Contingent. Once at the front, his reputation quickly grew. He was tireless in ministering to the men of the First Division, and was omnipresent in the trenches, spending long hours travelling the front on horseback or motorcycle. By war's end, Scott was the most popular chaplain in the Canadian Corps and one of the best-known and best-loved figures in the entire CEF.

The affection was fully reciprocated, and Scott developed a deep attachment to the soldiers in his flock. Their stoicism through hardship and suffering moved him deeply and reminded him of the object of his own faith. 'The sordid life has been transfigured before me,' he wrote, recalling the

Canon Frederick George Scott (centre, with walking stick) surrounded by men of the 1st Division. (Rev. L.G. Duby)

scene around Messines. 'The hill was no longer Hill 63, but it was the hill of Calvary. The burden laid upon the men was no longer the heavy soldier's pack, but it was the cross of Christ.'[19] For Scott, like Pickthall, the figure of Christ seemed the most natural metaphor for the sacrifices being made at the front. His beloved soldiers, with their calm resolve, selflessness, and determination to defend sacred principles, were not simply emulating Christ's example. They had become saviours themselves.

George Godwin's response to the war was very different from Scott's. While the canon revelled in his time at the front and grieved when it came to an end, Godwin's work suggests no such affection for service. He had been a subaltern during the war, the most dangerous rank in the army, and during the interwar years supplemented his earnings as a lawyer by writing freelance articles for newspapers and magazines in North America and Great Britain. In 1930, Godwin published *Why Stay We Here?*, a bitter and powerful tale of Stephen Craig, a British Columbia fruit grower, and his wartime odyssey. The novel is full of protest against the use of religion in war. In one exchange, Craig and his doomed friend Piers ponder the existence of God; Piers concludes that 'if He exists at all, then He must be an impersonal God who doesn't care a hoot about mankind.' Nonetheless, Godwin concludes his novel by admitting that the soldiers were universal victims like Jesus; in the final chapter, he leaves us with a powerful image: 'what were these marching men as, if not as Christ, Archetype of all suffering, sacrifice? ... A battalion of Christs bearing the sins of the world along a northern road of France.'[20] Godwin had clearly agonized over the relationship between Christianity and war and had concluded that there was no place for organized religion in the carnage at the front. There was, however, a place for Jesus. He, like the soldiers, had been condemned to suffer for the sins of others. Christ, then, was the quintessential symbol of the man at the front.

On the occasion of Remembrance Day 1937, the editor of the *Globe* pondered the comparison drawn by Pickthall, Scott, and Godwin: 'He is the flesh of our flesh and kinsman to us all. He is the incarnation of all the finest qualities of idealism ... He received all the wounds and endured all the agonies of the millions of the wounded, and he won all the victories bought at so great a cost ... [He was] the apotheosis of the ordinary man.' At first glance, it may seem that the editor was writing about Christ, yet the column referred to the Unknown Warrior entombed in Westminster Abbey to represent all empire dead who had no known grave. The degree to which the two figures became interchangeable is striking. The Unknown Warrior had been an ordinary man, yet by offering his life for civilization, he had transcended his own humanity. Deified by death in battle, he could look forward to the same reward for his sacrifice that Jesus had earned 2,000 years earlier: the assurance of resurrection and everlasting life.

II

IT WAS NOT ONLY the Unknown Warrior, however, whose immortality was guaranteed. Each Canadian who died for the cause could be assured of eternal life. Just as Christ's crucifixion had been followed by his resurrection, and as medieval crusaders believed that death in battle against the infidel sent them directly to the Kingdom of Heaven, so too was the death of a Canadian infantryman understood as his elevation to immortality.

This insistence on the immortality of the fallen was in part a consolatory act but, in a broader context, it was also part and parcel of making sense of the war. Having accepted that the war had been a crusade in defence of Christian principles, people simply could not conceive of 60,000 Canadians descending into oblivion after dying in a righteous cause. The memorial volume of a Toronto high school noted that the war had 'fortified the faith in a personal survival after death,' for the simple reason that one's sense of justice demanded it. 'They went down to save civilization, to save the whole world,' boomed a clergyman in 1921. 'These men could not die.'[21] The only alternative to a heightened belief in the resurrection of the soul was spiritual desolation. To have lost a loved one was bad enough; to lose faith as well was unthinkable.

As a consequence, Canadians frequently and fervently trumpeted the immortality of the dead soldier, in comments that are strikingly similar even down to their syntax. 'Dead? No! They are immortal!' T.R. Deacon assured fellow members of the Soldiers' Relatives Memorial Association in Winnipeg. Ottawa airman and poet Arthur S. Bourinot knew that 'they are not dead, the soldier and the sailor, / Fallen for Freedom's sake.'[22] On the contrary, they had already been resurrected:

> These graves are empty, their brief tenants gone,
> Though all unstirred heaves this unsodded clay;
> In living hearts of flesh is raised their stone,
> Let wooden crosses wither as they may,
> Then woman lave afresh your burning eyes;
> Sweet babe, be comforted, the dead arise.

Such men did not lie in Flanders or Artois. They were 'in the Conqueror's courts of glory, in the Gardens of the Lord!'[23]

This conviction was evident in war memorials, where resurrection and ascension imagery abounds. The National War Memorial in Ottawa, for example, was carefully situated so that the movement of the figures was from west to east under the arch. The symbolism was clear: those Canadians who sacrificed their lives, who had, in soldiers' slang, 'gone west,' would find everlasting life.[24] A particularly beautiful articulation of this notion exists in Knox United (formerly Presbyterian) Church in Calgary. The focal point of the memorial window is the risen Christ, who carries the banner of Triumph over Death and is surrounded by a scroll with the notation 'I am the Resurrection.' At the bottom of the window are a number of Canadian soldiers. One, cradled in the arms of a nurse, looks upwards with an expression of serene faith; another lies dying directly beneath the figure of Christ. The momentum of the window leads upwards, towards Jesus, affirming that the fallen will inevitably be carried to the Kingdom of God.[25]

Another powerful resurrection image can be found in Coeur de Lion McCarthy's three memorials designed for the Canadian Pacific Railway stations in Montreal, Winnipeg, and Vancouver. Executed in bronze, they portray an angel with a laurel wreath bearing the body of a dead soldier towards heaven. Far from subtle, the image was heartily approved as offering a positive vision of death in battle. Communities that could not afford the services of a sculptor of McCarthy's stature found it easier to affirm the immortality of the dead in a memorial's inscription. Phrases like 'Death is

The National War Memorial in Ottawa, unveiled in 1939. The figures symbolize the united nation, while their movement through the arch represents death and resurrection. (J. Peter Vance)

The memorial window in Knox United (formerly Presbyterian) Church, Calgary. The figures of the soldiers at the bottom are overshadowed by the knights, who typify virtues like Patience and Fidelity, and Christ surrounded by angels and cherubs. (Knox United Church)

swallowed up in Victory' (Riverfield, Québec) and 'These have won a deathless victory' (Cornwall, PEI) bore witness to the survival of the soul after death in battle.

Faith in the resurrection was also conveyed by the use of images of natural regeneration, especially the bud. Left on the branch where each leaf falls in the autumn, buds symbolized regeneration and, when used in connection with dead soldiers, the belief that they would be reborn. W.D. Lighthall articulated this theme in 'Deathless':

> At Passchendaele I sleep not,
> Only my leaves of autumn,
> My autumn leaves fell there,
> In the hour of farewell splendour
> In the sunset of the year,
> But when they fell I died not,
> For the wondrous spring was in me
> And the life I gave at Passchendaele
> Hid the life of morrow year –
> I am here.[26]

Images of natural regeneration had particular resonance when used in the language of remembrance. Trees were popular for war memorials, either singly or in the form of groves or avenues, because they represented the promise of everlasting life. Macdonald College planted a ring of oaks around the men's playing field, one for each member of the college who had been killed during the war. In Toronto's Coronation Park, veterans dedicated a

In Coeur de Lion McCarthy's memorial in the CPR station in Montreal, the Angel of Victory bears the fallen soldier to Heaven. (NAC PA30810)

grove of silver maples as a war memorial; separate groups of trees represented the four divisions of the Canadian Corps, with trees being dedicated to individual units.[27] Some cities, such as Victoria, Calgary, Montreal, Winnipeg, Saskatoon, Fort William and Port Arthur (now Thunder Bay), and North Bay, opted for tree-lined memorial avenues. Ironically, few of these avenues have survived; the symbols of everlasting life could not survive road-widening and urbanization.

The image of dawn was another important resurrection motif in Canada's memory. Paul Fussell remarked that, during the war, dawn was 'morally meaningful, as a moment fit for great beginnings' but insists that this use of dawn did not survive the war; it lived on in postwar fiction only as an ironic contrast to the horror of the battlefield that it illuminated.[28] In Canada, however, the use of dawn in an ironic sense is infrequent. It was much more common to aver that dawn continued to mean what it had meant in 1914, the promise of a new beginning and of God's infinite good. A memorial window in Carmichael United Church in Regina depicts the Great Sacrifice, with the gathering dawn behind the central figures. The significance of this was not lost on Carmichael's minister, the Reverend J.W. Whillan. A former battlefield chaplain, Whillan observed that Allied troops had looked across No Man's Land at the sun rising in the east for four years, and it never failed to impress upon them the rising hope of victory. For this reason, he found dawn to be entirely appropriate as an image, for it reflected the promise of goodness that would come from the war. Whillan was not just an optimistic cleric in idealizing the dawn. As the following passage demonstrates, others had similar views:

> I liked the keen damp air of the mornings of September ... The east would shoot with crimson. Birds would twitter. Then, like magic, the sun would glitter on the dew-covered weeds and wet wire. There would be mists in the hollows, often extensive, so that the distant slag heaps would appear dark islands in a woolly sea. Gradually the sun would gain strength, and the vapors would dissolve. Then we went back to our shelters and odors of tea and bacon would make each man happy.[29]

The author of this passage was not a chaplain viewing the front from the comfort of a rear-area billet, but Will Bird, the renowned Maritime folklorist who served as a corporal in the 42nd Battalion. Born in East Mapleton, Nova Scotia, in 1891, Bird had been helping with the harvest in Western Canada when war was declared; he immediately tried to enlist but was rejected on account of his bad teeth. After his younger brother was killed in action, however, he tried again and this time was accepted, reaching the front in December 1916. Bird spent most of the last two years of the war in the trenches, surviving some of the heaviest fighting experienced by the Canadian Corps, and, by his own admission, he was a bitter and discouraged man by the time the Armistice came. Yet the dawn never lost its power to inspire him; it meant renewal, and carried with it the promise that the new day could not possibly be as bad as the old.

The resurrection was even implied by the rituals performed at memorial unveilings and on Armistice Day. The focal point of such ceremonies was the sounding of the last post, the observance of a moment of silence, and the blowing of reveille. Each of these acts was deeply symbolic. The last post, the bugle call that marked the end of the day and the setting of the sun, was also used at front-line burials and thereby came to represent the death of a soldier. The moment of silence was an opportunity to reflect upon the dead, but it also suggested Christ's time in the tomb. And then came reveille, the bugle call that awakened soldiers at the front and, by extension, would resurrect the fallen and signal their ascension. The sounding of reveille recalled not simply a line from Rupert Brooke's 'The Dead' ('Blow out, you bugles, over the rich Dead!'), but also a verse from Paul's first letter to the Corinthians, which affirmed the immortality of the soul: 'For the trumpet shall sound and the dead shall be raised incorruptible.' This brief, three-part ritual, lasting only a matter of minutes, was enacted time and time again across the country, and it remains the centrepiece of Canadian Remembrance Day ceremonies. Its original symbolism may be forgotten now, but it once offered a simple metaphor for the journey of the fallen soldier through sacrifice to immortality.

III

THE PERSISTENCE of resurrection imagery in Canada's memory of the war and the enduring faith that the fallen soldier gained immortality had a significant impact on the entire attitude towards death in battle. No one enunciated this attitude more clearly and comprehensively than John Daniel Logan. Born in Antigonish, Nova Scotia, in 1869, Logan was educated at Dalhousie and Harvard before setting out as a dabbler in teaching, advertising, publishing, and literary criticism. None of these fields brought him either financial or emotional security, and in 1916, with no immediate prospects, he joined the army at the age of forty-six. He was eventually promoted to sergeant, and fought at Vimy and Passchendaele before a knee wound won him a discharge. For the brilliant but somewhat shiftless Logan, army life was a revelation. He loved the comradeship of his unit, the 85th Battalion, took immense pride in performing duties of substance (in contrast to the often aimless scribblings of his prewar life), and drew new spiritual energy from the sacrifices being made for the cause.[30]

It was this last element that underlay many of Logan's reflections on the meaning of the war. In two collections, *Insulters of Death* (1916) and *The New Apocalypse* (1919), he assembled a body of poetry that was inspired by 'the vision of death, and especially heroic death, as the supreme venture and consummation possible to the soul of man.' Poems like 'Timor Mortis' and 'For an Only Son' were avowedly consolatory; they were intended 'to give the living who had been robbed of their beloved new and reasonable solace for the spirit, by making death beautiful.' As strange as it sounds coming from a veteran of Passchendaele, Logan's vision drew praise from critics. A reviewer from the *Halifax Herald* said of *The New Apocalypse* that 'every line is redolent of highly spiritual experiences … [S]o full is it of poignant sweet-

Proposed title page for J.D. Logan's *The New Apocalypse*. (Acadia University Archives, J.D. Logan Papers, box 10, f. 97)

ness and ineffable consolation that it may be likened to healing balm poured gently on stricken hearts.' Horatio Crowell of the Halifax *Morning Chronicle* was scarcely less adulatory: 'If the nation as a whole can glimpse the war in the perspective in which Logan views it, our future is safe; our sacrifice will be justified.'[31]

Crowell would have been gratified to learn that much of the country did view the war from Logan's perspective. Though few people were quite as enthusiastic as Logan, many believed that, of the various ways to die, death in battle was by far the best. In believing this, they were able to separate the significance of death from its physical realities. A body bloated by gas, sliced apart by shrapnel, or pulverized into atoms by artillery did not necessarily mean that the death was a hideous one. Indeed, if the ideals behind the death were pure, the physical ugliness was irrelevant. For this reason, the myth considered it a mistake to view death in battle as a loss; rather, it was a sacrifice willingly made. As a Vancouver clergyman and former military chaplain said, 'in one sense the thing that strikes us most about the war is the appalling wastage, beyond all computation, of life and substance. But there are wars and wars, and we must distinguish between loss and waste and sacrifice.' He referred to a veteran who stated indignantly that he did not lose his arm, but rather gave it; such 'was not loss or waste, but sacrifice! And it was sacrifice exultantly rendered.'[32] By the same token, war memorials almost never refer to the dead as having lost their lives. Loss suggested a hap-hazard event, something that occurred by chance, and so did not accurately describe death in battle. Rather, the fallen invariably gave their lives.[33] There is a sense of purpose inherent in this notion that affirmed the war as a mean-ingful event and its participants as willing actors. To lose one's life was a tragedy; to give one's life by making the supreme sacrifice was the ultimate in selflessness.

Because the fallen soldiers had offered their lives of their own free will, Canada's memory discouraged mourning for them. Exhortations against public displays of grief are common. 'Why mourn thy dead?' wondered Duncan Campbell Scott.[34] Remembering the fallen was no occasion for weeping: 'no funeral dirge or plaintive strain forlorn / Should sound the passing of their chivalry,' wrote the Vancouver poet A.M. Stephen. This was abundantly clear to next of kin entering the Soldiers' Tower at the University of Toronto, for the planners of the memorial had chosen as an inscription a passage from Milton's 'Samson Agonistes':

> Nothing is here for tears, nothing to wail
> Or knock the breast; no weakness, no contempt,
> Dispraise, or blame; nothing but well and fair,
> And what may quiet us in a death so noble.

When Militia and Defence Minister S.C. Mewburn suggested striking a com-memorative cross to present to mothers who had lost sons in the war, Sir Edmund Walker assumed that it would be a Maltese cross, for 'a Latin cross which a woman would wear in memory of some sorrow would not, it seems to me, serve the purpose.'[35] Not sorrow over a loss, but gratitude at having had something to give for the cause was the correct emotion.

In the myth, grieving Canadians who took the time to ponder their be-reavement rationally would realize at once that sorrow was inappropriate: if they embraced the myth, they could not help but be struck by the contrast between the temporal world inhabited by the war's survivors, and the Elysian Fields where the fallen passed eternity. 'Peace brought my father restful days, with love and fame for wage; / War gave my son an unmarked grave and an unwritten age,' mused Isabel Ecclestone Mackay. 'Who shall declare which gift conveyed the greater heritage?'[36] Few thoughtful Canadians could doubt which was the more precious gift. Those people who survived the war did so only to toil meaninglessly in the workaday world. The years might bring them 'love and fame for wage,' but they might just as easily bring disappoint-ment, disillusion, and heartbreak. Each day they might wake to 'the inglori-ous morrow / That mocks our anguish and our victory.' The peace might well be unkind to them, bringing only old age, a slow decline into decrepitude, and a lingering death. 'Yours is the warm soft scent of poppy leaves,' said another poet to the dead, 'Ours the ceaseless war of hopes and fears.'[37]

Dolly Cayley pondered these matters as she watched an Armistice Day service at the end of Sydney Arthur's bizarre college romance *A Man's Worth*. She considered those soldiers 'who returned to outlive their glory, to struggle on for a living under a handicap,' and was overcome by gratitude that her lover, George Norton, had been killed in action: 'He will always be young, and perfect, and we will never live to mar love's golden dreams.' Countless other Canadians professed to draw solace from this fact. 'He died more gloriously than if he had lived out his allotted span, and died at last in his bed, his loved ones weeping at his side,' rejoiced a relative of William George McIntyre, killed in action in 1917.[38] 'We who remain shall grow old,' wrote a McGill alumnus,

> We shall feel the snows of cheerless winter;
> But you shall be forever young,
> With you it shall be forever spring
> Where you wander through the willows.[39]

By dying in God's battles and in the prime of life, they had won freedom from the petty strictures of life on earth; they had secured eternal youth.

The answer to Mackay's question, then, was self-evident. 'Who dares to pity their lost youth?' queried the editor of the *Globe*, who already knew the answer to his own question: 'They did not lose their youth. They took youth with them from the world ... Envy them. They won clear, with their youth undimmed upon them.' Roger Thornewill, the hero of ex-soldier Harold Baldwin's *Pelicans in the Sky*, agreed. He thought of the comrades he had left in France, and concluded that they were the lucky ones:

> Mine's a harder life, for I didn't die
> But I live to envy the happy dead,
> Yes envy the luck of my old chum Bill
> Who merely died upon Dead Man's Hill.'[40]

In light of this tendency to envy the dead, one might expect Canada's memory of the war to be characterized by a sense of pity for the survivors. After all, the figure of the ruined veteran, the ex-soldier damaged in body and soul by his experiences, is common in the war literature of other countries. Eric Leed remarked that silence was a dominant characteristic of Great War veterans, caused either by a neurasthenic reaction to the horror of war or by an intellectual inability to convey the realities of battle.[41] Both variants exist in the Canadian canon. Sitting in their isolated cabin in northern

Saskatchewan, Hedwig, the German war bride of Lieutenant Davey Adams, tells her friend and fellow war bride that the fighting has left their husbands mute shells: 'We're married to shadows – merely walking shadows. The real men died – out there some where – in Flanders ... They seem to be hypnotized or something by the awful horrors they have seen. It keeps them forever chained.' Will Bird, who could rhapsodize about the beauty of a Flanders sunrise, could not speak of the horrors of Passchendaele. In one short story, 'The Prisoners Who Cannot Escape,' he relates the touching tale of Danny Dick, a mounted rifleman whose mind was so destroyed by battle and captivity that he is only capable of watching birds and animals.[42] Perhaps the most poignant evocation of the ruined-veteran thesis is found in Isabel Ecclestone Mackay's 'The Returned Man,' a powerful poem set in a town that assumed that the soldier would come back quieter and less boyish 'but still a hero with tales to tell':

> So, when there were no tales,
> Only blank silences –
> When he lay for hours
> Staring through leafing branches
> And forgot them
> Utterly –
> They tried to arouse him, saying:
> 'The war is over.'
> But when he turned on them
> His shadowed eyes
> They stammered –
> Knowing that they lied![43]

Mackay's poem is a fine character sketch of a figure who was probably all too common in postwar Canada, yet the ruined veteran had little place in the myth of the war. The envy of the dead was a consolatory technique to affirm for survivors the glory of the sacrifice; it was not to be taken in a literal sense, to suggest that the survivor should be pitied. Certainly some ex-soldiers experienced psychological problems in the years of peace, but in the myth these men were only the exceptions who proved the rule. When two French doctors decided in 1918 that the psychic constitution of the *poilu* had not been fundamentally altered by the war, they reached a conclusion that would have satisfied many Canadians.[44] The soldier could not have been coarsened by war because the cause was righteous: it was unthinkable that the twentieth-century crusader could have been transformed into an animal or an empty shell by fighting God's battles in Flanders.

But Canada's myth went even further than the French psychologists.

The soldier's soul was not hardened by war, or even left unchanged. On the contrary, it was remade in a finer form. If death had freed the fallen from 'the ceaseless war of hopes and fears,' the simple act of enlistment did the same. It liberated men from materialism and earthly concerns and ennobled them in a righteous cause. The war, wrote Rupert Brooke in his 1914 sonnets, had 'caught our youth, and wakened us from sleeping.' It had washed away evil and, in so doing, had brought a generation into its heritage. Writing from the front in August 1914, the tempestuous French poet Charles Péguy agreed. The war had cleansed him: 'vingt ans d'écume et de barbouillage ont été lavés instantanément.'[45]

Canada had its own Brookes and Péguys, people who saw in war an improving force for the individual. In 1916, Lieutenant G.R. Forneret delivered a eulogy for the nation's fallen:

> The guns and shells are playing the most magnificent requiem that it is possible for a man to have. His name ranks with the heroes and martyrs of all ages. And he was just a common man who was used to going to his office, to tea in the afternoon and to the theatre. By one stroke he has achieved what has been sought for by all the greatest men who had a goal ... to do some one thing with that gift he calls his life to make that life worth living – to make his own country and his own Empire a little cleaner, the better and the freer.

For Peregrine Acland, who would later write the antiwar novel *All Else Is Folly,* 'the hardships and bitter sufferings of open strife were not so appalling as the monotony and miseries that so frequently beset that life of peace.' Ensnared in that life, prewar Canadian men had been 'dwellers on the plain' until the call of war rang out, when 'they suddenly find themselves struggling towards the mountain-tops.' By allowing them to devote their lives to the defence of sacred principles, the war gave a 'background of magnificence' to their lives.[46]

The horrible realities of trench war gave few Canadians cause to rethink the potential of war for human improvement, and this theme remained potent in the interwar period; even huddled in water-filled dugouts, the soldier could still be 'struggling towards the mountain-tops.' On Armistice Day 1936, Sir Andrew Macphail said that 'war evolved the best qualities with which man is endowed, fortitude, courage, fidelity in duty, and loyalty to comrades, respect for our enemies, and humanity towards them when they come into our power.' It did so by offering the common man a chance to demonstrate that he could reach beyond his own petty concerns when called to a greater task. 'His care was all for simple, selfish things,' wrote Robert J.C. Stead of one of his beloved farmers:

His home, his wife, his horses, and his child;
No thought had he for conquerors and kings,
    Or reeking power and innocence defiled.

Then in an hour his soul was born again;
    He saw himself the nation's instrument.[47]

Stead's farmer was replicated across Canada. He appeared on Robert Tait McKenzie's war memorial in Almonte, Ontario, as the keen-eyed Volunteer, captured in 'that electric moment that magnetized a million spirits, freeing them for the instant from material preoccupations.' He stood on Frances Loring's memorial for the Law Society of Upper Canada, at Osgoode Hall in Toronto, in the figure of a youth about to shed the robes of everyday life to offer himself to the higher cause of humanity.[48] He was the fop of the 1919 popular song, the unremarkable individual who had been ennobled by donning the uniform of the king. He was Harry Amoss's Efficiency Jim, the coldly rational businessman who was humanized by the comradeship of the trenches.[49] The Great War, then, was a purifying force that could transform anyone, even the most hard-bitten wastrel, into a soldier for righteousness. It was a refining force that 'revealed the pure gold' of Canadians by burning off sham and insincerity and laying bare the true nature of the individual.[50]

Implicit in this notion of war's redemptive power was a recognition that it was at once destructive and constructive: for the refiner's fire to work its purifying magic, it first had to reduce the subject to an elemental state. Postwar literature is full of characters who found in the war their initial ruination but ultimate redemption. In Theodore Goodridge Roberts's novel *The Fighting Starkleys,* Jim Hammond succumbs to fear and deserts from his unit while still in Canada. His shame is only temporary, however, for he seizes the chance to join up again, goes to France to fight, and returns home a hero with a shattered knee. Bob Seward, in Janet Cox's short play *The Coward,* is also overcome by fear. While guarding an ammunition store with two comrades, Seward panics and has to be knocked unconscious to avert disaster. When he regains his senses, however, he has been somehow transformed and gives his life by throwing himself on a bomb to save a friend.[51] Even Gray Thornton, the hero of Leslie Roberts's *When the Gods Laughed,* finds in the war not only his destruction but also his salvation. He is court-martialled and cashiered after getting drunk in the front lines, but he eventually rejoins his old unit and reveals his true nature, that of the selfless hero.

For Thornton, Seward, Hammond, and countless real-life Canadians, the crusade of 1914 was a unique opportunity. It gave them the chance to stand as defenders of Christianity, in line with the storied soldiers of the faith throughout history. Those who died for the cause gained immortality; those who survived were purified by the trial. By allowing Canadian men and women to offer their lives for humanity, the war had afforded them the rare opportunity to emulate Christ. As J.D. Logan wrote in terms that would not have been considered hyperbolic, the war enabled Canadians to make a very public expression of 'Christlikeness in self-slaying love for the perfection and happiness of humanity.'[52]

IV

CANON FREDERICK GEORGE SCOTT might well have approved of Logan's philosophy. In September 1918, the canon was ministering to the men of the First Division near its headquarters at Warlus. He travelled between battalion billets in a motorcycle sidecar, sharing meals with the soldiers, watching them play, and lending a sympathetic ear to their concerns. Looking back on those days from 1922, Scott recalled thinking 'that a new and mysterious light that was born of heaven hid behind the sunshine, and cast a glory upon men and even nature.'[53] For the canon, everything that surrounded him was redolent with meaning. Spirituality was everywhere: in the men he counselled, in the battered fields and ruined villages, and in the dawn that broke on the scene every morning. It had been illuminated by the Christlikeness of the sacrifice, to use Logan's term.

The light that Scott divined in 1918 continued to suffuse Canada's memory of the war in succeeding decades, giving every facet of the memory of the war a spiritual significance. The battlefields of Belgium and France were no longer Flemish fields or Picardy orchards; the blood of Canada's youth had sanctified the very earth, transforming the Western Front into a new Holy Land. J.W. Dafoe called Vimy Ridge 'holy ground, for here men by the tens of thousands died for mankind!' while George Fallis referred to the blood that had consecrated the slopes of Vimy. Even in 1939, just a few months before the outbreak of the next war, the Hamilton *Spectator* confirmed the religious interpretation by proclaiming in a large headline, 'The Land is Holy Where They Fought and Fell.'[54]

Because the Western Front had become a Holy Land, it was assumed that all good Canadians would want to journey there to pay their respects. 'To many Canadians,' wrote Mary MacLeod Moore in 1920, 'it is the dream of their saddened lives that they may some day cross the ocean and the Channel to stand beside the grave of a boy who offered his life for others.' Certainly many people undertook the journey for personal reasons, to visit the grave of a loved one, but the pilgrimage was also a show of reverence and fidelity to the war's sacrifice. As J.W. Dafoe put it, 'generation after generation for centuries to come, will follow the Canadian way of glory over the battlefields of France and Flanders, with reverent hearts and shining eyes, learning anew the story of what will doubtless always remain the most romantic page in our national history.'[55] Even during the war, Canadians were prepared to follow Dafoe's direction and undertake a pilgrimage once the fighting had finished. In January 1916, Dr. J.J. Mackenzie wrote to his wife from Salonika that 'we are going to see a lot of France when the war is over. Wouldn't it be fine if it should end before the summer, and if you and I could make a pilgrimage through the war zone before we go home.' The idea of touring the battlefields may seem strange to present-day minds, but it was a goal that many Canadians held. 'When peace has come, and I return to France,' wrote poet Arthur Bourinot, 'I know the places that I'll long to see.'[56]

Even before the peace treaty had been signed, tourists began arriving on the battlefields, as many as 60,000 in the summer of 1919 alone.[57] Soon, an entire industry sprang up to service these visitors. For those people who wished to explore on their own, any number of guidebooks were available; the first Michelin guide to the Western Front was published in 1919. Less adventurous travellers could procure the services of a professional guide, frequently an ex-soldier trying to capitalize on the pilgrimage movement, or could book cheap tours from various tourist agencies in England. Others could wait for any of the huge, organized pilgrimages that occasionally descended upon the Western Front. In 1927, 15,000 Americans took part in the American Legion pilgrimage; the following year, 11,000 members of the British Legion attended the unveiling of the Menin Gate in Ypres. With these opportunities, next of kin and curious tourists came to the battlefields in huge numbers – 140,000 in 1931 and 160,000 in 1939.[58] Canadians were certainly not immune to the appeal of the battlefields, and the Overseas Military Forces of Canada were deluged with requests for travel permits to visit 'the devastated areas,' as they were called. The first organized pilgrimage from Canada was apparently a group of thirty veterans from the Maritimes who made the trip in 1927. The great event, of course, came nine years later with the Vimy Pilgrimage of 1936, when 6,000 Canadians journeyed to Artois for the unveiling of Walter Allward's memorial on Hill 145.

This event reveals the peculiar character of battlefield pilgrimages. Typically, they bore little resemblance to what is normally understood by the term. They did not constitute a rehearsal of one's own demise, nor were they punctuated by hazards to test the faith of the pilgrim.[59] Instead, they had spiritual meaning on another level. Just as the soldiers had discarded petty material preoccupations to direct their energies to a higher cause, so too would pilgrims leave their homes to pay tribute to that higher cause. A pilgrimage to the Western Front could 'refresh ... heart, mind and body ... by

'With an old ammunition box as table: a party of sightseers lunching in a camouflaged shelter on the former battle front in France.' Michelin guidebooks would direct them around shellholes and away from roads still blocked by rubble. (*Illustrated London News,* 14 June 1919, 853, courtesy of Illustrated London News Picture Library)

Canadian nurses pose for a group photo during a sightseeing trip to the ruins of Ypres, January 1919. (NAC PA3933)

Pilgrims and spectators await the dedication of the Vimy Memorial, July 1936. The view faces northeast, towards the coal fields which were bitterly contested in 1917. Note the fields in the foreground, still badly cratered nearly twenty years after the battle. (NAC PA803934)

thoughts directed towards all that was great and lofty.' With this, the pilgrimage became a re-enactment of the war as crusade.[60] The soldiers had shown their faith by going to war; the pilgrims could show their faith by retracing the paths of the crusaders. They would undertake this sacred act as 'worshippers venturing upon a service that inspired within them the noblest elements of their being.' Vimy Ridge became a new Mecca or Canterbury; it was a magnet to the faithful, who made the journey in the same spirit of Christian piety that had animated the soldiers.[61]

If the journey to the battlefields took on strong religious overtones, so too did the ultimate destination, for the war cemeteries, which drew so many Canadians, were the equivalent of shrines. They were holy sites, each grave 'the sacred altar / Between every man and God,' and one should approach those cemeteries with the same reverence as one would approach 'the most bejewelled crucifix in the noblest fane of Christendom.'[62] The construction of these shrines was the responsibility of the Imperial War Graves Commission (IWGC), authorized at the Imperial War Conference of 1917. The driving force behind it was Fabian Ware, who laboured tirelessly to establish the commission and then recruited some of Britain's finest creative minds. Sir Edwin Lutyens designed a number of cemeteries as well as the Stone of Remembrance placed in the larger burial grounds, while Reginald Blomfield built the first three model cemeteries and also designed the Cross of Sacrifice common to all plots. The two most famous inscriptions used by the IWGC ('Their name liveth for evermore' on the Stone of Remembrance and 'A Soldier of the Great War – Known Unto God' on stones with unidentified remains) were chosen by Rudyard Kipling, whose only son was lost at Loos in 1915.

The commission's work was based on two fundamental principles. In the first place, no repatriation of bodies from the war zones was permitted. The bodies of Canadian soldiers who died in England could be returned to Canada, but those buried at the front would remain there. This stipulation was partly symbolic. It reflected not so much the notion that a soldier should lie where he fell (the reorganization of the cemeteries to eliminate isolated plots meant that many soldiers did not in fact lie where they had fallen) but that he should rest with his comrades. Allowing the repatriation of soldiers' bodies for interment in municipal or parish cemeteries across Canada violated the unity of dead soldiers. The other reason for the prohibition of repatriation was logistical. Because of the chaos on the former battlefields and the sheer number of bodies, the repatriation of human remains would have created immense administrative difficulties. The American government committed itself to offering next of kin the choice of repatriating remains or leaving them in the battle zones (roughly 70 per cent of families chose repatriation) but may have had cause to rue this decision; Fabian Ware reported that the head of the American graves service in France resigned because he could not guarantee that the right bodies would go to the right relatives.[63]

The second guiding principle was that all graves, regardless of the individual's rank or social station, would be marked with a standard headstone, a slab of Portland stone with a gently curved crown. Next of kin could select a short motto to appear on the bottom of the headstone, but no other personalization was allowed. This regulation was partly aesthetic, for the IWGC had no desire to see its cemeteries littered with elaborate grave markers erected by wealthy relatives. But again, there was a strong symbolic motive as well: standard markers affirmed that all soldiers were equal in death. The general and the private may have had little in common in life, but both had died for the same principles. One sacrifice had not been any greater or more selfless than the other.

Much of the commission's early existence was spent defending these

Contemplating the death of comrades: a lone soldier surveys the bleak Canadian cemetery at Vimy Station in December 1917. (NAC PA2281)

two principles, and it worked quickly to complete and beautify cemeteries so that relatives would not press for remains to be repatriated. In the spring of 1919, Robert Borden urged Lloyd George to accelerate work on the larger cemeteries or the IWGC would face a public outcry. He had recently received a report from his High Commissioner in London, Sir George Perley, who had toured the cemeteries and found those near Amiens in good shape but those around Ypres in need of quick work, so visitors would not get 'a bad impression of the manner in which the cemeteries are maintained.' Indeed, the reason most often given for denying permission to visit a given ceme-

The transformation of Maple Copse Cemetery near Zillebeke (Ypres) from a swampy burial ground into a tidy cemetery. Not all graves were aligned in rows; the Imperial War Graves Commission did not exhume bodies simply to achieve neatness. (Commonwealth War Graves Commission, *before* B/W 21401[8], *after* COL12822[s])

tery was that it was not yet in a fit condition to be seen by relatives. By 1920, Ware could report to Perley that the work was progressing well and that if requests for repatriation of bodies could be resisted for another two years, people would be satisfied with the cemeteries and would drop their requests.[64]

This, of course, assumed that relatives of the dead would act rationally, an assumption that was not always valid. Indeed, two lurid incidents reveal the lengths to which determined individuals would go to evade IWGC regulations. Private G.C. Hopkins had been killed at Passchendaele in November 1917 while serving with the Princess Patricia's Canadian Light Infantry, and his body laid to rest in Tyne Cot Cemetery. In January 1919, the soldier's father applied for a permit to visit France and apparently spent some time trying to locate his son's grave. The experience must have convinced him that the IWGC was badly organized, and that his son's body should be brought home where it could be properly cared for. Of course, he came up against the Commission's refusal to allow the repatriation of remains, and all of his efforts were fruitless. Finally, Hopkins decided to take matters into his own hands. On the night of 17-18 May 1921, Private Hopkins's body vanished from Tyne Cot; cemetery workers noticed that the grave had been disturbed, and they dug up the coffin to find that the remains (few enough to be carried in a small valise) had been removed. They were eventually traced to a mortuary in Antwerp, where they were seized by IWGC officials. Private Hopkins's bones were reburied, and proceedings were instituted against the individuals responsible for the desecration.[65]

The second instance was even more bizarre. In January 1921, a Toronto woman named Anna Durie began to enlist support for a campaign to have her son's remains repatriated; she was particularly incensed that the families of Canadians who had fought in the American forces could arrange for the repatriation of remains. As in the case of Hopkins, her efforts came up against the stone wall of IWGC policy. A letter from Hugh Guthrie summed up all of the commission's arguments:

> Those who fought and fell together, officers and men, lie together in their last resting place facing the line they gave their lives to maintain ... [T]he dead themselves in whom the sense of comradeship was so strong would have preferred to lie with their comrades. These British cemeteries in foreign lands would be the symbol for future generations of the common purpose, the common devotion, the common sacrifice of all ranks in a United Empire.

Frustrated, Durie took the same course that Hopkins had. In July, she went to France and let it be known that she intended to remove her son's remains from Corkscrew British Cemetery. The local IWGC superintendent warned cemetery staff and visited the woman in an effort to dissuade her. The interview was not a success. Durie refused to listen to reason and insisted that IWGC officials were all liars; she fully intended, she said, to return to Canada and denounce the commission and its treatment of relatives of the dead. She had more in mind than a publicity campaign, though. Durie hired two French workers, and, on the night of 30 July 1921, they removed her son's body from its grave and placed it in a coffin on a hired horse and trap. Captain Durie, however, did not get as far as Private Hopkins. At some point in the operation, the horse bolted, breaking the trap and leaving the coffin lying on the road. The workers hurriedly returned the remains to the grave and beat a hasty retreat. Put off by the mishap, Durie returned to Canada and evidently made no further attempts to reclaim the body.[66]

These bizarre but isolated incidents, involving only two of Canada's 60,000 war dead, reveal the IWGC's success in holding to its principles. Certainly once the cemeteries were completed, few relatives could have wished for better resting places for their loved ones. Colonel H.C. Osborne, secretary-general of the commission's Canadian agency, predicted that 'visitors to the cemeteries will be struck first by their order and beauty, by the nobility of the plan, by the profusion of flowers.' The sight of an IWGC cemetery would evoke Shelley's lines, written when he first glimpsed the grave of Keats: 'It might make one in love with death to think that I should be buried in such a plot.'[67] Saskatoon schoolteacher Evelynn Aitchinson visited the cemeteries in 1922 and called them 'a picture ... a mass of flowers with not a weed in sight.' Nova Scotian Florence Murdock, who went to France for the unveiling of the Vimy Memorial in 1936, made a similar comment in her diary: 'The horror of so many graves, is taken away by the beauty of the cemetery and the flowers are marvellous.'[68]

These two remarks reveal how the character of the cemeteries conditioned perceptions of the war. The determination to delay battlefield visits until the cemeteries had been beautified was not a calculated scheme to hide the horror of war from families; this was merely an unplanned consequence. The IWGC had only wanted to render the cemeteries so appealing that people would not insist on the repatriation of bodies. It was so successful in this task, however, that its work had an important bearing on the mythicization

Garden of the dead: Tyne Cot is the largest British military cemetery in the world, with nearly 12,000 burials. The names of a further 35,000 soldiers who have no known graves are inscribed on panels at the top of the cemetery. The Cross of Sacrifice is built on a ruined German bunker. (Jonathan F. Vance)

of the war. By turning soldiers' graveyards into gardens of the dead, the commission helped the relatives of the fallen to avoid the reality of death in battle. The ordered and charming cemeteries meant that visitors never had to confront the ugliness of their relative's death.[69]

Consequently, Aitchinson's comment on the absence of weeds can be interpreted in a symbolic sense as well. There were no weeds in the cemeteries – no mangled bodies, gassed faces, or bloated corpses – to blight the beauty of war. As Florence Murdock realized, the horror of so many burials was muted because each war cemetery became a sort of botanical exhibit. Visitors strolling through cemeteries with quaint and rustic names such as Nine Elms, Wailly Orchard, and La Plus Douve Farm would have had little trouble reconciling God's grace with the tragedy of war. Everything around them offered reassurance of the healing power of natural regeneration and the transcendence of God's abiding love. The nature of the cemeteries thus gave strength to the religious interpretation. It was difficult to find spiritual inspiration in the ossuary at Verdun or in rows of corpses wrapped in blankets; in an IWGC cemetery, it was difficult to avoid it. Visiting a war graves cemetery became a religious experience more profound than anything possible in church or chapel. 'Have you seen those graves in Flanders?' asked Toronto poet Oliver Hezzelwood:

> Sixty thousand graves in Flanders,
> Where the flower of our manhood sleeps beneath the poppied sod?
> Have you measured their devotion,
> Sensed their love and consecration?
> Then you've glimpsed a glorious vision of the boundless Love of God.[70]

The cemeteries assured visitors that, whatever concerns they may have had about the losses of war, God was in his place and all was right with the world.

The war cemeteries were not the only shrines for pilgrims to the Western Front; dotting the landscape were a handful of memorials erected by governments and private groups to commemorate specific battles or units. Though only a few of these were overtly religious in character, they all inspired the same sort of spiritual response that characterized the battlefield pilgrimages and cemeteries. In a speech at the dedication of the Cross of Sacrifice in Thélus Military Cemetery in July 1921, Arthur Meighen spoke of 'the quiet of God's acre' and the sacrifice of the fallen, who had 'sheathed in their hearts the sword of devotion.' The scene had the same impact on Hamiltonian Lily Hendrie:

> We arrived at the dear little plot of God's Acre ... [I]t was a glorious day, the larks still singing and the poppies! beautiful they were beyond

description! besides which it was one of those quiet Sabbath mornings and you can imagine my thoughts were of those splendid men who had died that we might live ... [W]e were brave till the 'Last Post' was sounded on the side of the little hill, it seemed far away, as if it were some heavenly benediction.[71]

The description of the ground as God's acre, the apprehended significance of the Sabbath, the characterization of the trumpet call as a heavenly benediction – all point to the degree to which spiritual overtones dominated these monuments.

The same aura of spirituality emanated from the government-sponsored memorials erected by the Canadian Battlefield Memorials Commission (CBMC), established in September 1920. The CBMC took on the task of marking the most famous battlefields of the Canadian Corps and, acting on the recommendation of a committee of senior officers, chose eight sites: St. Julien (the site of the Second Battle of Ypres), Crest Farm (captured in November 1917 to end the Battle of Passchendaele), Hill 62 (Sanctuary Wood, which the Canadians had defended through the summer of 1916), Hill 145 (Vimy Ridge), Dury (where Canadian troops broke the heavily defended Drocourt-Quéant line in August 1918), Bourlon Wood (to commemorate the attack across the Canal du Nord in October 1918), Courcelette (captured in November 1916 to end the Battle of the Somme), and Le Quesnel (marking the Canadian Corps' successful attack east of Amiens in August 1918). The notice soliciting entries for the design competition pointed out that they should have 'a cumulative effect due to similarity in scale and general form as landmarks. Each monument should, however, be individual in character as to its base and the composition of its immediate precincts.'[72]

The imprecise instructions created a dilemma for the CBMC: should there be a single design, repeated at each of the eight sites, or should one of the sites have a larger and more distinctive memorial? H.M. Mowat, the member of Parliament for Parkdale, and Cy Peck, the Vancouver MP, who had commanded the Canadian Scottish during the war and had won the Victoria Cross, both wanted a distinctive memorial at Vimy, but Arthur Currie frowned upon this plan. 'I do not want to have the impression left ... that Vimy was our greatest battlefield,' he told the commission, but he admitted that if Canada were to erect only one monument, it should be on Hill 145. In the end, the committee chose Vimy as the site of the major memorial, though the souvenir booklet put out by the commission incorporated Currie's concerns. Vimy was not 'the greatest achievement of the Canadian Corps either in strategic importance or results obtained,' it stated, but 'there it was that the Canadian Corps first fought as a unit and, as its components were drawn from all parts of the country, Vimy may be considered as the first appearance of our young nation in arms.'[73] Mackenzie King agreed, predicting that Vimy Ridge would be the crown jewel of the overseas memorials in 'conserving to future generations enough of this consecrated ground to disclose at a glance something of the nature of the activities, as well as of the sacrifices, of our Canadian soldiers.' To that end, King suggested that his government obtain title to the entire crest of the Ridge, between two strong points known as the Pimple (Souchez) and the Commandant's House (Farbus), a distance of some five miles. In fact, only a part of this land was available, the Farbus section having been returned to cultivation. The French government had already expropriated the rest, and eventually decided to present it to Canada as the site for the memorial.[74]

In some ways the outcome of the CBMC's deliberations was governed by the designs submitted in the competition. Many worthy proposals were received, but two stood far above the others. Regina sculptor Frederick Clemesha proposed the figure of a soldier emerging from a granite pillar; his hands rested on his upturned rifle, and his helmeted head was bowed in an attitude of repose. In time, the design came to be known as the Brooding Soldier. The other outstanding design came from Walter Allward of Toronto. It was a massive structure built on a series of long walls that were intended to symbolize a line of defence. Around the base stood figures representing the Breaking of the Sword, the Sympathy of the Canadians for the Helpless, and Canada mourning her dead. Two huge pylons rose from the base; between them, a figure symbolizing the Spirit of Sacrifice threw the torch to his comrades, while the figures of Peace, Justice, Truth, and Knowledge looked down from the pylons. The proposed memorial was a tour de force, the culmination of the sculptor's distinguished career. A.Y. Jackson rightly observed that Allward had gone 'beyond and above anything the framers of the competition conceived of.' The designs by Clemesha and Allward were of too high a standard to be rejected and were too original to be repeated eight times; Allward's design especially captured the imagination of the assessors, who judged it to be 'of such individuality and complexity that its character precludes it from the possibility of repetition.'[75] The only alternative was to have two distinctive memorials and six smaller, identical monuments. These would be simple inscribed blocks, each sitting on a terrace in a small landscaped park.

Not everyone was impressed by the CBMC's decision. Garnet Hughes, the son of the former Militia minister, carried on a running battle against Clemesha's Brooding Soldier and Allward's Vimy memorial. He called the former 'a most ghastly jack-in-the-box' and embarked on a campaign to have a 'simpler and more suitable design' adopted instead. To Peter Larkin he disparaged the Brooding Soldier as 'most inappropriate and most unfortunate artistically ... I think every Canadian who saw the monument considered that it approached grotesqueness.' Hughes was no more complimentary about Allward's Vimy memorial. He called it 'another enormous thing with steps and railings' and intimated that 'I would not mind this edifice being erected if I had the contract, but I do think it is [a] waste of money as well as being a tribute to vanity.'[76]

Despite Hughes's carping criticisms, Allward's memorial went ahead, though the project was plagued by delays. It took some time to decide on the type of stone to be used, and then longer still to locate supplies of the stone in a disused quarry in Dalmatia. With the discovery of the quarry, however, the problems only multiplied. Allward's correspondence reveals growing tension with Walter Jenkins, the Englishman who supervised the quarrying operation. They quarrelled over the quality of stone being shipped to Vimy, Allward insisting that all blocks be flawless and Jenkins countering that

The Vimy Memorial from the front. The effect of Allward's massive stone base, intended to symbolize the walls of defence, is evident. (NAC PA183629)

such expectations were unrealistic. The contractor also complained about Allward's refusal to specify the exact size of blocks required; in response, the sculptor insisted that sizes not be stipulated until prices had been agreed upon, for Allward considered that Jenkins's quotes were exorbitant. Finally, labour and transportation problems meant that Jenkins's costs were over three times higher than what he had contracted for, and he frequently pleaded for a renegotiation of the terms, so that his company could avoid financial ruin.

Allward certainly appeared obstinate to Jenkins, but his stubbornness grew from a recognition of the importance of his task and a determination to use only the finest materials. He was content to let sixteen years pass between the announcement of the competition and the unveiling of the monument because he knew that the Vimy Memorial would assume immense importance in the coming years. Indeed, once dedicated it became the cathedral for Canadian pilgrims to the Western Front. Like the pilgrimage that marked its unveiling, the memorial was surrounded by religious phraseology and symbolism. In Allward's vision, the walls and pylons suggested the upper part of a cross; in the afternoon, the play of sunlight between the pylons illuminated the sculptures and suggested a cathedral effect.[77] At the unveiling ceremony, speaker after speaker drew attention to the cross on the pylons, the sacred precincts, or the hallowed ground that surrounded the memorial. Some Canadian clerics complained about the absence of a religious service in the unveiling ceremony, and others might

Sculptural groupings on the Vimy monument. The grouping on the left shows the Breaking of the Sword. The figure with the bowed head is Canada mourning her dead. The figure on the right represents the Spirit of Sacrifice throwing the torch. (Mike Bechthold)

have lamented that the original plan to erect a chapel at the memorial was never realized.[78] Such accoutrements were redundant, for the Vimy Memorial was clearly a place of worship. It was the nation's primary altar to the fallen of the war.

Of course, a relatively small proportion of Canadians had the where-withal to undertake a pilgrimage to the Holy Land of British Arms. However, if many Canadians could not go to the battlefields, it was always possible to bring the battlefields to them. Pilgrims took great pleasure in filling their suitcases with souvenirs gleaned from the old front, all of which were borne home with the same reverence and tenderness accorded to the bone of a saint or a piece of the True Cross. These relics came to serve the same purpose as war cemeteries and overseas memorials: each could become an object of veneration that symbolized the meaning of the war to Canadians.

Battlefield crosses were especially highly valued in this regard, in part because of their rarity; for logistical reasons, the IWGC decided that it would not honour requests received after 1 September 1920 for the return of crosses.[79] A few of these rough crosses, used to mark war graves before the cemeteries were reorganized and the stone markers erected, found their way back to Canada to be hung piously on the walls of churches. There, they existed as substitute graves whose configuration represented the ideals for which the soldiers had died.

More common was the practice of incorporating relics from the battlefield into local war memorials. The memorial window in Carmichael United Church in Regina has a piece of glass brought back from Ypres, and the plaque in Christ Church Cathedral, Fredericton, includes a cross made of stones from the cathedrals in Arras and Ypres that had been brought back by Bishop John Richardson in 1918. St. Paul's Church in Toronto is a verita-ble treasure trove of war relics. There are some 600 pieces of glass from sev-enty ruined European buildings in its memorial window, and the church is also adorned by a broken marble column, part of the altar rail of Arras Cathedral, and dozens of other similar items, all brought back by parish-ioners. Arthur Currie's grave marker in Mount Royal Cemetery includes a stone from the chateau at Camblain l'Abbé (where Currie lived for a time) and bags of soil from Vimy, Ypres, the Somme, and Mons, all brought back by pilgrims to be incorporated into the monument.

The popularity of battlefield relics reveals the degree to which Canon Scott's 'new and mysterious light' illuminated Canada's memory of the war. Bits of rubble, shards of glass, and bags of dirt were endowed with a spiri-tual significance; as artifacts taken from the new Holy Land, the detritus of war was transformed into objects of veneration. People could touch a piece of Arras Cathedral, or see a shaft of light beaming through a piece of the Cloth Hall, and be enriched by the experience. For many Canadians, it was the closest they would get to the Great Crusade.

IN 1921 HARRY AMOSS, an ex-soldier supplementing his teacher's salary with earnings from freelance writing, published a short story called 'The Padre Who Was Born Again.'[80] It tells of a chaplain who constantly chastised his men for their swearing and drinking, the very stereotype of the padre who ministered to men's morals rather than their souls. One evening, though, he is called to the stretcher of a dying soldier who had given his life to save his comrades. The experience was a revelation for the chaplain. 'For one brief moment, beside his tortured body,' he mused, 'I saw the glory of the transfiguration ... In that brief moment the darkness was illumined. I saw the glory of a thousands Christs all about me.' His personal faith rekindled by the experience, the chaplain resolves never to preach to the troops again about their morals, but rather to focus his efforts on instilling in them the love of Christ that had been reborn in him. In a dim dugout in Flanders, he had come to the realization that Jesus, and not the social reform and moral improvement that he and so many other chaplains had preached, had to be the focal point of religion at the front.

Amoss was certainly not alone in viewing the entire edifice of organized religion more sceptically after four years of war. 'The returned soldier looks at the minister with scrutinizing eyes,' wrote one veteran in 1919. So, too, did an alarming number of Methodist chaplains and probationers who had gone overseas; nearly 10 per cent resigned their orders upon returning to Canada and over a quarter disappeared altogether, choosing to have no further contact with the church.[81] This inability to reconcile organized religion with what occurred at the front runs through much postwar writing by veterans. Soldier-writers such as James Pedley and Archie Gray railed at the irony of holding church parades at the front, and Theodore Goodridge Roberts was even sceptical about the Christ-in-Flanders image. In one poem, he gazes up at the crucifix on the wall of his billet but is not filled with wonder as the scene takes on a spiritual light. Instead, he is touched by something approaching pity as he observes that 'poor Christ languished, pale and small, / In agony on the mildewed wall.'[82]

Yet if soldiers were dubious about the church and the ardour with which it exhorted men into the inferno, their doubts did not extend to the figure of Christ. In the memory of many soldiers who lived through the war, Jesus became distinct from twentieth-century Christianity and the churches that claimed to practise it. Institutionalized religion, which chastised them for engaging in the few pleasures open to them, held little appeal for the average soldier. Jesus, on the other hand, was someone he could relate to; He was a fellow sufferer whose agonies could be a source of strength and comfort.[83] After all, implicit in Roberts's verse is the realization that Christ and the poet shared the same mouldy billet.

If soldiers were most attracted by the suffering of Christ as a source of consolation, non-combatants were drawn to the example of his sacrifice and resurrection. Whatever troubling dilemmas the war had raised about the Canadian church or modern Christianity, notions of sacrifice, redemption, salvation, and resurrection were strengthened. The sheer size of loss experienced by the country demanded it. To abandon these ideals was to abandon oneself to despair; to embrace them more fervently than ever was to give meaning to the war.

CHAPTER 3

O Death, Where Is
Thy Sting?

The bells of hell go ting-a-ling-a-ling,
For you but not for me.
And the little devils how they sing-a-ling-a-ling,
For you but not for me.
O death, where is thy sting-a-ling-a-ling,
O grave, thy victory?
The bells of hell go ting-a-ling-a-ling,
For you but not for me.

Trench song

DESPITE ITS undeniable emotional appeal, some Canadians may
have found the religious interpretation of the war to be somewhat unsatisfying. Yet few quarrelled with what that interpretation was intended to
achieve: the supremacy of a positive, uplifting version of the events of 1914-
18. The religious interpretation drew the sting from the war by affirming
that physical discomfort and death were insignificant when compared with
the issues at stake and the meaning of the sacrifice. Those people who were
troubled by the image of Jesus in khaki, however, could achieve the same
end within a secular framework.

If the focus on the figure of Jesus Christ grew out of a determination
to demonstrate the relevance of Christianity through the Great War, the secular strategy was rooted in a need to conceptualize the war in a broader
sense. This was no easy task, and several factors limited the range of options
available to those people, be they ex-soldiers or non-combatants, who sought
to construct a vision of the war they had just endured. An understandable
reluctance to relive the tragedy of 1914-18, the desire of veterans to recall
only the positive aspects of life at the front, the physical separation of all but

a small number of Canadians from the realities of the battlefield, the absence of any historical precedent to aid in understanding the war – all of these factors contributed to the creation of a version of the war that avoided the painful memories in favour of positive, light-hearted recollections, and that retained essentially nineteenth-century images to describe a twentieth-century war. No less than the religious interpretation, the emphasis on humour and traditional modes of discourse drew the sting from the war by making it seem non-threatening and familiar.[1]

I

CANADA IN 1919 was tired of war. Recruiting drives, thrift campaigns, and fuel shortages had become all too common features of life. So, too, had the lengthening casualty lists in daily newspapers, the letters of condolence either sent or received, and the sight of telegram delivery boys who were the heralds of doom. Even in the worthiest of causes, these things began to grind down the soul. When St. Andrew's Church in Cowichan Station, British Columbia, inscribed its war memorial window with the phrase 'It is finished,' the parishioners did not merely echo the last words of Christ; they also conveyed their own deep sense of relief that the conflict had concluded.

After four years of war, most people had simply had enough of tragedy, death, and misery. In January 1919, University of Toronto president Sir Robert Falconer declared himself to be 'tired of reading about the hideousness of war,' a sentiment that appeared to change little over the course of the next two decades. Even in 1938, the editor of a newspaper in Vancouver announced on Armistice Day that there was 'no profit in recounting the horrors and the miseries and the privations to which this day, twenty years ago, brought a temporary cessation.'[2] Significantly, neither Falconer nor the editor of the *Vancouver Daily Sun* said that he was tired of reading about the war: they merely said they were tired of reading of its hideousness and miseries. In fact, there was little desire in postwar Canada to lay to rest the events of 1914-18. Robert Graves and T.E. Lawrence might have agreed never to discuss it, but lesser mortals were not interested in consigning the war to the realm of the unspeakable.[3] It was too immediate and had touched too many lives; the war was simply too big to be swept under the carpet. That did not mean, however, that the entire experience was suitable for discussion. First, it had to be tidied up to accommodate the desires of countless Canadians who had had enough of horror and tragedy.

After all, it was only natural to want to spare the feelings of bereaved relatives. The death of a loved one was enough of a trial; there was no need to remind relatives that the weeks that preceded the death were a misery of water-filled trenches and the ever-present stench of decaying corpses. This was certainly the feeling of Marguerite Taylor, who sculpted the Next-of-Kin Monument in Winnipeg. 'I wanted to do a happy soldier,' she stated, 'so the bereaved wives and mothers would not be too much saddened when they looked at it.'[4] The war memorial committee in Brantford, Ontario, was governed by the same consideration for the feelings of the townsfolk. It originally selected a sculptural group showing a broken field gun and a wounded soldier leaning against the leg of a woman. The committee, however, discarded the design as too depressing and in its place approved a grouping that was more positive. As the committee described it, the sculpture showed 'the wounded figure of a recumbent youth gazing up at the cross, while a mother, with head held high, typifies unbroken faith and patriotic fervour; a third figure is in the attitude of prayer.'[5] By opting for allegorical rather than realistic figures, by eliminating the debris of war in favour of personifications of its values, the committee had effaced the negative from its version of the war. The committee members were neither the first nor the last people to adopt this strategy.

In 1936, Sir Andrew Macphail was invited to speak at the Armistice Day ceremony in the city of Saint John. The favourite son of Orwell, Prince Edward Island, Macphail had left McGill University at the beginning of the war to join the Canadian medical services overseas. In 1921, he was commissioned to write the official history of the medical services; this highly partisan volume, harshly critical of the battle between civilian and military leaders for control of the Canadian Army Medical Corps, appeared in 1925. Macphail's remarks in Saint John would have found favour with Marguerite Taylor or the Brantford committee. He spoke of the 'secret joy there is in the soldier's life of poverty, temperance, chastity, and obedience' (veterans might have recalled the pains they took to avoid the last three; the first was often inescapable, even on $1.10 a day), and stated that 'a sense of pleasure dominates us to-night as we regard the war in retrospect. We remember sunny skies, summer fields strewn with poppies; and in the several springtimes, the hawthorne hedges that concealed the guns breaking in waves of white flowers.' It is easy to chuckle at Macphail's naivety and dismiss his remarks as the ramblings of a Victorian gentleman who never got closer to the trenches than a hospital in the rear area. Yet there was much truth in what he said. For many ex-soldiers, life in the trenches did take on what Stephen Leacock called 'the soft glory of retrospect.'[6]

Just a few months before Macphail's address, Charles G. 'Chubby' Power spoke at the unveiling of the Vimy Memorial. Power, the garrulous and hard-drinking minister of Veterans Affairs, had served at the front until

September 1916, when he was wounded by a rifle grenade explosion and invalided out of the army. Though he saw considerably more of the sharp end of war than Macphail, his remarks to the Vimy pilgrims were strikingly similar. He, too, referred to the soldiers' light hearts that saw them through the hard times: 'Difficulties dissolved before the timely jest; hardships lightened with a merry quip; they faced danger with a smile.' This, for Power, was his most enduring memory of the men who had served with him: 'Ignoring, as we feel they [the dead] would have us do, the dull, weary, miserable hours; erasing from our memory the hateful, degrading manifestations of brutish inhumanity; forgetting the hardships, the horrors; dispersing the inevitable fog of gloom, depression and despair, we see them emerging, even now, through the dull mists of passing years, gay, cheerful, happy comrades, loyal, true, faithful friends.'[7] Power's comments cannot be excused on the grounds that he had no desire to depress his listeners on such a momentous occasion, for his theme recurs too frequently in veterans' writings to support this explanation. In fact, Power spoke for a significant segment of the veteran community when he admitted the horrors of war but insisted that there was little to be gained by dwelling upon them. 'I guess we look at life optimistically,' mused cartoonist Jimmy Frise, 'the same way we remember the funny things in war. You never hear us old soldiers telling sad stories.' Dennison Grant, the creation of Robert J.C. Stead, spoke little of his time at the front but 'when he drew on his experience at all it was to relate some humorous incident.' And when Kim Beattie published a collection of his war verse in 1929, he did so not 'to stir an old stern sorrow / Nor probe old wounds of grieving and of pain'; on the contrary, he merely wanted to stir some memories in his readers.[8]

The memories to be rekindled, then, were highly selective. It was best to remember only the good times, when the hawthorne hedges bloomed, the poppies splashed across No Man's Land, and the men drowsed in the sun or bathed in nearby streams. Those were the times that ex-soldiers like the fictional Alan Gadsby wanted to remember: 'he recalled not war scenes but vistas of the countryside where they had sat drinking red wine; the village thick with orchards in the spring sun; the little stream where they had washed their shirts and fished in the fall.' Such memories were punctuated, not by the whine of bullet and shell, but by the calls of songbirds and the laughter of soldiers. In J.D. Logan's mind, 'not the thunders of the battle and not the slaughter are the imperishable experiences, but the jesting and laughter of "the boys."'[9] Through the bright glass of memory, the average soldier was not 'a moody fellow given to much bitter and silent contemplation of his tragic fate,' as memoirs by upper-class English officers suggested. On the contrary, he was a jolly fellow with a ready smile and a cheery song on his lips, a man 'who laughs in the face of hardship – makes a joke of pain – and immortalizes his own weakness in a jest.'[10] So, for every volume of poetry like Robert T. Anderson's *Troopers in France,* filled with thoughtful and sometimes bitter poems about the tragedy of war, and every novel like Peregrine Acland's grimly realistic *All Else Is Folly,* soldier-authors turned out half a dozen books like A.C. Joseph's *Rhymes of an Old War Horse* or Will Bird's comic novel *Private Timothy Fergus Clancy,* intended by its author to recapture some of the lighter moments of the war.

Underlying these accounts was a strong sense of nostalgia. They tended to idealize the atmosphere at the front and carried with them a wistful yearning for days when life was dangerous and uncomfortable but was characterized by comradeship, selflessness, and egalitarianism, qualities that seemed all too rare in peacetime. An illustration on the menu from one veterans' luncheon shows a man seated behind a desk, poring over budget papers; the thought bubble reveals that he is remembering life at the front. The drawing captures the contrast between the petty paper-pushing of the workaday world and the higher purpose of life in the trenches. Kim Beattie captured this contrast in a poem about the conclusion of a veterans' reunion:

> They're breaking up! – yet linger and seem sorry
> To turn to petty things from epic days,
> From sad days, mad days, of grieving and of glory,
> From storm and stress and triumph and high praise!
> The pride of proven men within them's burning;
> They scatter now and leave these high-played parts.[11]

A desire to recapture those days of 'high-played parts' was one of the dominant features of the veteran movement in the interwar period.

Veterans, for example, jumped at the chance to revisit the battlefields they had known on the Western Front. It might be wondered that, having shaken the mud of Flanders off their feet, soldiers would want to return to places with names like Dead Man's Trench, Casualty Corner, and Stinking Farm. Indeed, some ex-soldiers were puzzled by the hold that the battlefields had over them. James Norman Hall, an American who served in the CEF, envisioned a return to France that left him mystified:

> Little could his body guess
> Why spirit found that stricken plain
> So beautiful, or why it said,
> 'Home! Home again!'

It may have been inexplicable to Hall, but the attraction was very real, and at any given time thousands of ex-soldiers from all nations could be found roaming the old front. Journalist and ex-soldier W.W. Murray likened them to exiles who were drawn back to the land of their birth; in the same way, the veteran was 'moved to seek that indefinable something which can be derived from nowhere but in France and Flanders.'[12]

Unlike Hall and Murray, most veterans were clear about the purpose behind their return to the old front: it was to rekindle the treasured memories of the war years. Future minister of National Defence J.L. Ralston, who saw his share of fighting with the 85th Battalion, wished that he had some men from his old unit with him on a 1930 battlefield tour 'to chew over the memories of those wonderful days.'[13] Tourists like Ralston wanted to revisit the trenches they had won, the billets they had inhabited, and the roads they had trudged. When their old stomping grounds had been rendered unrecognizable by the passage of time and the healing power of nature, they were keenly disappointed. But when they found things unchanged, as was often the case when they travelled the old rear areas, it was a source of great joy. Will Bird's lengthy account of his wanderings

Turning to 'petty things from epic days': the menu from a 1931 veterans' reunion. Does the ex-soldier wish he were back in the trenches with his comrades? (*Caduceus* 12, no. 1 [April 1931]:49)

through France and Belgium in 1931 is full of trench names, inside jokes, and descriptions of local characters the troops would have known during the war. He recalls fondly a night spent in a Hazebrouck restaurant, and delights at touring an old billet and finding a nail on which a pal had once caught his shirt. 'And do you remember the old corner café at Lozinghem?' he queried.[14]

Only a small proportion of Canadian veterans could afford to return to the Western Front. Those who could not had to satisfy their yearnings by periodic reunions with their comrades. Unit reunions began within a year of the Armistice and continued through the interwar period. Modest at first, they quickly gained popularity, and by the 1930s the monster reunion was the order of the day. In 1934, 90,000 veterans converged on Toronto for a three-day reunion; four years later, over 100,000 came to the second great Canadian Corps reunion. These reunions were remarkable for the degree to which they attempted to recapture the war years. In essence, they sought to re-enact those portions of service life that veterans valued most highly. The 1934 Canadian Corps reunion, for example, included a concert by the Dumbells, a concert troupe that had entertained the soldiers in France, and a sports day modelled on the Dominion Day athletic competition held between the four divisions of the Canadian Corps at Tincques, France, in 1918. At the 1938 reunion, teams representing Montreal and Ontario played a rematch of the corps baseball championship of 1918.

The most popular venue of both corps reunions, however, was a reconstruction of a French village, suggestively named Partout. It was not rebuilt as a shattered ruin, as every village in the path of the war inevitably became, but as an intact, thriving community, complete with half a dozen licensed *estaminets* that attracted tens of thousands of reunion goers. The *estaminet* had been the focal point of a soldier's life out of the trenches. In these rough cafés, the men could feast on home-cooked eggs and fried potatoes, soothe their nerves with bottles of beer or 'van blong,' flirt with barmaids, and sing bawdy songs. It was a setting that came to symbolize much that was good about the soldiers' war. Indeed, if the symbols revered at unit reunions are any indication, the metaphor for the Great War was not mud, or barbed wire, or an endless row of headstones; it was the *estaminet*.

Though one officer lamented the glorification of café life and the fact that 'our line of narrative rather runs to the door of an estaminet than to the grim bargaining in hardware that left us the ownership of trenches,' divergence from this narrative line was rare. A typical account was *You're Lucky If You're Killed,* a play written by Norman Craig, formerly of the Royal Flying Corps, as a benefit for the Fergus, Ontario, war memorial tower. Performed 'for the dead men to whom it is reverently and affectionately dedicated,' the only scenes set in France took place in an *estaminet* behind the front lines, in 'a little moment of happiness snatched from death and disaster.'[15] For their first revue, the Dumbells reprised a sketch entitled 'Behind the Lines.' The program notes for the sketch outline the meaning of the culture of the *estaminet*: 'To those who were there [at the front], who found momentary forgetfulness of their troubles in the Estaminet's general atmosphere, the picture will perhaps bring memories of some of the things that helped them forget what had been yesterday and what was to be tomorrow; memories of warmth and light; laughter and music; fun and fellowship of friends.'[16] In short, the *estaminet* represented what the ex-soldier wanted to remember about his war experience.

The idealization of *estaminet* life, so characteristic of the veteran movement, was just as prevalent in popular culture, where it was the strongest element of what might be called the vaudevillization of the war experience. Thanks to the efforts of soldier-writers like J.D. Logan, Theodore Goodridge

Soldiers enjoy a meal at an *estaminet* in Mericourt. Often little more than a room in the home of a villager, the *estaminet* served as a welcome refuge for soldiers out of the trenches. (NAC PA4503)

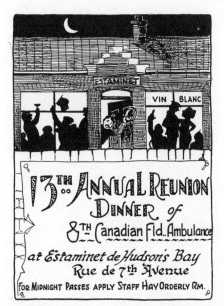

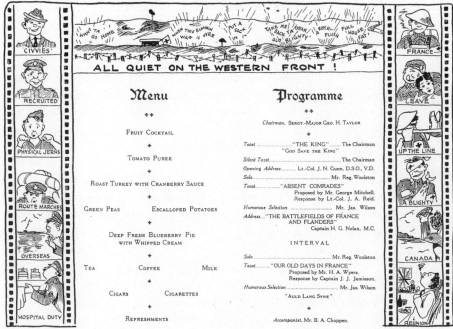

Veterans of a Calgary field ambulance unit celebrate the culture of the *estaminet* by converting the Hudson's Bay Company banquet room into a French café for their 13th reunion dinner. The only reference to battle is to a 'blighty,' the neat and tidy wound that earned the soldier a trip home. (Glenbow Museum and Archives, William Guthrie Papers M6342)

Roberts, and Will Bird, light wartime yarns were staples of magazines in the interwar years. The articles often followed the same basic formula. The protagonist, invariably a ranker, was a bit of a schemer whose plans to liberate a cache of liquor or keep an assignation with a local mademoiselle were frustrated by the tough-as-nails sergeant (often with a handlebar moustache to twist at crucial moments) or the weak-kneed (and even weaker-chinned) officer. In the end, after many hilarious trials and tribulations, the conniver with the heart of gold realized his goal, and his tormentors got their comeuppance.

These short stories were entirely typical of a music-hall approach to reconstructing the war. They relied on broadly drawn caricatures for comic effect, and the plots, such as they were, often turned on wildly improbable situations. The same far-from-subtle devices awaited theatre- and cinema-goers in search of entertainment. They dominated attempts to place the war in a serious dramatic context and turned earnest efforts into cloying melodramas full of dashing heroes, vulnerable heroines, and story lines that guaranteed the ultimate triumph of truth and right. Jean Renoir's *Grand Illusion* (1937) and the screen version of Erich Maria Remarque's *All Quiet on the Western Front* (1930) are frequently mentioned as the most significant war films of the interwar era, but they were heavily outnumbered at Canadian cinemas by more traditional treatments of the war, like *Carry On* (1929), a stirring epic of the Royal Navy, which awakened 'the best emotions ... [and left] a heartening and grateful memory behind,' and *Under the Black Eagle* (1928), a melodrama that followed the adventures of a police dog on the Western Front.[17]

The few portrayals of the war that attempted some form of critique drew ambivalent responses from Canadians, who seemed determined to interpret any version of the war in a music-hall context. Certainly the renowned play *Journey's End*, by R.C. Sherriff, and Lewis Milestone's film version of *All Quiet on the Western Front* played to wide audiences during the interwar years, but the reaction to these acknowledged antiwar classics was hardly what their authors would have expected. *Journey's End* was a favourite of local veterans' organizations, who enjoyed it not because it documented war's impact on the human spirit but because it offered them the chance to dress up in khaki and pretend to be back in the trenches again. When veterans in Peace River, Alberta, staged it, one ex-soldier admitted that they all 'liked the idea of donning our khaki again and portraying on the stage what we had all once done in grim reality.' He sincerely regretted the end of the play's short run, for 'the memories and comradeship of the trenches had been revived – old names, old faces came crowding back from across the years.' Veterans and serving militia members also mounted a production of the play as a fund-raiser for the London, Ontario, branch of the Canadian Legion. None of the cast members or audience apparently discerned any irony in an antiwar play being put on by militiamen, with musical accompaniment by the band of the Royal Canadian Regiment.[18]

Returning to the trenches: Peace River, Alberta, veterans stage Sherriff's *Journey's End* in the summer of 1930. (*Caduceus* 11, no. 2 [July 1930]:56)

The response to the Toronto screening of the film version of Remarque's novel reveals the same ambivalence. In the *Globe* a reviewer observed that it expressed the futility of war but went on to note approvingly that romance and comedy, the staples of popular culture versions of the war, were present 'in a surprising degree.' As if to confirm the fact that *All Quiet* had satisfied the urge of Toronto society to take a critical glimpse at the war, the film was followed at the Royal Alexandra Theatre by the British film *Splinters,* a rollicking comedy 'in which there is a laugh for every shrieking bullet of "All Quiet on the Western Front."' The reviewer went on to muse, 'A realistic war comedy? Impossible! and yet it was laughter and the unfailing sense of humour that carried the army from Mons to Victory.'[19]

Regardless of the accuracy of the reviewer's contention, laughter and an unfailing sense of humour certainly carried a wave of war films and plays to immense popularity. A stage version of *The Better 'Ole,* based on cartoonist Bruce Bairnsfather's grizzled but lovable soldier Old Bill, played in Toronto to rave reviews in 1918, 1919, and 1926; a film version, starring Charlie Chaplin's brother Syd, was ranked by *Saturday Night* as the 'comedy classic of all times.' Another popular film was *Alf's Button* (1920), based on the novel by W.A. Darlington, in which a typical Tommy discovers that one of his buttons is made from Aladdin's lamp; Samuel Morgan-Powell of the *Montreal Star* called it 'more fun, more clean, wholesome mirth, than in the "Better 'Ole."'[20] In the same vein was *The P.B.I., or Mademoiselle from Bully Grenay,* a play written by four soldiers of the First Contingent and first performed at Hart House Theatre at the University of Toronto in March 1920. Peopled by the same stock characters and improbable situations that graced short stories in popular magazines, it was such a hit in Toronto that it later toured Ontario and was eventually serialized in *Canadian Forum.*

Theatregoers could get even closer to the life of the *estaminet* by spending an evening with the same concert troupes that had delighted the troops in Flanders. Constituted during the war from soldiers (many of them pulled from the trenches) to entertain units out of the line, a number of these musical comedy ensembles reunited after the war to tour concert halls across North America and Britain. Their shows, too, relied on stock characters, vaudeville techniques, and impossibly happy endings, while giving little hint of the negative side of trench life. The most popular and enduring of these troupes was the former Third Division concert party, the Dumbells. Established by Captain Merton Plunkett at Vimy in 1917, the Dumbells reformed after the war and toured Canada, the United States, and England, playing to packed houses virtually everywhere. Though their revues were written to appeal to civilian audiences rather than soldiers, the war experience was never entirely absent; indeed, critics often found the trench sketches and songs the most appealing part of the production. Their first major success, 1921's *Biff! Bing! Bang!* relied heavily on soldier material and included such songs as 'Good-bye Khaki' and 'Medals on my Chest.' *Cheerio,* which opened in Montreal two years later, was described by its promoter as 'very much overseas, harking back to the original show in its tendency of bringing out the bright side of trench life.' In 1928, the theatre reviewer in *Saturday Night* reserved his highest praise of the revue *Why Worry?* for a rollicking skit entitled 'A Night in the Barracks Room.'[21] In each of these productions, the Dumbells constructed a vaudeville version of the war, with plenty of light songs and harmless jokes; just like in popular magazines and films, it was a war without battles, death, or destruction.

Theatregoers, then, could be forgiven for believing that the war consisted primarily of an extended stay in a local *estaminet*, and that brief bursts of battle were overshadowed by endless days of singing, joking, and drinking (in moderation, of course). This tendency to make light of the war experience was both a cause and an effect of the war's prominence in all aspects of life in the 1920s and 1930s. If the war experience could be softened by

The all-male Dumbells in full costume. Their wartime shows were immensely popular with the soldiers, and their notoriety propelled them to years of successful touring in the 1920s. (NAC PA5741)

adapting it to the music hall or the pages of a popular magazine, it could also be softened by mining it for metaphors to sell, entertain, explain, and describe. In each case, the images were carefully employed to erase any negative connotations; even the most frightening aspects of life at the front were endowed with positive significance.

War images, for example, were commonly used in advertising. In a Chiclets advertisement, a soldier relaxes in his living room while his son marches around in his tin helmet. 'They steadied our nerves and eased our thirst in some pretty hot corners overseas,' reads the caption. O'Keefe's Stone Ginger Beer went a step further by asking veterans, 'Remember how good the water back in France tasted when, tired, muddy, nerves just a little ragged, you stopped for a refreshing drink on your way out of the lines? … you'll find all the thrill of that most refreshing drink you ever had in O'Keefe's.' Other advertisements reminded consumers that they could purchase the same coffee that had been served to 'the boys in the trenches,' or that Goodyear tires were just as good as 'an extra ration of rum or ten days in Blighty.'[22]

This advertisement for coffee was typical of the way the war was used to sell products. It bridged the gap between home and front by reminding people that they could enjoy the same coffee that had comforted the soldiers in the trenches. (*Manitoba Free Press*, 11 April 1919, 2)

Such advertisements minimized the difference between a soldier's life at the front and his family's life at home by creating clear parallels between the two. A soldier returned home with an air of well-being fostered by 'plenty of good, wholesome food and lots of fresh air and exercise'; his family could achieve the same glow of health from a bottle of Dr. Chase's Nerve Food. In an advertisement for McLaughlin Motor Cars, a nattily dressed quartet admire a war memorial from the comfort of their convertible. In this way, the sacrifice of Canadian soldiers was brought down to the same level as the McLaughlin Master Six: both were 'Symbolic of Canadian Ideals.'[23] In each instance, consumer products bridged the gap between home and the front. Buying a McLaughlin automobile was the next best thing to having one's name on the war memorial; when chewing the soldier's gum or drinking the soldier's coffee, an afternoon digging in the garden was not unlike an afternoon digging a trench.

Outside of advertising, the war was put to every conceivable use. Vaudeville routines might include such songs as 'The World is Simply Mad on Uniform' (with the memorable line 'And there's goin' to be some hollerin' from the House of Hohenzollern, / Ere they finish with the khaki uniform') or 'Cakes (The Dry Toast),' which suggested that the miseries of trench life could be cured by treats from home: 'Here's to the little girl full of fun / Who her love sent in packages of chewing gum. / "Here's Tutti-

Frutti, boys, do your duty, never look glum.'"[24] Another popular song, 'The Battle at the Gates of Love,' employed war images to describe a courtship, a tactic that Stephen Leacock used with effect in 'Some Startling Side Effects of the War,' in which a man's marriage proposal is described entirely in military language.[25]

The phraseology of war was co-opted and distorted to such an extent that meaning was often completely inverted. Even 'over the top,' the worst nightmare of many an infantryman, came into usage as a term of encouragement. The Army and Navy Veterans of Winnipeg predicted they were 'Going Over the Top' with their season's finale in 1919, and, in extending his best wishes for an ex-soldiers' reunion, a Toronto alderman expressed the hope that 'this Worthy Pageant [would] go over the top.' A proponent of aggressive evangelism urged fellow Baptists not to settle down into trench

warfare but to go 'over the top for Christ.'[26] In this way, an action that every soldier would have avoided, given the chance, had been transformed into a goal to be sought after.

The use of 'over the top' as a term of encouragement acknowledged, however obliquely, that battle had been an integral part of the war. Regardless of the number of nights they spent singing and laughing in the *estaminet*, soldiers did occasionally have to fight and die. Even this unpalatable reality could be softened by reducing battle to stylized shams or tableaus. During the war, this was usually done for recruiting or fund-raising purposes. One such event was announced in a southern Ontario newspaper in October 1914: 'A sham battle will take place ... next Monday afternoon by the local volunteers. Captain D.D. Gunton with F Company will defend the farm, which will be attacked by C Company.' To complete the irony, the notice pointed out that 'after the battle sandwiches, cake and coffee will be

All across Canada, dry and tidy trenches, like these in downtown Winnipeg in 1916, were built to encourage enlistment or to raise money for philanthropic causes. When they reached the front, these soldiers would find the trenches to be much less comfortable. (Provincial Archives of Manitoba, Foote Collection 2310, Neg. no. N2972)

served.' In 1917 the Vancouver branch of the Great War Veterans' Association choreographed a mock bomb attack on German trenches as part of the Dominion Day celebrations, and the Canadian National Exhibition (CNE) of that year erected trench displays for recruiting purposes.[27]

Such displays were ideal as patriotic or fund-raising enterprises during the war, but their continuance after the war might be considered in poor taste. Nevertheless, continue they did. At Saskatoon's Peace Day celebrations in 1919, the white doves released to symbolize peace had to share the skies with airmen re-enacting battle formations and aerial skirmishes. At a 1923 celebration in Sault Ste. Marie, Ontario, visitors could watch carefully sanitized re-enactments of a daylight attack on enemy lines or night manoeuvres on the Western Front; for those who wanted to get even closer to the action, a display representing a typical trench system allowed them to see what life was like on the firestep.[28] The firestep, of course, was free of ankle-deep mud, bits of human body, and flying shrapnel.

Visitors to the CNE in 1919 could also experience a carefully contrived version of the war. They might begin in the Process Building, which featured a series of life-size dioramas showing the fate of disabled veterans through history. The first six tableaus revealed the piteous condition of veterans from the Middle Ages to the Boer War, but the last two depicted the happy situation of 1919: a limbless ex-soldier fitted with a prosthesis of the finest material and workmanship; and a mad veteran whose mind had been reclaimed by the careful ministrations of charming nurses. Passing outside again, fairgoers might pause to watch Canadian airmen Billy Bishop and W.G. Barker, both winners of the Victoria Cross, re-enact dogfights over the Western Front in British and captured German aircraft. Then, in the Railway Building, they could marvel at a huge diorama of Canadian troops attacking near Ypres. 'By means of electrical mechanism,' read one press account, 'the fighters are shown leaping over the top and charging across No Man's Land, led by lumbering tanks, spitting fire and death from their steel sides.' While all this was going on, ingenious lighting simulated the shell-

Victoria Cross winners Billy Bishop and W.G. Barker with a captured German Fokker DVII at Leaside, 1919. In aircraft like this, they re-created wartime dogfights for the crowds at Toronto's Canadian National Exhibition (NAC C3538)

bursts.[29] A day at the CNE reduced war to the level of theatre: the disabled became smiling mannequins, the duelling aces would soon land to share lunch, and the battle could be stopped with the flick of a switch. It was all very amusing, and there was hardly a better way to spend a warm afternoon in the summer.

II

THE DETERMINATION of veterans to recall primarily the happy times at the front, and the public's thirst for light entertainment based on war themes, went a long way towards drawing the sting from the war experience. In both instances, the war was perceived as a form of theatre, full of light moments and jolly songs. But such trivialization could never entirely ease the pain of the war; the very real horrors of the trenches could not be wished away with a humorous ditty or a flippant joke. A confectionary vaudeville song could not erase the blight of Passchendaele. Celebrations of victory, even in a just cause, could not fill the vacant chairs at the kitchen table or hide the fact that almost every big city street corner was home to a disabled veteran. 'What of the thousands of unglorified men whose eyes were blinded, whose lower jaws were shot away, who are still paying for it?' queried Theodore Goodridge Roberts.[30]

For many recent critics, there was no easy answer to Roberts's rhetorical question. As a result, they see the First World War as marking a caesura in human expression. For Paul Fussell, pre-1914 Western society was 'a static world, where the values appeared stable and where the meanings of abstractions seemed permanent and reliable. Everyone knew what Glory was, and what Honour meant.' Those abstractions created positive, uplifting equivalents for occurrences that were either mundane or inherently negative: the dead became 'the fallen,' the front became 'the field,' and to die became 'to perish.' Fussell called these equivalents the vocabulary of High Diction.[31]

In the view of many critics, High Diction was a spent force after 1918. Machine-made death on a grand scale rendered the traditional forms of expression obsolete; they could no longer have any resonance or even meaning when applied to human conflict. 'Sacrifice' could not begin to describe the 60,000 British casualties sustained on the Somme on a single day in the summer of 1916, and 'field of honour' was irrelevant to what German soldiers called *das Leichenfeld von Loos,* the corpse-field of Loos. There was nothing in the vocabulary of High Diction to represent these new ways to die; it was simply not possible to refer to a small clump of mangled flesh and bone as 'the fallen.' As John Cruickshank argued, to respond to something as shattering as the First World War with such rhetorical techniques was inadequate and even immoral; any writer who attempted to fall back on nineteenth-century forms of expressions about the war is today unreadable.[32]

Cruickshank writes as a literary critic and bases his judgments on aesthetic grounds. For the historian, however, the readability of a book or poem is irrelevant; just because Peregrine Acland's antiwar novel *All Else Is Folly* is a much better book in a literary sense than *Shrieks and Crashes,* W.B. Kerr's very conventional war memoir, does not mean that Acland's view of the war should be taken more seriously than Kerr's. Furthermore, value judgments based on literary merit are not borne out by the weight of evidence. On the contrary, if all Canadian accounts of the war are considered on equal terms, a very different picture emerges than the one discerned by Fussell and Cruickshank. What emerges is a literary landscape with far more Kerrs than Aclands, one in which modernist critiques of the war are the exception rather than the rule. As one of the few observers to take this approach has pointed out, an examination of the entire body of Canada's war literature, rather than just the best works in a literary sense, reveals that Canadians continued to use nineteenth-century forms of expression to describe the war experience. The war had not discredited High Diction, but had validated it. If the trivialization of the war served to make the events of 1914-18 palatable, the continued use of traditional abstractions served to make the war comprehensible. It placed the Great War firmly in a context that Canadians could understand, the context of a Victorian or Edwardian world. In doing so, the war became even more familiar and non-threatening.[33]

It is tempting to ascribe this state of affairs to non-combatants foisting their unrealistic views of the war experience upon an unsuspecting public. In *Why Stay We Here?* George Godwin addressed this very question:

> The war as it looked from England, from the prairie, from the bush, a thrilling affair, studded with great moments, what was it? Only a trudging in mud, waiting for the inevitable packet. Dirt and vermin, heartache, ache of body, wet, sickness, a weary waiting – and then; the terror of gun fire. Yet, with some, fancy triumphed in a way over reality ... Couldn't see how exactly, but this was heroism. This was being a hero. For King and Country. Being plugged at, sitting tight. Living underground or in an open grave. Suffering wet, cold ... No matter, nothing could destroy those illusions of the home-folk which they carried with them.[34]

In some respects such illusions are entirely understandable. The distance of Canadian civilians from the fighting meant that they could not experience the war directly, even with the death of a loved one. Strict censorship and government control of the press, the desire of soldiers to avoid alarming relatives, the inability of human imagination to conceive of the landscape in which soldiers lived – all of these combined to prevent civilians from constructing a realistic frame of reference in which to interpret and understand the war. As a consequence, they were forced to imagine the war in the only frame of reference that they possessed, that of the nineteenth-century empire.

This explanation, though, is entirely too simplistic; High Diction was retained as an interpretive framework not only because it was the only framework available, but also because of its emotional appeal. Alexander Falcon, the hero of *All Else Is Folly,* returns from the trenches a physical and emotional wreck, yet cannot help being attracted by the lure of war. Huddled in an armoury in 1924, he is strangely moved by the sight of the local regiment returning from drill: 'with the skirling of the pipes in his ears, he could have signed away his liberty, his life, for another war.'[35]

Falcon was certainly not an impartial observer, yet he was not the only person to find pageantry and military display more appealing than the horrors of war were repellent. A powerful essay written by Roger Sarty in 1936 begins in the trenches, as a raiding party of ten soldiers clambers over the parapet and into No Man's Land; moments later, the sole survivor returns, leaving the bodies of his comrades littering the cratered earth. With 'nine souls blasted to their Maker,' silence settles again on No Man's Land. The scene then shifts abruptly. It is twenty years later, and another generation is marching off to war. The town square has been transformed into a carnival: streamers cascade across the streets, a brass band blares a battle march, and adoring crowds cheer the ranks of young men in khaki. The echoes of 1914 are inescapable, as is the message. The passage of twenty years has been sufficient to dull the sting of No Man's Land; the 'gold braid, glistening, twinkling spurs, shining buttons and bright buckles' again carry the day.[36] Sarty is at once saddened by and resigned to the fact that military trappings have more power to inspire than the horrors of war have to shock.

The other paradox regarding the persistence of traditional paradigms is even more problematic: the tendency of many people, especially soldiers with first-hand knowledge of the realities of war, to dismiss the High Diction vocabulary and then, in the very next breath, celebrate all of the values that it symbolized. In the introduction to his melodramatic novel *The Towers of Mont St. Eloi,* Archie Gray condemned the perpetuation of notions like glory in the face of the horrors of war; it was he who wondered how glory could fill the empty chair at the kitchen table. The introduction, however, evidently salved Gray's conscience, for the novel is a highly conventional tale of 'a great love, a great feeling of patriotism, a great sense of duty'; its story line validates all of the High Diction ideals the author had decried.

The writings of Theodore Goodridge Roberts convey the same ambivalence. Thede, as he was known to friends, was a member of one of Canada's most prolific literary dynasties, the Robertses of New Brunswick; the family (Roberts and his siblings Sir Charles G.D. and Elizabeth Goodridge MacDonald, his nephews Lloyd Roberts and Cuthbert and Goodridge MacDonald, and his cousin Bliss Carman) was a fixture on the Canadian literary scene for the better part of a century. Born in Nova Scotia and educated in Fredericton, Roberts covered the Spanish-American War for the *New York Independent* and went overseas in 1914 with the First Contingent. He spent some time as the aide-de-camp to Arthur Currie before eventually transferring to the Canadian War Records Office, where his talents could be put to better use. A poet and essayist of no mean talent, Thede has the dubious distinction of being the most underrated writer of the Roberts clan.

Much of Roberts's work is highly critical of notions of military glory and patriotism, and it carries overtones of cynicism and disillusion that would have done credit to Siegfried Sassoon or Robert Graves. Roberts once described the last resting place of the Unknown Warrior in Westminster Abbey as 'England's glory-heap of wornout things.' In another disturbing essay, he dreamt of battalions of children, with specially made miniature rifles, preparing to march to their deaths in battle. Roberts pleaded against the manufacture and sale of weapons but lamented that it was 'business as usual – while Jesus weeps.'[37] In spite of these sentiments, Roberts wrote much that was in a very traditional vein. His newspaper columns, 'Under the Sun' in the Saint John *Telegraph Journal* and the syndicated feature 'Soldiers, Then and Now,' were built around jolly glimpses of life at the front and a cavalcade of caricatures who could have stepped directly from any vaudeville version of the war. His war novels, *Tom Akerley* and *The Fighting Starkleys,* were both very conventional tales that could easily have been written by the most unrepentant flag-waver.

Accounting for Roberts's contradicting visions is not as difficult as it may seem. He was a very keen observer who could not have failed to appreciate the realities of modern warfare; his serious essays are too perceptive to be anything but completely sincere. However, as a man who made his living with the pen, Roberts was also attuned to the realities of the marketplace. He always kept his eyes open for a profitable venture, and inundated Lorne Pierce of Ryerson Press with suggestions for marketing his books more effectively.[38] Roberts knew what would sell and what would not, and he obviously realized that a traditional vision of the war was considerably more profitable than his antiwar critique. So, he saved his cynicism for specialist publications and filled his novels and syndicated columns with all of the humour and High Diction ideals that he knew the reading public would appreciate.

There were countless Canadians who, like Roberts, were either unwilling or unable to sustain a modernist critique of the war. The fact that popular culture had embraced a war experienced largely in *estaminets* and inhabited by a cast of vaudeville characters probably had something to do with this. The traditional allure of military trappings, something that could not be washed away even by four years of bloodletting, was likely an element as well. Civilians, who had not experienced the war personally, had no choice but to fall back on the only interpretive frame of reference they had available to them, the comforting words of the past that could make the present comprehensible. And ex-soldiers realized that it was impossible to describe something like Passchendaele and probably did not relish the soul-searching that such an attempt demanded. Preferring instead a less painful nostalgia for the *estaminet*, they acquiesced in the tendency to minimize the negative aspects of the war. Finally, anyone who had lost a loved one to the war must have wondered if the war could be criticized without casting shadows on the memory of the fallen. In the face of these powerful tendencies, the survival of High Diction in Canada's myth of the war was virtually guaranteed.

In many accounts, the story of the war assumed an almost supernatural aura. As the chancellor of Victoria University put it, 'the great events of four years of war on the most stupendous scale crowd the canvas ... flaming against the blackness of it all, deeds of bravery and heroism, and nations stirred and thrilled with sublime passions.' It was the example of selflessness set by the fallen that was the source of light; the war record was 'illumined by the glory of their unselfish devotion.'[39] 'The light that shines for their example,' said Arthur Meighen in a speech about Colonel George Baker, the only member of Parliament to be killed in action during the war, would be treasured by all future generations. Theirs was 'a shining tale ... one which we believe our children and our children's children will read with glowing faces and swelling hearts.'[40]

A single thread runs through all of these comments: light or brightness. Canada's war record shines forth from the pages of history, suffusing everything around it with an unearthly glow; it is at once a beacon and a light of inspiration. With its fine emotions and high purpose, the story of the war could be an object lesson for future generations. It would 'warm the blood of all true Canadians,' proclaimed University of New Brunswick chancellor

Cecil Charles Jones, and 'make us all better men and women.' All that was required of Canadians was that they study the war story; by drinking deep from that fountain, wrote J.W. Dafoe, they would learn lessons in valour, sacrifice, patriotism, and national pride.[41]

But the war story was as entertaining as it was edifying. According to one school text, 'as the glorious tale unfolds of Canadian valour and Canadian victories, your pulses will quicken and your hearts will swell with pride at the thought that these mighty men of battle were your countrymen.' A reviewer raved about George Drew's *Canada's Fighting Airmen* for possessing 'all the drama, thrills, and suspense to be found in a whole library of fiction ... [N]othing in thrill-picture, or the annals of Nelson and Drake, ever surpassed this sensational story.'[42] With this, the Great War was reduced to a story by G.A. Henty or Rider Haggard, a Boy's Own yarn that stirred the blood and filled the reader with admiration and wonder. By lumping the experience of the Western Front with every battle the British Empire had ever fought, the First World War was firmly placed in a Victorian context. Gallipoli, the Somme, and Passchendaele could take their places alongside the Charge of the Light Brigade, the relief of Batoche, and the Battle of Paardeberg. The same adjectives and superlatives were applicable, for in Canada's memory the Great War belonged more to the nineteenth century than to the twentieth.

Not only in prose is such an interpretation evident. The frontispiece of one unit's history is an ink sketch entitled *Faithful to the Last,* a highly conventional scene of dead artillerymen slumped over their gun. But for a few minor details, it could easily be set at Waterloo, Balaklava, or Colenso. The Dundas, Ontario, war memorial, designed by Hamilton McCarthy, is a Victorian sculpture by a Victorian artist; it depicts a soldier 'with rifle and fixed bayonet defending the flag, which is seen in the background covering the broken wheel of a gun carriage,' and is reminiscent of McCarthy's Boer War monument in Quebec City.[43] A few miles away, the memorial in Stoney Creek, Ontario, exudes a similar feeling. A hatless soldier stands erect, head held high, clutching a furled flag. Both memorials convey the very Victorian lesson captured in the immensely popular patriotic song 'We'll Never Let the Old Flag Fall.'

Having established the nineteenth-century context, the discourse of High Diction proceeded to describe everything else about the war in Victorian terms. The battlefield became precisely what we now know it was not: full of vitality and colour. According to Arthur Chute, readers would find that 'lives lived in those trenches shall shine forth with colors of romance.' In his introduction to *Canada's Hundred Days,* J.F.B. Livesay admitted that he sought 'to clothe these [technical aspects of war] with the pulsating life and colour of the battlefield.'[44] Victorian redcoats may have made a battlefield pulsate with life and colour; few Canadian infantrymen looking out from the trenches at Hooge or Vimy would have used those words to describe their view across No Man's Land.

Filling the landscape created by writers such as Livesay was an army of that most nineteenth-century of characters, the Happy Warrior. In 1805, after hearing the news of Lord Nelson's death at Trafalgar, William Wordsworth began work on a poem that he entitled 'Character of the Happy Warrior.' Published in 1807, it is a paean to military heroism, a description of the ideal soldier that abounds with High Diction concepts like glorious gain, noble deeds, and high endeavour. 'This is the happy Warrior' it concludes; 'this is He / Whom every Man in arms should wish to be.' A century later, the Imagist poet Herbert Read wrote a bitterly ironic reply to Wordsworth that has been deservedly praised by recent critics, but in the postwar decades Wordsworth's version held sway. An Ontario school text describing acts of heroism on the battlefield noted that many stories contained therein 'recall

"Faithful to the Last!"

A Victorian image transplanted to Flanders. Only the equipment places this scene in the twentieth century. (J.A. MacDonald, *Gun-Fire: An Historical Narrative of the 4th Brigade, Canadian Field Artillery* [Toronto: Greenway 1929], frontispiece)

Wordsworth's fine word-painting of "The Happy Warrior,'" and even the unmilitary Mackenzie King borrowed a few lines from Wordsworth for a 1921 speech honouring Marshal Ferdinand Foch. Stuart Armour, one of the Vimy pilgrims, heartily approved of Edward VIII's use of the poem in the unveiling ceremony: 'No more beautiful resting place could possibly be found than these British cemeteries in France and Belgium. And are their occupants not truly happy warriors?'[45]

Even if the poem itself was not cited, accounts frequently suggested that the soldiers enjoyed every minute of life at the front. Much of this notion was conveyed by published volumes of wartime letters written by soldiers, which gave the impression that life in the trenches had been a delight from start to finish. 'I am back in the mud again,' wrote Victor Gordon Tupper in November 1916. 'It is the place where I am most happy and contented.' A volume in honour of Major J.M. Langstaff expressed his satisfaction with trench life:

> I view the panorama in a trance
> Of awe, yet colored with a secret joy,
> For I have breathed in epic and romance,
> Have lived the dreams that thrilled me as a boy.[46]

Armine Norris would have agreed; he wrote to his mother that 'the danger is not terrible nor have I in my personal experience of over two months in the trenches seen any "horrors" ... This beats sailing or fishing.'[47]

Of course, these comments from doomed young men must be read carefully. Censorship prevented the disgruntled soldier from filling letters home with tales of abysmal food, days spent hip-deep in icy water, and chums being sliced apart by shell fragments. At the same time, the soldiers exercised a form of self-censorship, attempting to allay the fears of loved ones by persuading them that life at the front was not all that bad. Finally, the grieving parents published these memorial volumes to provide a measure of consolation and a fitting epitaph to a young life lost. To do so, it was necessary to remember the fallen in the best possible light; it was not suitable to remind people that one's son had passed his time at the front huddled in a water-filled hole and counting the hours until his unit was relieved.

For these completely understandable reasons, memorial volumes give an overriding impression of intense joy felt by soldiers at the front. Canadian soldiers carried light hearts into battle; active service gave them 'a liberty of spirit such as they never before experienced,' proclaimed Queen's University principal Reverend R. Bruce Taylor, who had spent a year as the chaplain to the 42nd Battalion. The cheeriness of the infantrymen was one of their distinguishing qualities, as observers were prone to note. J.F.B. Livesay wrote that 'hot-blooded youth doesn't care how long the war goes on; it is his great adventure; to him it is "a lovely war."'[48] Livesay had missed the good-natured sarcasm of the popular trench song and interpreted it in a literal sense.

A dominant image to sum up this great adventure was the identification of war as a game. Popularized by Henry Newbolt's 1892 poem 'Vitaï Lampada' ('Play up! play up! and play the game!'), this very Victorian tendency to blur the lines between war and sport has been deemed by some observers as one of the casualties of the Great War. Literary critic George Parfitt maintained that, because war and sport do not share enough common ground for their connection to be illuminating, 'the only analytically useful comparisons are ironic.'[49] In Canada, though, the sporting metaphor was rarely used in the ironic sense, nor was it used to draw direct comparisons between battle and sport. On the contrary, it referred to a mode of conduct and confirmed that the virtues described by the term 'sportsmanship' were transferable to the battlefield. 'Playing the game' meant carrying out one's duty honourably, faithfully, and selflessly. The battlefield was not the same as the playing field, but virtues like playing fair, not letting down the side, and pulling one's weight were as applicable to war as they were to sport.

So, the transition from athlete to soldier was a natural one. For Montreal poet Alfred Gordon, there was no irony in writing a verse honouring the All-Montreal baseball team on the first anniversary of the Battle of Vimy Ridge. Entitled 'Play Ball!,' it has much in common with Newbolt's poem, for one is never entirely certain whether a given stanza talks of Vimy Ridge or a Montreal baseball diamond.[50] 'The cannon ball has replaced the football and the one mile race and hundred yard dash have given way to "over the top" and the bloody charge of the battlefields,' declared a Maritime writer. 'The roar of mighty guns is now heard instead of the cheering of bygone spectators on the bleachers.' Ralph Connor, too, found the comparison entirely apt: 'They [the attacking soldiers] were all sportsmen, and had all experienced the anxious, nervous thrill of the moments preceding a big contest. Once the ball was off, their nervousness would go, and they would be cool and wary, playing the game for all they had in them.'[51]

The connection between sport and war was perpetuated in another way: the erection of sports facilities as war memorials. The football stadium at Queen's University, still in use today, was funded by Winnipeg businessman James Richardson as a memorial to his brother, who had been killed in action. Acadia University had planned to build a gymnasium before the war, to replace an earlier building lost to fire; after the war, the university's board of governors decided that the gymnasium should be erected as Acadia's war memorial. Sports-minded citizens of Toronto had less luck with their plans.

A proposal to erect War Memorial Stadium on the waterfront never got past the design stage; the $150,000 price tag was too high for city council, even after organizers suggested that the stadium's name be changed to Flanders Field.[52]

If the connection between soldier and athlete remained as potent after the war as it had been during, so too did the device of relating a soldier's blood to wine. The athlete who was willing to accept a few hard knocks for the sake of the team was of a piece with the soldier who was willing to 'pour out ... unstintingly, / A poppy-red libation' for the sake of his country.[53] This metaphor had been brought into the canon of Great War poetry most forcefully by Rupert Brooke, whose lines 'These laid the world away; poured out the red / Sweet wine of youth' were among his most enduring contributions to the discourse of High Diction. Like the rest of that discourse, the image was as popular in Canada through the 1920s and 1930s as it had been in 1914. Brooke's lines appeared in the inscriptions of many Canadian war memorials, and the metaphor was a favourite of professional and amateur poets alike. Regardless of the deftness of the usage, the image was taken entirely seriously. When George Gibson wrote of the 'soil dyed purple with an imperial stain,' no one commented that his prose was the same shade as the earth.[54]

The purple-dyed soil, of course, implied the death of the happy warrior, and, true to form, he greeted death 'with a proud and tranquil smile,' as Arthur Currie put it in 1920. The ability to die smiling was assumed to be a general characteristic of Canadian soldiers. A government pamphlet even

PROPOSED MEMORIAL STADIVM

A sketch of Toronto's proposed War Memorial Stadium. Despite the emotional appeal of the project, city councillors balked at the price. (City of Toronto Archives, PT000851)

advised Victory Loan speakers to conclude their remarks with a reference to those men who went to their deaths 'with a smile on their lips because they had faith in their comrades and you.'[55] There was no room for agonizing deaths from phosgene gas or gaping stomach wounds; the final blow had to be quick and painless. The typical cliché in letters to next of kin, that poor Billy had been shot through the heart and died smiling, was more often than not used to hide from relatives the horror of the facts. After the war, this subterfuge was accepted as reality. Victor Gordon Tupper died at Vimy Ridge with 'the faint flicker of a smile spreading from his half-opened lips.' The poet Bernard Freeman Trotter, too, had 'a suspicion of a smile on his lips' when his body was retrieved by fellow officers. It was not just the poets and the dreamers who met death with a smile; Dave Elden, Robert J.C. Stead's cow puncher, also 'went out with a smile' at Courcelette.[56] The beauty of the passing, manifest in a beatific smile, grew out of a sense of deep satisfaction of a job seen through to the end. For the happy warrior, there was much pleasure in fighting and dying for a good cause. 'You shout as the blood gushes, red as a rose; / There's no joy like the joy that the fighting man knows,' wrote Cecil Francis Lloyd, capturing the happy warrior in full flight towards eternity. In 1933, an editor remembered the fallen in the same way: 'when they died, it was with a heroic smile upon their faces and the unspeakable joy in their hearts of honor unbetrayed, and duty well and nobly done.'[57]

It was the rectitude of the cause that allowed the happy warriors to die with a smile on their lips; according to the myth, they died in the comforting certainty that the words of the Latin epigram were still valid. 'Dulce et decorum est pro patria mori,' the poet Horace had written in 27 BC to instruct the youth of Augustan Rome in their duty to the state: it is sweet and seemly to die for one's country. Discredited as 'the old lie' in Wilfred Owen's poem of the same name, the Latin maxim lost none of its resonance in postwar Canada. It was inscribed on a host of war memorials and honour rolls across the country, and was used on the programs for dedication services; along with Pericles, whose funeral oration was a fixture in war memorial unveilings, Horace was the most popular of the classics in the language of commemoration. Far from deriding his proverb, writers more frequently affirmed that the sacrifice of Canada's soldiers had demonstrated its validity. Even Archie Gray's *The Towers of Mont St. Eloi*, which he claimed was an antiwar novel, accepted it. The motto of the Cordray family is 'Ma Vie est a Ma Patrie,' and Charlotte Cordray reveals late in the book that, even after the tragedy of the war, it retained its validity: 'What did life mean beside the overwhelming presence of patriotism?' she cries as her world falls to pieces around her.[58]

All of the stars in the High Diction firmament, then, remained in their proper course after the war: the vivid and vibrant field of honour; the happy warriors jousting on the battlefield, just as they had on the playing field; the earth stained by the rich wine of sacrifice; and the beauty of a patriotic death. One of the most complete articulations of this discourse came from the pen of William Douw Lighthall, the lawyer, former soldier, and one-time mayor of Westmount. Lighthall had been a founder of the Society of Canadian Literature and by 1918 was one of the most venerable of the Canadian literati. Behind him was a broad range of poetry, essays, historical fiction, and factual accounts of early Canadian history; ahead was his continuing quest to strengthen Canadian nationhood through the written word. As he said in a December 1918 address, the war was a unique opportunity in this regard:

> Young men and women of genius – some probably returned from the contest – will celebrate its glorious deeds, will drink deep inspiration from that brilliant band of heroes who are already beginning to render our circles illustrious with their presence ... This is our Homeric Age ... The poets may perhaps not yet be born who shall invent utterances that shall be truly worthy of the innumerable heroic achievements, the Galahadic dedications to the supreme sacrifice, the wonderful idealism of the whole crusade. The story is too grand to be forgotten. It will sound the trumpet of the breast until it finds and calls out to our supreme minstrel to supremely chant our Idylls of the Heroes.[59]

This passage, and indeed the entire article, harkens back to the previous century. The notion of a Homeric age in modern times, the use of the Arthurian adjective, the oblique reference to Tennyson – all of these characterize the author as eminently Victorian.

And yet the essay cannot be dismissed as a pathetic anachronism from a man unable to cope with modernism. Granted, Lighthall's writings on the Canadian nation were never known for their restraint, but the tenor of his remarks should not be dismissed as the excessive and fanciful musings of an elderly bookworm. That such diction was not deemed archaic in the postwar years is evident from the reception given to Sir Arthur Currie's famous dispatch of 27 March 1918, at the time of the German spring offensive, which brought the Allies closer to defeat than they had been since 1914. Because of its significance, the dispatch is worth quoting in its entirety:

> Looking back with pride on the unbroken record of your glorious achievements, asking you to realize that today the fate of the British Empire hangs in the balance, I place my trust in the Canadian Corps, knowing that where Canadians are engaged, there can be no giving way.

Under the orders of your devoted officers in the coming battle, you will advance, or fall where you stand, facing the enemy.

To those who fall, I say: 'You will not die, but step into immortality. Your mothers will not lament your fate, but will be proud to have borne such sons. Your names will be revered for ever by your grateful country, and God will take you unto Himself.'

Canadians, in this fateful hour, I command you and I trust you to fight as you have never fought, with all your strength, with all your determination, with all your tranquil courage. On many a hard-fought field of battle you have overcome this enemy, and with God's help you shall achieve victory once more.

The phrases might be different from Lighthall's but the thrust is the same: it validates all of the traditional assumptions about the war.

Of course, Currie's dispatch was written as a morale booster at a time of dire emergency, and it would be odd indeed if he had not couched it in such terms. Furthermore, the soldiers to whom it was addressed were not impressed by it. James Pedley called it a 'ludicrous bombastic sham-Napoleonic message ... done in the most approved opéra-bouffe style.' He recalled that the troops laughed and sneered when it was read, saying 'He won't die, not likely' and calling Currie a 'bloody old bomb-proofer.' Brigadier Alex Ross refused to read the order to his troops, realizing that it would not appeal to them. A battalion commander went even further, maintaining that the soldiers would have no idea what Currie was talking about.[60]

More notable than the derision that the dispatch drew from the troops, though, was its tremendous popularity in postwar Canada. The Department of Militia and Defence thought enough of it to have copies done up on parchment and signed by Currie, as had been done with Haig's stirring dispatch issued to the Canadian Corps after the capture of Vimy Ridge in April 1917; the department also printed cheaper copies in 1920 for public distribution. Historian W.S. Wallace called it 'worthy of being ranked with Napoleon's famous manifesto to the army of Italy,' and the Reverend Charles W. Gordon thought it should be prominently displayed in 'every institution of learning where our Canadian youth are being trained in those qualities that make for high and noble character.'[61] This was never done, but the dispatch did appear in countless school texts and, next to John McCrae's 'In Flanders Fields,' was probably the most reproduced piece of Canadian writing to come out of the war. The town of Marksville, Ontario, even asked for a wax cylinder recording of the dispatch to place in its memorial obelisk. The popularity of the dispatch proves that its phrases had great resonance for Canadians. They reiterated the spiritual interpretation of the war and affirmed that those who gave their lives did so in a just cause. Furthermore, the comparisons to

Napoleon, made either in criticism or in praise, are telling; the popularity of the dispatch lay in the fact that it interpreted this most modern war in a very nineteenth-century framework.

The persistence of the High Diction discourse was not confined to poetry and prose. We have seen echoes of it in memorial sculpture and popular songs, and its equivalent in pictorial art existed in the collection assembled by the Canadian War Memorials Fund (CWMF). From its inception in the perpetually active mind of Lord Beaverbrook, the CWMF was to be a historical record. According to Beaverbrook, painting was 'the most permanent and vital form in which the great deeds and sacrifices of the Canadian Nation in the war could be enshrined for posterity.'[62] Thus, the motivation behind the creation of the collection was not primarily artistic. Contributors to the CWMF were certainly chosen for their skill and the quality of their work, but their art was only a means to an end. It was just another way to record the story of the war. When the deputy minister of National Defence prepared a memorandum on the CWMF in 1928, he took pains to stress that 'the collection contains actual battle scenes historically accurate and the pictures depict the type of warfare, materials and conditions of warfare [sic] and locations very correctly.' Clearly, art had become the handmaiden of history; the deputy minister was referring, not to works of art, but to historical documents. Those documents, as Sir Robert Borden put it, would relate 'the meaning of the war as it was and as it would be understood.'[63]

That interpretation, however, could only be done in the vocabulary that artists had at their disposal. For many of them, that vocabulary was traditional. This was particularly true for landscape artists like J.W. Beatty and David Y. Cameron. Beatty, who had seen action at Fish Creek during the North-West Rebellion, must have found the experience of modern war bewildering. Unable to come to terms with it, he retained his landscape style unchanged; the war was purely incidental in his canvases, and often only the title revealed that his subject was the scene of a battle.[64] Even an artist less entrenched in the traditional landscape genre, such as Eric Kennington, found the war a difficult subject: '[I] did not attempt to depict any of the horror and tragedy, realising that it was too vast, and that I was not capable ... Intended to get as much as possible of the magnificence of the men [and] all their fine qualities.'[65]

It was not that artists like Beatty were immune to the horror of the war. On the contrary, Beatty's letters reveal that he was deeply affected by the devastation around him. Nevertheless, he could only work with the vocabulary he possessed, and there was nothing in it to describe what he saw in Flanders. In fact, only a few CWMF artists commanded the forms of expression necessary to capture the war on its own terms. The Vorticist Percy Wyndham Lewis, the Cubists David Bomberg and William Roberts, future Group of Seven member F.H. Varley, the Nash brothers, the Futurist C.R.W. Nevinson – only these and a handful of others possessed an artistic vocabulary suited to conveying the true essence of modern warfare.

J.W. Beatty, *Liévin from Vimy Ridge*. There is little in this scene to suggest that a battle has taken place here. The crater in the foreground is simply a chalk pit. (Canadian War Museum, 8103)

Some viewers applauded the few artists who tried to bring a modernist vocabulary to war. A critic in *Canadian Forum* praised their work for driving home 'the fact that this great war was not a glory-getting, come-on-boys sort of struggle, but a very filthy mess, a tangle of garbage-like residue, tortured earth, and pitiful heroic victims.' Accompanying such praise was a condemnation of those works that used the traditional vocabulary. Arthur Lismer dismissed Norman Wilkinson's canvas of the First Contingent sailing from Canada as 'a tame transcript of a steamship company on review,' and rejected *The Flag* by Byam Shaw as 'a decorative illustration in drab tones, uninspired, totally lacking in warmth of feeling.' Such works, wrote Barker Fairley, would appeal to that section of the public that wants the 'act of perception ... transformed into a sort of spoonfeeding.'[66] A.Y. Jackson was just as critical as his Group of Seven colleague Lismer. He believed Richard Jack's paintings showed the 'futility of fine craftsmanship used without passion or dramatic conception' and considered them to be largely irrelevant:

> They give one a feeling of being left over from previous wars, the same old popular poses, the same old bits of debris painted like still life, with a considerable amount of smoke wherever composition was giving trouble ... We got sick of literary heroics long before the war was over, but in painting it will continue for some time to come ... The difficulty will be to choose between the works which have a popular appeal and no artistic value, and the ones that do not glorify war but might live as works of art.[67]

The implications of Jackson's final comment were also clear to Hector Charlesworth, a man who admitted that his own views on art tended towards the conservative: 'Who shall say but that to future generations the panels which strike us as wantonly hideous will not carry a more effective message of what Canadians endured in the great war, than some of the works in which nobility of treatment is obvious.'[68]

Jackson and Charlesworth had happened upon the problem of balancing aesthetic quality with popularity. Regardless of its artistic merit, modernism was not a vocabulary that most Canadians in the 1920s and 1930s approved of to describe the war. The Vorticist and Cubist painters realized this fact even before they began work for the CWMF. In a letter to Paul Konody, the British art critic who advised the CWMF, William Roberts recognized the artistic leanings of the selection committee: 'I will send you on some more things that will have less "Cubism" in them but should a meeting of your committee take place before these reach you, will you only exhibit those that you think would not puzzle too much the meeting.' The committee, which eventually engaged Roberts, warned him that 'Cubist work is unacceptable'; David Bomberg ignored a similar warning and found himself having to repaint *Sappers at Work* in a more naturalistic style.[69] Augustus John admitted that Wyndham Lewis's attempt 'to reduce his "Vorticism" to the level of Canadian intelligibility' was a 'hopeless task,' and Eric Kennington gloomily predicted that it could take 200 years for Canadians to appreciate

Richard Jack's *The Second Battle of Ypres, 22 April to 25 May 1915* includes all of the clichés of battlefield painting: the wounded officer in the centre right who calmly exhorts his men on; the simian-looking enemy soldier at the left; the kilted soldier to the right who moves stalwartly into the line; and the stretcher-bearer helping a wounded soldier to the rear. (Canadian War Museum, 8179)

the fine modernist works they were receiving from people like Roberts and the Nash brothers.[70]

It has not taken 200 years, but Canadians certainly did not appreciate such works in the interwar period. Robert Borden admitted to his wife that he neither understood nor appreciated the modernist works, and those of a similar mind responded in a variety of ways.[71] Some people endeavoured to interpret the modernist works in traditional terms. As the caption for Roberts's *Gas Attack,* the catalogue for the 1919 CWMF exhibition in New York used an excerpt from *Canada in Flanders,* Beaverbrook's official history of the war, published in 1916 and written in the best gripping prose. There was no comment on the painting's style at all; it was treated as if it were a canvas by Richard Jack. The same guidebook excused Lewis's *A Canadian Gun Pit* with the statement that 'it is an experiment of the painter's in a kind of painting

In *A Canadian Gun Pit,* Percy Wyndham Lewis emphasized the technology of war, not only through the dominance of machines in the painting, but also by rendering the gunners in a jagged, mechanistic style. (British, National Gallery of Canada, Ottawa, 8356, Transfer from Canadian War Memorials, 1921)

not his own.' The implication, of course, was that Lewis was not very adept at the mode of expression that he helped pioneer; with a little more practice, inferred the guidebook, *A Canadian Gun Pit* could be more naturalistic.[72]

An alternative strategy was to maintain that traditional works were in fact modern. Notes on the CWMF issued to William Orpen pointed out that 'artists who paint Canadian fighting subjects go to France to make their preliminary studies and drawings. There are no "studio-concocted" pictures.' The inference, of course, is that all of the paintings executed for the fund were starkly realistic.[73] And this is precisely what many observers believed. Sir Edmund Walker advised that 'the public of the future is not likely to appreciate such a realistic treatment of war,' while the *Globe* went a step further. 'Life at the front is shown with shuddering realism,' it said of a CWMF display. 'Dying men, wounded men, smoke, flame, horror but always the spirit to fight on, visible on every side.' The comments referred to the paintings by Jack, those in the collection that bear the most obvious hallmarks of being studio concoctions.[74]

The most common way of coping with the modernist works was to construct a two-tier hierarchy of the CWMF. At the bottom were the modernist pieces, often lumped together under the term 'decorative panels.'[75] They were acknowledged to be closer to art than history; because they had more in common with painted balusters and sculpted columns than with the other pieces in the collection, they were by definition less important. They did not tell the story of the war; they merely added a touch of colour and variety to whatever gallery hosted a CWMF exhibition.

By dismissing these works as merely decorative, many viewers could then ignore them altogether and focus on the traditional works, those that were the visual equivalents of High Diction. They did this for the same reason that they preferred traditional accounts in literature: the traditional works transformed modern warfare, which was characterized by disorder, confusion, and chaos, into a rational and comprehensible activity.[76] The paintings by Richard Jack, Norman Wilkinson, and Kenneth Forbes were applauded for this very reason. They depicted, not a war of stalemate or random slaughter, but a war in which each individual action made sense. The progress of an engagement could be easily followed in the battle scenes; each soldier played a vital and identifiable role; and both the outcome and consequences of that engagement were clear. Paintings with titles such as *Void* and *For What?* were problematic, for they suggested confusion, senselessness, and amorality. *Canada's Answer* and *The Defence of Sanctuary Wood,* however, offered no such difficulties, for they clarified events and explicated their meaning. They introduced to the war a sense of order, coherence, and distinctness.

Their very titles filled Nash's void with a call to arms and answered Varley's question with a statement of fact. In short, they made the war make sense.

The centrality of these works to the CWMF is evident from accounts of its exhibitions. The description of the Burlington House exhibition in the *Canadian Annual Review* dwells on the traditional works, such as Jack's *The Taking of Vimy Ridge* and *The Second Battle of Ypres,* Louis Wierter's *The Battle for Courcelette,* Wilkinson's *Canada's Answer,* and William Orpen's portraits. W.B. Kerr dismissed the Cubist and Vorticist works reproduced in Paul Konody's *Art and War* ('modernistic to the point of nightmares. Of little value from the standpoint of either art or war'), while the *Globe* was anxious to interview Konody 'to find out whether anyone could be found who would defend the impressionist and expressionist paintings in the War memorial exhibit at the [Canadian National] Exhibition.'[77]

The wider public appeared to be just as sceptical. Unwilling to place

F.H. Varley, *For What?* The fallen soldiers in Varley's painting are heaped unceremoniously in a cart as they await burial beneath a row of tiny crosses. As the title suggests, the picture gives an impression of utter pointlessness. (Canadian War Museum, 8911)

themselves ahead of their time, they lavished the greatest attention and praise on a single work: James Byam Shaw's *The Flag*. This richly coloured oil depicts a Canadian soldier, draped in the Red Ensign, lying across the feet of an immense lion. He is intended to be dead, though his attitude is more reflective of a peaceful repose. Beneath him, a crowd of women, old men, and boys are seen in traditional attitudes of mourning. One woman is prostrate on the plinth; another raises her hands to the sky imploringly. An elderly man, perhaps a veteran of some earlier war, stands erect in the foreground as if to salute the fallen. Behind him, a young boy gazes at the flag with an expression of wonder. The image, so redolent with symbolism, struck a chord with Canadians. The *Canadian Bookman* called it 'a remarkable composition,' while the *Montreal Star* said it 'captured the sacrificial spirit in which the sons of the Empire laid down the greatest gift they had to give that freedom might triumph.' The *Toronto World* averred that, of all the works, Byam Shaw's left 'the most lasting impression' on visitors. It was the most popular work in the CWMF shows in London, Toronto, and Montreal.[78]

AN ADVERTISEMENT for the 1919 CWMF exhibition referred to the paintings of Richard Jack in inviting viewers to 'see the most dramatic conflicts – the horrors, the pathos, the humor, the glory of the Great War ... Know what war means. See it with your own eyes. Look into the hell of death that faced

Norman Wilkinson's *Canada's Answer* typifies resolve and commitment. In contrast to Varley's *For What?* a sense of purpose is implicit in this painting of the fleet carrying Canadian soldiers to Europe. (Canadian War Museum, 8934)

the Canadians at the Second Battle of Ypres ... Watch the flaming barrage of shell and machine gun fire that failed to melt the khaki line which rushed and overwhelmed Vimy Ridge.' Commenting on the earlier London show, the *Vancouver Daily Sun* predicted that 'certain exhibits are likely to arouse criticism on account of their too faithful rendering of the horrors of war.'[79]

These short comments summarize the persistence of the discourse of High Diction. Canadians were not interested in a faithful rendering of the horrors of the war. Instead, they wanted to remember the war as Richard Jack had painted it, as Currie's March 1918 message had described it, and as the Dumbells had acted it. In this regard, there was no significant dissonance between veteran and non-veteran. The light-hearted and disarming picture of war, which veterans perpetuated in their organizations and reunions, and the High Diction version of the war as a Victorian conflict were not mutually exclusive, nor were they fundamentally antagonistic. Certainly soldiers snorted at Currie's 'sham Napoleon' dispatch and might have laughed at people who characterized them as happy warriors, rushing with a smile towards death. By the same token, non-combatants may have been uncomfortable with the idealization of the culture of the *estaminet*, wishing that veterans spent a little less time describing carousals and a little more time recounting how they stoically guarded the line against the kaiser's armies. In reality, however, the two views fed each other. The veterans' entirely reasonable desire to remember the happy times of the war and forget the

John Byam Shaw's *The Flag*. This immensely popular painting symbolized what many Canadians wanted to believe about death in battle. In contrast to the corpses in Varley's *For What?* this dead soldier conveys a feeling of peace and tranquility. (Canadian War Museum, 8796)

horrors provided fertile ground in which the Victorian view of the war could flourish. Ex-soldiers and non-combatants were not speaking different languages; rather, their discourse took them from the same starting point to the same destination along two different routes.

In the early 1920s, no one in their right mind wanted to wallow in the horrors of the war just ended, but neither could they go on as if the tragedy had never happened. The only solution was to construct carefully a version of the war experience that showed consideration for the sensibilities of Canadians but also satisfied their desire to keep the war in the forefront of public consciousness. Veterans, who saw little point in reliving the horrors of trench warfare in their memoirs and reunions, achieved this by submerging the negative aspects in the positive. The sights they saw in Flanders might have taken precedence in their private thoughts, but in their public discourse the good times spent in *estaminet* and billet dominated.

It was not such a big step from the cult of the *estaminet* to using the war as a source of light entertainment, and it is notable that ex-soldiers from Theodore Goodridge Roberts to the Dumbells were quite prepared to profit from the contemporary taste for music-hall versions of the war. By doing so, they took their nostalgic, vaudeville memory of the war into the public domain. There, it found a ready audience simply because it offered civilians a comprehensible way to interpret the war: Flanders could be accommodated in the repertoire of the Victorian music hall simply by changing the dates and place names.

But the popularity of the veterans' version also accorded with the more serious view of the war, a view that was also solidly Victorian. The characters of a Dumbells review or Will Bird's Timothy Fergus Clancy were simply coarser versions of Wordsworth's happy warrior. Their masks of hilarity were easily dropped and, once the battle began, they embodied all of the characteristics that the Victorians liked to see in their soldiers. Private Clancy put aside his bottle of 'van blong' to become Currie's idealized Canadian soldier, ready to step into immortality to stem the foe, and the cast of *Biff! Bing! Bang!* ceased their good-natured grumbling and became the central figures of Jack's *The Second Battle of Ypres*. In the myth, they all stood together.

CHAPTER 4

Accurs'd They Were Not Here

We few, we happy few, we band of brothers;
For he to-day that sheds his blood with me
Shall be my brother; be he ne'er so vile,
This day shall gentle his condition;
And gentlemen in England, now a-bed,
Shall think themselves accurs'd they were not here;
And hold their manhoods cheap whiles any speaks
That fought with us upon Saint Crispin's day.

Henry the Fifth, 4.3

READING THIS AFTER THE WAR, many a Canadian might have wondered if Shakespeare's Henry had actually stood at Ypres or Vimy Ridge instead of Agincourt. According to the religious interpretation of the myth, the Great War had indeed 'gentled the condition' of more than a few tough nuts by turning their lives to a higher purpose. But Henry's famous speech had resonance on another level as well. The 'band of brothers,' whether at Agincourt or Arras, was an exclusive club, membership in which was held by a select few. All Canadian men of military age had been given the opportunity in 1914 to join that club, and those who had leapt at the chance were forever a breed apart. In the myth, the 'happy few' were a privileged body on a different level from the rest of society; those who had declined to accept the challenge would indeed 'hold their manhoods cheap.'

In 1934, a Winnipeg doctor and amateur playwright named Simon Jauvoich wrote *Dawn in Heaven*, about a soldier facing court martial for allowing his pal to sleep while on guard duty. In a thoughtful passage, Captain Waightman, one of the main characters, wonders aloud, 'after the war who is going to wield the authority on Man? Those few who are now ready to give their lives away on some dream, or those who are merely applauding because they are looking on from a brave safe distance?'[1] In the context of the myth, Waightman's question need not have been asked at all, for the answer was abundantly clear. In 1916, Dominion archivist Arthur G. Doughty wrote that 'to have been on Active Service in this great war will confer a mark of distinction more favourable than that which wealth may purchase or merit may attain.' Some years later, Gilbert Nason, the Winnipeg businessman in Douglas Durkin's novel *The Magpie,* held forth to his dinner guests about the impact of the war on society. 'The man who hasn't a clean war record to show,' he declared, 'will have to keep his mouth shut or take a beating.'[2] Many an ex-soldier, informed by a prospective employer that veterans made unreliable workers, might have glumly dismissed Doughty's prediction. But in the myth, participation in Canada's first world war was a cachet of inestimable value. It would drive communities to great lengths as they endeavoured to memorialize the townsfolk who enlisted. It would create a hierarchy of service in which the front was the only conceivable place for the true patriot. And it would move veterans, the happy few, to preserve wartime ties of comradeship and to demonstrate whenever possible both their solidarity with each other and their distinctiveness from the 'stay-at-homes.'

I

FOR MUCH OF THE WAR, the able-bodied adult male ventured into Canada's streets in civilian clothes at his peril. At every corner, he ran the risk of being accosted by a crowd of drawing-room patriots who demanded to know why he considered himself to be above enlistment. These self-appointed recruiting sergeants might even follow him through the city streets, brandishing the white feather that was the universal symbol of cowardice. Ironically, his only defender might well be a wounded and demobilized soldier who saw the white feather as infinitely preferable to death or dismemberment. Even in his own home, the man of military age was not safe from criticism. He might receive a white feather in the mail, like Dan Thatcher in Philip Child's *God's Sparrows,* or his newspaper or magazine might be full of attacks on the slackers who sat comfortably at home while their betters did their duty. He might read Montreal poet Alfred Gordon's 'The Coward,' which told him that the only proper course for the shirker was suicide, or any of the many vituperative anti-slacker poems by Robert Stanley Weir, like 'Were You Not There?' ('But you – Go hang yourself! – you didn't care').[3] Not even popular music offered a diversion for the man who failed to answer the call. Anti-shirking ditties were staples of vaudeville routines and sheet-music collections, and

Canadian toes were kept tapping to such favourites as 'There's A Fight Going On, Are You In It?', 'He's Doing His Bit – Are You?', and 'Why Don't You Wear a Uniform?'

It would be comforting to think that, after 1918, Canadian society recognized the injustice of shaming men into enlisting for service, and repented its actions. There is little indication, however, that this occurred. Indeed, ridicule of the shirker remained a significant element in postwar discourse, and fiction and non-fiction perpetuated the notion that men who had failed to join up should indeed hang their heads in shame. Those people who had declined to join the band of brothers remained, as they had been during the war, either unpatriotic scoundrels or shallow cretins.

Anti-shirking poetry stayed in vogue in the postwar years, many poets implying the continuing validity of such verse by reprinting it in postwar collections. Far from ruing their actions, Canadian poets also produced a considerable body of new work in this vein after the Armistice. Some of it, like Oliver Hezzelwood's 'Eat Christmas Dinner in Khaki,' was light-hearted:

> But unless you are a Kitchener recruit
>> Do not call me chum and comrade,
>> For I would not give a fag
> For the chaps not eating dinner in a khaki suit.

Other pieces, though, were as bitter as anything produced during the war. Take, for example, a poem called 'The Slacker,' written by an Ontario clergyman, the Reverend A. O'Malley:

> You slaves and serfs! Don't kiss his wooden hand!
> Touch not his hobbling crutch and empty sleeve!
> Shout not the frenzied shout with those who may!
> Think of the ignominy and the brand
> Of Cain that's on your brow! You can't deceive.
> Your cowardice, it's clear as the noonday.[4]

These are strong and perhaps unchristian words, but they were after all directed at men who had decided against joining the Great Crusade.

Reverend O'Malley was not a lone voice, for postwar literature is filled with characters for whom enlistment was the only conceivable course of action. Such figures are in no way drawn in a critical manner, as jingoistic buffoons rushing gleefully into the cannon's maw at the drop of a hat. Rather, they come across as decent, rational Canadians who recognized that, to paraphrase Rupert Brooke, God had matched them with his hour. Peter Starkley, a creation of Theodore Goodridge Roberts, believed that 'the only man worth pointing out was the man who had enlisted to fight.'[5] Anyone who had not accepted God's commission did not deserve notice.

For countless Canadians, imaginary and real, August 1914 constituted the challenge of a lifetime. Few people were granted the opportunity to defend the values of Western civilization and the principles of Christ. By giving it this chance, fortune had indeed smiled upon the generation of 1914. Forever after, one's character could be gauged by a simple criterion: how one responded to the test. For the characters in postwar fiction, this fact could not have been clearer. 'If you don't go,' declared a Victoria Cross winner in Child's novel, *'that's* something you'll remember all your life.'[6] Walter Blythe, the sensitive aesthete in L.M. Montgomery's *Rilla of Ingleside,* was moved by similar feelings: 'I'm going for my own sake – to save my soul alive. It will shrink to something small and mean and lifeless if I don't go.' Fear also motivated the protagonist of Harry Amoss's poem '1914.' Would his wife still honour and trust him if he failed to enlist, he wondered? 'Would not we twain / Dread in the sleeping child the coward stain?' The possibility was too terrible to contemplate, and he chose the chance of death at the front over the certainty of years of regret. 'Better that life leave love than love leave life,' he concluded.[7]

Like his fictional counterparts for whom a failure to enlist would have been a source of eternal shame, New Brunswick soldier Walter Brindle was immensely proud that he answered the call:

> I know that I played a man's part there
>> For two years, a month and a day,
> While many who might have been with us,
>> Cheered war films each night at the play.[8]

His soul would never be small and mean and lifeless; merely by joining the colours, he had demonstrated a greatness of spirit. Many other soldiers, just as proud as Brindle that they had demonstrated a rare quality of soul, expressed gratitude to the war for allowing them to do so. Edgar McInnis was grateful to his experiences as a gunner for showing him 'the love of strong men and the glory we else would have missed,' while Ralf Sheldon-Williams, who served with the Canadian Machine Gun Corps, spoke of soldiers having been 'granted the privilege of taking part' in the war.[9] William Howey spent two years in hospital on account of his war service, and must have spent many long hours pondering the experience. One result of his reflections was a poem he entitled 'Blessings':

> To have had the strength to serve in the Great War,
>> Oft missing Death by inches, scarcely harmed;
> And having lived to know that victory was ours – ...
>> These are the blessings that lay claim each day,
> To grateful recognition which I gladly own.

For L. Moore Cosgrove, an artilleryman and later Canadian trade commissioner to Australia, Armageddon taught soldiers 'that which we sometimes do not achieve in a lifetime! We learned to know ourselves and read our souls.'[10] The fear of so many soldiers on all sides, that the war would end before they had a chance to get into action, may have died a grim death in 1915. Yet in the postwar myth this fear survived, albeit in a different guise. It had been transformed into a feeling of gratitude that they had been able to take part in an event of almost cosmic significance.

The war, then, was a test of character; those who had passed could look back upon their experience with immense satisfaction. August 1914 had been their moment of destiny, their once-in-a-lifetime opportunity to experience the making of history, and those who had participated in this shift in the tide of human affairs felt a deep pride at their involvement. Just as Union soldiers of the American Civil War had worn their service with General Grant as a badge of honour, said Nova Scotia parliamentarian Daniel McKenzie, 'the day will come when the gallant veterans of the Grand Army of Canada will be proud to tell their children, "I was with Currie."'[11]

It had not always been so. In fact, pride in a nation's soldiers, individually rather than collectively, was a fairly recent innovation. Before the nineteenth century, the soldier was a nameless, faceless man, barely respectable and certainly not worthy of note on an individual basis. In uniform, he was an unsavoury character who was only restrained by the strictures of the garrison and the often inhuman exercise of military discipline. Once discharged he became even more sinister. Skilled in the use of arms, inured to the taking of human life, and accustomed to plundering whatever took his fancy, he constituted a potential threat to the social order. Everyone may have been proud of the heroics of the Thin Red Line, but few people would have been willing to invite a private of the King's Own into their parlour.

Through the 1800s, however, this view changed. The emergence of the war correspondent during the Crimean War moved the individual soldier into the spotlight. Thanks to the sympathetic reporting of journalists like William Howard Russell, the soldier's valour on the battlefield and his stoicism through hardship generated an emotional response that had scarcely existed before within the general public.[12] More importantly, the tradition of voluntarism spawned by the great revolutions in Europe and America created a new version of hero: the citizen-soldier. The man who rallied to the cause might be a clerk, a tradesman, or a student who had temporarily downed the tools of his profession to take up arms for his country. No longer was he an anonymous ruffian who had donned the king's uniform to escape poverty, a debt, or the long arm of the law. He was a patriot whose identity was worthy of note; he became an individual.

In Canada, this metamorphosis created what might be called the cult of the service roll, an obsession with listing the names of those soldiers who had joined the colours. In contemporary accounts of the North-West Rebellion and the Boer War, the identity and individuality of the soldier were paramount concerns. The accounts that appeared in newspapers and patriotic volumes relied heavily on letters written by soldiers, and usually included detailed lists of the members of the local regiment who had offered their services to the colours. Publications like *The History of the North-West Rebellion of 1885* and *Canada's Sons on Kopje and Veldt* not only outlined the issues at stake and the course of the conflict, but also included lists of the soldiers who had served. Engraved portraits of soldiers were commonly added to reinforce the human element.

The Great War was tailor-made to elevate the cult of the service roll to an even higher level, and the practices that had taken root in the Victorian wars were invigorated by the experience of 1914-18. Service rolls started to appear before the war was six months old. From February 1915, for example, each issue of *The University Monthly* began with a list of University of Toronto students serving at the front. Churches, too, began compiling rolls early in the war. Significantly, most of these started as blank scrolls, with names being added as the men departed. In this way, one could immediately tell which parishioners had been the first to answer the call. As well, many communities published a souvenir volume to commemorate the departure of the local battalion. They described the raising of the unit and usually provided a full list of its soldiers; ironically, more often than not these proud battalions were broken up for reinforcements as soon as they reached England.

The war's end saw no abatement in this commemorative activity. Indeed, the successful defence of Christianity and Western civilization made it even more imperative to record the names of those Canadians who had served the cause. As a consequence, the compilation of rolls became an important ritual in postwar Canada. Sometimes enlistment registers could be obtained from the Ministry of Militia and Defence, but in most cases advertising campaigns had to be mounted to secure the necessary information. When asked by the government of Nova Scotia to compile the province's war record, for example, Horatio Crowell placed a notice in every newspaper in the province, asking the relatives of Nova Scotia's fallen to write to him with details.[13]

A process that relied on assistance from well-meaning friends or relatives rather than official information was often fraught with difficulty. Local committees first had to decide what means of death was sufficient to secure a place on the honour roll. The Law Society of Upper Canada (LSUC) wondered if it should include on its roll only those who lost their lives at the hands of the enemy, or everyone who died while in uniform. Into the last category fell several men who succumbed to illness after enlistment, a recruit who was killed in an accident at Camp Borden, and a lieutenant who was shot by his father in Port Arthur, Ontario. Parkdale Collegiate Institute in Toronto decided against adding to its honour roll the name of Lieutenant John C. Scott, who accidentally killed himself while cleaning a German revolver he had captured.[14] The war memorial committee in Colborne, Ontario, solved the honour roll dilemma by giving pride of place to those soldiers who had been killed in action; those men and women who died on active service of other causes had to settle for a spot at the bottom of the roll. Having decided on the criteria for the honour roll, the committee then had to check and recheck the names for spelling and accuracy. Even the best efforts could not guarantee against embarrassing mistakes. After experiencing considerable difficulty in completing its honour roll for the Osgoode Hall memorial, the LSUC included in its list the name of Captain Henry C. Draper. Later, the secretary informed sculptor Frances Loring that 'I had an interesting conversation yesterday afternoon with the said gentleman who is very much alive.'[15] Loring's correction is still visible on the memorial; similar corrections, additions, and deletions can be seen on monuments across the country.

Despite such gaffes, the publication of service rolls peaked in the years immediately after the Armistice and continued at a healthy pace through the interwar period. The number of memorial volumes, honour rolls, and service registers that appeared in Canada, as books or pamphlets, in newspapers or magazines, or on war memorials or plaques, is remarkable. Not surprisingly, veterans' organizations played a prominent role in this process, and the preservation of full nominal rolls became an important consideration behind the publication of unit histories. Indeed, some books that claimed to be histories were in fact nothing more than lists of members of the unit. The 16th Battalion Association went to great trouble and expense to include a full nominal roll in its history; Hugh Eayrs, the president of Macmillan of Canada, said it was the most intricate publishing job he had ever encountered. However, despite the fact that the roll threatened to push the volume's price to more than twice what the association had anticipated, there was never a thought of printing the book without it.[16]

Schools, communities, churches, businesses, and service clubs also devoted considerable time and effort to ensuring that their citizen-soldiers were listed for eternity. Indeed, it is difficult to find an organization that did not compile a service roll as a tribute to its warriors, and few local newspapers failed to print a full honour roll in a special edition shortly after the Armistice. Commemorative magazines published in late 1918 and 1919 are frequently filled with advertisements from local businesses that list the names of workers who had enlisted for active service. Larger concerns, with correspondingly greater resources available, produced more elaborate honour rolls. Regardless of their origin, these memorial volumes are strikingly similar. Typically, they are sumptuous, expensive tomes that begin with fulsome praise of the war from a leader of the town, school, or business concerned. They frequently trace the course of the war through letters received from the front and always provide a complete list, usually with biographies and photographs, of all members who lost their lives while on active service. More touching are the many memorial volumes printed (usually privately and for limited circulation) to commemorate the lives of individual soldiers. They, too, follow the same basic format. They are essentially eulogies and relate the life story of the soldier from birth through service at the front to death. These volumes are usually epistolary, relying heavily on

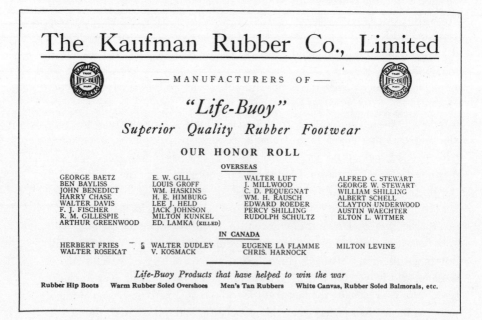

The honour roll of the Kaufman Rubber Company reveals an interesting ethnic mix among its soldiers, including a good number of men of German extraction. (Frederic Yorston, *Canada's Aid to the Allies and Peace Memorial* [Montreal: Standard 1919], 120)

extracts from the individual's letters, and they invariably end with excerpts from letters of condolence received from the soldier's comrades.

The effort that went into assembling nominal rolls suggest that they were central to the nation's attempt to construct a memory of the war. This was especially true for honour rolls and memorial volumes. These were in part consolatory; the ability of the bereaved to speak the name of the dead signified a coming to terms with the death, after which the emotional healing process could begin.[17] More importantly, the emphasis on naming the dead was intended to insure that the identities of the fallen remained prominent in the public consciousness; if the names were forgotten, the memory of the sacrifice would inevitably slip away as well. Indeed, it would be difficult to overstate the importance attached to recording the names of the dead. A souvenir pamphlet on the return of the 22nd Battalion to Québec regarded it as 'le pieux devoir déterniser les noms de ces vaillants et de ces martyrs.' A disgruntled citizen in Saint-Hilaire, Québec, expressed his commitment to that pious duty more forcefully. In August 1922 he dynamited the town's war memorial, apparently unhappy that it had not been inscribed with the names of the dead.[18]

The damaged memorial in Saint-Hilaire, Québec, dynamited by a local man who was displeased with the inscription. Atop the memorial sits a captured enemy machine gun, to symbolize the victory of Canada's citizen-soldiers over German militarism. (*Monuments commémoratifs de la province de Québec* [Quebec City: Commission des Monuments Historiques 1923], 1:259)

The civic pride that surrounded the recruiting of local battalions naturally fostered a desire to mark what was the most momentous event in many a community's history. The service roll emerged as a way, not simply to commemorate the event, but to gauge the community's response. A version of municipal boosterism developed after the war, with towns and cities across the country putting forth claims of their pre-eminence with respect to enlistments. In Ontario, both

Brantford and Galt claimed to have the highest enlistment rate in Canada in proportion to its population. Springhill, Nova Scotia, claimed the second highest per capita enlistment rate in the country.[19] In provincial terms it was Nova Scotia that claimed to have 'surpassed the other Provinces of the Dominion in promoting the successful conclusion of the great conflict – not only by the number of splendid troops it supplied in proportion to its population.' St. John's Church in Ancaster, Ontario, was proud that all of the men on its service roll were volunteers; not a single parishioner had waited to be conscripted. The minister also grumbled that other churches had padded their honour rolls by including the names of people whose connection with the parish was tenuous.[20] His complaint is noteworthy, for in each of these examples, the service roll was the yardstick of performance. A town or social group whose young men and women had responded promptly and eagerly to the call could find in that response a source of great pride; a town with a long honour roll in proportion to its population was a good town. If, however, the youth had tarried or declined to offer themselves at all, it reflected badly on the community for not cultivating a sufficient sense of civic duty. As James Gray later wrote, 'it was a mean and inconsequential hamlet ... that had no war dead to mourn.'[21]

II

THE SIGNIFICANCE of the service roll as a gauge of conduct demonstrated the degree to which Canada's memory of the war came to focus almost entirely on the front. In this, it paid scant heed to reality. There were other ways to serve the war effort than at the front. It was not necessary to be in uniform to 'do your bit'; you could do it in countless other ways, such as supplying comforts to the troops, growing more crops, or paying more taxes.[22] At the end of Robert J.C. Stead's novel *The Cow Puncher,* Dave Elden tells Irene Hardy not to remain in England as a nurse, but to return to Canada and farm: 'it will be neither soldiers nor nurses that will win the war ... it's the plow that's going to win ... Think of every furrow as another trench in the defences which shall save your home from the fate of Belgium's homes. It's not as easy as going to the front; it hasn't got the heroic ring to it ... But it's the thing that must be done.'[23] The wisdom of this comment, of course, had been made quite clear long before the fictional Elden was killed in action at Courcelette. Among the tens of thousands of Canadians who flocked to join the First Contingent in 1914 were countless skilled workers whose enthusiasm was admirable but whose talents Canadian industry could ill afford to lose. Many a factory owner, driven to considerable effort and expense to train new workers in order to fill war contracts, would have agreed with Elden wholeheartedly.[24] The skilled worker, like the skilled farmer, was of much more use at home than in the trenches.

Elden's argument, however, was a very hard sell. For the able-bodied woman, there was no other acceptable response to the war than to don the uniform of the king and proceed overseas. No amount of rationalization could change the fact that serving in field or factory simply could not carry with it the same honour as serving in the trenches. It was being *with* Currie that counted, not growing the crops that fed the Canadian Corps or making the rifles that armed it. The young man who stayed at home, no matter how honourable his motive, carried the stigma of failure. Like Rupert Stillwell in Ralph Connor's *To Him That Hath,* whose flat feet kept him out of the army but did not keep him from tireless war charity work (or, for that matter, from improving his tennis game), he would always suffer by comparison with those men who had gone to the front and 'gambled with the ultimates.'[25]

Unfair though it may have been, this assumption underlay many fictional portrayals of Canada's war. George Cummings, in Grace Blackburn's *The Man Child,* warns his pal of the lie that 'a man has got more of the right stuff in him when he wears the king's colours than he has when he is in civilian clothes,' but his pragmatism does not ring true, and his life follows an entirely traditional course. He enlists in the army and dies in an effort to save Jack Winchester; only by meeting a gallant soldier's end could Cummings demonstrate that he had 'the right stuff' in him.[26] His friend Jack was cut from the same cloth, one of the many fictional heroes who forsook important non-combatant careers to join the ranks of doomed infantrymen at the front. Winchester left his medical studies, through which he could have made a significant contribution to the war effort and to humanity, to enlist and die with thousands of other infantrymen. Thor Lindal, in Laura Goodman Salverson's *The Viking Heart,* also left medical school to perish in the trenches, while Gregory Vant, the hero of Beckles Willson's *Redemption,* quit his job as a government minerals expert to enlist in the infantry. The nation had more use for someone with such detailed and specialized knowledge of strategic materials, but this was irrelevant; Vant knew his place was in the firing line.

The most fully rounded example of this type of character was created by Robert J.C. Stead. Born in Middleville, Ontario, Stead had moved to the Prairies while a child and eventually joined the editorial staff of the *Calgary Herald.* His reputation, however, was built not on his journalism but on immensely popular novels like *The Homesteaders* and *The Bail Jumper,* which turned Stead into one of the pre-eminent bards of the prairie experience. During the war, his patriotic verse drew high praise, while his novels *The Cow*

Puncher and *Dennison Grant,* both set against the backdrop of the war, sold well. Eight years after the publication of *The Cow Puncher,* Stead's novel *Grain* appeared. It is of considerably more literary merit than the earlier work and reflects a sharp shift in opinion on the part of the author. *Grain* (Stead toyed with titling the book *A Soldier of the Soil* or *Half a Hero* but eventually rejected these more suggestive alternatives) tells the story of Gander Stake, the not entirely likeable son of a western farmer.[27] Stake is not impressed by the war heroes of a Boy's Own story. His heroes are people he knows, like his weather-beaten father and Bill Powers, who runs the steam thresher. When war is declared, Stake decides it is none of his business; although his sweetheart despises him for failing to enlist like the other local men, he decides that he can be more useful doing what he knows best, producing grain to feed the Allies. Gander is certainly right, and in real life he would have deserved the exemption from conscription that was promised to the sons of farmers. Yet as a literary creation, he is plagued by guilt that his decision brands him as a shirker: 'Down underneath was a gnawing sense – a sense that he was running away from something, that he was a fugitive, taking refuge on the farm!' At the end of the novel, Gander finally surrenders to his guilt and finds a way to expunge it: he resolves to devote his life to helping the wounded war hero Dick Claus, as a way to make up for 'doing less than his share in the great struggle.' Once Claus is provided for, Gander decides to leave his beloved farm for the city, a further act of penance, which he rationalizes as expanding his horizons. Significantly, he does so as a soldier: 'now you will take your medicine, and you will take it from yourself. Form Fours!'

Gander Stake, the man who felt shame at spending the war farming (at which he excelled) instead of soldiering (for which he had little aptitude), was not simply a literary artifice. He had his counterparts in the real world, in men who believed that their absence from the front lines followed them like a cloud. The historian A.L. Burt admitted to feeling 'sad and somewhat shamefaced that though I am in khaki I have not served in France.' Graham Spry felt the same sense of inadequacy; outraged and humiliated that service in England did not earn him the badge given for service at the front, he disguised his failure by joining a veterans' organization whose badge resembled the service badge.[28] J. Lucien Dansereau took great pains to answer charges that he was the only former student of the Royal Military College not to offer his services during the war. He went to the trouble of securing a letter from the former deputy minister of Militia and Defence Eugène Fiset affirming that Dansereau had indeed volunteered but had been rejected.[29]

No one in a position of influence was more dogged by such charges, though, than Mackenzie King. In the years before the war, his promising political career had apparently stalled. Defeated in the general election of 1911 after serving as Laurier's minister of Labour, he had drifted until being asked to take over management of the Liberal party's information office; he passed his days making speeches, organizing conferences, preparing pamphlets, and editing the *Canadian Liberal Monthly*. It was a thankless task that paid him a meagre salary and scarcely challenged his considerable reserves of energy. At the same time, he dabbled in pacifism, associating himself with American peace movements and earning himself a reputation in some cir-

cles as pro-German. Then, in June 1914, King's ship came in. The Rockefeller Foundation invited him to New York to discuss various aspects of industrial relations, an emerging field in which King was something of a pioneer in North America. It soon became clear what the Rockefellers had in mind for King and on 13 August 1914, just nine days after Canada entered the war, he became head of the foundation's new department of industrial relations. For the next five years, King acted as a labour relations troubleshooter with some of the largest corporations in the United States on labour-management issues.

By all accounts, King was very good at what he did, and his successes in securing industrial peace during the war should not be underestimated. Yet there was no getting around the fact

Mackenzie King in 1910. Was he young and fit enough to join the infantry four years later? (NAC PA25970)

that he had not offered himself for service at the front, and a whispering campaign that King had shirked his duties during the war started soon after he was elected Liberal leader in 1919. He was quick to tackle the charges. In his first public address as Liberal leader, in his adopted riding on Prince Edward Island, King defended his 'noble, heroic, and self-sacrificing part' in the war and was gratified by the crowd's response: 'I challenged any one present (of the 3 to 4000) to say I had not done my full duty during the War. Not a person spoke ... The silence in that vast gathering was impressive. I said I hoped it might be heard throughout the Dominion.' He also received wholehearted support from the *Island Patriot,* which 'venture[d] to assert that no single man did greater work in our country or in the US, to assist the Allies in winning the war, than did Mackenzie King.'[30]

King's enemies were not easily placated. At a meeting of the Montreal Progressive Club, McGill classicist John Macnaughton again questioned King's role: 'So far as the returned man was concerned, ... how could he expect to receive any concessions from a Liberal leader who had deserted Canada in her hours of crisis in search of Standard Oil millions?' This time, King defended himself in the House of Commons. He read into the record many letters from American industrialists testifying to his good work during the war, and then recounted his own personal trials; his father had gone blind just before the war and died in 1916, his sister had died in 1915, his brother had contracted tuberculosis, and his mother had died in 1917. 'As I look back upon those years of war,' he mused, 'so full of poignant suffering for the whole of mankind, I cannot but experience a sense of gratitude, that in that world ordeal it was given to me to share in so intimate a way the sufferings of others, and, with it all, so large a measure of opportunity to do my duty, as God gave it to me to see my duty, at that time.'[31]

Losing family members to illness and old age, however, was not a sufficient contribution to the war, and the suggestions of shirking refused to fade. In December 1921, in Holland Landing, Ontario, the Liberal leader was back on the defensive. Stressing the aims and ideals of the Rockefeller Foundation, he described his work in solving labour problems at Bethlehem Steel and Bethlehem Shipbuilding, which he claimed had built 60 per cent of Allied vessels during the war.[32] An early biographer of King also leapt to his defence, writing that the prime minister was an internationally recognized expert in labour relations; such men were essential to the production of war materials, and King's decision to continue with the Rockefeller Foundation during the war had been based on a realization that this was the best way he could serve the Allied cause. Even this did not mark the end of the whispering. In the 1930 election campaign, Ontario premier Howard Ferguson stirred a minor controversy by raising further questions about King's conduct during the war.[33]

Throughout this episode, Mackenzie King and his defenders were entirely right. A forty-year-old paunchy academic with no aptitude for things military would have been no asset to the CEF; his talents were much better utilized in industrial relations.[34] Nevertheless, King continually had to defend himself from charges that he had shirked his duty in his country's time of need and, like Gander Stake, felt the need to expunge his guilt in other ways. He went to great lengths, for example, to secure documentary evidence that he had played a leading role in the creation of the Vimy

Memorial. His persistence in pursuing the administrative paper trail suggests more than just an appreciation of the political advantage to be gained from leadership of the scheme. It suggests King's desire to remove the perceived stain of failing to enlist by ensuring that those Canadians who had done so were memorialized on the Western Front.

King would have had an easier time of things had he been able to claim a close relative (a younger brother would have been ideal) among the fallen. In the House of Commons in 1923, the prime minister's mention of the sacrifices of war drew this comment from Opposition leader Arthur Meighen: 'I am moved by one regret, that the feelings of this parliament, as embalmed in the resolution [thanking the French government for the gift of a portion of Vimy Ridge], feelings of undoubted gratitude and appreciation, cannot be expressed, rather than by me, by one who like yourself, Mr. Speaker [Rodolphe Lemieux], or many others assembled here, is linked by memories more sacred with all that sacrifice.'[35] Like many of Meighen's remarks, this one implied much more than it said. His humble claim to be unworthy to move the resolution inferred that he was at least more worthy than the prime minister. Though he was the same age as King, Meighen escaped the criticism that hounded King because, as a staunch and vocal supporter of the war and the primary drafter of the Military Service Act, he had done everything legislatively possible to prevent shirking. More importantly, the comments also revealed the degree to which the glory of service could be shared. King could not even claim to have given a close relative to the war, so he was hardly fitted to speak of sacrifice. Rodolphe Lemieux, however, was a different matter. His age obviously prevented him from enlisting, but he had something of almost equal value: his eldest son, Rodolphe, had been killed in action at Courcelette while serving with the 22nd Battalion. Through the death of his son, Lemieux could share in the glow that was emitted from the pantheon of fallen heroes.

For older Canadians whose age barred them from military service, the enlistment of a child allowed them to participate vicariously in the crusade; if they could not die for the cause, they should at least send someone to die in their stead. The personification of this assumption in Canada's memory of the war was the parent who revelled in the child's enlistment and in whom the fateful telegram produced sorrow but an even stronger rush of pride. This figure, like the young man of promise whose life was snuffed out in the trenches, was a staple of postwar literature. Gander Stake's parents were ambivalent about his decision not to enlist: 'not that they were anxious for [Gander] to go, but it would have been a solace to their pride if he had *wanted* to go.' *Rilla of Ingleside* is full of women who gladly dispatch their sons to war. Even Rilla's mother, who eventually sends three sons to France, feels this way. When a neighbour (whose son remained at home) asks her how she could stand to watch her son marching away to war, Anne replies 'it might have been worse, Mrs. Drew. I might have had to urge him to go.'[36] For these characters, the sadness at watching the troop train pull away was balanced by a deep pride that a part of them had joined the crusade. They were all like the Montreal man who took great exception to Currie's use of the word 'sacrifice' to describe the offering of Canadian men for the war. This gentleman had five sons overseas, and 'neither the Father [nor] Mother ... of those Boys consider[s] their going as a Sacrifice but rather as a God given privilege that we had the boys willing to go.'[37]

In 1919, a local worthy in northern Ontario told the townsfolk at the unveiling of a memorial tablet that 'in Canada today we only recognize two classes.'[38] The first consisted of those people who, because of age or infirmity, could not themselves go to France and so were forced to stay at home and support the troops in spirit. These were the Arthur Meighens and Susie Stakes of Canada, people whose conduct and public statements left no doubt about their wholehearted support for the war effort. They threw all their energies into recruiting, made frequent affirmations of their willingness to sacrifice a child to the war, or, like the poet Camilla Sanderson, expressed a seemly envy for the fiancée, wife, and mother who had lost

Sharing in the glory of sacrifice: four proud mothers ride in a Warriors' Day parade. (Pringle and Booth, NAC PA60562)

their men in battle.[39] Such people could not join the band of brothers at the front, but at least they could appreciate the almost magical quality of that select group.

III

THE BAND OF BROTHERS WAS, of course, the only other class of Canadians worth recognizing, at least according to the myth. Those men and women whose names appeared on the nation's service rolls were set apart from the rest of society by their membership in the crusade. In this way, the cult of the service roll served to accentuate the already profound estrangement of the returned man from the rest of civilian society. It turned veterans into a sort of caste, in society but not of it. In virtually every nation that had fought, postwar social relations were marked by a schism between ex-soldiers and the 'stay-at-homes.' Robert Graves divided British society into the Fighting Forces and the Rest, with the line between the two groups lying somewhere just west of No Man's Land. In Germany veterans were the *Frontsoldaten* who were united in a *Schicksalgemeinschaft,* a community of fate. 'Only we know, no one else,' wrote Paul Alverdes in *The Whistlers*.[40] Will Bird agreed. 'We, of the brotherhood,' he wrote, 'could understand the soldier but never explain him. All of us would remain a separate, definite people.'[41]

Many Canadians foresaw this gap while the war was still in progress. When a Methodist chaplain wrote to his superiors in 1918 that 'the men at home can never understand the soldier. The people at home can never understand what the war has meant to the soldier,' he might have been dismissed as an alarmist.[42] Yet, as his superiors may not have recognized, he was speaking with the voice of a soldier, not a clergyman. Ten years later, Theodore Goodridge Roberts admitted that the gulf had not closed in a decade of peace, and he offered some advice to fellow veterans: 'Do not talk about the war, truthfully or otherwise, to people who weren't there. You will be misunderstood if you do ... Keep your war-talk for old soldiers.' The war was the bailiwick of the ex-soldier, and the battlefield was 'a place of precious memory – mystic – unearthly – a place the stay-at-homes can never know.' Only veterans had the authority to speak of battle. If the war was a crusade, they became its only legitimate chroniclers, granted the powers of articulation by their presence at the front. When a Victoria Cross winner took the stage at a patriotic meeting in *God's Sparrows,* a hush fell on the crowd as they realized that he was the only man in the room with the authority to talk of the war: 'they could tell he believed what he said: he had been in France; he had a right to speak.'[43] Experience in the trenches had conferred upon soldiers the sole right to talk of the war; it had brought knowledge, and it was knowledge that separated the veteran from the rest of society.

But separation from the rest of society had not always meant unity among ex-soldiers. Indeed, tensions between officers and other ranks ran high in the immediate postwar years. The soldier's jealously guarded right to grumble about his officers, the inability of many ex-soldiers to find a secure job or a decent home while their officers prospered, inequalities in the pension system – all contributed to bitter feelings for many rankers and led Currie to despair over the future of Canadian veterans' organizations should those feelings not be soothed. By the mid-1920s, a certain equanimity had come over the veteran movement. The disappearance of the controversy over payment of war bonuses to ex-soldiers played a significant role in improving relations, for it removed what had been a major bone of contention among veterans.[44] At the same time, the cult of the service roll had exerted a powerful influence on ex-soldiers, confirming in their minds that officer and ranker alike shared something with each other that they could never share with the stay-at-homes. Gradually, the factors that appeared to divide veterans became less important than the single factor, participation in the crusade, that united them and separated them from the rest of society. They began to celebrate that separation as a source of great pride, cultivating and proclaiming it through frequent and very public demonstrations of their distinctiveness and solidarity.

That solidarity was summed up in a single word: comradeship. Comrade was not simply a synonym for friend; there was a qualitative difference between the two words. Friends were linked by common interests and tastes; friendship was mutable, and could dissolve if interests and tastes changed. Comrades, on the other hand, were joined in a common fate. The strength of their relationship lay in a shared response to the conditions they experienced at the front and an acceptance of the fact that only in a spirit of cooperation and tolerance could those conditions be endured. Unlike friendship, comradeship was permanent; even when the war experience ended, it remained the bedrock upon which the relationship was based.

The importance of the bonds of comradeship stemmed from the fact that they were formed in a climate of complete honesty. As Charles W. Gordon put it, service in the trenches meant 'the casting away of any mask.' Education, social status, wealth, physical appearance – none of these mattered in the valuation of a soldier at the front. 'Snobbishness died miserably in the trenches,' wrote Will Bird. 'No artificial imposition could survive in the ranks where inherent value automatically found its level; all sham of superiority fled before such an existence of essentials.'[45] All that counted was a soldier's conduct. 'France, take it all in all, was hell,' observed James Pedley, 'but in it was the *camaraderie* of the damned, and he who entered there might know that he would be presumed to be a real man until he had proved himself less.' Whatever else could be said about army life, at least it 'involved a factor of living that seems to be impossible in peace, the factor of honesty between men and the rating of a man for what he is, not for what he has.'[46]

It was that factor of honesty that made comradeship so special. Officially adopted for use between veterans at the 1927 Canadian Legion Convention in Winnipeg, the word comrade was 'a simple but meaningful term born of endearment and common sacrifice on the battlefields of France and Belgium.' Its significance, as the vice-president of the Great War Veterans' Association (GWVA) said in 1921, was something that non-combatants could never appreciate: '[comrade] to us means fellowship of a most sacred kind formed by ties that cannot be broken but are written in blood, ties that we formed in days of trial that cannot be broken now by anything else, ties that are sacred to those who have gone and to those who still live.'[47] Comradeship became 'the most precious heritage of the struggle,' for it was a relationship of a rare kind. 'Better associations were never formed, truer friendships were never made, and these must not, they cannot, die,' proclaimed a unit history.[48]

And in many cases they did not, for ex-soldiers were determined to perpetuate the spirit of their units after demobilization. There is little evidence to substantiate the conventional wisdom that ex-soldiers only wanted to forget the war years and consequently shunned reunions and unit associations. If the history of the veteran movement in Canada is any indication, ex-soldiers displayed no desire to fly from their past. Even before demobilization, the men of the CEF vowed to preserve the spirit of their units by establishing associations once they returned to Canada, and dozens of such groups began convening reunions in 1919 and 1920. In 1920, the 137th Battalion Association enrolled 293 former members of the Calgary-based reinforcement unit, nearly 40 per cent of the battalion's survivors. Their first reunion was paid for by R.B. Bennett, who had sponsored the unit's establishment, and annual gatherings continued until 1958. As a reflection of the comradeship of the trenches, no tickets were sold; each attendee chipped in what he could afford, and the wealthier members of the unit made up the shortfall.[49] By 1932, the 31st Battalion Association had 1,200 members, nearly a third of the unit's survivors, and even national organizations boasted sizeable memberships. In the mid-1930s, the Canadian Legion claimed to have more than 150,000 members, over a quarter of Canada's surviving veterans.[50]

It would be tempting to ascribe a simple economic motive to the formation of these organizations, and indeed much of the impetus for the establishment of early veterans' groups came from a desire to ensure that members were treated fairly by the government. The first such organizations, formed by wounded and demobilized soldiers in 1916 and 1917, were mostly concerned with ensuring that veterans received adequate medical care, pension benefits, and employment assistance. Furthermore, when the majority of veterans' groups came together into the Canadian Legion in 1925, it was under the assumption that only through unity could ex-soldiers become a strong and effective lobby group. The importance of the economic motive was confirmed during the 1930s, when the Depression spawned dozens of new, independent veterans' organizations, like the Canadian Soldiers' Non-Pensioned

Widows' Association, the Veterans' Dependants' Mutual Assistance League, the Canadian War Remnants Association of British Columbia, the War Veterans' Independent Advocate, the Disabled Veterans' Association of Saskatchewan, and the United Ex-Servicemen's Association. Almost without exception, these organizations were essentially lobby groups attempting to secure relief, employment, or other provisions for ex-soldiers and their dependants. The common denominator among members was not trench experience but economics. The fact that they were veterans was largely incidental; the real link was a common need for financial assistance.

As a consequence, such organizations came and went as the economy fluctuated. The true veterans' organizations, like the Canadian Legion, the Canadian Corps Association, and countless unit associations, survived through the boom and bust cycles of the interwar period and beyond. They were able to do so because they owed their existence not to specific discontents, but to a desire to perpetuate 'the close and kindly ties of mutual service' in the trenches.[51] The larger of these organizations still exist today, their ranks filled by veterans of later wars. The unit associations literally died out, many meeting through the 1960s and 1970s, until the last members died or were too frail to attend reunions. They survived for so long because they were not lobby groups, but comrades' clubs. They did perform some philanthropic function, assisting members of the association who had fallen on hard times, but generally they existed as vehicles to ensure that the comradeship of the trenches was preserved.

These groups had a number of characteristics, all of which served to emphasize the distinctiveness of veterans and perpetuate the comradeship of the trenches. In the first place, the unit associations did everything possible to set veterans apart from the rest of society. Victor Odlum advised that 'active membership [in the 11th Brigade battalion associations] should be marked by an emblem, unobtrusive but always visible, the right to wear which should be jealously restricted to and guarded by the active members.' When veterans of the 111th Battalion began holding yearly reunions in Preston, Ontario, on the anniversary of the Second Battle of Ypres, they were encouraged to wear their uniforms to the accompanying church service. British Columbia veterans frequently secured permission from the Department of Militia and Defence to wear their uniforms to war memorial unveilings.[52] This tactic served a dual purpose. It affirmed the bond between those participants who had served during the war and, at the same time, set veterans apart; the ex-soldier was immediately distinguishable from the 'stay-at-home.' The larger the gathering, the more important this tactic became. At the great Canadian Corps reunions in Toronto in 1934 and 1938, veterans received red, blue, grey, or green berets, which corresponded to the colour of their divisional patch. For the Vimy pilgrimage of 1936, former soldiers were issued with khaki berets; everyone else wore navy blue berets. Again, the use of coloured berets was a conscious attempt to emphasize the solidarity of ex-soldiers and also to ensure that the veteran was instantly distinguishable from every other member of society.

If a distinctive dress was adopted to affirm the solidarity and distinctiveness of ex-soldiers, so too was a unique mode of discourse. Veterans communicated in a sort of code language, as Theodore Goodridge Roberts had said, that often made their utterances incomprehensible to outsiders. Many unit histories freely admitted that they were written entirely for former members, and that the general reader would find them bewildering; the slang was unintelligible, the anglicized place names unrecognizable, and many of the incidents meaningless to the uninitiated. Hector Charlesworth, in a review of the soldier play *The P.B.I.*, admitted that he did not understand many of the jokes that drew roars of laughter from the veterans in the audience.[53]

One of the strongest elements of the veteran discourse was the grim, fatalistic humour of the trenches. The sort of vaudeville soldier jokes that punctuated *The P.B.I.* were certainly common, but veterans' humour often

Vimy pilgrims await the unveiling ceremony. Coloured berets distinguished veteran from stay-at-home, and round badges divided pilgrims into 'companies.' (NAC PA803934)

had a harder edge. Instead of simply relying on broadly drawn stereotypes for comic effect, it took some of the most horrific aspects of the war and transformed them into objects of laughter. In the programs for veterans' dinners, for example, this humour was given free rein. Veterans of the 8th Canadian Field Ambulance dined on 'Bed Rolls and Waggon Grease, Remy Siding Turkey, and No. 9 Peas,' while former members of another Alberta battalion, the 31st, celebrated their sixteenth reunion with Creme de la Somme soup and Dead Cow Corner milk. A dinner reunion of the 15th Battery, Canadian Field Artillery was even more macabre. The meal began with Bucket of Blood, Shell-hole Special, and Fish-guts; the choice of pies included Ypres Fish-tail, Vimy Mud, or Passchendaele Slime, while Cambrai Muddle or Mons Coal pudding was also available.[54] To the civilian, the tendency to make jokes about dismembered corpses or artillery bombardments might have seemed callous or perverse. To the soldier, it was essential to the psyche if one was to survive the war with wits intact. The perpetuation of this sort of humour after the war was not so much an attempt to shock stay-at-homes, although some veterans probably took a perverse delight in the squeamishness of civilians. It was primarily to celebrate a significant facet of

Ex-artillerymen re-muster for a reunion dinner on the ninth anniversary of the Battle of Vimy Ridge. Stay-at-homes might well have been offended by the menu. (Jonathan F. Vance)

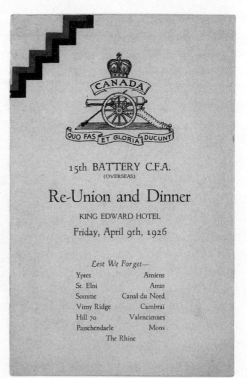

15th BATTERY C.F.A.
(OVERSEAS)

Re-Union and Dinner

KING EDWARD HOTEL

Friday, April 9th, 1926

Lest We Forget—

Ypres	Amiens
St. Eloi	Arras
Somme	Canal du Nord
Vimy Ridge	Cambrai
Hill 70	Valenciennes
Passchendaele	Mons
	The Rhine

MENU

Bucket of Blood, Shell-hole Special, Fish-guts

~

Canal du Nord Eels, Tickled Soles, Tripe

~

Mules' Innards, Frozen Rabbit, McConachie, Bully

~

Romp de Cheval — Ox a la Buttock

~

Mangels, Weeds, Musical Fruit, and Pommes de Terre
(Battered, Slivered, Burnt or Gypoed)

~

PIE:—Ypres Fish-tail, Somme Chalk, Vimy Mud, Passchendaele Slime,
Arras Pip-squeak, Amiens Sunshine

~

PUDDING:—Cambrai Muddle, Valenciennes Camouflage,
or Mons Coal

~

Heavy Drag-rope Cigars, Cigarettes, "Arf a Mo," "Three Witches,"
"Life Rays," "Ruby Queens"

~

Char Sandbagged, Cafe Noir, Klim

~

Fromage a la Sewer, Massey-Harris Binder

~

SOLDIER'S FAREWELL

trench culture. By cracking the same jokes that had helped them endure life at the front, veterans paid tribute to the healthy relationship that had grown up among the happy few.

A third characteristic of veterans' organizations was their constant affirmation of solidarity with the fallen. It was almost an article of faith among veterans that any gathering of ex-soldiers brought together not simply the survivors, but the fallen as well. 'The spirits of those men who lie in Flanders Fields,' said a veteran of the 21st Battalion, 'have come across the ocean, and they are in our midst to-night.' They could be felt at Armistice Day ceremonies, unit reunions, anniversary dinners – one ex-soldier sensed them at the memorial arch of Royal Military College:

> Beneath the curve of a beautiful arch
> I stood, and thought I saw them march,
> Ghostly regiments marching by ...
> Yet still I saw them marching on
> Laughing and singing – when all had gone
> Quietness settled down.[55]

Not surprisingly, these strange meetings were invisible to the stay-at-homes. As Kim Beattie wrote of an Armistice Day parade,

> The World knows not the Dead went thro'
> To rouse and to revive
> And steel the steel-stern bond anew
> With them that did survive.[56]

The comradeship of the trenches had forged bonds between soldiers that were infinitely stronger than death. 'We, who outmastered death and all its fears,' wrote Frederick George Scott, 'are one great army still – living and dead.' He called ex-soldiers the unbroken line, reflecting both their stalwartness in battle and the enduring bonds between them. In recognition of these bonds, reunions invariably included toasts to fallen comrades, or some affirmation of the presence of the dead. Eric Leed called this a 'cowed subjection' of survivors to the ghosts of the dead, but few veterans would have described it this way.[57] Such rituals were the most solemn part of a reunion and affirmed that the veteran community was a closed society. Like the coloured berets and the grisly humour of the trenches, the rituals in honour of fallen comrades became vehicles to demonstrate the solidarity of soldiers. Only the veteran could see the spirits of the fallen as they passed on Armistice Day; only the veteran could commune with them in armoury or Legion hall. These rituals verified that the brotherhood of the trenches remained intact. Death had no power over the ties that linked the happy few.

LIKE THE DETERMINATION to downplay the negative aspects of war in favour of a positive, uplifting version of history, the cult of the service roll reflected a complex mix of fact, fiction, nostalgia, and wishful thinking that easily accommodated the feelings of veteran and civilian alike. The cult itself was a very real force in the nation's memory of the war; there is no denying that Canadians were intent upon recording the names of everyone who had enlisted. But here the memory began to depart from reality. Contrary to what Doughty had predicted in 1916, service in the war did not necessarily confer anything of substance. There were few guarantees of preferential treatment in postwar Canada, and many veterans' benefits programs were of dubious value. Civil service jobs that had been reserved for ex-soldiers turned out to be menial and low-paying, while men who tried to become farmers under the Soldier Settlement Act found themselves facing heavy debt and falling prices for their products, disabilities that forced more than half of Canada's soldier-settlers off their land by 1930.[58] By the same token, failure to enlist was no real obstacle, in spite of Gilbert Nason's warning. Having spent the war as an industrial relations consultant certainly did not hinder the public career of Mackenzie King, Canada's longest-serving and most successful (at least in electoral terms) prime minister.

And yet the cult of the service roll allowed veterans to construct a memory that downplayed these unpalatable realities. It was fertile ground in which the distinctiveness and solidarity of the ex-soldier could be cultivated. The cult gave them a tangible starting point: a list of names. From there, as the passing years brought no sign that ex-soldiers would receive special treatment for offering everything to the cause, they turned to that list as a reward in itself. With few material considerations coming their way, ex-soldiers could at least celebrate an equally important gift, the gift of comradeship.

In this, society as a whole was quite willing to accommodate the veteran. There was no denying that the ranks of ex-soldiers made an impressive show on Armistice Day, and the sea of coloured berets at the big reunions conjured up fond memories of the great response of 1914. An ex-soldiers' bonus may have been too much for the taxpayer to swallow, but civilians could take great pleasure in applauding public demonstrations of the ties that held together the band of brothers. A few people, watching the ranks file proudly by once or twice a year, might even have wished that they, too, could march in coloured beret or musty tunic.

CHAPTER 5

The Soldier as Canada

I F THE CULT OF THE SERVICE ROLL transformed veterans into a breed apart, separated from all other Canadians by the experience of war and united in the brotherhood of the trenches, it in no way alienated the ex-soldier from the nation. On the contrary, those men who had been willing to fight to defend Canada, Western civilization, and Christianity entered into a special relationship with the country. In a very real sense, the CEF became the nation in arms, the life-force of Canada transported overseas. With similes taken from his native Nova Scotia, the poet Archibald Mac-Mechan had one way of putting this when he wrote that Canadian troops 'charged like the tide of Fundy, / Like Blomidon they stood.' Canon Frederick George Scott was more explicit. Describing the First Contingent's departure for Europe, he recalled that 'it seemed as if Canada herself were steaming across the ocean.'[1]

Here, the canon captured the essence of the myth. It was not just that the individual soldier represented Canada; he was Canada personified. Healthy and vigorous, the citizen-soldier's stubborn individuality stood in stark contrast to the automatons of militarized Europe and the inhuman mechanization of war. His attachment to a mother figure paralleled the nation's relationship to Mother Britain and confirmed him as the heir to 300 years of Canadian history, while his youthful vitality hinted at immense potential in the coming decades. In short, he was the nation's past, present, and future, and the embodiment of all its aspirations and potential. The soldier *was* Canada.

I

THE FINAL SUMMER OF PEACE has become a season with two distinct personalities. On the one hand, it stands out as the last gasp of the old order. The West had been sliding downhill for decades and reached its nadir in the summer of 1914. It was a time when the egocentrism and decadence of pre-war society peaked in a frenzy of materialism and vacuous pleasure seeking. Everywhere, lamented Rupert Brooke during a visit to Canada in 1913, was 'corruption, irresponsibility, and disastrous individualism.'[2] The wealthy spent their riches ever more pointlessly, while the underclasses became progressively more downtrodden. People troubled by the obvious inequities searched for moral direction, or even some sense of certainty in societies that appeared to be spiralling out of control, but there seemed so little of substance to hold on to. 'Are there not enough signs that have been always heralds of the dissolution of empires with us now to give us pause?' wondered British historian K.G. Feiling in an apocalyptic mood. 'Towns instead of country ... machines instead of men ... faith dim and luxury gross – are not these enough to send us to the old paths and seek the Ark of the Covenant on our knees?' Dostoyevsky, too, craved a way out of the 'Stygian hell of pointless and abnormal existence' but for him, unlike Feiling, it was not so simple as returning to the old gods.[3] Nor were they alone in despairing over the lack of direction. 'A surfeit of materialism,' observed Teddy Roosevelt, 'has produced a lack of spiritual purpose' in the United States. According to Sir Robert Falconer, the road was not clear because the waters of Canadian life 'had been growing turbid'; people had simply lost their way in the moral fog that blanketed the West.[4] Whether from the severely respectable Falconer or the turbulent Dostoyevsky, the concerns of the pre-war years took on the same overtones: everything appeared cloudy, dark, clogged. It was as if the Western world was choking on its own excesses. But into this suffocating atmosphere burst the war, bringing everything that society craved: purpose, meaning, certainty, clarity. In this way, August 1914 constituted an escape route. The millions of young men who flocked to enlist in the first days of August were rushing, not just towards war, but away from the decadence, materialism, and emptiness of Western society.

But there was another side to the last season before the coming of war. 'How often have we heard the cynics prate / Of our proud empire toppling in decay,' chided Loftus MacInnes, 'Our youth grown sickly and degenerate, / And valour with our grandsires passed away.'[5] Too often, thought the poet. Moral complacency and enervating laziness were simply the inventions of a discontented minority. For every hard-working and right-thinking individual, the last few months of peace constituted the legendary Golden Summer of 1914. It was a time of innocence and promise, of perpetual sunshine that was impervious to the gathering clouds of war. 'Golden grain fields billowed in a limitless expanse,' rhapsodized the narrator of Canada's official war film. 'The produce of farm and orchard ripened in abundance.'[6] Industrial unrest, deepening social problems, political schisms, spiritual despair – all were subsumed into a season of bounty, tranquillity, and contentment. Adjectives like dark and turbid had no place in this vision; there was only brightness, clarity, and plenty. As the world slipped closer to the abyss, Western society blithely enjoyed the fruits of its earnest labours. When war came, it was time to settle accounts. Volunteers rushed to the colours not to escape the horrors of a stagnant peace, but to defend all of the gifts they enjoyed during the Golden Summer. F. Scott Fitzgerald spoke of the Great War being punctuated by love battles; the final season of peace symbolized the objects of that love.

The notion of the Golden Summer has persisted in the Canadian consciousness for a variety of reasons. In historiographical terms, the prosperity of the Laurier years was carried forward to 1914 simply to compartmentalize the past more efficiently. That year was so obviously a watershed that it seemed inconvenient to place another turning point at 1912, when the Laurier boom actually began to tail off. On another level, to Canadians looking back at 1914 after the tragedy of war, the disappointment of the peace, and the dislocation of the Depression, the last summer of peace must have appeared as a golden age, if only in contrast to what followed it.[7] The season of bounty, however, was also essential to Canada's myth of the war; it was one of the props on which the entire edifice rested. The Golden Summer was the only milieu in which the idealized version of the Canadian soldier could exist.

Not surprisingly, the myth all but excises urban Canada from the summer of 1914. When war came, it was not to a nation of city dwellers but to a nation of outdoorsmen, healthy, vigorous, and in harmony with their natural surroundings. In remembering the Golden Summer, Canadians turned most frequently to two motifs. One that recurs in accounts of the coming of war is the wilderness expedition. It exists in many variants, both in life and in art, but the elements are always the same. It is early in August 1914, and we are introduced to a small group of military-aged men travelling, usually by canoe, through the northern woods. Invariably, they have been isolated from civilization for some time and are blissfully unaware of the coming tragedy as they commune with nature. News of the war, though, does reach them, either in a chance meeting with other travellers or by returning to civilization to catch up with the newspapers. As soon as they learn that hostilities have broken out, they decide to enlist. Often, they take this decision in the course of a fireside discussion beside a rushing river.

In a motif analogous to the wilderness expedition, an agrarian Canada is diverted from its harvest by the call to arms. Typically, the agriculturalist is bringing in the crops when news of the war reaches his farm. He quickly drops the implements of peace to come to the defence of humanity. The 4th of August catches the protagonist of Manitoban Cecil Francis Lloyd's poem 'The Reason' as he is going out with his team to plow his fields. 'I left my team, saying the land could wait, / Freedom is more than life,' he declares.[8] The people of Beaver Dam, New Brunswick, the fictional home of Theodore Goodridge Roberts's fighting Starkleys, were also 'busy with their haying when Canada offered a division to the mother country.' Roger Thornewill, the semi-autobiographical hero of Harold Baldwin's *Pelicans in the Sky,* learns of the war when a Native trader brings the newspapers to his isolated Prairie farmstead. He and a friend immediately drop everything and journey to Saskatoon to enlist.[9]

The agrarian motif was at its most effective in the hands of Peter McArthur, a man whose love of working the land was as strong as anyone's. This is the beginning of his unfinished poem 'A Chant of War':

> John Smith, the farmer, riding on his disk harrow,
> Disking his bean ground for wheat, was busy, yet idle.
> Jolting over the field he watched the blades cutting the soil –
> Smelled the damp earth, watched the weeds being worked under
> He clicked to his horses and slapped them with the lines to keep them moving.
> He heard the crickets chirping in the dry grass on the headlands.
> He heard the hens cackling at the barn.
> He saw the spider webs sparkling in the sunshine.
> There were flocks of cow-birds around the cattle in the pasture ...

Paul Wickson, *Your Country Calls.* In a typical motif, news of the war reaches a Canadian farmer as he brings in the harvest. (Metropolitan Toronto Reference Library, J. Ross Robertson Collection MTL2119)

And because there was nothing to think about there came a thought of the war ...

He whistled to drive away thought – a thin tuneless sound.
But the war thoughts would come.
At last they touched him with their magic.
His imagination opened until he was at one with the universe
Till he saw more within him than the world about him –
Saw the Great War, felt the urgent thought of mankind.[10]

John Smith is typical of Canada's generation of 1914. He was a man of peace whose life was dedicated to bringing forth food from the earth. His horizons stretched no further than the fence of his bean field, yet when the call of war opened the wider world to him, he reacted to it instinctively. His place in the great scheme of things now obvious, Smith realized that war was imperative to preserve all that surrounded him.

The wilderness and agrarian motifs affirm the Canadian soldier as a child of nature in harmony with his environment, but they also highlight the contrast between a militarized Europe and a pacific Canada. The summer of 1914 saw the nations of continental Europe engaged in petty politicking, building up armies, and rattling sabres. Canadians, however, were people of peace who spent that summer communing with nature in forest and field. 'When war broke out,' said George Perley in a farewell speech before retiring as high commissioner to Great Britain, 'the people of Canada were wholly engaged in developing their great national resources and building up a strong self-governing Dominion under the British flag.'[11] They were tending their fields, developing the nation's natural wealth, and fostering their political institutions. Peace-loving by inclination, they had little interest in the standing armies and power struggles that preoccupied Europe.

This contrast was captured particularly well in two very different contexts. Elizabeth Wyn Wood's war memorial for Welland, Ontario, consists of figures representing Sacrifice and Service standing in front of a wheat-sheaf, pine boughs, and a trench mortar; a soldier stands in defence, his arm out to protect the woman behind him. A newspaper description of the sculpture captured its meaning: '[the] informal sincerity of the young soldier's stand to defence proclaims that his actions had nothing in common with mere belligerence or routine militarism.'[12] The memorial is entirely consistent with the myth: the symbols of farmstead and wilderness confirm the soldier as the man of peace, forced to resort to the trench mortar only to protect the things he loved.

Another enunciation of this theme is Robert J.C. Stead's 'We Were Men of the Furrow,' a poem that describes the response of Canadians to the advent of war. It begins with the image that McArthur, Lloyd, and dozens of other observers had used: Canadians quietly going about their business of 'laying the lines of a nation.' They ignore the warlords of Europe and their brinkmanship, preferring to keep 'dreaming our dreams and our visions, planning the way we should go.' Upon this idyllic scene bursts the war: 'in a flash, it was on us; blazed, and it dazzled our eyes.' But Canadians did not shy away when the war shattered their reveries, and the poem ends with a warning to the militarized nations of the world:

> Well may the world read a lesson, well may it learn, and be wise;
> Not to the strong is the battle; not to the swift is the prize;
> Loud is the boast of the despot, clanking his nations in arms,
> But beware of a peace-loving people when they sweep from their forests
> and farms![13]

Like Wood, Stead emphasized the symbols of farmstead and wilderness. The pine bough and wheatsheaf, rather than the despot's boast, defined the Canada of 1914.

The contrast between pacific Canada and militarized Europe served to heighten the identification of Canadian volunteers as citizen-soldiers. Because he had been canoeing or tilling the land in the Golden Summer of 1914, rather than drilling and forming fours, the citizen-soldier became the central figure in the myth. The Canadian Corps was an army of amateurs, eventually commanded by the modestly successful Victoria insurance sales-man Sir Arthur Currie. Everyone under him, aside from the small core of regulars, was a civilian in uniform, someone who had enlisted for the dura-tion of hostilities and for whom the end of the war meant, not a posting to some dismal garrison, but a return to field or forest. According to A. Fortescue Duguid, herein lay the secret of the CEF's success. Canada's war effort amply demonstrated that 'civilian soldiers when discreetly disciplined, carefully trained, vigorously led and above all when imbued with a resolute and unflinching determination to make their cause triumphant, could com-pete with and vanquish the product of a Military Autocracy.'[14]

The character of the citizen-soldier was essential to the development of the myth because it stressed the humanity of the soldier. It is axiomatic that the very fact of military service implied the submergence of individual desire into the will of the group, and many observers discussed this in neg-ative terms as a loss of selfhood.[15] The military machine was an entity that demanded that its constituent parts, the soldiers, be stripped of their human-ity and transformed into cogs in the engine of war. Conflict on the Western Front became a massive technological exercise in which personal will was meaningless; the soldier was a mere game piece to be manipulated by the forces, human or otherwise, that controlled the machine.

Recent Canadian critics have tended to accept this interpretation, but the myth of the war experience does not substantiate such a negative assessment.[16] Veterans celebrated the submergence of the individual will into the larger community of the battalion as one of the most positive aspects of the war. Comradeship was a form of social contract that implied the surrendering of at least a degree of selfhood, for only in the resultant spirit of cooperation could the experience of the trenches be endured. The demands of war, however, did not mean that a soldier was transformed into an automaton; as Chubby Power put it, 'no external restraint could entirely irradicate [sic] their spiritual heritage.'[17] Indeed, the cult of the service roll was a product of the desire to recognize the humanity of each soldier and preserve his identity as an individual, a desire that governed the public response to CWMF exhibitions as well. Donald Buchanan, of the League of Nations Society, praised Paul Nash for capturing the 'mass attrition of men hopelessly entangled in the rigid product of their own organization and machinery,' but most viewers were not interested in such futuristic visions of technological battle.[18] They preferred the work of Richard Jack and Louis Wierter, who filled their canvases with identifiable individuals, each of whom could be picked out and his actions examined.

As the human side of the war was highlighted, so too was the mechanistic nature of the war downplayed, not simply by a refusal to consider the war as a machine but also by avoiding the machines of war. In stark contrast to the judgment of history, Canada's memory declined to interpret the Great War as a technological nightmare of man-destroying machines; instead it was a contest between human beings in which technology played a secondary role to the gallantry and élan of the soldier. Virtually everything in the canon points towards this interpretation. The individual is celebrated; the machine ignored.

For example, the tank, one of the most potent symbols of twentieth-century machine war, held no fascination for Canadian observers. It is conspicuous by its absence in fictional works, one of the few exceptions being Archie Gray's *The Towers of Mont St. Eloi,* which concludes with a tank battle at Arras. Even then, the final duel between two huge tanks ends inconclusively, giving Mark Draco the opportunity to escape his steel cocoon and charge gallantly across the battlefield towards the enemy. He is killed, but dies in the knowledge that he has asserted both his individuality and his freedom from technology. Only a handful of pieces in the CWMF collection depict tanks, and in at least two of them the tanks are wrecked. Alfred Bastien's *Cavalry and Tanks Advance at Arras* is noteworthy in this regard. The eye is drawn immediately to the cavalryman in the centre, whose horse is bathed in ethereal light; he and his comrades are caught at the moment of jumping over an abandoned trench and charging past a destroyed German field gun. Silhouetted against the horizon, scarcely identifiable as such, are the tanks, indistinct blobs that may or may not be moving. Even after four years of war, the cavalry still represented force, energy, and movement. The tank, whose advent had already changed the face of modern war, was all too often a symbol of stasis or, at the very least, barely perceptible motion little better than the snail's-pace advance of the infantry.

Other depictions confirm that the cavalry remained the focus of interest. In contrast to the half-dozen renderings of tanks in the CWMF collection, there are dozens of cavalry subjects, by Bastien, Gerald Spencer-Pryse, Algernon Talmage, and, most notably, the British landscape artist Sir Alfred Munnings. In his most well-known cavalry painting, *Charge of Flowerdew's Squadron,* Lieutenant G.M. Flowerdew leads a squadron of Lord Strathcona's Horse across lush fields near Moreuil Wood in March 1918. The canvas quivers

In Alfred Bastien's *Cavalry and Tanks Advance at Arras,* the cavalry clearly represents movement and action. The tanks in the background, in contrast, might just as easily be mounds of earth. (Canadian War Museum, 8092)

with movement. The horses' hooves are indistinct blurs, and their heads strain forward against the reins; the riders lean down, peering from under their tin helmets and thrusting their lances, merely white slashes, towards the enemy. At the head of the squadron, Flowerdew holds his sword aloft and exhorts his men forward. It is an impressive work and almost makes the observer believe that Sir John French and Sir Douglas Haig were right in thinking that the cavalry could indeed win the war.

The potency of the *arme blanche* was accepted by others as well. Will Bird was moved by the sight of Canadian cavalry units charging at Parvillers, 'riding like mad, sabres flashing, lances glittering, all in perfect formation.' The tanks that followed the cavalry elicited barely a flicker of interest from Bird. The report of the Overseas Military Forces of Canada included a passage that revealed the persistence of the myth about the use of cavalry in

Sir Alfred Munnings, *Charge of Flowerdew's Squadron*. The strong horizontal lines in the horses and riders emphasize their speed and give the painting a sense of action and excitement. (Canadian War Museum, 8571)

modern war: 'it was discovered that the German infantry with machine guns, which invariably held out to the last against an Infantry attack, readily surrendered to the cavalry. The prisoners captured confessed that they were seized with a great fear when they saw mounted troops charging down on them with the sword. It established a triumph for the sabre.'[19]

Aircraft and artillery, two other symbols of the changed face of war, appear frequently in the Canadian canon, but they also contribute to the interpretation of the war as a human rather than a technological exercise. The airplane was popular with writers and artists not because it transformed warfare by opening up new possibilities for long-distance killing, but because it was deemed to represent a return to traditional modes of conflict. The aviator was a knight of the air, jousting with the enemy in the clouds according to a complex but well-understood code of chivalry. For flyers, technology

F.H. Varley, *Knights of the Air*. The airman's jaunty gesture and the sunbeams radiating from behind the clouds give a carefree and optimistic air to what was in fact an extremely dangerous job. (Canadian War Museum, 8922)

was a liberating force, not a constricting one. It freed them from the constraints of the battlefield and, just as importantly, allowed them to assert their individuality through garishly painted aircraft, lone-wolf tactics, and colourful nicknames. Archie Gray's Julien Corday (a French version of Billy Bishop, nicknamed Le Diable), Theodore Goodridge Roberts's Tom Akerley (who, predictably, went overseas as a cavalryman), Bertrand Sinclair's Wes Thompson, Laura Goodman Salverson's Manfred Marcusson, the real-life heroes in George Drew's *Canada's Fighting Airmen* – all are strongly drawn characters whose flying machines allow them to exaggerate their individuality.[20] So much is clear in the titles that F.H. Varley chose for his aviation sketches: *Knights of the Air, The All-Seeing Aviator,* and *Personality Counts in the Air.* In his flying machine, the airman transcended the anonymity and stagnation of the trenches by taking to a realm where personal action clearly determined the outcome of events.

The captured artillery pieces that came to Canada as war trophies also conformed to this interpretation. Hundreds of Canadian communities clamoured for a trophy to place in their park or schoolyard, but not out of

Sir Arthur Currie inspects German artillery pieces captured at Amiens in August 1918. Many of these guns would eventually reach Canada as war trophies. (NAC PA3017)

a recognition that technology had played the most important part in the war. German field guns and mortars were craved for precisely the opposite reason, because they proved that Canada's citizen-soldiers had overcome the enemy's engines of war. For Victor Odlum, who commanded the 11th Infantry Brigade for the last two years of the war, the captured guns served as 'physical and tangible reminders of the courage, fortitude and skill of Canada's sons.' The public display of German trench mortars, howitzers, and field guns was intended to remind townspeople, not that such machines had taken over war, but that they were no match for Canada's citizen-soldiers.[21]

The individual soldier, then, was central to the mythologized version of the Great War. Battles were won by men, not machines; tanks and machine guns did not perform acts of gallantry. Establishing the humanity of the individual soldier was crucial because he had to stand for Canada. A tank could not represent the pacific nation called to war from its fields; a uniformed automaton, his identity squeezed out by close-order drill, could not stand for the peaceful country that emerged from its northern isolation to help defend civilization. Only the citizen-soldier who had an identity independent of the military structure could do this.

II

BECAUSE THE INDIVIDUAL SOLDIER was invested with such a responsibility, it was inevitable that an idealized image of him should evolve. Arthur Currie characterized the Canadian soldier as 'vigorous, clean-minded, good-humoured, unselfish, intelligent and thorough.' One local worthy in central Ontario was even more laudatory; the soldiers were all 'perfect gentlemen,' he told an audience in 1919. They were all like Chaucer's 'perfect gentil Knight,' said the *Manitoba Free Press,* who 'lovede chyvalrie, trouthe and honour, freedom and courtesie' and possessed 'courage like a lyon's.'[22] But two characteristics stand out in reflections upon the nature of the Canadian soldier: his youth and his attachment to a mother figure. Both of these attributes, of course, can apply to the country as well. The youth of the soldier paralleled the youth of Canada, while his devotion to his mother extended into devotion to his country and also symbolized the devotion of Canada to Mother Britain. The metaphors were so closely related that a certain amount of interchange in terms was inevitable; indeed, in this complex discourse the lines of distinction between the soldier and his country became blurred.

In Canada's memory of the war, the soldier's mother is a figure of considerable importance. The conventional wisdom had the infantryman spending many an hour propped against the side of a trench, penning a cheery note to his mother. Or, in an image used on sheet music and postcards, he shared a tender embrace with his mother as he prepared to join his comrades marching off to war. Poems and popular songs in a maudlin and cloying Edwardian vein were frequently dedicated to the mothers of soldiers, and many memorial volumes highlighted the subject's devotion to his mother or, as W.D. Lighthall put it, 'his childlove of his mother / Illumining his strength.'[23] This 'childlove' was at the heart of Jean Blewett's poem about a soldier's return home:

> He wasn't the bugler strong and true,
> Who had bugled boldest and best –
> He was just a little, homesick lad,
> Flying straight to his mother's breast.

Because of the bond between soldier and mother, it was not uncommon to maintain that the soldier's last thoughts before death were of his mother.[24]

The mother was a vital part of the equation because her strength played the major role in moulding a good soldier. 'Show me a boy with a capable, good, God-fearing mother,' wrote Sir Archibald Macdonell, 'and I will show

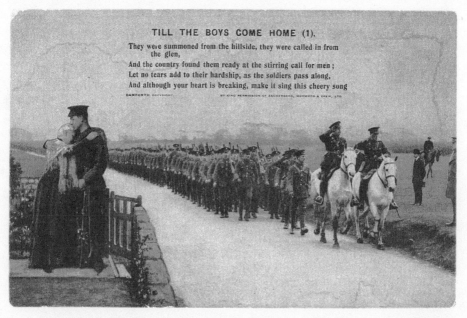

This postcard, with a verse from the sentimental song 'Keep the Homes Fires Burning,' was sent by a woman to her son serving with the 4th Canadian Mounted Rifles in France. The mother is depicted in her conventional role, stoically supporting her soldier son despite her sadness at his departure. (William H. Wiley)

you a boy, if he wins through, with a name in the Honour Lists.'[25] Jean Blewett put it rather more lyrically, declaring that the soldier who became his country's pride owed his 'courage strong / To her who sang his cradle-song.' The family of Armine Norris, in publishing his wartime letters (entitled *Mainly for Mother*), included one that bore out what Macdonell and Blewett said: 'I want to thank you for the Mother you have been to me and if all Canadian mothers were like mine, there would not be any shortage of men for reinforcements.'[26]

Because the mother played such a significant role in the life of the soldier, she was often singled out for special consideration when it came to memorializing the dead. On more than one occasion, observers noted that the mothers of the fallen exerted a disproportionate influence in discussions about what form a memorial should take. They were also accorded pride of place in the spectator section at unveiling ceremonies. At Yarmouth, Nova Scotia, the prime seating directly in front of the memorial was reserved for mothers; all other family members, including fathers, had to sit on the other side of the monument.[27] Songs were occasionally sung about them, like at the unveiling of the memorial in Queenston, Ontario, when

A Toronto woman mailed this sentimental postcard to her son in France. The verse captures the widespread belief that the war was being fought to defend home and hearth. (Rev. L.G. Duby)

local schoolchildren sang 'Just Before the Battle, Mother,' a sentimental song that included the lines

> Farewell Mother, you may never
> Press me to your heart again
> But Oh, you'll not forget me mother
> If I'm numbered with the slain.[28]

In many ways, the mother almost equalled the veteran in the depth of her connection with the fallen soldier.

The bond between soldier and mother was more than just a literal one, however. It is tempting to explain its prevalence, as Graham Dawson does, by referring to the symbols in nationalist discourse of domestic femininity requiring the protection of martial masculinity, but the mother of the Canadian soldier is a very different symbol than the wife in Dawson's reading. In this context, the mother comes to symbolize, not female frailty in need of male protection, but stability in turbulent times. She is the personification of traditional, even immutable, values, her strength and constancy lending a sense of continuity to events. As the progenitor of the next generation of Canadians, the mother affirms the logical progression of history. She is at once the symbol of the past and the creator of the future.[29]

In this context, the soldier-mother bond symbolized the relationships between the individual Canadian and his country, and Canada and Britain. For George Godwin, the motivation of the soldier could be understood in these terms: 'The Major was a tired little boy dragging himself out to the wood pile at the close of a long day to chop the needed kindling and stovewood for a weary widow woman. Only the little boy was now a grown man, and his mother had become his country. In a word, duty. Duty and love; piety. Love of mother projected into love of country.'[30] If Christ became the spiritual symbol of the ideals for which Canadian soldiers fought, an allegorical maternal figure became one of the most potent secular symbols. In countless recruiting posters, patriotic cartoons, and sheet-music covers, she was a lioness or bear whose call for aid brought her cubs running from the corners of the globe. She was celebrated in a whole array of poems, which might be called the 'Mother Britain' school of Canadian literature. The elements are always the same. The children of Mother Britain have been scattered around the globe yet remain tied to England by bonds stronger than steel. When the call goes out in August 1914, they all answer 'Ready, aye, ready,' and come running to the aid of Mother Britain. As poetry, these works are mostly unremarkable, even in the hands of someone as gifted as Wilfred Campbell, but as historical documents they are revealing.

The Mother Britain school, and the maternal symbolism generally, played a crucial role in the development of the myth. The devotion to mother looked back at a glorious past; it revealed the soldier's sensitivity to his ancestors and, by extension, the nation's fidelity to the memory of its founders. In short, the emphasis on a maternal figure gave the memory of the war a sense of history. By placing the soldier and his war in what Paul Fussell has called 'a seamless, purposeful "history" involving a coherent stream of time running from past through present to future,' the myth affirmed the primacy of continuity over change.[31] The forces of innovation and modernity became less significant than the security and reassurance provided by an appreciation of heritage.

ANSWERING THE CALL

Answering the Call. Mother Britain summons her children to war. (Vancouver *Province,* 5 August 1914)

The same sense of security and comfort could be fostered by setting the war firmly in the context of Canadian history and portraying it as a natural outgrowth of the past. The heroic past could be used, not in an ironic sense to point away from itself, but to provide an interpretive context. Historical events that were familiar to everyone could be invoked to insulate Canadians from the shock of the new and to allay their concerns that a profoundly different type of conflict had emerged.[32] The modernity of machine-made warfare could be glossed over by linking the struggle to its precedents from the nation's past.

Some of the most important commemorations of the war went to great lengths to affirm the continuity of Canadian history. The Memorial Chamber, in the Peace Tower on Parliament Hill, tells the story of Canada's war on panels that are adorned by carved insignia of all French and British regular regiments, colonial forces, and militia units that served in Canada since the days of the *ancien régime.* In this way, the chamber commemorates not just the dead of the Great War, but 'all who strove for Canada, from the dawn of the country's history to the present.' The Royal Military College intended to convey the same message with its war memorial arch. In the original plans, reliefs on the arch depicted Frontenac's arrival in North America, the Battle of the Plains of Abraham, and the Battle of Queenston Heights. Statues of Wolfe, Montcalm, Brock, and de Salaberry stood at the four corners of the arch.[33] Ridley College in St. Catharines, Ontario, chose a similar pantheon of historical heroes for the reredos in its memorial chapel: La Vérendrye, Cartier, La Salle, Wolfe, Brock, and an infantryman of the CEF. In each case, Canadian history was made manifestly linear and contiguous; the memorials confirmed that the events of 1914-18 entailed no break with the past.

The Canadian Memorial Chapel in Vancouver is the most comprehensive attempt to give the Great War a comforting sense of historical context. It was the brainchild of George Fallis, who was first struck by the idea of erecting a war memorial chapel while conducting a front-line burial in the Ypres Salient in November 1915.[34] When a nurse made the same suggestion after the burial of victims of the bombing of the Canadian hospital at Étaples in May 1918, Fallis became even more determined to proceed with the project and began to plan a chapel that would place the war firmly in an historical context. Beginning in 1925, he almost single-handedly raised the money required to build the chapel, which officially opened on Armistice Day 1928. It remains in use today as a living memorial to Canada's war.

The great treasures of the chapel are the provincial windows, funded by the nine provinces and the Yukon. Each illustrates a biblical tale but, more importantly, also depicts two important events from the province's history. The Nova Scotia window, for example, shows the landing of John Cabot in 1497 and the decree of the expulsion of the Acadians in 1755; the Alberta window illustrates the Great March of the North West Mounted Police in 1874 and the arrival of Sir George Simpson at a Hudson's Bay Company fort. The most significant national events are reserved for the All-Canada window, above the chapel's main entrance: the arrival of Jacques Cartier, the death of General Wolfe on the Plains of Abraham, the coming of the United Empire Loyalists, the founding of Fort Garry, and the driving of the last spike at Craiglachie. Taken together, the windows serve as a textbook of Canadian history, but they do more than that. By connecting the commemoration of the Great War with these events, the chapel reminds people that history is indeed teleological. The war was no different than the arrival of Cartier or the driving of the last spike. They were all steps on Canada's journey through history, no one event more significant than another. In this way, the First World War was confirmed as a culmination of the past, not a break with it.

The Canadian Memorial Chapel is only the most sustained example of a common strategy for interpreting the war. Across the country, significant events from Canada's past were cited to give an interpretive context to the war. The Battle of the Plains of Abraham was an obvious metaphor, and General James Wolfe (Montcalm was mentioned only occasionally) was connected to the Great War at every opportunity. Canadian battalions had laid their colours on Wolfe's tomb in Westminster Abbey before they left for France, a highly symbolic scene that was captured by a number of artists.

The Nova Scotia window. The main scene, depicting the empty tomb of the Risen Christ, was meant to symbolize immortality, while the historical scenes, the landing of John Cabot in 1497 and the Decree of Expulsion of the Acadians in 1755, emphasized significant events in the province's history. (Canadian Memorial Church)

This simple act, which linked Wolfe with the CEF, had such impact that the GWVA petitioned the government for a grant so that Canadian battle colours could be placed on the tomb in perpetuity.[35]

Emily Warren, *Placing the Colours of the 38th Battalion on Wolfe's Tomb.* By the end of the war, the tomb was almost invisible beneath the battle standards of Canadian units. (NAC C103341)

By the same token, the inclusion of Benjamin West's *The Death of Wolfe* in the Canadian War Memorials Fund was carefully calculated to bring 'the Second Battle of Ypres into touch with the Battle of the Plains of Abraham.'[36] The acquisition of portraits of Alexander Mackenzie and Joseph Brant (not to mention Edgar Bundy's painting of Champlain landing at Québec in 1603, done as a companion piece to his canvas showing the landing of the First Division at St. Nazaire in 1915) fulfilled the same purpose of linking Canada's past to the modern age. This was so important to the CWMF that both Mackenzie King and Lord Beaverbrook reacted with alarm when Arthur Doughty attempted to transfer the historical paintings to the Dominion Archives; such a move would 'be disastrous to [the] whole conception' of the CWMF, wrote Beaverbrook, for it would rob the collection of its historical context.[37] General Wolfe also came to be a spokesman for the 1919 Victory Loan campaign. In a pamphlet written by the poet and novelist Arthur Stringer, the ghost of Wolfe visits Canadian industrialist John Hardy, who believes that his son has died a meaningless death in Flanders. In a stirring speech, Wolfe convinces him that this was not so; 'to die, victorious, on the field of honour, to go gloriously, in the hour of triumph,' is hardly a meaningless death, he declares. In the end, the industrialist is convinced. General Wolfe has opened Hardy's eyes to the value of the sacrifice; a death at Québec in 1759 has given meaning to a death in Flanders 160 years later.[38]

The War of 1812, particularly the death of General Isaac Brock at Queenston, was also a popular historical event to provide context to Canadian achievements in Flanders. Like Wolfe, Brock had died 'on the field of honour, in the hour of triumph' and, what is more, he had died defending Canada from foreign invaders. These facts made the War of 1812 an obvious analogy. One observer noted that the men of the CEF were animated by 'just the same fine steadfast courage as carried their forefathers up the hill at Queenston Heights.' For that reason, Arthur Chute believed that Ypres and Langemark would become as significant as Queenston Heights and Lundy's Lane as 'touchstones for the maple Leaf.'[39] At the unveiling of the war memorial in Queenston, a speaker drew attention to the fact that the monument stood in the shadow of Brock's column. And when the town of Stoney Creek, Ontario, prepared its honour rolls, it placed them, not in the town hall or a local church, but in Battlefield House, on the site of the Battle of Stoney Creek in 1813. Clearly there was no significant difference between the War of 1812 and the First World War; as Nathaniel Benson wrote, Brock gave his 'English hero's blood' at Queenston Heights in the same way that the soldiers of the CEF had given theirs 'on the crimsoned Somme.'[40] Though a century separated them, their sacrifices were identical in all respects.

The Conquest and the War of 1812 were the most popular events of

The band of the 13th Battalion (Royal Highlanders of Canada) pipes the First Contingent onto French soil in Edgar Bundy's *Landing of the First Canadian Division at Saint-Nazaire, 1915.* (Canadian War Museum, 8121)

Canadian history to link to the Great War; but any incident that had particular local significance could serve equally well. Mayor James Dawson of Sault Ste. Marie, Ontario, found it appropriate to hold a soldiers' reunion on the 300th anniversary of the discovery of Lake Superior and St. Mary Rapids by Étienne Brûlé: 'have not these men [the soldiers] by practical demonstration nobly upheld the glorious traditions of the past by a display of those same qualities which have made it possible for Canada to attain the place it now so proudly boasts among the nations of the world?' he asked.[41] French Canada had its own pantheon of heroes beside which to place the heroes of the Great War. In a speech dedicating the memorial at Rimouski, Brigadier-General T.L. Tremblay observed that the gallant acts of Jean Brillant and Joseph Kaeble, both Victoria Cross winners from the district, compared well with the heroics of Adam Dollard des Ormeaux and Charles de Salaberry. The exploits of French-Canadian soldiers were even praised on St. Jean Baptiste Day, the national holiday of French Canada. To unveil the Terrebonne memorial, as part of the 1922 *fête nationale*, the town brought in a certain Colonel de Lanaudière, a direct descendent of Madeleine de Verchères, the youthful heroine who had defended her family's fort against an Iroquois attack in 1692.[42] A book published for the 1918 fête spoke of the dead and returned soldiers, wondering 'n'ont-ils pas ouvert une nouvelle

Edgar Bundy's *Landing of the French under Champlain at Quebec, 1603* (Canadian War Museum, 8122), done as a companion piece, draws parallels between the two events by echoing the structure and perspective of the 1915 scene.

page de notre histoire héroïque qui avait été interrompue à Chateauguay' and calling them 'les dignes descendants de ceux qui ont combattu à Carillon et à Chateauguay.' But the heroes of the Great War were superior to the earlier heroes of French Canada, for 'nos ancêtres se battaient pour eux-mêmes, pour leur pays, leurs biens. Nos "gars" se sont battus pour une idée, pour la paix du monde civilisé, pour le triomphe de la justice.'[43]

The focus on the war's historical precedents merely continued the process begun by the emphasis on the soldier's devotion to his mother: both served to accentuate the connection between the soldier and his country and to affirm the continuity of historical events. This constant invocation of individuals and events from the heroic past ensured that the Great War and its soldiers remained firmly within a linear version of history. The First World War was not a break with the past; it was a fulfilment of the principles by which Canada had evolved as a nation. The scale, technology, and unprecedented nature of the war were irrelevant in the face of this sense of history.

III

IF THE MYTH TRANSFORMED the individual soldier into the culmination, and in some respects the personification, of Canada's history, it also turned him into the symbol of Canada's future. His devotion to his mother and his relationship to figures and events from Canadian history gave the soldier firm roots in the past, but his youthful exuberance pointed ahead to a bright future. His enthusiasm and vitality hinted at his own immense potential and, by extension, that of his country. While other societies perceived service at the front as a rite of passage in which childlike energy and enthusiasm were converted into manly power and strength, a very different assumption held sway in Canada.[44]

It was not the manhood of the soldier that was stressed, but rather his boyishness. Furthermore, boyishness was not a quality to be lost in the maturing process; it became something of a national treasure. The emotions were not stirred by the soldier who proved his manliness in battle, but by the soldier whose strength lay in his boyishness. 'How much more inspiring a figure is the Boy than the Man today!' declaimed Toronto author Nellie Spence in the first of a number of paeans to the schoolboy-soldier: 'The Boy who went forth ... to slay Goliath!' Even when engaged in the man's task of vanquishing the foe, the Canadian soldier was ever the schoolboy. They were 'little-boys-at-war in Valor's Upper School' and when the day was won, they returned to their horseplay and hijinks, as carefree as they had been in the sixth grade. 'These men are fresh from battle and yet like schoolboys,' read the caption to an official war photograph showing exhausted infantrymen resting by a roadside.⁴⁵ Even as he lay dying, the soldier's last thoughts (if they were not of his mother) were of the playing fields he had loved as a schoolboy.⁴⁶

Like so many other metaphors used in the myth, the schoolboy figure had meaning on a number of levels. It captured a degree of innocence that, in William Blake's vision, existed before the spirit was crushed by experience. With that innocence came optimism, an outlook that was untrammelled by the pressures and obligations of maturity. The character of the schoolboy reflected the enthusiasm of a soul going out into the world for the first time, and the energy of a young body whose vitality had not yet been sapped by the demands of the workaday world. The soldier's boyishness was a state of mind and a quality of character that had been fostered by the nation. As Anglican cleric R.J. Renison put it, 'Canada is the home of youth. We saw our destiny far off, and the consciousness that our morning hours were only dawning made those boys of ours doubly dear to us. The world needed them and this new century was to be their arena, and now they sleep by the Arras–Cambrai road. But their youth has made their country forever young.'⁴⁷ The products of a young nation, Canada's fallen had amply repaid the gifts that the nation had conferred on them. By dying in the flower of youth, they left their youth to enrich the country.

In Renison's vision, the soldier and his country were all but indistinguishable from each other. In this, the former battlefield chaplain had captured another of the myth's fundamentals. Because he represented the nation's future, the soldier was the essence of Canada. If American war narratives frequently use two stock characters, the stoical Yankee and the raw, powerful frontiersman, to capture the breadth of American society, Canadian accounts use two similar paradigms to stand for the soul and spirit of Canadian society: the sensitive intellectual and the rugged backwoodsman.⁴⁸

In 1915, Robert Falconer had great praise for the sensitive intellectuals carried away by the tide of war: 'It is not merely the adventurers who have enlisted, but men of sensitive mind who will feel most poignantly the physical suffering, – delicate and cultured youths with vivid imaginations to magnify the distress by forecasting it, who have had the brute indifference to death refined out of them.'⁴⁹ Canadian accounts are full of these characters, though they are not usually cast with such condescension as this. In the body of fiction, Walter Blythe in *Rilla of Ingleside* comes immediately to mind. One also thinks of two real-life Walter Blythes, the poets Bernard William Trotter and Frederick Charles Manning.

The sensitive young man at war, however, was less inspiring than the scholar-backwoodsman, the man who bridged the gap between the two paradigms to embody the breadth of Canadian society in a single person. A photograph of Victor Gordon Tupper in his memorial volume shows him standing on a rocky outcrop, the very picture of a rugged outdoorsman; reading the text, we find that he was well educated, well bred, and sensitive, an admirable representative of the upper-class intelligentsia. Another memorial volume noted that William George McIntyre was a 'student in arms,' but, lest any reader imagine that education had softened McIntyre, the author hastened to add that 'there was plenty of good red blood in him.' On at least two occasions, speakers dedicating Bank of Commerce war memorials stressed that bank clerks were not generally thought of as robust, outdoors types, yet the war had proven they were of the same mettle as men in less sedentary occupations.[50] This not entirely successful attempt to bridge the gap between the paradigms points out how important it was to turn the soldier into a Canadian Everyman.

It is in the body of fiction, though, that the complete Canadian comes out most strongly, and the protagonists of many war novels move between library and mountain crag with consummate ease. Ralph Connor's Barry Dunbar, in *The Sky Pilot in No Man's Land,* is sensitive and well educated, yet he loves the backwoods life and, indeed, finds it more congenial to him than his career in the church. George Norton, in Sydney Arthur's *A Man's Worth,* is a university student who spends his summers on wilderness treks. Alexander Falcon of Peregrine Acland's *All Else Is Folly* is an eastern college student who goes to Alberta to work on a ranch. Craig Forrester, the hero of Douglas Durkin's *The Magpie,* unites the paradigms in a slightly different way; he is a young farmer whose father bought him a seat on the Winnipeg Grain Exchange.

Not even these figures carried the same force as the identification of the Canadian soldier as a pure and rugged backwoodsman who lived his life far from the stultifying influence of city and university. Arthur Currie used this image in 1919, seeing in it the archetype of the strong man toughened by exposure to the outdoors. It also made a deep impression on A. Fortescue Duguid. In a long manuscript on the Canadian as a soldier, he breathed life into Currie's image.[51] The hardships of Canadian life had produced a distinctly Canadian type: a man of great physical strength and endurance who was mentally alert, fearless, and fiercely independent. Such men possess 'those indelible signs with which Nature graces the bodies and souls of those who have pitted their will, their strength, and their determination against her elemental forces.' The unfit were weeded out by the harsh climate, the weaklings turned away by the hard work, and the lazy reformed by the 'incessant activities' of the community. 'The invaluable gifts of our deep forests and lofty mountains, of our rolling plains and our great waterways and of the clear light of our northern skies,' Duguid went on, had created in Canada a race of giants.

Poets were moved to the same heights of emotion as the pragmatic Duguid. Montreal writer Esther Kerry captured this feeling in a tribute to the soldier called 'He Is a Canadian':

> 'He is a Canadian' – I wonder has he stood
> In some thick forest, on a mountain slope
> Silent beneath a pine
> And looking out across a valley seen,
> Nothing but bristling tree trunks far below
> And stony-scarred grey mountains
> Whose snow-caps
> Rise to a sunswept blue?

Her answer is decidedly in the affirmative. Because he *is* a Canadian, he knows

> the keenness of our winter's icy blast ...
> That bites and purifies
> And clears away
> The murk and greyness of too sordid lives.[52]

He is the very giant who inspired Duguid.

Theodore Goodridge Roberts was also profoundly affected by this figure, whom he immortalized in two fine poems. 'Private North' recalls the origins of one backwoodsman-soldier:

> I've seen his home, low-set and grey
> In black woods thousands of miles away,
> Where he lived from the loud, mad world removed,
> Masterless, gentle and gladly loved.

Another poem, 'A Cook-house at Reveille,' puts the soldier in the context of his prewar work:

> And here is one who worked, last year,
> With Mitchell's crew on Beaver Lake,
> Where the dark spruces lift their spires;
> Where axes flash and white frosts ache.[53]

In both poems, just like in the writing of Duguid and Kerry, the soldier is typified as a child of nature, someone who is intimately connected to the untamed wilderness. He is what we believe the essential Canadian should be.

In his immensely popular play *Brothers in Arms*, Merrill Dennison created a version of this paradigm. A backwoodsman who was discharged from the army as an incorrigible because he despised drill and only wanted to kill Germans, Syd White stands in stark contrast to J. Altrus Browne, the money-hungry businessman who spent the war trying to obtain his release from the Army Service Corps in England. Browne's wife Dorothea is fascinated by White. 'Don't you love his sturdy independence?' she gushes. 'It's so Canadian.'[54]

Precisely what it means to be 'so Canadian' comes out clearly in George Godwin's novel *Why Stay We Here?* Stephen Craig, the British Columbia fruit farmer, is posted to Kent and marvels at the contrast between the British soldiers and the men of his unit: 'No anaemic men, these, drawn from office stools or shop counters. No. But men whose clear eyes have that look in them that comes only in the eyes of those whose horizons have been wide. Men of the prairie, of the mountains, of the timberlands. Canadians.'[55] Such figures are more than just individuals. They are distillations of the essence of Canada. Compelling and larger than life, they reveal the degree to which the myth had made the soldier and Canada virtually interchangeable. Innately peaceful yet willing to fight for a principle, the soldier possessed the same youthful vigour and vitality that marked his homeland out for greatness. He was the heir to traditions that extended back three centuries. In his person he embodied the strength and the soul of the nation. He was the complete Canadian.

IT WAS OF NO CONSEQUENCE that this inspiring image had little basis in fact. Frederick George Scott's belief that the First Contingent was Canada itself steaming overseas carried more force than the fact that 70 per cent of the contingent were British-born and bred, or the fact that of the 470,224 soldiers who served overseas with the CEF, fewer than half had been born in Canada. By the same token, the characterization of Canadian soldiers as rugged backwoodsmen carried more weight than the statistical evidence, which told a different tale. Generally speaking, the soldiers of the CEF were not 'men of the prairie, of the mountains, of the timberlands.' They were more apt to be 'drawn from office stools or shop counters,' and even more likely to come from factory, mill, and workshop. Of the soldiers who had enlisted by 1 March 1916, only 6.5 per cent were farmers or ranchers; 18.5 per cent were clerical workers, and nearly 65 per cent were manual workers. Even by the war's end, the reality had not changed to meet the myth. In November 1918, fewer than a quarter of the men in the CEF were farmers, hunters, fishermen, and lumbermen. Over 36 per cent were industrial workers, and there were more white-collar workers than farmers in the CEF.[56]

It was in the nature of the myth, however, to transmute the facts into a more usable fantasy. Australian official historian C.E.W. Bean helped to fashion an enduring notion that the typical Australian soldier was a bushman and that bush skills had made the digger a great fighter. Bean's myth was much more appealing than the truth – that many Australian heroes were townsmen who may never have seen the bush. By the same token, British propaganda fostered the belief that the war was being fought to save a pastoral, rural England. This also carried more weight than the reality that less than a quarter of the population lived in rural areas and that, if anything, the war was being fought to save overcrowded urban terraces and dark Satanic mills.[57]

It was no different in Canada. Few people were interested in the fact that the CEF had more British-born factory workers than Alberta trappers. The image of a lathe operator popping around the corner to enlist after his shift ended was accurate but unromantic. The soul was moved, however, by the picture of a prospector or lumberjack hearing rumours of war, downing his tools, and trudging through the wilderness to offer his services for God, King, and Empire. The lathe operator was a prosaic, unlovely character; the backwoodsman was a figure to stir the blood. In the myth, only he could capture the essence of Canada going to war.

CHAPTER 6

Safeguarding the Past

THE INTIMATE CONNECTION forged between the soldier and Canada gave the story of the war a special place in the Canadian consciousness. Because the CEF had been the soul of the nation transported overseas, it was imperative that its deeds be chronicled. The government had every intention of doing so, but while Canadians waited for the official record, they set about compiling their own story of the war, in countless local and battalion histories, poetry collections, novels, and short stories. They took their mythicized version of the war, with all its inaccuracies and half-truths, and gave it legitimacy as history. Their memory was transformed into a gospel, and the worth of any account of the war was judged on the degree to which it approximated the ideal.

This version of the war, enshrined in poem, novel, and history book, was not subject to variation, nor was it conceded that another version could be just as valid. On the contrary, Canadians refused to recognize the existence of alternative interpretations of the events of 1914-18, insisting instead that such interpretations were inaccurate, misleading, and untrue. Notably, this stout defence of the received version was not always made in defence of truth. Strict adherence to historical fact was desirable, but only if such facts did not contradict the myth. It was the myth, not fact, that was paramount; it had to be safeguarded against anything, even an indisputable truth, that threatened to undermine it.

I

FROM THE EARLIEST DAYS OF THE WAR, two influential individuals recognized the importance of keeping an exhaustive record of Canada's great crusade. The first was William Maxwell Aitken, the self-proclaimed native son of New Brunswick who had in fact been born north of Toronto. Aitken made his first million before the age of thirty and, by the time the war was declared, had transplanted himself to England, where he became the member of Parliament for Ashton-under-Lyne, a textile town near Manchester. In 1917 he added a peerage, as Lord Beaverbrook, to a list of accomplishments that included extensive investments in the British press and a host of prominent friends like Andrew Bonar Law and Rudyard Kipling.

Medically unfit for military service, Aitken turned his energies in other directions but initially met with only polite refusals in Britain. Undaunted, Aitken sailed for Canada and came away with an invitation to act as the Borden government's unofficial representative in Britain, publicizing Canada's war effort to anyone who would listen. It was a task that Aitken relished; he secured for himself a commission in the militia and went to France as the Canadian Eye Witness. It was a very modest beginning to what would become an information empire centred on his London offices. By 1918, much of the publicity surrounding Canada's war effort could trace its origins to Aitken's fertile mind and deep pockets. The centrepiece of his empire was the Canadian War Records Office (CWRO), created in January 1915 when Aitken was appointed to superintend the records of the CEF. In January 1916, after a year of collecting material and depositing it hodge-podge in his London office, Aitken requested a grant of $25,000 from the Canadian government to bring some order to the chaos. In March, the CWRO was put on an official footing with an initial establishment of over sixty writers, researchers, camera operators, and support staff.[1]

Because the CWRO was primarily engaged in maintaining the historical record of the war, Aitken was bound to encounter the other person deeply concerned about its archival heritage: Arthur G. Doughty, who had amply demonstrated his own energy and determination as Dominion archivist, a position he had held since 1904. In May 1916, Doughty arrived in London to assert his claim, on behalf of the Dominion Archives, to all records generated during Canada's war effort. What could have been a ruinous power struggle between the two men fortunately never materialized. Doughty was immediately impressed by Aitken. 'Evidently a man of action,' he recorded in his diary. 'In earnest about it [the CWRO], and is determined to make it a success. He is full of enthusiasm, of quick judgement. Whatever may be his motive he is doing the work well ... [H]e appears to be the right man in the right place.' Aitken, for his part, handled Doughty very adroitly by promising that all records would become the property of the Dominion Archives after the war ended. Converted, Doughty joined the CWRO and received Ottawa's permission to place the entire London staff of the archives at the office's disposal.[2] So began a prodigious archival partnership.

Over the course of the war, the CWRO managed such diverse enterprises as the Canadian War Memorials Fund, the photographic and motion picture records of the war, and a collection of CEF badges. Most of its effort went into publishing, and the office mobilized the talents of some of Canada's best-known writers, including the Nova Scotia-born novelist Henry Beckles Willson, Theodore Goodridge Roberts, and his brother Sir Charles G.D. Roberts. The CWRO was incredibly prolific. Its flagship publication was the three-volume *Canada in Flanders: The Official Story of the Canadian Expeditionary Force* (1916-18) but it produced a host of other books and pamphlets as well, including short histories of Canadian battalions, the *Canadian Daily Record* (a domestic and world news digest, 22,000 copies of which were published every day for distribution throughout the CEF), souvenir books of official war photographs, patriotic periodicals like *Canada in Khaki,* and a storybook of deeds rewarded with the Victoria Cross.

Despite such successes, Aitken's vision of the CWRO's mandate probably did not sit easily on Doughty's orderly and precise mind. When its work was completed, declaimed a CWRO document, its official history 'will be a wonderful romance, woven from hundreds of thousands of threads of slender but drastically tested information.' Precisely what 'drastically tested' meant was open to debate. The CWRO accepted criticism that its form of contemporary history was often based on incomplete or partial information, but it made clear its attitude towards the competing claims of reportage and objective history: when a choice had to be made, journalism came out on top.[3] A 1917 report conceded that CWRO accounts of the war sacrificed accuracy for vividness, and Aitken himself (by now Lord Beaverbrook) admitted that the main purpose of the second volume of *Canada in Flanders* was not to document a period of the nation's history but 'to further the Imperial cause by stimulating recruiting in Canada.'[4]

Largely for this reason, much of the CWRO's work did not stand up to critical scrutiny. During the war, Beaverbrook frequently fielded complaints that CWRO books were plagued by inaccuracies, and Currie warned that *Canada in Flanders* would have 'no value whatever as an historical document' because it bore 'no more resemblance to the true story of the period it depicts than a mutton stew does to the sheep itself.' Historian W.S. Wallace praised the third volume, by Sir Charles G.D. Roberts, but criticized the first two volumes of the series, those written by Beaverbrook, for having too much purple prose and excessive flattery of senior officers and politicians.[5]

Doughty likely found some merit in these criticisms, for CWRO accounts did tend to be closer to romance than history. The Dominion archivist might have been more satisfied with the publications that emanated from other government offices, like the Overseas Military Forces of Canada

(OMFC), the Department of Militia and Defence, and the Office of Public Information. These accounts were as dry as the CWRO books were florid. One reviewer admitted that the OMFC's 1918 report, an imposing grey volume filled with tables and figures, would be 'of little interest to the general reader.'[6] Currie's report of the Canadian Corps' operations in 1918 was similar but had the advantage of being considerably shorter. Another such item was a slim pamphlet by the Department of Public Information entitled *Canada's Part in the Great War,* a straightforward, clinical summary. Despite its plainness, it was snapped up. By July 1919, the government had distributed half a million copies of the booklet, and a new run was in press to meet the huge demand. Less than two years later, a third edition had to be published.

Most Canadians assumed that these publications were only precursors to the exhaustive official history that would detail every aspect of the war effort. When this volume failed to appear, complaints began to surface. Not surprisingly, historians were among the first to demand action. William H.C. Wood, a chronicler of the War of 1812, advanced an ambitious scheme involving a series of document volumes, a multi-volume comprehensive history, and a single-volume history for 'every intelligent Canadian.' He said that 'our [war] record system should bring in every scrap of authentic original evidence that throws any light on Canada's connection with it' and combine it 'into one vast but well co-ordinated whole.' W.B. Kerr, a historian at the University of Buffalo and a former artilleryman, castigated the government for failing to produce an official history. By not having done so, wrote Kerr, 'Canada is in a class with Turkey, Russia, and the United States as most backward of the contending nations ... Such a condition of indifference to the greatest conscious effort of the nation's history seems unique.'[7]

Kerr was not the only veteran to raise such criticism, and prominent ex-soldiers and veterans' groups were tireless in their efforts to prod the government to action. Resolutions calling for the publication of an official history were common at Canadian Legion conventions, and hardly a day went by, reported an Ottawa newspaper, without the Legion receiving a new batch of queries from veterans about the status of the official history. Tiring of these enquiries, Legion president J.S. Roper suggested that, if the Department of National Defence's Historical Section was not up to the task, the government should appoint a new official historian from the ranks of veteran writers. A Prince Edward Island branch of the Legion suggested Will Bird or George Drew, the lawyer and ex-artillery officer who would later be Ontario premier, for the job.[8] Bird would likely have jumped at the chance, for he had already added his voice to the chorus of complaint. The war records were too closely guarded, he maintained in 1932, and should be open to any

Canadian who wished to use them. By the time the official history appeared, all of Canada's veterans would be dead. 'Then who will read them? ... We, the men who served, want them NOW, have wanted them for years ... Within twenty years the vets will have gone to their last roll-call – then they can bury for ever, with the spiders and stale tobacco, everything regarding the Great War.'[9]

It may have appeared that the government was trying to bury the historical record, but this was not the case. In January 1917, Brigadier-General E.A. Cruickshank had been attached to the CWRO to begin work on compiling the official history; shortly after the Armistice, he became director of the Historical Section of the General Staff. In May 1921, the historical section's duties were confirmed: to compile the official history of Canada's war effort and to supply 'authentic information concerning the military history of Canada.' This second task proved to be the section's undoing. Because the order-in-council was so vague, the section found itself doing every conceivable research task connected with war history: proofreading the manuscripts of private regimental histories; advising local war memorial committees on lists of battles, names of fallen soldiers, and suitable inscriptions; supplying information to the Imperial War Graves Commission; and answering queries from politicians, journalists, and members of the public. In the first eight years of its existence, far from being idle, the historical section sorted and indexed 135 tons of documents, indexed over 7,000 war photographs, compiled skeleton histories of every unit of the CEF, answered over 8,000 enquiries, and published dozens of short histories and summaries of the war.[10] Just about the only thing the historical section had not done was complete the official history. In short, the section had lost its direction. Colonel A. Fortescue Duguid, Cruickshank's successor, was evidently frustrated and advised that virtually all of the section's tasks be curtailed until the official history had been completed. The minister of National Defence was not sure that even this was sufficient and struck a committee to determine if the historical section should proceed with work on the official history or transfer the task to the Dominion Archives. He even raised the question of whether the history should be completed at all.[11]

The committee, made up of Henry Marshall Tory, recently retired as president of the University of Alberta, Major-General P.E. Thacker, former adjutant-general of the Canadian forces, the historian Adam Shortt, Norman Rogers, former secretary to Prime Minister King and a veteran of the Canadian Mounted Rifles, and Wilfred Bovey, commander of the Canadian Section at GHQ in France and now McGill University's director of Extramural Education, tendered its report in January 1929. The members expressed confidence that the historical section could perform the task, but Duguid must have been a little alarmed at the committee's vision. It suggested that a strict narrative of military campaigns was not enough; instead, the country deserved 'a history of the national effort of Canada in the face of a great emergency.' It should provide a 'clear-cut picture of the progressive efforts of the Canadian people during a critical and formative period in our development as a nation.' This massive undertaking could only be realized under the stewardship of an advisory committee composed of staff officers and academics. The entire process, thought the committee's secretary, would take at least seven years.[12]

The historical section was probably relieved that this project never went beyond the discussion stage, and that Duguid's advice about curtailing the work of the section was accepted. With a clear mandate at last, he and his staff began the task of laying out the planned eight general volumes and two or three supplementary volumes.[13] From that point, the work of sifting through the mass of documents progressed relatively smoothly. The records of the section suggest that further delays resulted from Duguid's quest for accuracy, for they are filled with correspondence with historians and former soldiers who had received drafts of the first volume for comment.

This fact checking took time, and it was June 1938 before the first volume (in addition to a volume of appendices) appeared. The book covers just over a year, from the weeks before the declaration of war to the formation of the Canadian Corps on 13 September 1915, in 550 pages of text. Though reviewers praised it as a fair and balanced account, it is somewhat uneven in the depth of its critical enquiry. Duguid candidly admitted in the book that over a quarter of the Canadians hospitalized in Britain in the winter of 1914-15 suffered from venereal disease, but he glossed over in a few short sentences the appalling conditions endured by the First Division on Salisbury Plain. The central section of the book, comprising some 150 pages, deals with the Second Battle of Ypres, a convoluted and confusing series of events that would have challenged the ablest of chroniclers. Here again, Duguid was selective in his exposition of the First Division's weaknesses. The appendices volume reprinted dozens of field messages from the battle which make it possible to discern problems in the handling of certain units, especially Currie's 2nd Brigade and Turner's 3rd Brigade. However another controversial episode, the conduct of Lieutenant-Colonel John A. Currie of the 15th Battalion and his subsequent dismissal, goes unmentioned, despite the fact that it generated much discussion in the division at the time. In this regard, one reviewer observed that 'even at this date it is not possible or perhaps even desirable, for the official historian to tell everything.'[14]

Most people considered the first volume to be well worth the wait. Newspaper and magazine reviews were, almost without exception, overwhelmingly positive. The *Northern Miner* considered it 'the most valuable set of war books in Canada alike for the students and the mere seeker after thrills.' W.B. Kerr, in the *Canadian Historical Review,* judged Duguid's work to be 'so good that it will never need to be done again.'[15] The book's warm reception led Minister of National Defence Ian Mackenzie to promise that the rest of the volumes would appear faster than the twenty years it took to prepare the first, but he proved optimistic. The rest of the series was never completed, the government having decided after the Second World War to abandon the project. Only when the official history of the later war was well advanced did attention return to Duguid's labours. Even so, Canadians had to wait until 1962 for the publication of George Nicholson's single-volume official history of the CEF.

If Duguid's official history had a tortured birth, Canada's official war film had an even stranger one. Cinematography had been another of Beaverbrook's pet projects, and the success of the CWRO's first motion picture, *The Battle of Courcelette* (1916), led indirectly to the creation of the War Office Cinematograph Committee, which assumed responsibility for all empire film production.[16] By the war's end, thousands of feet of film had been shot by CWRO camera operators in Canada and overseas, but much of it apparently disappeared after the Armistice. Nearly fifteen years later, the lost footage resurfaced. George Drew was sifting through the storage rooms of the Ontario Motion Picture Bureau in Toronto in search of entertainment for the annual gathering of the Canadian Overseas Artillery Officers' Association. He found a few reels of guns in action and showed them to Andy McNaughton, the former commander of the Canadian Corps heavy artillery and now Chief of the General Staff. McNaughton was astonished to see that the films were part of the missing archives. Another search was made of the vaults, and eventually over 25,000 feet of film was discovered. They were not the original prints but rather copies made by some far-sighted but anonymous individual.

Immediately, plans were set in motion for reconditioning, copying, and editing the films into a form that was fit for public viewing. To superintend the work, National Defence created the Great War Motion Picture Committee (GWMPC), made up of Doughty, McNaughton, Duguid, and F.C. Badgley of the Canadian Government Motion Picture Bureau. The fruit of the committee's labours, entitled *Heritage,* was scheduled for release in August 1934, but delays plagued the project. Committee members debated every conceivable aspect of the film, from the amount of aerial footage to be included to the title, until finally Hollywood forced the government's hand. Twentieth-Century Fox and MGM both had similar films in progress, and the company that had contracted to distribute *Heritage* in Canada predicted that the American films would be completed and distributed before *Heritage* could reach Canadian screens; as a result, Canadians would be stuck with an American interpretation of the war.[17] The government speeded up the production process and eventually offered *Lest We Forget* (as the film had been retitled) to the Canadian Legion to show, on the understanding that the Legion would reimburse the government for all production costs. The Legion accepted the terms, and the film finally premiered in Ottawa in March 1935.[18]

Like Duguid's official history, *Lest We Forget* drew praise for its balance and its refusal to shy away from the more disquieting realities of the war, yet it too was selective in its coverage. The rousing send-off given to the Princess Patricia's Canadian Light Infantry (PPCLI) enjoyed more screen time than the miseries on Salisbury Plain, and the devastation of the Flanders countryside was emphasized more than the toll in human terms. In most cases, the focus was on the victory, not the cost. In one scene, the camera lingers on corpses in the ruins of Courcelette, but there are few mentions of casualties. In another scene, the narrator's solemn description of war as 'ghastly – pitiless – diabolical' is followed jarringly by the celebration of Dominion Day 1918, when the four divisions of the Canadian Corps gathered for a day of sports, concerts, and merriment. Similar contradictions punctuate the film: protestations of war's horror and wastage are juxtaposed against affirmations of the glory of the sacrifice, the appeal of military display, and the cheery demeanour of the troops.

Though some observers expressed concern that the Ottawa premier, intended to be a tribute to the sacrifices of Canada's war, turned into a glittering society gala, critics' reaction to the film was positive. Helen Allen of the *Toronto Telegram* liked it because it depicted 'not too much of the horrors' of the war, while Roly Young in the *Mail and Empire* found it completely neutral and classed it as 'an historical souvenir.'[19]

Young was more prescient than he might have imagined, for the film and the official history soon became little more than historical souvenirs. *Lest We Forget* generated little public interest when it went into general release, the Legion admitting that it 'completely failed to appeal in our largest centres.'[20] The same might be said of the official history. As a work of history it was a considerable achievement, yet the *Northern Miner* was overly optimistic in predicting that it would appeal to 'the mere seeker after thrills.' Again despite favourable reviews, its unadorned prose, occasionally dry subject matter, and often hour-by-hour narrative structure could have had little

Audiences stayed away from *Lest We Forget* in droves, despite sensational advertisements. Were they turned off by the prospect of seeing 'war, stripped of its gaudy trappings – fearful in its grim reality'? (*Hamilton Spectator*, 25 April 1935, 4)

appeal beyond a specialist audience. Indeed, Duguid's volumes now repose largely in reference libraries, where they are consulted rather than read. *Lest We Forget* suffered a worse fate and is now all but forgotten.

Had Duguid's official history and *Lest We Forget* appeared fifteen or even ten years earlier, they might have played a significant role in shaping Canada's memory of the war. Instead, they give every indication of having been shaped by that memory. With their reluctance to tackle directly the mismanagement of the war and their insistence on proclaiming war's glories in fortissimo and war's horrors in pianissimo, they were entirely consistent with the version of the Great War that had developed up to the mid-1930s. In this instance, the official memory followed where the popular memory had led.

II

THIS WAS THE FUNDAMENTAL REASON why these official versions failed to catch on. By the mid-1930s, Canadians no longer had any need of an official story of the war, because by then they had crafted their own history. *Lest We Forget* and Duguid's volumes may have added visual shadings and new details, but they told Canadians little that they did not already know. The nation's collective memory of the war was by then fully formed. Canadians had not been content to wait for the official version of 1914-18. The time to tell it was immediately after the event, and, while government departments debated the duties of the historical section and pondered the wisdom of editing out this or that footage, amateur historians turned their energies to recording the war history of battalion, community, church, and business. Virtually every unit of the CEF, from famous infantry battalions like the PPCLI to supporting units like the 2nd Canadian Divisional Ammunition Column, published its history in the interwar period. Some, like the history of the 4th Canadian Mounted Rifles, were published with regimental funds and distributed free to all members and next of kin of the dead.[21] Others appeared on a subscription basis or as commercial ventures. Community, organization, and business histories poured forth as well. The province of Nova Scotia, the county of Lennox and Addington in eastern Ontario, the Canadian Patriotic Fund, the Knights of Columbus Catholic Army Huts, the Canadian National Railways, the diocese of Antigonish, and a host of other special interest groups published detailed and sometimes lengthy accounts of their activities during the war.

A distinguishing feature of these unofficial histories is their lack of a critical element. They used as a starting point the terms of the myth and, rather than testing their validity, merely gave them a local flavour. Instead of questioning the veracity of atrocity stories, a church history told of a local boy who suffered unimaginable abuse at the hands of his German captors. Instead of suggesting that the war had ushered in a new age of technological conflict, a railway history affirmed the strength of historical continuity by reminding readers that General Wolfe's fleet had stopped near Valcartier on its way to besiege Québec.[22] In this regard, these unofficial histories are merely extensions of the cult of the service roll. They are overwhelmingly positive and focus on cooperation, unity, and a determination to put the cause ahead of everything. Their intent is to supplement the honour roll in demonstrating that the town, church, or company concerned acquitted itself well in the great crusade.

Unit histories are no more critical. They have little to say about the political or strategic decisions that killed off so many of their members, and they rarely question the ability of Allied generals to carry out their duties. Such histories confine themselves to relating the facts in such a way that is consistent with the myth. Repeated bayonet charges against well-defended trenches demonstrate the tenacity of the infantryman, not the tactical bankruptcy of his commanders. Even the bayoneting of surrendering Germans reveals, not that Canadian soldiers were capable of war crimes, but that the enemy had acted treacherously and brought this fate upon themselves.[23]

This is not to suggest that the compilers of these histories were either stupid or naive; it is simply that they never pretended to write objective history. 'Our purpose is not to write "history,"' noted Ham Warren, one of the driving forces behind the 38th Battalion chronicle, 'but to put on record ... the story of a Battalion with an honourable record but particularly the story of all those who served with it and were found worthy.'[24] Such writers made no effort to detach themselves from the events they wrote about for the simple reason that their work did not require it. These amateur historians were essentially writing tribute volumes, designed to honour the contributions of their subjects. Examining events critically would have jeopardized this goal. If Canadian soldiers occasionally bayoneted prisoners, it could mean that they were no better than the Hun, and few battalion associations wished to pay tribute to the unit's war record with a volume that admitted that their boys were just as brutal as the enemy. Because it threatened to undermine the foundations of the nation's memory of the war, critical enquiry had no place in these local and unit histories. There was no need to be negative when a much more positive hue could be put on events. Such histories should be stories of cooperation and self-sacrifice, not greed and mismanagement. They could stand as examples of what could be achieved when people pulled together. An ideal history of the war should not seek to warn or admonish, but rather to enrich and inspire.

But the memory of the war was not found only on the non-fiction shelves of library and bookshop; poetry and novels also shaped, and were shaped by, the myth. Like amateur historians, poets, novelists, and playwrights lost no time in turning their talents to a consideration of the war, and through the 1920s and 1930s they produced an immense quantity of literature that dealt either directly or indirectly with the war. Many poets gathered into collections the verses they had published in newspapers and magazines during the war, and there were few active poets who did not write at least one new verse on the war. Fictional war stories appeared in periodicals as diverse as *National Home Monthly* and *Canadian Defence Quarterly*, and playwrights fully exploited the dramatic potential of war situations. Dozens of novels dealt with the war directly, and countless more relied on it for plot development.

Despite the great variety in literary accounts of the war, this body of work was governed by the same sort of unofficial rules that applied to non-fiction accounts. The histories strove to honour the sterling qualities that saw Canada through the war; a good factual account of the war was distinguished by the panache with which it described those qualities rather than by sound historical method or discerning judgment. By the same token, literature endeavoured to discern the emotional and psychological factors that won the war. The right way to craft a fictional account of the war had nothing to do with meter, construction, or any other technical aspect; it was all about tone and feeling. In 1924, J.D. Logan evaluated Canadian poetry of the Great War in these terms: 'It is relatively great in noble ideals. In it we see clearly and vividly what Canadian men and women, at home and in the field of war, really thought and felt ... [It is] originally conceived, winningly suffused with beauty of sentiment, rich in noble ideas and spiritual imagery, engaging in verbal music, and technically well wrought.'[25] Recent scholars have contended that, after 1918, those works imbued with notions of 'beauty of sentiment' and 'noble ideals' did not constitute good war literature. Such concepts, with their decidedly pre-twentieth-century connotations, were irrelevant to the realities of the trenches. To employ them was not only misleading but positively immoral.[26]

For many Canadian critics, however, it was precisely these qualities that characterized fine war literature in the 1920s and 1930s. It is instructive to note, for example, the war poems that prominent Canadian literati rated as the best. Lorne Pierce of Ryerson Press accorded the honour to Robert J.C. Stead's 'Kitchener,' a eulogy to the British minister for War, which begins with the exhortation 'Weep, waves of England! Nobler clay / Was ne'er to nobler grave consigned.' *Canadian Bookman* heartily approved of the deep feeling shown in Alfred Gordon's 'Vimy Ridge,' which informed Canadians that 'henceforth we shall lift a higher head / Because of Vimy and its glorious dead.'[27] One columnist, in judging the ten best Canadian poems of the war, produced a list that was entirely traditional. It included 'In Flanders Fields' and 'Kitchener' as well as other entries in the same vein. Norah Holland's 'New Year's Eve, 1916' affirmed the ineradicable bond between soldiers by describing an infantryman who greets the new year with the shades of two dead comrades. Her 'Home Thoughts from Abroad' was a pseudo-Georgian offering that juxtaposed the glories of an English spring with a nineteenth-century view of battle. Robert W. Service's 'The Man from Athabaska' tells of an old backwoodsman who quits his trapline, tramps in from the wilderness, and joins the infantry. Lilian Leveridge's 'Over the Hills of Home,' a tribute to her younger brother who died of wounds in France, imagines the fallen soldier as a boy at play. Main Johnson's 'Wind – and the Dust of Death' tells of a grieving mother who communes with the spirit of her aviator-son as she scatters his ashes from a mountain top. In 'Ici Repose,' Bernard Freeman Trotter expresses envy of the fallen from the standpoint of the living, who 'shall grow old, and tainted with the rotten / Effluvia of the peace we fought to win.' 'The Fifes of Valcartier' by Theodore Goodridge Roberts is a stirring patriotic recruiting verse in the best Victorian tradition. The only unconventional choice was A.C. Stewart's poem 'The Shell,' a vaguely Futurist paean to 'the nation-wrecking, race destroying, world-engulfing' artillery shell.[28] Read together, these ten poems capture virtually every aspect of the myth of Canada's war. Although it appeared shortly after the Armistice, the list could have been compiled at any time in the interwar period. Indeed, the war poetry most often reproduced and quoted in the 1920s and 1930s partook of just those qualities that Logan identified.

What was true of poetry was also true of fiction, and the same qualities were expected of a good fictional account of the war; it too had to be 'suffused with beauty of sentiment, [and] rich in noble ideas.' Few novels approximated this ideal more closely than L.M. Montgomery's *Rilla of Ingleside,* the tale of the village of Glen St. Mary's journey through the Great War as seen through the eyes of Rilla, the daughter of Anne of Green Gables. It opens in the Golden Summer of 1914, capturing the innocence and purity of prewar Canada, and proceeds to provide a directory of the stock characters that peopled Canada's memory of the war: the sensitive Walter Blythe, a Canadian version of Rupert Brooke, who dies a glorious (and painless) death in battle; his brother Jem, the outdoorsman who went to war as an adventure; the mothers who rejoice that they do not have to urge their sons to enlist; and Mr. Meredith, who believes that the sacrifice of young men will give the country a new vision. As a piece of literature, it is not one of Montgomery's best; some reviewers dismissed it as a 'spun-sugar creation' or a formula novel.

Far more critics, however, raved about the novel, not for the author's finely drawn characters or deft handling of plot, but for a very specific reason: it captured the essence of small-town Canada during the war. One reviewer praised the book for presenting 'a faithful and worthy picture of war years in Glen St. Mary, which could be a thousand other small towns in Canada.' The *Regina Post* said that it 'possesses in a very high degree that natural, life-like semblance of being a chronicle of actual happenings.' According to another critic, 'most Canadians lived and felt those months very much as did the Blythe family.' R.W. Douglas, a Vancouver librarian, agreed, lauding Montgomery for 'visualiz[ing], if such a thing can be said, the soul of the Canadian people in the war; you have given a true picture of what we went through during five long years of agony.'[29] In essence, these reviewers universalized Montgomery's view of the war. Glen St. Mary became Anytown, and each character was deemed to have its counterpart in villages across the country. By praising the novel's verisimilitude, reviewers shifted *Rilla of Ingleside* from fiction to history: it became a 'true' record of Canada's war, and the fictionalization was merely an artistic device that only served to accentuate the book's authenticity. Obviously, L.M. Montgomery had hit upon the right way to tell Canada's war story in fiction. Canadians evidently thought so too, for they purchased 27,000 copies of the book in the interwar years.

III

IF THERE WAS BROAD CONSENSUS on the right way to tell that story, there was even greater agreement on the wrong way. Indeed, the defence of the accuracy and balance of the right story against the challenge of alternative versions of the war was remarkable in its stoutness. The most significant attacks came from three different quarters: from south of the border; from a small Ontario newspaper; and from a new genre of war literature. On each occasion Canadians from across the social and political spectrum allied to preserve a version of the war that had become an article of faith.

Many Canadians despaired of the degree to which the story of their war was filtered through an American lens. Even before the United States entered the war, Canadians read more war books by Americans than by Anglo-Canadians.[30] Not surprisingly, many of these books overemphasized the American contribution to the war, often to the detriment of everything else. When the Detroit *Free Press* and other newspapers began to inflate the

American role in victory still further, J. Castell Hopkins decided enough was enough and devoted five pages of the 1919 *Canadian Annual Review* to a meticulous demolition of the American claims. Other interested Canadians took up the same battle and 'Who won the war?' – a call raised by the author of a 1919 broadsheet – echoed across the country in the interwar years.[31]

In the American pulp war magazines such as *Battle Stories* and *War Stories,* which flooded across the border in the 1920s, there was only one answer: the doughboy had won the war. Soldiers from other nations had no role in the Allied triumph, and Canadian contributors soon learned that, if their articles were to be accepted, their heroes would have to be American; they solved the problem by writing of Americans in the CEF, and poking fun at the British to appeal to American readers.[32] This bothered Canadian veterans who read the magazines. One proclaimed that he was 'heartily sick of war stories, as dished up in American magazines,' and another complained of 'the hot air from the other side of the line. Although they are nice people, they outdo themselves in conceit.' W.D. Stovel had a solution. The only reasonable response to American claims, he thought, was simply to ban any fictionalized accounts of the war produced in the United States.[33]

W.C. LaMarsh, a veteran of the First Contingent, was equally troubled by the distortion of history fostered by American pulp magazines and was determined to establish a Canadian equivalent. With his own money and some support from a local member of Parliament, LaMarsh launched *Canadian War Stories* in March 1929, operating in a small office above the town hall in Chatham, Ontario. Advertised as 'an alert Canadian magazine depicting romance, fact and fiction, gallant acts and deeds of war heroes,' the magazine featured contributions from some of Canada's best soldier-writers,

'An alert Canadian magazine.' During its short lifetime, *Canadian War Stories* published work by some of Canada's most popular soldier-writers. (*Canadian War Stories,* 15 Sept. 1928, Acadia University, Eric R. Dennis Collection)

such as Kim Beattie, Will Bird, and Edgar McInnis. LaMarsh's timing was unfortunate, though. The magazine went bimonthly in September 1929, reverted to monthly in November, and finally ceased publication in February 1930, a victim of the stock market crash that killed many of its competitors as well.[34]

Canadian War Stories thus passed into oblivion, but other, better-funded voices had already taken up the battle to safeguard a uniquely Canadian version of the war. The occasion was the publication in 1927 of a series of articles in American periodicals that suggested that the British Empire had shirked its duty in the war and that the United States had picked up the pieces and forced Germany to come to terms in November 1918. In a number of widely discussed articles, Brigadier-General Henry Reilly claimed that in the last stages of the war, there were more American than British troops facing the enemy. The reason for this was that Britain kept too many troops at home and guarding the Channel ports and did not institute conscription early enough in the war.

The reaction to these articles was not long in coming. An Ottawa editor insisted that Germany had been beaten well before American troops reached the front and that the final victory had been won by 'the guns and bayonets of Britain and France.' Will Bird tackled the claims that, because American casualties were higher than Canadian, the United States must have played a greater role in defeating the Hun. He pointed out a fact that should have embarrassed American authorities, that over half of American casualties died of disease, many in their own training camps. Stephen Leacock poked fun at the tendency of the American media to portray the Great War as the Great American War, which was won entirely by the doughboys who rushed overseas to put Europeans in their place, with the blessing 'of God, of Abraham Lincoln, the Southern Confederacy and the Middle West.'[35]

In its Dominion Day 1928 issue, *Maclean's* magazine brought its heavy guns to bear on the American claims. In an article entitled 'The Truth about the War,' George Drew provided a meticulous demolition of the American version of the war. He produced statistics from a variety of sources, including one American historian who maintained that for the United States to have matched the empire's commitment of soldiers, it would have had to put thirteen million men in uniform. But Drew did not stop with troop statistics. He went on to munitions and aircraft production, enemy prisoners captured, merchant shipping losses, enemy divisions in opposition, and a host of other categories to prove that the American contribution on the Western Front was considerably smaller than that of the empire. Drew hastened to point out that he had no desire to belittle the American effort; he merely wanted to provide a plain statement of the facts so that future generations of Canadians, many of whom read American periodicals, would know the truth about their history.

Drew's article touched the wellspring of anti-Americanism that lies in the Canadian psyche. The Dominion Day issue of *Maclean's* quickly disappeared from the news-stands, and the magazine published a special run of 100,000 offprints to cope with the demand. Single copies were available at no charge, or they could be purchased in quantity at twenty-five cents a dozen. Legion members in Dartmouth, Nova Scotia, distributed copies of the pamphlet to local schoolchildren, while the branch in Bridgetown, Nova Scotia, opened a competition for the best student essay on Drew's article.[36] *Maclean's* was flooded with enthusiastic letters; 'in almost every case,' editor H. Napier Moore wrote to Currie, 'the wish is expressed that the article should be placed in the hands of every school child in Canada.' Colonel A.T. Hunter would have approved of this suggestion. He told an Armistice Day audience in Cobourg, Ontario, not to 'growl at the Americans for their propaganda. But, whenever they mention one of their pet shows, just bring out in parallel columns three bigger and better shows put on by the Canadians.'[37]

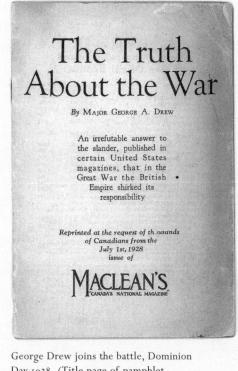

The Truth
About the War

By MAJOR GEORGE A. DREW

An irrefutable answer to
the slander, published in
certain United States
magazines, that in the
Great War the British
Empire shirked its
responsibility

Reprinted at the request of thousands
of Canadians from the
July 1st, 1928
issue of

MACLEAN'S
CANADA'S NATIONAL MAGAZINE

George Drew joins the battle, Dominion Day 1928. (Title page of pamphlet reprinted from *Maclean's*, 1 July 1928)

The response generated by Drew's 'The Truth about the War,' however, was more than just a manifestation of anti-Americanism. It was a reaction to an assault on the memory of the war. Articles that overemphasized the American role in the victory belittled everyone else's and thereby threatened to undermine the preferred version of the war. If Canada's contribution was as insignificant as the American articles suggested, the nation's sacrifice was open to question. The defence of Ypres in 1915, the capture of Vimy Ridge, the Hundred Days – all were reduced to minor and relatively unimportant skirmishes that had little real impact on the outcome of the war. If these battles were insignificant, then the deaths of Canadian soldiers must also have been insignificant. For the countless Canadians who had lost loved ones to the war, such a suggestion was intolerable.

IV

IT IS AN ODD COINCIDENCE that Colonel Hunter's remarks were made in Cobourg, for the small town on the north shore of Lake Ontario became the scene of an even more dramatic episode in the battle to safeguard the received version of Canada's war. This time, the attack came from within, and its object was the former commander of the Canadian Corps. It was in Cobourg's Victoria Hall, at the 1928 spring assizes for Northumberland and Durham Counties, that the final act in the strange and rather tragic postwar odyssey of Sir Arthur Currie was played out.

When the pear-shaped Victoria insurance salesman returned home in August 1919 after commanding the Canadian Corps since June 1917, he received anything but a hero's welcome. Currie debarked from the SS *Caronia* onto a darkened Halifax pier, deserted save for two Toronto reporters and the same small knot of officials and local philanthropists who had met every returning soldier, and proceeded through empty streets to be greeted by barely a hundred people at the civic reception at city hall. It was no better in Ottawa; there were no cheering crowds or bands lining the streets, and the reception on Parliament Hill was decidedly chilly. There was no ringing praise of Currie's successes, and Deputy Prime Minister Sir George Foster's speech was restrained and unenthusiastic.[38] No cash gratuity was presented to Currie by a grateful nation. He did not even receive an official resolution of thanks from the House of Commons immediately upon his return.

Yet by the time of his death in December 1933, Currie's reputation was higher than it had ever been. He was the greatest personality in the Dominion, wrote Leslie Roberts, 'the only outstanding figure on our public horizon, a figure beside whom our Meighens and our Mackenzie Kings and our captains of Commerce were dwarves and puppets.' Charles Vining, a former editor at the Toronto *Star Weekly*, called him 'one of the few really great men this country has,' and *Saturday Night* was even more effusive: 'the commander whose work appeared great during four years of gruelling combat, and has continued to seem great through fifteen years of the most searching subsequent examination, is surely the nearest thing to a certified great man that we can get without awaiting the judgement of the centuries ... [T]he greatness of Sir Arthur Currie seems to us to be assured in a way which cannot yet be predicated of any other Canadian of the 20th Century.'[39] In an unprecedented step, Currie's Montreal funeral was broadcast live, coast-to-coast, on the radio. One-quarter of the city's population attended his funeral, and the courts and Protestant schools were closed for the day. Robert Borden said that neither Sir John A. Macdonald nor Sir Wilfrid Laurier had received such accolades; Sir Edward Beatty predicted that the tributes would be unparalleled for decades.[40]

What had brought about this remarkable metamorphosis in the standing of the former commander of the Canadian Corps? The answer was simple: his reputation had been publicly attacked. In 1919 and again in 1927-8, Currie was the object of serious allegations regarding his handling of the Canadian Corps, and each time he emerged from the fray with his reputation strengthened. Former soldiers, who were by no means unstinting in their love for the general, closed ranks around him when he was attacked, and the general public also rallied to Currie's defence. Though the attacks undoubtedly shortened his life, they contributed immeasurably to his heightened stature.

The allegations against Currie first surfaced in October 1918, when Sam Hughes, the fiery former Militia minister, complained to Borden about the 'useless sacrifice' of Canadian troops at the Battle of Cambrai. The whispers raced through the CEF, finding an eager audience among staff officers jealous at Currie's rise and soldiers who regarded it as their special privilege to grouse about their generals. Currie knew that these accusations were gaining force, and early in 1919 he learned that his primary antagonist was about to mount a public assault.[41]

On 4 March 1919, Hughes rose in the House of Commons to deliver his reply to the governor general's address. It began harmlessly enough, with a list of those MPs who had enlisted for service or whose sons had joined up, but the member for Lindsay soon got into his stride with what was obviously his major theme. He began to question the casualties sustained by the Canadian Corps, particularly during the Hundred Days of 1918, and spoke of the 'useless massacre of our Canadian boys' at Cambrai. He referred also to Lens and Passchendaele, 'where the only apparent object was to glorify the General in command,' and then launched an attack on the Canadian capture of Mons. 'You cannot find one Canadian soldier returning from France,' he thundered, 'who will not curse the name of the officer who ordered the attack on Mons.' Hughes stopped short of naming names, but everyone knew to whom he was referring: Arthur Currie.

The attack won few friends for Sam Hughes, in the House of Commons, among veterans, or in the general public. Member after member took the floor to sing the praises of Currie, but Hughes's strongest opponent was the charismatic Colonel Cy Peck, the member for Skeena. Peck had commanded the 16th Battalion during the Hundred Days, had won a Victoria Cross in September 1918, and had fought at Cambrai. Of all the members in the House that session, he was the most qualified to answer the charges that had been levelled. With the aid of a map of Cambrai, he did just that; but it was the tone of Peck's remarks that was noteworthy. His greatest concern, he said, was for the feelings of those Canadians whose sons, fathers, and husbands lay buried in Flanders; those feelings would be hurt by Hughes's accusations. He questioned the propriety of the honourable member for Lindsay in raising them: 'Any man who says anything to cause these wounds to bleed afresh should have behind him the most indisputable facts, should be able to guarantee his statements to the utmost, and should be absolutely convinced that what he says is absolutely necessary to be said in the public good.' When Hughes promised to continue his investigation into Currie's conduct, including his time as a brigade commander during the Second Battle of Ypres, Peck replied, 'it will be unfortunate for the reputation which the Canadians have won for themselves, and which should be cherished in the heart of every true citizen of this country.'

In Peck's view, Hughes had not merely questioned the tactical judgment of one general. He had called into question everything Canadian troops had accomplished during the war and had tarnished the sparkling reputation they had built. Furthermore, even if Hughes's remarks were accurate, Peck was not convinced that it was in the public interest to reveal the truth. The truth, after all, might compromise the received version of the war story. Even a few months after the Armistice, the myth of Canada's war had built such a cachet that it was more important than the facts.

The daily press took an equally dim view of the former Militia minister's allegations. The *Montreal Gazette* criticized Hughes for impugning Currie's 'bravery, courage and judgment,' while the *Toronto Daily Star* averred that the charge made by Hughes was 'so atrocious that it discredits himself and everything else that he has uttered.' The paper quoted a number of soldiers who said they had never heard any criticism of Currie's conduct of battles, though they heard plenty of complaints about Hughes's Ross rifle.[42] The *Globe* wrote bitterly that 'the enemy never dealt a fouler blow than that directed by Sir Sam Hughes against the leaders of the Canadian Army still in the field.' Enraged by the attacks against Currie, J.F.B. Livesay began work on the highly laudatory *Canada's Hundred Days,* which he hoped would set the record straight; he took up the cause, in part, because Currie was reluctant to enter the fray himself.[43]

Eight years later, Currie was finally drawn to battle. The occasion was an unsigned editorial on the capture of Mons published by the Port Hope

Evening Guide in June 1927. The editorial maintained that Currie had ordered that Mons be attacked on the morning of 11 November simply so he could say that his corps had fired the last shot of the Great War. His only motive was 'to glorify the Canadian Headquarters staff.' Thanks to this 'worse than drunken spree,' Canadian troops who had survived 'the whole four years of war lie buried in Belgian cemeteries as the result of the "glories of Mons."' The editorial also stated that official photographs of Currie reviewing the Canadian troops in Mons concealed a different scene; headquarters staffers were, in fact, warned to leave the town without delay before the soldiers turned their rifles on their generals.[44]

Currie was on holiday when he learned of the editorial, and he agonized over the course of action to take. The *Evening Guide* was an unremarkable small-town journal with a limited circulation, and there was every likelihood that the editorial would be quickly forgotten. Consequently, many of Currie's friends advised against pursuing the matter. Currie, however, could not take the charges lying down. He had endured the accusations since 1918 and finally decided that the opportunity had arisen to clear his

Sir Arthur Currie and his generals take the salute in Mons, 11 November 1918 (NAC PA 3524)

reputation once and for all. He retained a Toronto solicitor and directed him to launch a libel suit against the paper's owner and publisher, Frederick W. Wilson, and W.T.R. Preston, the editor who wrote the piece.

The trial began on 16 April 1928 in Cobourg and became front page news across the country, with up-to-the-minute reports clattering off telegraph equipment installed on the second floor of Victoria Hall. Dozens of former soldiers of all ranks appeared as witnesses, and cross-examination was often spirited and even acrimonious. Finally, a little before 4 PM on 1 May, the jury returned its verdict. With one dissenter (an ex-artilleryman who had twice been wounded in action), the jury awarded the judgment to the plaintiff, with damages of $500 plus costs.

One might suggest that, though the judgment went in Currie's favour, the small damages awarded meant that he was really the loser. Canadians certainly did not interpret the verdict this way, and newspapers across the country revelled in the outcome of the trial. 'Every red-blooded and patriotic Canadian will be pleased over the verdict,' trumpeted the London *Free Press*. The editor of the Toronto *Evening Telegram* believed that relatives of the men who had died at Mons would be relieved to know that their boys had not died in vain; the editor may well have been right, for the father of Private George Price, the last man killed in the war, had earlier written to Currie of his 'humble hope that you will succeed in bringing to justice those responsible for bringing this case before the public.'[45] The Brantford *Expositor* was obviously correct in stating that Canadians 'keenly resented the aspersions cast upon the integrity and military genius of the commanders ... It is now almost ten years since the war ended, and the publication of this discreditable gossip served no good purpose whatsoever.' The *Calgary Albertan* made the same point and took satisfaction from the fact that, though the damages awarded were negligible, the costs would be substantial. Currie's vindication was complete, thought the *Halifax Herald:* 'he emerges from the situation a bigger and stronger man than when he went into it ... [T]here never was a time when he was as popular with the men he led as today.'[46]

Currie himself predicted that 'one of the happiest results of this trial will be an even closer union between all men who served overseas,' and the case certainly did rally Canadian veterans to his defence. A reunion of the 4th Battalion passed a resolution in April 1928 affirming that 'at no time did we feel that in any way you failed to carry out the interests of the men under you.'[47] The *Toronto Daily Star,* which had found many veterans to defend Currie against Hughes in 1919, repeated in 1928 that it had not met anyone who had served with the Canadian Corps in November 1918 who thought the corps was mishandled. Leslie Roberts was more explicit in his comments: 'I am unable to understand how a mere politician-civilian like Mr. Preston could be in any position to set up in business as a critic of our military strategy.'[48] Clearly, it was not the privilege of stay-at-homes to criticize anyone who had served overseas.

The trial was so important to Canadian veterans because the Mons editorial was more than just a criticism of Currie; it touched everyone who served in the CEF. This sort of guilt by association may seem illogical, but it was deeply felt by many people. According to the London *Free Press,* 'Sir Arthur Currie was fighting in the libel suit not only for his own good name, but for the good name of the Canadian staff, the Canadian officers, and the Canadian army.' Indeed, Currie publicly admitted as much, so when the judgment came down in his favour, it marked a vindication not just of his conduct of the operations at Mons, but of the entire record of the CEF. In Currie's view, the trial was the last victory of the Canadian Corps.[49]

But Preston's editorial was even more than an attack on the Canadian Corps. As Peck said in 1919, allegations against Currie had implications that extended far beyond the reputation of a single general. When Sir Archibald Macdonell wondered 'why they should try to deprive Canada of the Glory he [Currie] won for her,' he was articulating a widely held belief that Hughes and Preston had gone beyond merely libelling the former commander of the Canadian Corps, to attacking everything that the corps achieved. For this reason, as *The Legionary* put it, 'it was essential that [Currie] not only secure personal vindication, but that he should safeguard the heritage which the service of Canada's sons ... created.'[50] By questioning the value of one day's sacrifice, Preston had cast a cloud on that heritage. In suggesting that the war could be a source of shame for Canadians, he threatened to undermine the very foundations of the myth.

V

GEORGE DREW and Arthur Currie defended their versions of the war with facts. 'The Truth about the War' amounted to a statistical rebuttal of the American articles; indeed, Drew was able to summarize his argument in two columns of figures at the front of the pamphlet. Once all of these facts were presented, Drew inferred, a single truth would emerge: his story. The Currie trial was the same. Duguid and an assistant from the historical section descended on Cobourg with crates of documents covering the final days of the war. Inside Victoria Hall, casualty tables were discussed, the timing of signals and messages debated, and the statements of veterans tested and retested. The events around Mons in November 1918 were broken down into their constituent parts, and each was examined in detail. The plaintiff took the position that these facts spoke for themselves; they were not open to interpretation. Viewed in their entirety and in context, they told one story, and one story only, that related by Currie. In both instances, Canadians appeared to agree.

The third significant assault on the received version also revolved around notions of truth and historical accuracy, yet in a strikingly different way. At the heart of this debate was the canon of antiwar literature. According to the conventional wisdom, soldiers returning home after the Armistice were initially incapable of putting their war experiences on paper. Ten years passed, and finally veterans began to articulate their experiences. In doing so, they created a new war discourse, one characterized by disillusionment, horror, and disenchantment. The products of this decade of reflection came to be known collectively as the war book boom. It began in 1928, when ten war novels were published in Britain and dozens elsewhere. The best of the 1928 crop were Edmund Blunden's *Undertones of War,* Arnold Zweig's *The Case of Sergeant Grischa,* and R.C. Sherriff's play *Journey's End.* The following year saw a flood of antiwar books, the most important being Erich Maria Remarque's *All Quiet on the Western Front,* released in English in March 1929. In the two years after the publication of Remarque's work, a host of other books joined the canon, including Richard Aldington's *Death of a Hero,* Ludwig Renn's *War,* Robert Graves's *Goodbye to All That,* Siegfried Sassoon's *Memoirs of an Infantry Officer,* and Henry Williamson's *A Patriot's Progress.* Of the Canadian contributions, the most notable were Peregrine Acland's *All Else Is Folly* (1929), Will Bird's *And We Go On,* and Charles Yale Harrison's *Generals Die in Bed,* the latter two published in 1930. As the story goes, the reading public around the world immediately pricked up its ears, jettisoned a previous fondness for stirring patriotic accounts of the war, and embraced this new vision.

Like much conventional wisdom, this is deeply flawed. In the first place, it is not true that the postwar years saw a general unwillingness to write about the war experience. In fact, more war books were published in Canada between 1919 and 1921 than in the rest of the interwar years combined. It is also misleading to suggest that the antiwar novel was an innovation of 1928. John Dos Passos and e.e. cummings both published important war protest novels in the early 1920s; similar books appeared in England, France, and Germany, so that by 1928 there was already a substantial body of work that could be considered protest literature. Most significantly, the public response to the antiwar books was not as enthusiastic as has been suggested. The checkered life of one antiwar novel is instructive in this regard. Walter Redvers Dent was a Torontonian who had enlisted for overseas service at the age of sixteen. During a period of postwar illness, he began work on a manuscript which he entitled *Why Smitest Thou Men?*, later changing the title to *Cry Havoc* and then to *Show Me Death!* It was under this title that the book, after extensive rewriting, finally appeared on 7 July 1930. It tells the tale of Lionel Thor, who enlists and reaches the front just in time for his unit (apparently the 4th Canadian Mounted Rifles) to be wiped out at Mount Sorrel on 2 June 1916. Thor survives to fight at Vimy Ridge only to lose an eye and a leg at Hill 70. His injuries revive a latent hatred of God, whom he accuses of preserving him so that he can be crippled, and Thor returns to Toronto a bitter and disillusioned man. Even that does not end the tragedy, however; at the sight of her horribly disfigured son, Thor's mother collapses and dies of heart failure.

The book, capable though unexceptional, drew critical acclaim, *Saturday Night* writing that it was 'based on a finer conception of the tragedy of war' than Remarque's book. Such luminaries as the poet and critic E.J. Pratt and Macmillan of Canada chief Hugh Eayrs also thought highly of it.[51] In Britain, the *New Statesman,* the *Times Literary Supplement,* and the *Spectator* all lauded the book, while the *Army Quarterly* predicted that the Canadian public would approve of Dent's vision. That public, however, was not convinced, and Macmillan's initial print run of 2,000 proved to be optimistic. Just 360 copies of *Show Me Death!* were sold in the first six months of release, and only five in the whole of 1931.[52]

In the absence of credible sales figures, it is difficult to say with certainty how the more famous antiwar books fared in Canada. Certainly *All Quiet on the Western Front* was deemed popular enough to be serialized in a number of daily newspapers, and Remarque and other antiwar authors garnered many favourable reviews in Canada. However, at least one critic questioned the real popularity of bestsellers, arguing that the public 'read to order like automata,' and press comments point to the existence of a sizeable body of opposition to these books.[53] Indeed, the canon of antiwar literature became a battleground, rallying the defenders of Canada's war myth just as 'The Truth about the War' and the Currie trial had done. At the heart of this battle lay a blurring of the lines between fact and fiction, memoir and novel. Recent scholars have debated endlessly the veracity of certain books, and contemporary readers had the same difficulty in determining whether a book was intended as history or fiction. For opponents of these books, however, the distinction was irrelevant. Fictional or not, they were simply bad history; any book that did not adhere to the accepted interpretation of the war was a dangerous falsehood.

Many Canadians dismissed these books as invalid for the same reason that they rejected the charges made against Currie by Sam Hughes and W.T.R. Preston: because they cast Canadian soldiers in a bad light. One of the distinguishing features of the canon of antiwar literature was its negativity. Generally speaking, it refused to recognize anything positive in the war experience, seeing it as a destroyer of human body and spirit. Battle was not a refiner's fire but an insatiable beast that chewed up soldiers and left only shattered and insensate hulks in its wake. With its parade of characters who drank, swore, and fornicated their way through Flanders, the canon revealed the power of war to bring out the worst in humanity. Obviously, this version of history could not go unchallenged in Canada. How could the soldier of Jesus Christ have been brutalized or dehumanized by fighting God's battles? How could the Canadian volunteer, who personified all that was fine and true about the country, have been transformed into an amoral animal by offering his life for the cause? It was simply not acceptable to suggest that the war had been so ruinous for all who experienced it.

Of course, it was no more reasonable to suggest that the war experience was entirely positive and that Canadian troops had been paragons of virtue. Rather, accounts of the war had to relate both the positive and the negative. This was at the crux of a debate between Malcolm Cowley, the American literary historian who had served as an ambulance driver in France, and the poet Archibald MacLeish. Cowley approved strongly of the trends in war fiction, but the conservative MacLeish (a former officer whose elder brother had been killed in action with the Royal Flying Corps) railed against the canon for lacking totality and balance. Life at the front did mean discomfort, agony, and death, but it also meant heroism, glory, and humour. To emphasize the former at the expense of the latter, MacLeish believed, was to do a disservice to the memory of the soldier.[54]

This argument was at the centre of the campaign to defend Canada's preferred version of the war. Any memory of the war, whether it was presented by a Canadian, a British, or a German writer, was judged on the degree to which it painted a balanced picture. When Reverend Edgar McKegney, wounded and captured in 1918 while serving as chaplain to an infantry battalion, reminded his listeners at a 1928 Armistice Day service that to recall the terrible life at the front was also to recall the wonderful spirit of fellowship that prevailed there, he was merely giving voice to what many people had accepted as the obvious criteria for evaluating any memory of the war.[55] Those versions that gave equal emphasis to the harrowing artillery bombardments and the evenings spent drinking *vin blanc* in a café were acceptable; those that dwelt only on the horrors were invalid. Simply put, an acceptable version of the war experience had to recognize the positive significance of comradeship and the culture of the *estaminet* in the soldier's life.

Perhaps not surprisingly, the standards demanded were high, and the soldier-author had to walk a very fine line to write a book that pleased reviewers. Those writers who struck the correct balance were warmly praised. James Pedley's *Only This: A War Retrospect* is one of the finest Canadian memoirs of the Great War. Pedley, a lawyer and later assistant city editor of the Toronto *World,* went overseas with the 216th Battalion and was eventually posted to the 4th Battalion; he was wounded in the attack on Amiens in August 1918 and invalided home. *Only This* is a memoir of exceptional quality, with neither the unrelieved gloom of the antiwar novels nor the wide-eyed optimism of more propagandist accounts. Pedley is hardly the stainless warrior; he candidly recounts his own petty dislikes, drinks heavily on occasion, and admits to a conspicuous lack of patriotism. His comrades are capable of great heroism, but they also have very human flaws; they plunder German bodies for souvenirs and can be churlish, dishonest, and greedy. In short, the book captures the totality of the war experience in unusually realistic tones: the horrors of the battlefield and the grumbling soldiers who question why they are there, but also the comradeship of true friends and the riotous evenings spent in local *estaminets*.

Critics reacted positively to the book's balance. *Saturday Night* was enthusiastic, applauding Pedley for relating all aspects of trench life, including 'the bits of fun, ... the sleeping quarters, the carefree hours off duty.' Another reviewer was just as impressed. Pointing out that too many recent war books had been a 'medley of blasphemy and butchery without the reliefs of rest and fugitive pleasures that helped to colour the monotony,' T.D. Rimmer commended Pedley for not neglecting the times 'when the troops lived gloriously.'[56]

In contrast, authors who were unable or unwilling to present this balanced portrait of the soldier and his war were given a rough ride. The most common response was to dismiss their vision as unrepresentative. F. Wells Johnson, an Anglican minister in Moose Jaw, 'deplored the present tendency to write unsavoury war books, depicting things which did not represent in any way the great mass of the army which fought in the Great War.' In *Canadian Forum* in 1930, H.J. Davis took up Archibald MacLeish's argument, insisting that 'most men maintained a certain buoyancy and mastery of circumstances which made their experiences of the war strangely mixed; horrible, disgusting, intolerably monotonous, but also exciting, pleasant, amusing, even triumphant.' This element was missing from much of the recent war literature, thought Davis.[57]

Reviewers often cited a single reason why certain authors had been unable to achieve this balanced viewpoint: they were not of sound mind. Their conflicting version of the war was not the result of a decade of reflection or a different perspective; it was simply a product of mental instability. The antiwar books, wrote one battalion historian, were full of misleading generalizations because they inferred the emotions of all soldiers 'by the whimperings of neurotic sensationalists.'[58] Sir Andrew Macphail agreed. In rejecting the antiwar canon in its entirely ('it is the product of foreign filthy minds; and it is false besides,' he wrote in 1932), he declared that such books were nothing more than 'the hysterical writings of neurotic adolescents who should never have been allowed to enlist.'[59]

Those people who considered the antiwar vision as simply the product of sick minds also perceived it as a real threat to Canadian life. Mabel Clint, who served as a nursing sister in France during the war, despaired of people 'who have read *only German* books about the war!! How is it possible to understand anything of the British spirit of those days by studying a viewpoint ... dealing altogether with futility and disgust.' The chaplain of the Canadian Legion branch in Moncton agreed, lamenting that young people were having 'their patriotic impulses warped by the flood of a certain class of literature coming across the border.' The only way to deal with such works, believed more than one Legion branch, was to ban them.[60]

It was left to two officers, however, to launch the most full-throated attacks on antiwar literature. In 1930, Lieutenant-Colonel F.C. Curry, the commander of a militia unit in Brockville, Ontario, launched a spirited assault on the direction of the war novel in the *Canadian Defence Quarterly*.[61] He began with the insightful point that war books gave their authors a licence to describe in horrific detail incidents that would not otherwise be tolerated in literature; the remains of a labourer killed by a dynamite blast were no less obscene than the body of a dead infantryman on the battlefield, he reasoned, but the public would not tolerate such detailed descriptions of the former as they would of the latter. Curry believed that antiwar books were only popular with people who had no direct experience with life at the front; they were 'largely quoted by the man who stayed at home as being the real truth about the war, and by inference, the reason why he did not indulge in this patriotic form of sport.' He was not sure who else such books could conceivably appeal to. 'Possibly the peculiar type of mentality that produces prohibitionists, freak religionists and other "holier than thou" exponents, finds a queer pleasure in this type of book,' he surmised.

An even more vicious condemnation was launched by Cy Peck in the pages of *The Brazier*, the newsletter of the 16th Battalion Association.[62] In an all-out offensive, Peck condemned books by 'ten minute warriors' who appear to have had a short and very superficial knowledge of the front; their work was all shot through with an undercurrent of 'filth, demagogery [sic], morbidity and hopelessness' and said nothing about the sterling qualities exhibited by the troops in France. He dismissed virtually every work that is now recognized as a classic of the Great War. Sherriff's *Journey's End* was a libellous slander for including a scene in which an officer had to be driven into action at gunpoint. By describing trysts with prostitutes in *All Else Is Folly,* Peregrine Acland had put himself 'on a level with the filth-purveyors of other nations.' Robert Graves's *Goodbye to All That,* which claimed that Canadian troops occasionally murdered prisoners, was 'the product of an unstable and degenerate mind.' *All Quiet on the Western Front* was worse still. Canadian soldiers fought every bit as hard as the characters created by Remarque, claimed Peck, 'but it did not lower their spirits or throw them into a state of agonizing gruesomeness.' Mocking the book as something that was loved by the 'smart set' who talk about its naughtiness and 'think themselves quite the wickedest things that ever were,' he found nothing whatsoever redeeming in it. It was 'printed putridness,' he snorted.

These books were offensive to Peck, Curry, and countless other Canadians for the same reason that they so impressed later critics: they universalized the experience of the trenches. Remarque's Paul Bäumer might have served in any army; he represented the suffering of millions of other soldiers from all nations, including Canada. This, of course, was precisely the objection. To many people, universalization was in fact defamation: these books tarred Canadian soldiers with the sins of others by claiming that, like all other soldiers, the men of the CEF had been brutalized and dehumanized by war. The antiwar vision suggested that war erased the soldier's individuality and identity, transforming him into a pawn whose suffering and death were of little consequence to anyone, even himself. Many veterans and relatives and friends of soldiers found this suggestion unpalatable. It robbed soldiers of their sense of agency; instead of rational, purposeful human beings, they became dupes of forces they could not hope to understand, much less control. People did not want their loved ones to be identified as anonymous victims sacrificed in a pointless slaughter, nor did they want them to share guilt by association in crimes committed by their semi-fictional counterparts. At best, many people viewed this as an insult; at worst, it was slander.

The comments of one ranker sum up what many Canadians may have felt. F.W. Bagnall had enlisted at the age of fourteen and was wounded and invalided home before the end of the war. In a bitter and confused memoir published in 1933, he lashed out at the 'continual calumnies and a succession of lies' contained in films about the war (presumably he was referring to the screen version of *All Quiet on the Western Front,* released in 1930). Bagnall felt particularly aggrieved that he had fought 'doggedly against every form of discomfort living in ditches, only to be held up to the eyes of even your own people as belonging to a group who were as pictured on the screen horribly depraved.'[63] For Bagnall, the antiwar vision was not simply a different perspective on events; it was a vicious personal attack on the ex-soldier.

That is not to say, however, that Bagnall, Peck, and those of like mind wanted all war books to be 'spun-sugar creations,' full of jolly soldiers jousting at each other across No Man's Land. Peck would have been the first to concede that the Canadian soldier was only human and rarely wore the halo of sainthood. Former chaplain George Kilpatrick agreed, predicting a rude response from the soldier who was told that he was 'a veritable Sir Galahad – the embodiment of all Christian ideals.' Even Frederick George Scott admitted 'there was much evil thinking, evil talking and evil doing' among Canadian troops at the front. He hastened to add, though, that 'there was, underlying all this, the splendid manifestation in human nature of that image of God in which man was made.'[64]

Here, Scott had hit upon the real objection to the antiwar books. A distinguishing feature of the canon was the degree to which behaviour was an indication of deeper maladies. Drunkenness, lewd behaviour, violence against prisoners, and insubordination were all symptoms of something deeper: the destructive impact of war upon the human character. The experience of war destroyed everything it touched. The dead were ground into unrecognizable fragments, while the survivors were left crippled, embittered, and morally bankrupt. For countless Canadians, this interpretation was unacceptable. The occasional misdeed of a soldier was undeniable, as were the horrors of war that surrounded him. Yet the men were inherently good. Even the soldier of Christ could stray occasionally from the true path, but he always returned to the straight and narrow. 'When the heart's clean the feet will roam / At Truth's command,' wrote Lloyd Roberts. Furthermore, it was inconceivable that the soldier had been permanently scarred by war. 'Many noble Canadian lads,' insisted T.G. Marquis, 'went through the hell unsmirched and came back the same courageous, clean-living lads that went forth to battle.'[65]

Marquis's comment captured what Canadians were really looking for when they demanded balance in war books. They wanted books that did not paint an unnecessarily gloomy picture of war's impact on the individual soldier. A recounting of war's horror was fine (so long as it did not become gratuitous), but that horror could not be allowed to touch the souls of the soldier; his spirit had to remain inviolate. This requirement comes out particularly clearly in the critical reception given to two war books, both of which appeared at the peak of the controversy: Charles Yale Harrison's *Generals Die in Bed* and Will Bird's *And We Go On*.

A native of Philadelphia, Charles Yale Harrison came to Montreal just before the beginning of the war to join the staff of the *Star*. He lived only a short time in Canada before enlisting in the 14th Battalion and proceeding overseas in 1916 as a machine gunner. Harrison served in France before being wounded at Amiens in August 1918 and returning to Montreal; a few years later, he moved to New York City. Shortly thereafter, he began work on a manuscript that was eventually published in England in 1930 as *Generals Die in Bed*.

As a piece of literature, it is typical of the war book boom, though a little coarser than most. One by one, the narrator's comrades meet their deaths in ways that can only have been calculated to shock the reader. Clark, the officer, is shot in the back by one of his own men for trying to stop the platoon from retreating, while Fry has his legs cut from underneath him by shrapnel while charging an enemy position; he runs a few paces on his stumps before collapsing. The rest of the book is in the same vein. Prisoners are routinely murdered, the soldiers constantly grouse at one another, pausing only to berate their officers, and the survivors of one attack go on a drunken spree, looting the city of Arras until they collapse in a stupor on the streets. In one oft-quoted passage, the narrator bayonets a German soldier, only to find himself unable to extract his weapon from his victim's body. Each twist brings a fresh gurgle of pain from the mortally wounded enemy, and the desperate narrator finally discharges his rifle to snap off the bayonet and release them both from their torment.

Harrison's book received mixed reviews in other countries. Some critics loved it, but others believed that it said nothing that had not already been said by more capable authors. However, the book was guaranteed a rougher ride in Canada. Because it alleged that members of the 14th Battalion had pillaged Arras and murdered prisoners, *Generals Die in Bed* was bound to raise the ire of Canadians. Some people contented themselves with denouncing Harrison's story as a complete fabrication. W.B. Kerr contended that it 'is obviously fiction of the blood-curdling type,' while Nathaniel Benson wrote in *Saturday Night* that fully half of the incidents described in the book never occurred. He called it 'a book of very dubious literary merit ... very ugly reading indeed.' The Reverend T.N. Tattersall was surely referring to *Generals Die in Bed* when he told the patients at a Toronto veterans' hospital that 'there have been far too many untruthful pictures drawn of late – gross, brutal misrepresentations of the men whom I once knew.' The critic for the *Montreal*

Gazette agreed, accusing Harrison of doing a disservice to his comrades by emphasizing the evils of the war to the exclusion of the good.[66]

Others took the book considerably more seriously. Cy Peck attacked it as 'pure obscenity, totally unrelieved by the slightest flash of genius. It's a gross and shameful slander on the Canadian soldier, by a degenerate minded fool.' Journalist Doug Oliver dismissed it as 'that dastardly war novel ... [with] its numerous beastly allegations.'[67] Veterans' groups deluged Tommy Church, the Toronto member of Parliament and long-time soldiers' friend, with complaints and demanded that the government ban the book on account of its 'many libellous statements' about Canadian soldiers. Sir Archibald Macdonell became almost apoplectic with rage when he read it. 'I hope to live long enough to have the opportunity of (in good trench language) shoving my fist into that s—— of a b—— Harrison's tummy until his guts hang out his mouth!!!' Batty Mac fumed to Arthur Currie.[68] Currie, too, could scarcely contain his anger. The book was 'a mass of filth, lies ... [It] appeals to everything base, mean and nasty,' he raged to Batty Mac. 'A more scurrilous thing was never published ... The book is badly titled, has a weak style, no worth while matter, is full of vile [*sic*] and misrepresentation, and cannot have any lasting influence.' While Currie was perhaps not the soundest authority on literary style, he certainly had a right to comment on the title. He may have been thinking of two old friends who had been killed in action: Major-General Malcolm Mercer, killed at Mount Sorrel in June 1916 while leading the 3rd Division; and Major-General L.J. Lipsett, killed in September 1918 shortly after leaving the 3rd Division. This may explain the personal edge to Currie's bitter comments on *Generals Die in Bed*. 'There is not a single line in it worth reading, nor a single incident worthy of record,' he wrote. 'I have never read, nor do I hope ever to read, a meaner, nastier and more foul book.'[69]

Will Bird clearly agreed with these sentiments and wrote *And We Go On* as a corrective to war books that were 'putrid with so-called "realism."' Such books portrayed the soldier, he wrote in his preface, 'as a coarse-minded, profane creature, seeking only the solace of loose women or the courage of strong liquor. Vulgar language and indelicacy of incident are often their substitute for lack of knowledge, and their distorted pictures of battle action are especially repugnant. On the whole, such literature, offered to our avid youth, is an irrevocable insult to those gallant men who lie in French or Belgian graves.' *And We Go On* strove for a more balanced picture. It showed that 'the private in the trenches had other thoughts than of the flesh, had often finer vision and strength of soul than those who would fit him to their sordid, sensation-seeking fiction.'[70]

The book is more of a memoir than Harrison's and follows Bird through his enlistment with the 42nd Battalion and journey overseas, in October 1916, to his return to Halifax after the Armistice. It appears to be based heavily on his diaries, which offer considerable scope for storytelling; Bird was in the line almost continually for the last two years of the war, aside from the very occasional leave and a bout with mumps. The tone is different from his other books and short stories; there is little humour, except of a grim kind, and an abundance of tragedy. Indeed, Bird's narrative is filled with incidents that might not be out of place in *Generals Die in Bed*. Giger, the idiotic young reinforcement, bayonets a helpless German because he does not want to return to Canada without having 'killed a Heinie.' Moments later, he meets his own end, his head cleft from his body by an axe-wielding Prussian. Other prisoners are murdered as well; one soldier bayonets a wounded German POW whose moans kept him awake. Officers are frequently scorned and are threatened more than once by privates and NCOS exhausted from battle. By the book's end, Bird and his pal Tommy are bitter, sullen, and confused. Tommy wishes that he could join the boys under the white crosses, as he puts it; he gets his wish, dying of influenza a few days after the Armistice.

Despite this grim record, *And We Go On* received sparkling reviews. The *Moncton Transcript* approved of the book because 'there is no filth to be found [in it] and it lacks the amorous experiences which have been played up by other writers in an attempt to increase sales by pandering to depraved minds.' Another paper rated it the 'most realistic war story yet written ... Gloriously free from that indelicate vulgar side. It has no profanity, nor does it feature loose women. It is clean yet vivid and realistic ... War is pictured in all its horribleness, yet done by a man who went through the awfulness of it all and came through clean, like thousands of his fellows, and other thousands of clean heroes.' One critic called it 'a clean, stand-out story after the recent flood of vulgar sensationalism,' while a reviewer for the Halifax *Chronicle-Herald* praised the book for being 'without filth or favour ... [or] bitterness of spirit.' Raymond Mullens in *Saturday Night* wrote that it was 'in many respects a fine book; clean, unusually temperate and packed with action.'[71]

Why was *Generals Die in Bed* vilified and *And We Go On* praised? The answer lies in a single word that recurs in the reviews of Bird's book: clean. Not clean in a literal sense, for it has every bit as much mud and grime as any war book, but clean in a metaphorical sense. Despite the inescapable dirt surrounding their bodies, the souls and spirits of Bird's soldiers remain pure. They may gripe about their officers, their food, and the war in general, but

Doggy, Waterbottle, Sambro, and the rest of Bird's comrades retain an innate goodness. They are decent, clean-minded, and good-hearted. Whatever misdeeds they occasionally commit, they are not brutalized or dehumanized by war. Their violence is shed when they leave the trenches. Behind the lines and in billets, they are boys again, horsing around and bathing in streams like Brooke's 'swimmers into cleanness leaping.'

As his ship nears Halifax, Bird reflects on the war's impact upon him and his fellow soldiers. 'There would be many of the boys,' he predicted, 'who would be surly, taciturn, moody, resenting good intentions, perhaps taking to hard liquor and aimless drifting.' They would constitute a brotherhood that was forever 'branded by a monstrous despotism.' This might have been a suitable thought for Harrison or Remarque to end a novel, but not for Will Bird. 'I warmed as I thought of all that the brotherhood had meant,' he continued, 'the sharing of blankets and bread and hardships, the binding of each other's wounds, the talks we had had of intimate things, of the dogged simple faith that men had shown, flashes of their inner selves that strengthened one's own soul.' This, for Bird, would be the legacy of the war. He knew his bitterness would eventually give way to something precious: 'despite that horror which I could never forget I had equalizing treasure in memories.'[72]

The average reader evidently put down the book with a feeling of satisfaction. Will Bird had come through Passchendaele, Amiens, the Hundred Days – some of the toughest fighting experienced by the CEF – and had done so with his spirit and soul intact. He had succumbed to bitterness while at the front, but by his own admission that condition was only temporary; soon he would be able to focus on the inherent good in his Flanders adventure. With *And We Go On,* he had given Canadians a worm's-eye view of life in the trenches. He had captured the horror and degradation that punctuated the antiwar canon but had not allowed himself to wallow in it. Instead, he had crafted a memory of the war that recognized the gifts it conferred on those who took part. This sense of balance made Bird the quintessential articulator of Canada's war: obviously knowledgeable, certainly credible, and, most important of all, optimistic.

IN A REFLECTION on the character of the Canadian soldier, Hugh Urquhart summarized the views of those people who opposed the antiwar vision. The soldier was neither saint nor sinner, but 'one of a company of unconquerable spirits who treated life and death on an equality.' He might grow depressed, or criticize his generals, or complain about the food, but through it all his resolution remained unimpaired: 'whatever disillusion he met with he paid no heed to it.' This was the secret to the buoyancy and mental stability of the Canadian soldier; he 'found humour and contentment in fatigue and discomfort, where less stable and more selfish natures would have found sourness and hardship.'[73]

Six years later, Victoria Cross winner Milton Gregg agreed. The common soldiers were not 'mournful fellows, oppressed with sadness and horror,' who spent their days 'in lugubrious introspection, discussing their unhappy lot with all the dolefulness and the analytic persuasiveness of Greek philosophers.' But neither were they saints in arms. They were 'nothing more nor less than good-natured, wholesome youngsters, endowed with all the virtues of adolescence, and, let it be readily confessed, with most of its Original Sin.' They were simply ordinary people in extraordinary situations. 'Happy-go-lucky, harum-scarum, they were a good-hearted lot of courageous kids,' he concluded.[74]

This was the only characterization of the Canadian soldier that could be compatible with the memory of the war. If the war had been as negative as the protest literature suggested, neither the survivors nor the grieving families had anything to be proud of. Furthermore, if other armies had done the lion's share of the work in defeating the enemy, or if the generals cared less for human life than for their own personal aggrandizement, then the soldier's service, suffering, and sacrifice became meaningless.

If, however, the successes of Canadian troops overshadowed those of the great republic to the south; if Arthur Currie had every thought for the men under his command and for the reputation of the corps, but none for his own fame; if every soldier was like Urquhart and Gregg described and could find in the horror of the trenches the same 'equalizing treasure in memories' that Bird did – then the war was everything that Canada's memory had construed it to be. And after investing so much in that memory, Canadians were not willing to sit idly by while it was undermined. To do so was to dishonour everything they held dear about the war.

CHAPTER 7

If Ye Break Faith

I T WAS MAY 1915, and the First Division had just emerged from its baptism of fire at Ypres. Gas casualties, the walking wounded, and stretcher cases poured down the Menin Road and through the ruined Menin Gate, passing reinforcements going into the salient. Perched on the back of an ambulance near his dressing station, a Canadian doctor snatched a few minutes from his duties to ponder the loss of a friend who had been killed by a shellburst the day before. He tried to capture his feelings in verse but after twenty minutes tossed aside the three stanzas he had written and returned to his duties. The man who retrieved the scrap of paper was more impressed by the poem and submitted it to a number of periodicals in England. *Punch* accepted the piece and published it, unsigned, on 8 December 1915:

> In Flanders fields the poppies blow
> Between the crosses, row on row,
> That mark our place; and in the sky
> The larks still bravely singing, fly
> Scarce heard amid the guns below.
>
> We are the Dead. Short days ago
> We lived, felt dawn, saw sunset glow,
> Loved, and were loved, and now we lie
>   In Flanders fields.
>
> Take up our quarrel with the foe:
> To you from failing hands we throw
> The torch; be yours to hold it high.
> If ye break faith with us who die
> We shall not sleep, though poppies grow
>   In Flanders fields.

The poet's name was given in *Punch*'s yearly index (albeit spelled incorrectly), and John McCrae, the proud son of Guelph, Ontario, was thrust to the forefront of Canada's war myth.[1]

In his most well-known portrait, McCrae hardly looks the part of a myth-maker. His uniform fits poorly over too-sloping shoulders, his hair hangs in an undignified thatch, and his mouth has a strange, lopsided quality. Yet the exhortation of the dead in his final stanza became a battle cry, calling a people to arms to defend the high ideals of the crusade. George Drew, Arthur Currie, and Cy Peck held the torch high as they struggled to safeguard the received version of the war against competing memories that threatened to undermine it. It was up to all Canadians to make similar affirmations of their fidelity to the memory of the dead. They might raise memorials, or perform annual obeisance, or even allow the war's high ideals to govern their daily lives. In the name of keeping faith with the dead, no effort was too great.

I

'WHO DOES NOT bless God for the noble Poem, "In Flanders Fields"?' inquired a reader of a religious publication. Modern critics may be lukewarm to the poem, but contemporaries could scarcely find a superlative sufficient to describe it. Archibald MacMechan called it a 'perfect rondeau,' and one of the few pieces of Canadian literature that would hold up in the future. Thomas O'Hagan agreed that McCrae's poem would 'survive the teeth of time and live forever in Canadian literature, because it is the revelation of a great soul.'[2] Critics frequently referred to McCrae as the finest war poet in the world, one who was 'as truly inspired as any Hebrew

John McCrae, photographed while in command of the 16th Battery, Canadian Field Artillery in 1904. (Guelph Museums, McCrae House)

psalmist.' Parts of 'In Flanders Fields' had 'passed into our common language,' observed the *Globe*'s editor. 'Its thought was embedded in the thought of the generation for whom it was written; it has remained a heritage for the indefinite future.'[3]

The poem was indeed a tract for the times. 'Go forth and purchase "In Flanders Fields" [the collection of McCrae's verse assembled by Andrew Macphail],' commanded a reviewer in *Canadian Bookman*. 'The year has not produced and will not produce another book more desirable for a Canadian to possess.' Many people took the journal at its word. A single Toronto shop sold 1,200 copies of the poem in a month, and the Colonel John McCrae Memorial Branch of the Canadian Legion in Guelph distributed 5,000 copies of the poem to local schoolchildren.[4] In 1919, Macphail's book topped the non-fiction best-seller list, beating out such literary luminaries as Robert W. Service, Arthur Conan Doyle, and Stephen Leacock. The following year it was still in the top twenty, one of only three books to appear on the list in both years.

But sales of Macphail's book represented only a fraction of the poem's impact. It provoked countless 'responses' from around the world, earnest but usually amateurish efforts with titles such as 'Answer to Flanders Fields' and 'To Those Who Sleep in Flanders Fields: A Canadian Response.'[5] McCrae's poem was committed to memory by generations of Canadian schoolchildren, intoned at countless war memorial unveilings and Armistice Day ser-

Keep the faith ... by purchasing Victory Bonds. Similar images were used to publicize other philanthropic efforts, not just in Canada but throughout the Allied world. (City of Toronto Archives, James Collection 742)

vices, and repeated at many a veterans' reunion. It was even used, albeit rather tastelessly, in an advertisement for pharmaceutical supplies. Phrases like 'keep the faith' and 'hold the torch' entered the vernacular as exhortations to adhere to the high principles for which the just war had been waged.

But precisely how did one keep the faith? It was easy enough to admit, as many Canadians did, that the fallen became 'an obligating symbol for survivors'; it was more difficult to decide on the best way to discharge that obligation.[6] Guarding against alternative and potentially dangerous interpretations of the war experience was one way. Another was simply to remember the sacrifice of the fallen. To forget was to drop the torch and to fail the men and women who had given their lives. Remembering, on the other hand, constituted a perpetual tribute to the fallen. If the sacrifices were fixed firmly enough in the public consciousness through various forms of commemoration, the myth of the war would become self-perpetuating and would not need Canadians to defend it.

Remembering, of course, could take many different forms. One popular method was to commemorate the sacrifice by naming things after the war. Indeed, this was such a common practice that it was difficult to go anywhere or do anything in Canada without being reminded of the war. Cities and towns across the country looked to it for distinctive and meaningful street names. In December 1924, sewers were being dug for Foch and Haig Avenues and Place Joffre in Windsor, Ontario; the following autumn, services were installed for Lens, Vimy, and Ypres Avenues.[7] The same year, a Winnipeg newspaper reporter suggested changing the name of Pine Street to Valour Road, in honour of the three Victoria Cross winners who had lived there. In every province, heroes and battles lent their names to residential streets, new highways, and country roads: Ypres, St. Julien, Courcelette, Vimy, Currie, and a host of other local heroes and lesser engagements.

New settlements, like Somme in Saskatchewan and Manitoba and Vimy in Alberta, Québec, and Ontario, also owed their names to the war, and the Geographic Board of Canada found the war a useful source of names for physical features. A range of peaks along the Alberta-British Columbia border received wartime names, like Arras, Cambrai, Bishop (Captain W.A., Victoria Cross), Hooge, and Turner (General R.E.W., Victoria Cross), and a peak near Jasper bears the name of Private J.G. Pattison, awarded the Victoria Cross at Vimy Ridge. A mountain on the Alaska-Yukon border was named after one of Canada's lesser-known heroes, Private William Brooke, who died of pneumonia while in a German prison in 1917. In 1934 the Red Birds Ski Club even renamed the big hill at St. Sauveur in honour of Currie, calling it Hill 70.

But the use of people and places from the war as a source of names did not stop there. In the 1920s and 1930s, wartime Battle-Class trawlers plied the waters off Canada's coasts. Most of these, such as the *Arras,* the *Givenchy,* and the *Loos,* worked as fisheries patrol vessels; four, the *Festubert,* the *Thiepval,* the *Ypres,* and the *Armentières,* were the strength of the Royal Canadian Navy. The practice of naming Legion branches after battles or heroes also began in the interwar period. Among the branches established in Nova Scotia were the Passchendaele Branch at Clark's Harbour and the Vimy Branch at Harmony. Canadians even named their children after places or people from the war. The roll of Royal Canadian Air Force dead from the Second World War includes thirty-five men who were named for British wartime prime minister David Lloyd George, eleven for Earl Kitchener, ten for Sir Douglas Haig, and seven for the Battle of Verdun. The list also includes such inspired choices as James Armistice Castle, Rupert Brooke Fraser, Richard St. Julien Gregory, Ferdinand Foch Mcneil, Robert Mons Rumble, and Vimy Ridge Vincent.

II

BUT THE SPIRIT OF THE WAR could be made to live on in other ways, and indeed keeping the faith demanded more active participation than merely adopting a battle's name for baby or boulevard. 'Let us bring pungent wreaths of balsam,' wrote Duncan Campbell Scott,

and tender
Tendrils of wild-flowers, lovelier for thy daring,
And deck a sylvan shrine, where the maple parts
The moonlight, with lilac bloom, and the splendour
Of suns unwearied; all unwithered, wearing
Thy valour stainless in our heart of hearts.[8]

As Scott recognized, the sacrifices of 1914-18 deserved the sort of tribute that could stand as tangible proof of a community's determination to remember. Many Canadians accepted the poet's advice, and the interwar era saw a burst of memorialization that was unparalleled in the nation's history.

There was tremendous variety in the responses to the challenge of memorializing the dead of the war. Communities of all sizes erected monuments of every conceivable design, including some that defy description and logic. One especially bizarre design exists in Campbellford, Ontario; a massive column with three huge orbs suspended from a cube-topped platform, it is less a war memorial than a monument to the ingenuity of the stonemason who assembled it. Agassiz, British Columbia, and Sintaluta, Saskatchewan, erected memorial halls, while Wainwright, Alberta, and

Kamloops opted for clock towers. The parishioners of Trinity Church in Cornwall, Ontario, restored the building's interior as a memorial to the members of the congregation who had not returned from the war. A group of Hamilton citizens suggested a memorial hospital situated beside a monumental plaza, to be known as the Glorious Court of Honour. The scheme was deemed over-ambitious, and the city erected instead a copy of Sir Edwin Lutyens's cenotaph in London, England. The Bank of Montreal erected two very different memorials, in its head offices in Montreal and Winnipeg. Both by American sculptor James Frazer, they are highly symbolic of their setting. In the austere and elegant Montreal building, Frazer placed a white marble figure of Victory. Winnipeg, the bustling metropolis that marked the beginning of the new West, received a sturdy and highly realistic infantryman decked out in full trench gear. Much to the dismay of local veterans, the gear was American.

Of course, if Sam Hughes had had his way, there would have been no variety at all. He proposed a standard, mass-produced memorial to be issued to local communities in different sizes, according to the number of casualties sustained during the war. In this way, people passing through a town could immediately determine if it had acquitted itself well during the war. *Saturday Night* also recommended central control of memorialization in the form of a national committee to direct the construction of local monuments. Because memorials should commemorate not just the soldier but the nation, only great artists were capable of executing them; according to the editor, average citizens could not hope to do an adequate job unaided. Ontario

The bizarre memorial in Campbellford, Ontario. Was it intended as a monument or an advertisement for the stonemason who erected it? (J. Peter Vance)

sculptors did indeed establish such a committee, the Ontario Advisory Committee on War Memorials, under the chairmanship of Ontario College of Art principal George A. Reid, but it disbanded in 1922 after three years of issuing advisory circulars. Not to be put off, Frances Loring (in her capacity as convener of the War Memorial Committee of the Ontario Society of Artists) took up the call for a national committee to give referrals to qualified sculptors, provide judges for design competitions, and assist with choosing suitable sites for memorials. Loring's greatest concern was evidently to poach some of the contracts being won by commercial funerary monument firms and to ensure that the province did not become dotted with bad memorials.[9]

Such suggestions to impose control over local memorialization might well be dismissed as artistic snobbery; at the very least, the good intentions were misguided. Certainly many Canadian memorials fail in an artistic sense, and the London *Free Press* was right to describe them as 'sculptural monstrosities ... [and] the last word in ugliness.'[10] But to look at them as artistic objects is to miss their point. Rather, they were intended to express the feeling of local communities towards the war they commemorated. Indeed, it is the naive sculpture, amateur construction, and often melodramatic images that make these memorials so appealing and so evocative of local sensibilities. As Michel Ragon wrote lovingly of French memorials, 'though the creation of jobbing workmen, they have been transformed into popular sculptures, corresponding to the majority taste of the population ... [T]hey also express a taste for the melodrama, for the fine gesture, for the bawdy song. There is a certain old-fashioned vulgarity about them that betrays their plebeian and petty-bourgeois origin.'[11] A locally commissioned monument, however garish or ill-conceived, said more about a community's memory of the war than any design foisted on citizens by a committee in Ottawa or Toronto could ever have done. Attempts at centralized control of memorialization were rightfully deplored, for this would have undermined the whole purpose of raising monuments to the war. As Major-General S.C. Mewburn, the minister of Militia and Defence, wrote, 'different locations should erect their own monuments and if that involves some difficulty they will value them all the more on that account.'[12]

Mewburn was certainly correct about the difficulty involved, and the initial decision to raise a memorial was by far the easiest part of the process. Most importantly, the local committee had to decide what form the memorial should take. Generally speaking, they could choose a utilitarian or an aesthetic memorial. The utilitarian response held that memorials should perform some function while commemorating the dead; they could be hospitals, community halls, schools, athletic centres, or anything else that increased the social wealth of the community. Proponents of the utilitarian approach held that merely to erect a cenotaph, something that served no social function, was a waste of money; far better to put the money into some facility that was used on a daily basis. Opponents believed that this was merely a cheap attempt to capitalize on public sentiment to build a facility that might not otherwise have been built. They believed that war memorials should serve one purpose and one purpose alone: to commemorate the dead. Anything that detracted from this goal lessened the force of the memorial. They also made the point, borne out by later experience, that such social utilities would inevitably become outdated and need replacing. The town's war memorial would then suffer the ignominious end of serving as a storage shed or, worse, being pulled down.

The aesthetic and utilitarian impulses, however, did not need to be mutually exclusive, and there were a number of successful attempts (like the Canadian Memorial Chapel in Vancouver) to bridge the gap between the two. Two other successful efforts are less well known. In April 1919, on the second anniversary of the Battle of Vimy Ridge, Senator William Dennis of Halifax approached the Board of Governors of Acadia University in Wolfville with a proposal. As a memorial to his son Captain Eric R. Dennis, who had been killed in action at Vimy, he offered the university the sum of $10,000 to purchase the personal library of J.P. Edwards, a noted collector of Canadiana.[13] The offer was gratefully accepted, and the Eric R. Dennis Collection of Canadiana came to Acadia, where it remains one of the finest collections of its kind in the country. As a war memorial, it is entirely fitting. Its shelves filled with Susanna Moodie, Thomas Chandler Haliburton, Sara Jeannette Duncan, and Charles Mair, the Dennis Collection contained the breadth of the Canadian experience. By allowing library patrons to appreciate the nation that had borne the war dead, as well as the heritage they fought to defend, the collection illuminated both the achievements and the potential of the people of Canada. In celebrating the past, it also pointed to the future.

In Saskatoon, the staff and students of Nutana District High School undertook a similar memorial. They conceived of a war memorial art collection to begin with twenty-nine works by Canadian artists, each dedicated to a former student who had been killed during the war. As the gallery catalogue recognized, 'this living memorial is providing a medium through which the spirit of our heroes may continue to participate in the life and ideals of our dear old school.'[14] The collection, which has continued to grow since its creation, was one of the first of its kind in Western Canada and established Saskatoon as a centre of Canadian art for decades.

The original collection was curiously eclectic, reflecting the artistic predilections of the principals who advised the students-cum-art patrons. Alfred Pyke, Nutana's principal during the war, purchased very traditional landscapes, quaint glimpses of Canadiana, and Edwardian character studies by established artists like F.M. Bell-Smith, Laura Muntz Lyall, and Robert Ford Gagen. Aldis Cameron, who replaced Pyke in 1923, was less well versed in the arts than his predecessor yet plunged head-first into the struggle between the conservative and the modern in the Canadian art world. His own inclination, encouraged by advice from A.Y. Jackson and Lawren Harris, took Cameron in a different direction, to works by less traditional painters like Fred Loveroff and James H. Henderson. In this way, he gave the collection the same breadth that characterized the Dennis Collection. It paid tribute to the heritage that underpinned the nation but also hinted at the potential for future growth. It, too, looked forward as well as backward.

The collections at Acadia and Nutana were inspired solutions to the problem of balancing aesthetic value with utility, but the form of a memorial could just as easily create problems. In Kitchener, Ontario, citizens argued the relative merits of a cenotaph or a carillon. The mothers of some of the city's war dead strongly opposed the idea of a carillon, insisting that a set of bells hidden away in a tower did not constitute a proper memorial, but the opposing faction maintained that the mothers' opinion should have no more weight than anyone else's. 'The memorial is not that of relatives of the soldiers,' wrote one observer. 'This is a community affair, something that will symbolize the respect of the citizens for the memory of the fallen.' In Yarmouth, Nova Scotia, citizens originally planned to raise a memorial for the entire county but could not agree on a monument or something utilitarian, such as a library, hospital, or day-care centre. Tired of waiting for the town to reach its decision, the surrounding settlements erected their own memorials.[15]

Even a well-organized committee like the one in Winnipeg could generate controversy. Toronto sculptor Elizabeth Wyn Wood and the German-born sculptor Emmanuel Hahn had met at the Ontario College of Art and were married shortly after. In 1924, Hahn (who had created one of the most copied war memorial figures in Canada) submitted a design to the first Winnipeg memorial competition. His entry, a fine cenotaph flanked by hooded figures, was praised not only by the assessors but by the other entrants, and easily captured the competition. Hahn's triumph, however, lasted only until community groups, led by veterans' organizations, the IODE, and the secretary of the Winnipeg Board of Trade, learned of his ethnic origins and had him disallowed. Three years later, the committee announced a second competition, and this time assessors unanimously chose Wood's design, a muscular male figure dressed in loin drapery and brandishing a sword. They judged it to be 'remarkable in its originality and, by its heroic proportions, bound to arrest the attention of the passer-by. It avoids the similarity of so many War Memorials already erected … The rugged execution of the dominant figure is outstanding, breathing as it were the spirit of the West with its strength and confidence, at the same time a memory of the past, emblematic of the spirit of those who answered their country's call.' The critical approval of the design, however, was not enough to overcome the fact that Wood was married to the German-born Hahn. The decision was overturned, and the contract awarded to Gilbert Parfitt of Winnipeg.[16]

Having chosen the design of the memorial, a committee then had to decide where to put it. Even this was not as easy as it sounded. The citizens of Saint John vigorously debated the location of their memorial: should it be in King Square at the head of King Street, or somewhere else in the square? Many townspeople felt its rightful place was at the head of King Street, but this would have necessitated moving the Woman's Christian Temperance Union's Loyalist fountain, something that was bound to raise hackles in the city. In Ottawa, competing interests squared off over the location of the National War Memorial. Mackenzie King wanted it downtown, on Connaught Place opposite the Chateau Laurier, but consultants and engineers maintained that it was too heavy for that location and would create insuperable traffic problems. Other people wanted it on Parliament Hill or away from the city centre altogether, on a site near the government's experimental farm, which would be called Flanders Field.[17]

Disputes over form and location inevitably meant delays, which in turn tested the patience of the townspeople. When construction of War Memorial Hall at the Ontario Agricultural College was put off again, disgruntled students threatened to start digging the foundation themselves. In Shelburne, Ontario, the townsfolk watched their council, the County Memorial Committee, and members of the local GWVA branch argue over the site, design, and cost of the proposed memorial. In a 1922 plebiscite, the citizens voted to install memorial gates on the town's cemetery, but local veterans blocked the wishes of the townspeople and forced council to accept their own proposal for the figure of an infantryman mounted on a plinth near the town hall.[18] The National War Memorial suffered more delays than almost any other. The contract was awarded to English sculptor Vernon March in 1925, but the finished monument was not unveiled until May 1939, over fourteen years later. A host of problems held up the project, including the government's difficulties in procuring the site, the addition of extra figures to satisfy the demands of critics, the enlargement of the arch, alterations to the steps, and the death of the sculptor in 1930.

Other memorials were delayed, altered, or cancelled altogether when financial considerations intervened. Elaborate plans for a Saskatchewan War Memorial Museum were eventually shelved when cost estimates overwhelmed the provincial government. The city of Brantford, Ontario, dedicated the major part of its cenotaph in 1933; there was not sufficient money, however, to pay for Walter Allward's figures, and the cenotaph remained devoid of sculpture until 1992. Windsor, Ontario, suffered an even more marked diminution of its plans over time. The original proposal, for a memorial subway under the Detroit River, was eventually dropped in favour of a more modest memorial community hall. Unable to get cooperation from neighbouring municipalities, the city then opted for a twenty-foot shaft topped by a Cross of Sacrifice, surrounded by four figures and bronze tablets listing battle honours and the names of the fallen. When the memorial was finally unveiled, all of the ornamentation had been dropped, leaving the city with a very simple cenotaph.[19]

The cenotaph in Windsor, Ontario, is simple and dignified but a far cry from the city's ambitious plans for a memorial subway under the Detroit River. (Jonathan F. Vance)

Such controversies and delays, irritating as they were to the local citizenry, were the exception rather than the rule. They involved only a few communities and should not obscure the fact that thousands of towns, churches, schools, businesses, and special interest groups erected memorials quickly and without undue difficulty. Indeed, Mewburn was correct in suggesting that the raising of a monument would draw a community together. One Regina paper observed that the campaign to erect a memorial cairn gave the citizens a singleness of purpose that they had not shared since 1918: 'the tenacity of purpose and "esprit de corps" which carried the Canadian boys through the long eventful years of the Great War was never more exemplified than during the past year.' The choice of a cairn was significant, for it lent itself particularly well to community involvement; each citizen could play a personal role in the construction simply by bringing a stone to add to the memorial.[20]

Regardless of the form chosen, the campaign to raise a monument often replicated the war experience by bringing together diverse elements of the community and directing their efforts towards a common cause. Of course, it is impossible to say with any certainty whether labourers had the same voice as members of the Canadian Club in any given campaign, but there does seem to have been a genuine effort to represent as many different groups as possible on memorial committees. The committee in Guelph included delegates from the Trades and Labour Council, the Young Men's and Young Women's Christian Associations, the Teachers' Association, the Independent Order of Foresters, the Men's and Women's Canadian Clubs, the Rotary Club, the Independent Labour Party, city council, and the Knights of Columbus. Nor was memorialization the sole preserve of local males, for as many as a third of Canada's civic war memorials were erected by women's organizations such as the IODE, Women's Canadian Clubs, and Women's Institutes.

How was it possible to achieve such unity and turn the energies of all segments of society to a single purpose? The answer lay in the virtual unanimity on the meaning of a memorial and the necessity of erecting one. The raising of a monument was an act of devotion, love, and gratitude, but it was also a test for the living; their response to the challenge of memorialization demonstrated their fidelity to the legacy of the fallen. 'If we do not

Residents of Red Deer, Alberta, watch Lord Byng unveil their war memorial, 15 September 1922. The area beside the platform appears to have been reserved for the relatives of the fallen. (Red Deer Archives)

adequately remember those who served,' said Sir Edmund Walker in 1918, 'and erect a memorial that will cause the students for generations to come to realize that this was a great moment in the history of the University [of Toronto] ... then we shall be absolutely unworthy of the brothers and sons of the fallen in this war.'[21]

In this way, the act of commemoration stood as public affirmation of the people's desire to keep the faith: the erection of a memorial was a tangible sign of the community's determination to remember the fallen and, by extension, the values for which they had died. In many cases, the sentiment was expressed through implicit or explicit references to 'In Flanders Fields.' The original design for the memorial in Windsor, for example, included life-size figures holding aloft a beacon light 'indicating that theirs is the duty of carrying on the glorious traditions left by those whom the monument honours.'[22] In other cities, bronze or stone torches decorated the memorial or its precincts. More frequently, monument inscriptions quoted or paraphrased McCrae, or included a reply to 'In Flanders Fields.' In this category can be placed the monuments at St. Stephen, New Brunswick, (Quiet they rest / In this high hope supreme / That we for whom they died / Shall keep the faith) and Langley, British Columbia, (If ye keep not faith we shall not sleep).

It was almost redundant to include such overt references to the obligation to the fallen. Everyone knew that the monument symbolized a commitment to keep the faith, so there was little need to write it in stone or bronze. The war memorial was a didactic object that at once instructed passers-by in the values of the war and affirmed the town's desire to ensure that those values were passed on. The notes for Mackenzie King's address in appreciation of the Canadian Battlefield Memorials Commission referred to monuments as 'an attempt, not merely to memorialize

This bronze torch on the memorial in Cornwall, Ontario, was a reminder of John McCrae's injunction to the living to keep the faith. (J. Peter Vance)

valour and sacrifice of men, but to catch spirit which prompted them. In the disillusionment of succeeding years tendency to forget the idealism which motivated our war efforts; Younger generations not old enough to remember this spirit; Memorials therefore assume new significance; to recapture the idealism; to teach this spirit to the young.'[23] Arthur Currie saw things in the same light: the dedication of memorials was 'a trumpet call to service for our fellow men and for our country. It is as if the voices of the dead called to us across the Great Divide bidding us to take courage and to toil for the ideals for which they fell.' As a Hamilton cleric wrote, his church's memorial stood 'just a few feet from a busy thoroughfare, teaching a lesson of self-sacrifice to a selfish world.'[24] It is not too much to suggest that the inscription on the Vancouver memorial ('Is it nothing to you, all ye that pass by?') was intended to shame people into pausing to consider whether their lives were worthy of the high example set by the fallen soldiers.

III

IMPORTANT AS IT WAS, erecting a war memorial was only a part of society's obligation to the memory of the war. A bronze soldier or stone cross did serve as a constant reminder of the sacrifice, yet there remained the possibility that some townsfolk might pass it by without pausing to ponder its significance. To supplement the granite cenotaph or bronze soldier, society required an annual observance that could ensure that the lessons of the war remained at the forefront of the public's consciousness. Armistice Day provided that occasion. Like so many other aspects of the war·myth, Armistice Day became a test of Canada's fidelity to the memory of the war, the day, according to the *Globe,* when Canada faced 'the judgement of her dead.'[25]

The observance of the anniversary of the Armistice had first been suggested in April 1919, when Isaac Pedlow, the member of Parliament for Renfrew South, proposed setting aside the second Monday of November as a 'perpetual memorial of the victorious conclusion of the recent war.' The following year, H.M. Mowat, representing the Toronto riding of Parkdale, put forth a motion that the Monday in the week of 11 November be called Armistice Day; Thanksgiving Day would be the same day. In 1921 the government stepped in and converted Mowat's motion into an Armistice Day bill. After minor discussion on the wording, it passed third reading on 23 May 1921.

For most of its first decade, Armistice Day stirred little controversy. It was guaranteed to fill the pews of local churches and bring together veterans at the cenotaph, yet it often passed with little comment. Like the first frost or the onset of spring thaw, it came, its significance was remarked upon, and it then passed into the unconscious for another year. In a sense, observing

Armistice Day became more a habit than anything. But that did not mean that it was taken lightly, and Canadians did not stand idly by when their November ritual came under attack in the late 1920s. While harried *Maclean's* workers tried to keep up with the demand for George Drew's 'The Truth about the War' and Arthur Currie fought his libel action, with the full sympathy of most observers, Armistice Day in Canada was about to experience a renaissance. With the myth of the war being assaulted from so many quarters, Canadians embraced 11 November as a way to demonstrate publicly their fidelity to that myth.

The revitalization of Armistice Day began in 1928, when prominent Canadian citizens came together to found the Armistice Ceremonial Committee of Canada (ACCC) to promote the observance of the day. The ACCC's executive roster included distinguished names from a range of organizations: Ernest Lapointe, later Mackenzie King's Québec lieutenant; Senator Raoul Dandurand, who coined the famous characterization of Canada as a fireproof house; former Québec premier Sir Lomer Gouin; Conservative leader and soon to be prime minister R.B. Bennett; Lady Julia Drum-

Toronto's cenotaph is barely visible beneath the wreathes laid to mark Armistice Day, 1924. (NAC PA86925)

mond, the noted Montreal philanthropist; prominent Jewish leader Rabbi F.M. Isserman; W.T. Kernahan of the Knights of Columbus; and Henrietta Wilson of the National Council of Women. One of the ACCC's priorities was to create a universal service to be used on 11 November; in doing so, the committee turned to elements that were already in general use across the country. The suggested order of service began with Harvey Gaul's anthem 'Chant for Dead Heroes' and included hymns that are now staples of Remembrance Day ceremonies, such as 'O God Our Help in Ages Past.' A passage from the book of Revelation describing the multitude of the Lamb of God (it had been echoed by Laurence Binyon in his famous poem 'For the Fallen') was suggested as a suitable text. The proposed order of service was widely distributed, going out to 600,000 Canadian homes as a newspaper supplement in November 1928.

The formation of the ACCC, however, was only the first step in reinvigorating Armistice Day. More than a standard service was required to observe the occasion fittingly, thought many Canadians. The combination of Thanksgiving and Armistice Day stood in the way of this: there was a time for giving thanks and a time for remembering the dead of the war, but to attempt both on the same day merely clouded the issue. As Armistice Day 1930 approached, an alliance of veterans, women's groups, political clubs, and municipalities deluged the federal government with demands for an end to the combined observance. Against this impressive array of support, a small group of chambers of commerce and city councils opposed any change in the present practice, apparently concerned that if the days were split, workers would have to be paid for an extra holiday. The Legion and its supporters carried this first battle, and in June 1931 royal assent was given to legislation making Armistice Day a separate holiday and changing its name to Remembrance Day.

Soon, though, a more fundamental question came under debate: should Remembrance Day be a holiday at all? Those who answered in the negative recalled Armistice Day 1919, which had not been a statutory holiday. On that occasion, King George V had asked all British subjects to observe two minutes of silence at 11:00 AM. In the imperial capital, the response was astonishing: all traffic paused, power was cut to trollies, factories ceased operations, and pedestrians in the street stopped and removed their hats. For many people who reflected on Armistice Day, this simple yet powerful act in the middle of a normal business day was an ideal observance. Were Armistice Day a holiday, its meaning would soon be lost, as *Saturday Night* pointed out: 'The threats to "compel" observance were nauseating, and we do not believe that the public men who urged this course were moved by any real sentiment with regard to the fallen. They were merely making a bid for the soldier votes ... [W]hat percentage of those who took a holiday paid any attention to the observance it was supposed to promote?'[26] Obviously a very small percentage, implied the editor.

Not everyone was so sceptical, and when the government began to consider amending the Remembrance Day Act in 1932, the opposition against removing the day from the schedule of holidays remounted. The Legion encouraged its members to express their displeasure to their members of Parliament, and the National Council of Women, local trades and labour councils, and patriotic societies all made their feelings known to the government.[27] A Prince Edward Islander captured his thoughts in a poem entitled 'One Single Day':

> Who are these men who grudge the dead
> One day a year – and would offer instead
> Only two minutes? O who are they
> That we should listen to what they say?
>   ... ungrateful are we
> If one Remembrance Day is not kept free
> From our selfish toil, and our selfish gain,
> Then learned we the lessons of war in vain
> And it may be if we soon forget
> That another lesson awaits us yet.

In October 1932 ex-soldiers in Toronto formed the Remembrance Day Committee of Associated Veterans to ensure the proper observance of the day. Far from having it removed from the calendar of holidays, they sought to have Thanksgiving removed and placed on a weekend so that there could be no more opposition to a holiday on Remembrance Day. In the end, both holidays remained on the schedule.[28]

This three-year debate was significant for the simple reason that it was not about the value of observing Armistice Day; people on both sides of the controversy eagerly affirmed its value. Rather, the debate was about the form of observance that would have the most impact in encouraging Canadians to ponder the sacrifice of the fallen. Ironically, the best tonic for Armistice Day turned out to be those few people who opposed it altogether. When in the early 1930s certain pacifist groups suggested that the observance of Armistice Day be ended because it perpetuated militarism, they inadvertently galvanized support for the object of their attacks. The Reverend T.W. Jones told the congregation of Calvary Church in Montreal that those people who called for an end to the observance of Armistice Day should be branded 'traitors to the cause.' 'When humanity ceased to place wreathes on cenotaphs,' said a Kitchener cleric, 'mankind would be deteriorating and below the standards of the men who died in France.'[29]

The best indication of a determination to defend Armistice Day against all naysayers, however, was not the utterances of clergymen but the burgeoning support for the day. With Canada's memory under attack by American versions of history, by the Port Hope *Evening Guide,* and by the antiwar critique of Remarque and Harrison, growing numbers of Canadians turned to Armistice Day as a way to demonstrate that they had not been seduced by an alternative interpretation of events. Further exercised by the pacifist criticism of the ceremony and by the efforts of the ACCC, they made 11 November as important in the 1930s as it had been in 1919.

In 1930, Woodstock, Niagara Falls, and Oshawa, Ontario, set attendance records for Armistice Day ceremonies, while the crowd in Smith's Falls topped 3,000, or roughly half the town's population. That same year, Arthur Meighen's birthplace of St. Mary's, a town of fewer than 4,000, attracted over 2,000 people to its service. The following year, Calgary witnessed the largest patriotic gathering held in the city since the end of the war. In 1932, Private A.L. Bergeron of Chicoutimi took it upon himself to organize the first Armistice Day ceremony ever held in the town. He secured the attendance of two local war heroes and (according to his claim) as many as 2,500 others.[30] In mid-decade, attendance records were still falling. The 1935 service in Toronto drew 50,000 spectators, and the Toronto Transit Commission cut all power to its line for two minutes at 11:00 AM.

The Women's International League for Peace and Freedom leads a small peace march in Toronto, Armistice Day, 1935. (City of Toronto Archives, Globe and Mail Collection 38447)

Montreal's Dominion Square also hosted the largest ever Remembrance Day crowd in 1935; there, the entire city's power connection was interrupted for two minutes at the eleventh hour. On the Prairies, Saskatoon and North Battleford reported attendance records in 1936. The final Remembrance Day before the next war drew larger crowds still. Over 10,000 people turned out for Edmonton's service, more than twice as many as the previous year. It was the same in Vancouver, Toronto, and Halifax – in virtually every city in the country, 11 November 1938 saw the peak of Remembrance Day observance in Canada.[31]

What had Remembrance Day come to mean by 1938? Certainly the services of that year were tinged by feelings of gratitude at the recent conclusion of the Munich Agreement, which bought the world another twelve months of peace. But it was more than that. The eleventh of November had become a ritual, a symbolic act intended to focus the thoughts of observers on the war's sacrifice. As a typical ritual, Armistice Day did not commemorate the actualities of the war, or even the deaths of soldiers in battle. Instead, it commemorated the version of the war that existed in Canada's collective memory. In short, it became a public statement of the myth of Canada's war.

The official Armistice Day ceremony in 1935 drew an immense crowd to the cenotaph in front of City Hall in Toronto. (City of Toronto Archives, Globe and Mail Collection 38441)

Armistice Day observances invariably included hymns that strongly emphasized the religious interpretation of the war. Standards like 'God of Our Fathers,' 'O Valiant Hearts,' and 'O God Our Help in Ages Past' reminded worshippers that God had fought on the Allied side, and they affirmed that the war had been a simple struggle between good and evil. This focus on the triumph of good over evil, rather than the traditional Christian tenet of reconciliation that might have followed the war, gave Armistice Day ceremonies a very particular character.[32] A service built around 'Onward Christian Soldiers' and a sermon on Paul's second letter to Timothy ('Thou therefore endure hardness, as a good soldier of Jesus Christ') commemorated, not the death of young men in war, but the sacrifice of young men in a good and just cause.

This is not to say that Armistice Day ceremonies did not take on overtones of peace, especially when the possibility of another war began to loom large. In 1936, Mackenzie King's official Armistice Day address began with seven lines on remembering the dead of the Great War and five lines on the horror of war in general; the rest of the speech was devoted to the need to preserve peace. When in 1938 the National Council of Women and the

Mackenzie King lays a wreath at the Peace Tower in Ottawa on Remembrance Day, 1937. Despite King's desire to emphasize peace, the ceremony obviously retained a strong military character. (NAC PA127563)

Canadian Legion proposed to observe Remembrance Day as a day of thanksgiving for peace, in the wake of the Munich crisis, the prime minister found it an 'exceedingly good idea.'[33] As the 1930s drew to a close, more and more clerics used Armistice Day as an excuse to look forward, towards the danger of another war, instead of back at the war that was ostensibly being commemorated.

This growing emphasis on peace had to compete with the militarism of the occasion. Since the early 1920s, services had invariably included strong contingents from local militia and permanent force units, and the Armistice Night ball, a fixture of many a city's social calendar through the 1920s, was often little more than a celebration of the military arts. In Calgary in 1921, guests passed through a triumphal arch decorated with machine guns and bayonets into a ballroom festooned with Union Jacks, the crests of units that had served overseas, and 'swords and other trophies of war ... cleverly worked into the scheme of decoration.'[34] Ten years later, the Armistice Night program at the Canadian National Exhibition stadium in Toronto was more a garrison display than an observance; it included a display of officers' horse jumping, a tug of war, and a march past of all units in the Toronto garrison.

Even as international tensions mounted and Canadians hoped more fervently than ever for peace in their time, such hopes did not diminish the military tenor of Armistice Day. So much was clear to a Vancouver editor who observed the last ceremony of the interwar period: 'It seemed as though they rededicated themselves to peace. But there was present, too, the anomaly that is with every display of military strength. That strange, prideful stirring in the heart when bands play and fine young men march to their martial strain.' The year before, the *Edmonton Journal* had noted that 'cheery martial music and the brisk sound of marching feet offset the depressing influence of cloudy skies.'[35] It also, evidently, offset the depressing influence of the pacifists, for the military character of the ceremonies reaffirmed the soldier as the only true pacifist. When Mackenzie King decided in 1935 that parading military units should salute the Peace Tower instead of the prime minister's reviewing stand, as had been the practice in the past, there was no inherent contradiction in his suggestion.[36] The soldier was the guardian, even the servant, of peace, so it was only natural for him to salute a symbol of peace rather than the head of government.

The calls raised against the militarism of Armistice Day observances were voices crying in the wilderness, simply because such calls missed the point. In 1929, Archbishop A.U. de Pencier thought nothing about donning his wartime chaplain's uniform to read the bible lesson in Vancouver. Nine years later, at the same time as children from Vancouver and New Westminster were walking to the Washington State boundary to meet American children at the International Peace Arch, a full-scale military parade was under way in downtown Vancouver.[37] Neither of these incidents elicited any adverse comment in the mainstream press, because there was no inherent contradiction in them. Both reflected a recognition that the soldier was a true servant of peace.

As it evolved through the interwar years, Armistice Day became an affirmation of the myth of the war. The eleventh of November was a day to pay tribute to the men and women who had laid down their lives in a just cause and to reflect upon the nobility of the sacrifices made for Christianity and Western civilization. It was not an occasion to wonder if Canadian soldiers had died needlessly or to recall that many of them had suffered dreadfully in the trenches. It may have been a day to pray for peace, but it was not a day for pacifism. On the contrary, it was a day to honour those people who had been willing to fight for peace.

IV

BUT WAS OBSERVING Armistice Day enough? 'Can we in sheltered ease by mumbled prayers,' queried Charles W. Gordon, 'by vacuous requiems for the dead, / Keep in red flame alive that fiery Torch?' Many Canadians thought not. 'We shall not regard that action [laying wreathes on memorials each Armistice Day] as fulfilling our whole duty to our heroic dead,' said the Reverend E.J. McCorkell in 1930.[38] Paying due tribute to the sacrifice required more than donating a few dollars to the war memorial fund or turning up at the cenotaph every November. The only way to render adequate tribute was to complete the task that the soldiers had gone to Flanders to begin, by ensuring that the war was indeed the progenitor of good. Failure to do so reduced the deaths of 60,000 Canadians and the suffering of untold others to utter meaninglessness. 'If your sons, your brothers, only died, it means nothing,' said the Reverend S. Buchanan-Carey:

> Calvary itself means nothing. But if from their deaths as from the death of God on Calvary, we get a new vision of life, a view of sacrifice that inspires us to nobler living, then their deaths were not in vain ... God did not waste them, He called them to a higher service than we know. They have become a part of the splendor of the race that will thrill us to the end of time ... They, like Christ himself, are the messengers of God to us, telling us that life is to be lived in utter selflessness.

The crusade had not ended in 1918 with the defeat of imperial Germany; on the contrary, the war's conclusion only raised the stakes and made it even more imperative that its goals be realized. 'The ideals for which they fought and died,' wrote Halifax journalist Harold Ross in 1937, 'are a bequest to us, a trust which it is treachery to betray.'[39]

To realize those lofty ideals, Canadians had to start at home by putting their efforts towards building a better nation. The country could not be allowed to slide back into the old habits of dissent, suspicion, and greed that the crusade had banished. 'Die to the little hatreds; die to greed; / Die to the old ignoble selves we knew; / Die to the base contempts of sect and creed,' urged Ontario Supreme Court Justice W.R. Riddell in 1926. In their place must be 'the great principles of justice, freedom and fair dealing.'[40] The only kind of Canada worthy of the war's sacrifice was a generous and law-abiding Canada that was free of irreligion, infidelity, and the 'withering curse of materialism.' The nation's war dead had given their lives to teach their compatriots how to live; unless people heeded that lesson, the fallen could not sleep in Flanders Fields.[41]

Many Canadians, however, apparently had not followed the example of the fallen, and the country had indeed returned to the base contempts that Riddell had warned about. 'Those wonderful chaps died that we might "carry on,"' wrote Oliver Hezzelwood, 'and we who are left are shrieking "dollars" and "strikes" and "distrust the other nation" so loudly that the voice of the dead is lost.'[42] The disillusionment that the average citizen felt with postwar Canada was captured in a poem read at the dedication of the memorial in Priceville, Ontario, in 1921:

> We thought to catch the torch ye threw,
> And to the charge ye left – be true;
> But once the strife of arms was past
> Then high resolves were overcast
> With selfish greed. And lust to gain
> Has put to flight the sweet, sad pain
> Of sacrifice. And in its train
> Went noble deeds. Are ye aghast?
> In Flanders' fields.[43]

For the editor of a Halifax paper, a unique opportunity had been lost: 'The war brought out the finest sentiments of the Race. The aftermath is a return of all that shrivelled in the face of a common cause ... We are getting back to ... that ruthless and unthinking strife for the things that are neither permanent, nor important, – nor kind.'[44]

The bitterness at the return to old ways was keenest for ex-soldiers. Will Bird offered a lament for dashed hopes: 'We see – not the world of our early visions and high resolve – but a world first absorbed in riotous pleasure-seeking, followed by the bitter struggle for the very means of existence.' Too often, the loser in that struggle was the ex-soldier, reduced to 'plead[ing] hopelessly with soul-less powers who renege their promises made, who grind these broken veterans to starvation, shame and suicide.'[45] A poem in a British Columbia veterans' publication included a dialogue between two soldiers who in France had dreamt of a time without greed, folly, or war. Their dreams, however, had been shattered:

> Graft and corruption, poverty and shame,
> And patronage in all its bane we saw,
> And heartless profiteers, sucking the very blood
> From those we left behind to tender care.

'Al Pat,' another soldier-poet, set his conversation in heaven, between two dead soldiers who had asked to use St. Peter's telephone to call earth and see how things were going there. When Peter tells them that earth is going to pieces, they are crushed: 'They've "broken faith" with us m'lad, and now we *cannot rest.*'[46]

Similar echoes of McCrae's poem ran through many veterans' reflections on the peace. Edgar McInnis wrote a sad lament called 'Requiem for a Dead Warrior' that offered little comfort to the soul of a fallen comrade:

The disappointment of veterans with postwar Canada is evident in this march of unemployed ex-soldiers at Thanksgiving, 1920. (City of Toronto Archives, James Collection 903)

Sleep on, brave heart. Our cause is ours no longer
The world rolls on without our aid.
We fought for right, but hate and fear are stronger
We dreamed of peace, and dreams have been betrayed.[47]

The poetry of Robert T. Anderson, an Alberta veteran, is less polished than McInnis's but no less powerful. 'They fed us high on Glory / That lures men on to war,' he wrote in his poem 'Comrades of the War Years,' but the lure had tarnished quickly. The return to Canada had brought nothing but misfortune for ex-soldiers:

And home – Where ye had longed for
    New forces walk the street
Dejected ones – old comrades
    Who now must face defeat.

Anderson promised that he and his fellow veterans would try to hold the torch high but admitted that their hearts were not entirely in the task. 'But can we see old comrades / About us here go down?' he wondered.[48] In both of these poems, there is a veiled reference to McCrae's theme. McInnis's betrayed dreams and Anderson's shattered hopes indicate that Canada had indeed broken faith with those who died.

The vision of 'old comrades who now must face defeat' was as painful to Arthur Currie as it was to the rankers who served under him. In an Armistice Day address that he never gave because of illness, he wondered 'has the world – has our country – in the fifteen years since the Armistice kept its promised faith with the unreturning dead? Has the great sacrifice really turned to glory – the glory of a better time?' Sadly, Currie concluded that the faith had not been kept: 'Bitterness and hate, selfishness and greed are still entrenched in our social, economic and political life.'[49] Postwar Canada had become a land unworthy of its heroes.

Each of these veterans knew where to pin the blame for this state of affairs: not upon the leaders who had managed the war, but upon those who had mismanaged the peace. The culprits were not the dull general and the greedy profiteer of the war years, but the men who had dishonoured the fallen by their inexcusable conduct after the Armistice. 'There was no hatred at the Front,' said Andrew Macphail in 1936. Postwar discontents emerged from the peace, not the war; the evils of the 1920s and 1930s were not born on the Somme and at Passchendaele, but at Versailles. 'So you went to make the "world safe for democracy," did you?' wrote the poet and ex-soldier Eric Goulding to John Daniel Logan. 'So, of course, did I. We now have the pleasure of watching at our leisure the politicians trying to make it safe for nothing at all.' The world had been given a fresh start on 11 November 1918, wrote Leslie Roberts. 'What have our leaders done about it?'[50] Very little, in Roberts's view, and he devoted an entire book, entitled bitterly *So This Is Ottawa,* to describing the shortcomings of Canada's leaders in the postwar decades.

The outlook appeared grim, but Canadians had no shortage of remedies for what ailed the nation. William Irvine believed that the only alternative to social revolution was the abolition of party politics and the institution of a system of group government and proportional representation. From his farm in Paris, Ontario, W.C. Good preached the gospel of tariff abolition in favour of a tax on land values.[51] C.W. Peterson's wake-up call to the nation included suggestions for repairing virtually every aspect of Canadian life, from fixed terms for senators to subsidies for military bands. For Stephen Leacock, the answer to the riddle of social justice was greater state responsibility for the welfare of the individual.[52] Single taxers, One Big Unionists, social gospellers – postwar Canada was filled with armchair philosophers, each with a panacea for transforming the nation into a land worthy of its heroes.

For many Canadians, the remedy was closer than some dubious theory of economic readjustment or social organization. To put the nation on the proper course, Canada need look no further than the spirit that withstood the gas attack at Ypres in 1915 and stormed up Vimy Ridge on Easter Monday 1917. Only the example of the Canadian Corps could elevate the nation to a level where it was worthy of the fallen. In contrast to the unnatural economic and class divisions that rent society, the spirit of the corps was an organic communion based on the innate worth of the individual. Tolerance, unity, devotion to duty, fair play, the sharing of burdens – these had been the watchwords of the CEF. Only by uniting in a common cause had the corps taken and held Vimy Ridge; only through a spirit of tolerance and cooperation had its soldiers endured the horrors of Passchendaele. No Canadians were better suited than veterans to instil these qualities in society. Because they were at once the only legitimate interpreters of the war experience and the only direct link to the fallen, they alone could reanimate the spirit of the Canadian Corps for the good of the nation.

In 1917, J.O. Miller had predicted that 'the inspiration and the impetus for the coming years [will] find their vitality in the unselfish service and unstinted sacrifice of [the nation's] sons upon the battlefields of France and Flanders.'[53] These men would be 'the moulders of the world's thought' in the postwar years because 'they have seen the realities. They have found out the real values in life.' C.W. Peterson agreed: '[The veteran] represents all that is finest and best and noblest in our national life ... He has wandered through the valley of the shadow of death and has unconsciously imbibed wisdom, tolerance and higher aim from the very source of the fountain of life.'[54] The soldier had emerged from the purifying fire of Flanders in a finer form and stood ready to act as an example for Canadians struggling to find the true path. In the battles to come, in the fields of Saskatchewan, the factories of Ontario, and the churches of Nova Scotia, only he could help Canada realize its full potential. If the nation was to become 'the land without peer' that many Canadians confidently expected, veterans, 'having borne the load / On Flanders Fields, once more must bear it here, / To make for righteousness a sure abode.' The nation's greatness lay in the future, boomed Oliver Hezzelwood. 'Our returned men will be the ones to lead us over the top and on to our objectives.'[55]

It was a task that many ex-soldiers professed to relish. 'Let us set our faces steadfastly toward the goal of a sober, clean and pure life, as we did set our faces toward Vimy, Passchendaele and Cambrai,' wrote a New Brunswick veteran soon after his return home. Victor Odlum informed the demobilizing troops of a British Columbia battalion that 'the future influence of the old 7th in the homeland should be as great as has been its past fighting efficiency in France and Flanders.'[56] Not even the disappointments of the immediate postwar years or the strains of the Depression shook the faith of ex-soldiers that they could act as shock troops for Canada. On the contrary, as the nation stumbled and faltered through the 1920s and 1930s, it only confirmed the dire need for their leadership. 'The equally great adventure of Peace still lies before us,' proclaimed the history of an artillery brigade in 1928, 'and demands from us those same qualities which made the "Old Fourth" a source of pride to us all.' Victoria Cross winner Edward Bellew made a similar remark at an Armistice Day ceremony five years later: 'As we helped our country in the days of bitter and anxious strife, so we can help her now in these present days of worry and disorder, unrest and suffering. The memory of a great national vision can renew our strength and raise the whole standard of our values.'[57]

EDWARD BELLEW had pinpointed the very medicine that Canada needed. It was not the veteran per se but what he represented that could lead the nation out of its slough of despond. By focusing on his example, Canadians would focus on the 'great national vision' that could be their salvation. The country's collective memory of the war, as personified in the ex-soldier, was the guiding light for a society that had lost its way. It taught lessons of co-operation, tolerance, selflessness, and unity, and Canada never had more need of such teachings. Keeping the faith, then, meant perpetuating the spirit of service and sacrifice that had animated the Canadian Corps. In 1937, Milton Gregg predicted that only with the 'spirit of high enthusiasm and of dangerous living' that characterized the Canadian Corps could 'our country become what ... all of us thought it was going to be in 1919.'[58] This was precisely the message that Canadians needed to hear. If the courage and selflessness that soldiers had shown on the battlefield could be shown by civilians every day of their lives, the nation would indeed be worthy of the men and women who had given their lives in the crusade. If the mythicized version of Canada's war, at once didactic, humbling, and inspirational, remained at the forefront of the public consciousness, the nation's future knew no bounds.

CHAPTER 8

To Found a Country

Sometimes I'm not even sure that I have a country.

But I know they stood there at Ypres
the first time the Germans used gas,
that they were almost the only troops
in that section of the front
who did not break and run ...

And that's ridiculous, too, and nothing
on which to found a country.
        Still
it makes me feel good, knowing
that in some obscure, conclusive way
they were connected with me
and me with them.

Alden Nowlan, 'Ypres, 1915'

I N 1910, a journalist asked a number of prominent writers for their
views on Canadian literature. L.M. Montgomery, who had done as much as
anyone to show Canada to the world, replied that the nation 'has not yet
fused her varying elements into a harmonious whole. Perhaps she will not
do so until they are welded together by some great crisis of storm and
stress. That is when a real national literature will be born.' Reflecting upon
those comments in 1919, she wrote that the generation born of the war
years would produce that real national literature.[1]

Montgomery shared this view with many other members of the
literati. B.K. Sandwell, Thomas O' Hagan, William Douw Lighthall, M.O.
Hammond – all believed that Canadian culture would be invigorated by the
trial of war. For Lighthall, the impact of the war was incalculable. The finest

Canadian verse was not the nature poetry of the Laurentian school or the work of the Confederation poets, but the war poems of McCrae, Trotter, and Stead: 'No other verse is more bathed in the blood and agony of bitter struggle; none speaks from a soul of more uncompelled and undiluted chivalry; and none proceeds specifically from our Canadian point of view, and so to speak courses directly in our national veins.' For Lighthall, poetry was proof that the war as a constructive force had no equal in Canadian history, not even in 1867: 'as the war is a greater, wider, nobler event for us than Confederation, its influence will be so much the stronger.'[2] Confederation was merely an administrative arrangement between a handful of politicians interested largely in ending provincial deadlock. The Great War was much more. As Canadians remembered it from the 1920s and 1930s, it was a crusade that rallied the nation in defence of Western civilization and Christianity. Those men and women who took up the challenge in 1914 were true national heroes, at once standing apart from society and embodying the essence of the country. This made the war a rare moment in the nation's history, a time when Canadians were at one with their destiny.

This conception gave the memory of the war inestimable potential. If people embraced the conception of the war as a unifying force in Canadian life, that conception could do more than just rejuvenate the country's cultural life; it could rid Canada of sectionalism, dissent, and discord. 'Racial passions, appetites for domination, ignorance, cowardice, materialistic ideals, will receive strong shocks from the forces of the new crusade,' predicted Lighthall. The memory of the war could act as a citizenship primer for children and immigrants, providing a means of Canadianization unlike any other. It could even reconcile the seemingly unreconcilable and forge the basis of unity between Canada's founding peoples. In doing so, the myth of the war would achieve what Confederation had not yet been able to do, for one simple reason: Confederation was merely a political incident. The Great War was a national force.

I

MANY CANADIANS REALIZED early in the war that a great opportunity stood before them. For George Foster, 1914 was a unique time in the life of the country: never before had he encountered the feeling 'that we were one in the same sense as at this hour of our history.' Speaking at the Canadian Club of Winnipeg in December, Sir Robert Borden observed that the first four months of war had brought 'an awakened national spirit and consciousness in this Dominion.'[3] The unity of August 1914 was indeed impressive, for the declaration of war had drawn Canadians together across social, political, religious, and ethnic divisions. Even Henri Bourassa gave his support to the war in August 1914.

As the war progressed, Bourassa and other Québec nationalists grew disillusioned and turned against the crusade. But few people lamented the departure of such fair-weather friends, and the belief that the war offered a unique opportunity for Canada only deepened. There was tremendous interest in the benefits that the war would bring, and articles with titles like 'Canada's Mighty Gains' rhapsodized over the developing national identity that was being fostered by the war. In his influential and widely read book *The German Tragedy and Its Meaning for Canada,* Robert Falconer wrote that it meant more to be a Canadian after the Second Battle of Ypres than it had before. 'A new birth-song for Canada is already filling the sky,' wrote Lintern Sibley in 1915, and the stirring strains of that song caught the hearts of countless people, soldier and civilian alike. 'I'm much more of a Canadian now than I ever was,' Frank Underhill wrote to his mother in September 1917.[4]

Deeply rooted in the Canadian consciousness by the time of the Armistice, the idea that the war meant nothing less than the birth of the nation flourished afterwards. No one could deny that the Canadian contribution to the Allied victory had brought new recognition on the international stage. The war, thought Montreal journalist Frederic Yorston, had been Canada's 'supreme chance to spring magnificently into the ranks of the free nations.'[5] To its eternal glory, the country had grasped the opportunity and made the most of it. It became a truism to assert that Canada gained its status as a nation through the heroism shown by its soldiers on the battlefield. 'Le pays a bénéficié, par la guerre, d'une réputation qui n'a pas peu contribué à créer la place enviée qu'il occupe maintenant sur les marchés du monde,' observed Colonel J.H. Chabelle. The Great War had truly been a journey from colony to nation by way of Flanders. 'Four hundred thousand bayonets,' boomed Chubby Power, 'had written the name of Canada large and broad over the face of Europe and the world.'[6]

That formal, international recognition was only an outward manifestation of something more important: the awakening of a national consciousness. This was not unique to Canada but was paralleled in the other self-governing dominions of the empire. If the Great War had been an Australian epiphany during which the country came to know itself, as official historian C.E.W. Bean declared, and if New Zealand's consciousness was born out of the dust and heat of Gallipoli, then Canada became aware of itself in Flanders, Picardy, and Artois. 'The war marked the beginning of a new epoch in the history of Canada,' wrote Burton Hurd in 1928. It 'rid the public mind of the incubus of an insidious inferiority complex. From 1914 dates a new tradition, a new sense of power, a new spirit of confidence.' By the sacrifices of the fallen, said J.L. Ralston at the unveiling of the Halifax war memorial, 'there has been breathed into the formal verbiage of a legal constitution, a national spirit, a national pride, a national consciousness.'[7] W.D. Lighthall's assumption is implicit here: Confederation had merely provided the political and administrative structure of the nation; the Great War had given it life.

Signs of this re-created country were everywhere. The burst of nationalism that followed the war spawned dozens of organizations and publications dedicated to expressing uniquely Canadian viewpoints. Periodicals like *Canadian Forum,* the *Canadian Historical Review,* and *Canadian Bookman* were founded so that Canadian observers could debate Canadian issues for a Canadian audience. Organizations like the Canadian League (later the Canadian Institute of International Affairs), the revitalized Canadian Clubs, and the Canadian National Parks Association served the same purpose. Academics like Frank Underhill, Harold Innis, and Arthur Lower returned from active service with a heightened sense of nationalism. Underhill might have spoken for any of them when he called the war 'the visible demonstration that there has grown up on her [Canada's] soil a people not English nor Scottish nor American but Canadian – a Canadian nation.'[8]

Those people who believed that the war had almost single-handedly fashioned a national consciousness saw in the war tremendous potential as a constructive force in the life of the country. Just as the spirit of the trenches could be utilized to make Canada into a land fit for heroes, so too could the broader story of Canada's war effort be mobilized for the national good. It came to be the answer to Canada's problems, be they social, economic, political, or racial. It was at once an object lesson, a source of inspiration, and a focus for unity; it was the magic elixir that could cure the country of any ill.

The heritage of the war could, for example, defeat the subversive elements that menaced postwar society. Having vanquished the armies of the kaiser in the field, the Canadian Corps could turn its attention to 'the enemies within our Dominion, the paid agitator who would seek to disrupt the Empire, and upset all recognized authority.' There was no need to identify those enemies specifically. When a Toronto poet summoned home the spirits of the war dead to defend Canada 'from future threatening broil,' her readers would have nodded knowingly, fully aware that Bolsheviks, unionists, leftists, and a host of other undesirables were poised to infiltrate Canada. They would also have been aware that facing down the threat was part and parcel of honouring the fallen. As a Kitchener editor wrote, 'cherishing the memory and the example of our heroes who defeated the most powerful military machine in history ... Canada will defeat revolution as she has defeated militarism – so will our mother Canada honour her dead sons.'[9]

Naturally, veterans would stand in the vanguard of this movement to purge the nation of undesirables. 'There are no Bolsheviki soldiers in Canada,' declared the president of the Calgary GWVA in 1919. A military intelligence officer in British Columbia agreed, predicting that in the event of social unrest, 'the returned soldier would be the asset of the Government to clean up the situation at home.' Indeed, many Canadians believed that the very notion of a radical veteran was inconceivable. 'It is grotesquely absurd,' intimated the Fredericton *Gleaner,* 'to suppose that the returned soldiers have any sympathy whatever with the forces of disorder ... The veterans are not trouble makers anywhere; rather they are the soundest bulwark of the nation.'[10] Throughout the interwar period, this refrain was repeated at every opportunity. Armistice Day was seen as a chance for ex-soldiers, and indeed 'every stable and Patriotic element,' to stand firm 'in the face of subversive influences.' William Mulock took advantage of the dedication of the heroes' grove in Toronto's Coronation Park in 1938 to remind the crowd that neither left nor right extremism would find a foothold in Canada while the spirit of the Canadian Corps lived on.[11] At every turn, the potentially unruly were reminded that the memory of the war remained a powerful antidote to disruption.

Yet it was not always so simple to invoke the war as a bulwark against unrest. During the Winnipeg General Strike of 1919, the Returned Soldiers' Loyalist Association often faced soldier-strikers on the streets of the Manitoba capital. Determining precisely how many veterans supported each side, however, is less important than recognizing the effort that both sides made to claim that they spoke for the veteran community. In the House of Commons, Ernest Lapointe and Peter McGibbon argued over whether the majority of veterans supported or opposed the strike. Supporters of the Citizens' Committee of One Thousand could point to the decision of the Winnipeg GWVA to abandon its position of neutrality and place itself on the side of the authorities. Those ex-soldiers who remained with the strikers were dismissed as pretenders who had not served at the front or as gullible pawns who, as Ralph Connor put it in a novel that transformed Winnipeg into the Ontario industrial town of Blackwater, 'fell easy prey to unscrupulous leaders and were being exploited in the interests of all sorts of fads and foolish movements.'[12]

Strike leaders, on the other hand, maintained that a majority of veterans (perhaps as many as 80 per cent, according to Major G.W. Andrews, the MP for Winnipeg Centre) backed the demands of labour. They cited the 4 June demonstration at the Manitoba legislative building when 3,000 veterans demanded that the government pass a compulsory collective bargaining act, or the proposal put forth by a group of soldier-strikers that the city police take down its Great War roll of honour until the police force had been restored to its rightful position without prejudice. Indeed, the *Western Labour News* devoted considerable effort to demonstrating that most returned soldiers belonged to the working class and to winning over any waverers in the ranks of veterans.[13]

Ironically, in staking these claims, both sides were in fact arguing from the same assumption: that the voice of the veteran community could be the decisive factor in the strike. If the Citizens' Committee could keep veterans on side, the strike was doomed; if labour could prove that it spoke for ex-soldiers, the achievement of collective bargaining and a living wage was assured. In this respect, both capital and labour accepted that the soldier, and the memory of the war he represented, had the potential to banish unrest from Canada. The Citizens' Committee and its supporters contended that any form of revolution, even the most modest, constituted an assault on Anglo-Canadian values that was no different than the kaiser's attack of 1914. Potential revolutionaries would soon realize that the soldiers who had faced up to that threat would respond as resolutely to all subsequent threats. Seeing that any attempts at reform were rendered impotent by the memory

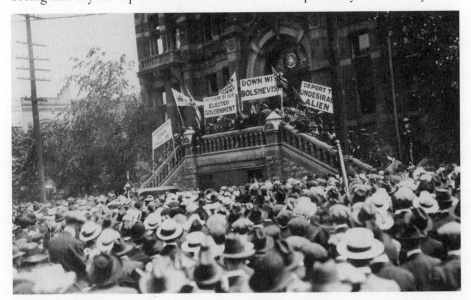

Veterans mobilize to defend authority during the Winnipeg General Strike. The banner on the left reads 'Canadian Corps Fall In.' (Provincial Archives of Manitoba, Winnipeg Strike 5, Neg. no. N12296)

of the war, agitators would soon turn their attentions to other countries and social peace would prevail in Canada.

By the same token, labour assumed that the support of ex-soldiers would make their legitimate goals irresistible. It attempted to place the strike's demands in the context of the liberties for which the war had been fought and to draw distinct parallels between the sacrifices of the soldier and the sacrifices of the worker.[14] Once the general public accepted this analogy and realized that the defenders of Western civilization supported labour's demands, they would understand that the strike could in no way be a Bolshevist-led revolution. Knowing that the men of the Canadian Corps would never associate themselves with such extremism, they would see through the fear mongering and become convinced of the justice of the strike.[15] They would pressure their leaders to meet the demands of workers and, with no further grounds for discontent, social peace would prevail in Canada.

On another level, the returned soldier as an individual was deemed to hold the key to industrial peace. The high ideals for which he sacrificed his youth, the bonds of comradeship he came to appreciate in the trenches, the habit of judging a man on his innate worth instead of superficialities – all of these characteristics made the veteran the natural conciliator between capital and labour. In Bertrand Sinclair's *The Inverted Pyramid,* lumber camps up and down the British Columbia coast are torn by labour disputes in the postwar depression. Industrial peace prevails only in the camp managed by Rod Norquay, an ex-soldier who learned in France that if the men under his control, be they privates or lumbermen, were treated fairly and with respect, they would reciprocate that treatment entirely. In Ralph Connor's *To Him That Hath,* Jack Maitland is the solution to industrial disputes in Blackwater. Respected by management and workers alike as a man of honour and judgment, Captain Jack is called upon to mediate the violent strike that is destroying the city. He can do so simply because, as an ex-soldier, he possesses the one skill that made him a success at the front: the ability to judge a situation on its merits, regardless of any personal interests that may be in play.

The war experience, then, had the power to keep political extremism at bay by calming the troubled waters that divided capital and labour. It also had the power to sweep aside provincial jealousies. Time and time again, observers emphasized that the Canadian Corps, and indeed each battalion, had brought together soldiers from every province in the spirit of unity in a common cause. In his final order before the demobilization of the 7th Battalion, Lieutenant-Colonel Fred Lister told his men that 'we started out a British Columbia unit; we return an Ontario battalion: but I defy anyone to note the point of cleavage. Welded together by many months of common danger, East and West have fused as one.'[16] In 1925, Arthur Currie wrote that the fallen 'went out to their death with no provincial prejudices and no racial suspicions in their hearts. For them, in their splendid service and in their heroic end, there was no Québec and no Ontario, no Nova Scotia and no Alberta, but one great country, – that beloved Canada, the land of their ancestral pioneers.' Four years later, he rang the same familiar changes: 'Over There, men did not care whether their comrades came from British Columbia or Ontario, whether the cook ... was a French-Canadian from Québec or an Irish-Canadian from Toronto. What mattered to us all was that we were men from the same country, bound by a common bond, with the same duty and the same objective, on the same great quest, and ready to give all, if need be, for the same ideal.'[17]

It was the image of provincial unity that gave the Battle of Vimy Ridge such import. The four divisions of the Canadian Corps, operating as a unit for the first time, brought together battalions from across the country. For many people, that battle came to symbolize the potential of Canada if such cooperation could be realized on an ongoing basis. In 1925, Viscount Byng told an audience in Vancouver that 'the boys at Vimy Ridge represented Canada as a whole. It was then that all the nine provinces walked up the hill as one, all with the same ideal before them and the same goal in mind.'[18] Mackenzie King also turned to Vimy Ridge in a 1926 debate on Maritime Rights. 'Surely we in this parliament representing the nine provinces of the Dominion,' he said, 'will not in these days of peace find it difficult to go up the hill together in the solution of whatever problems may still remain in the perfecting of Confederation and the great idea and ideal of national unity it was intended to serve.' For King, a man for whom national unity was a paramount concern, the image was one that he would use again and again. In 1938, at the Canadian Corps reunion in Toronto, he declared that 'the Corps revealed on the field of battle what a spirit of unity can achieve. The various units in the Corps preserved the names and traditions of particular localities, but all were engaged in a common national purpose.'[19] By contemplating the memory of that purpose, King and countless other Canadians believed that unity could be recaptured.

The power of the mythicized version of the war experience, then, was considerable. Before it, extremist subversion was reduced to impotence and provincial rivalries crumbled; it had the power to heal all that ailed the body politic. But the memory of the war was particularly powerful among those elements of society that were vulnerable to being led astray. And Canadians who looked for chinks in the social armour during the interwar period fastened upon four groups that were deemed to be especially needy of guidance: the youth of the nation; immigrants who required 'Canadianization'; members of the First Nations; and French Canadians.

II

FROM THE FIRST YEAR OF THE WAR, Canada's schoolchildren had been vital foot soldiers in the crusade against the kaiser's Germany. No student was too young to be educated in the issues of the war or to take a hand in winning it. In November 1915, the Ontario Department of Education directed its teachers to take up the study of the war in history classes and prepared an outline of the course for distribution to the schools each year. Sir Edward Parrott's *Children's Story of the War* and *Nelson's History of the War* by John Buchan could be found in most public schools across the country, while Sir Robert Falconer's *German Tragedy* was also adopted for use in Ontario schools in 1915. Near the end of the war, the New Brunswick Department of Education directed that *The Canadian War Book* be placed in the hands of all students over the age of ten. From it, they would learn all about the 'World Confederacy Against Barbarism' and the fact that Germany stood for militarism, tyranny, treachery, organized cruelty, murder, slavery, and robbery. The campaign to educate the youth evidently got off to a good start; one provincial minister of Education reported in 1918 that the children had been 'well taught the essential principles of the struggle, the part Canada has played, and the meaning of the British Empire to the whole world.'[20]

But the use of the war in classrooms could not end with the Armistice. The Reverend H.J. Cody, the Ontario minister of Education from May 1918 to November 1919, called history 'the great vehicle of patriotic instruction' and opined that 'the importance of direct and indirect inculcation of sound moral and patriotic ideals cannot be overestimated.' The Great War was tailor-made for this inculcation because, according to Currie, it had given students 'a Canadian history redolent with glory.'[21] Imparting that history to future generations was essential to the health of the nation; to keep it from them would do nothing less than stunt the development of the Canadian people.

At the very least, the war could provide Canadian schoolchildren with an appealing and potent example of the value of discipline. In 1919, New Brunswick students were exhorted in these terms by the Department of Education: 'it is asked of you that you remember these deathless heroes, who so faithfully did their part in clearing the world of tyranny and oppression, and that by hard and honest work, by prudent living, by habits of thrift, by private well-living and public integrity you prove yourselves worthy of the principles of freedom and honour for which they fought and died.' Those principles were too precious 'to be frittered away in the foolish pursuit of unnecessary pleasures.' Instead, children must take advantage of every day in school to prepare themselves to fill the places left by the fallen.[22] In 1938, T.E. MacNutt told the pupils of a Prince Edward Island elementary school that they could serve their country just as the war heroes had done. He interpreted that service, however, in very narrow terms: 'First it is your duty to obey your parents, teachers and all others placed in authority over you. It is your duty to take every possible advantage of your educational facilities.'[23]

But the war could be more than just a sort of classroom monitor; it could mould the character of youth in the widest possible sense. People who pondered the ways to instil in Canadian children the values that were deemed worthy of transmission saw no better medium than the memory of 1914-18. That version of the war as a traditional, Victorian conflict, full of all the High Diction concepts that had been validated by the experience of the trenches, dominated in history texts. They tell a compelling story, but one that has little to do with the reality of the First World War and everything to do with the Great War as it was interpreted in the myth.

Hearing of the war in their isolated fastnesses, Canadian pioneers 'threw down their tools and tramped fifty, a hundred, even two hundred miles to "do their bit."'[24] They did so because the war was manifestly just: Germany constantly revealed its inherent barbarism, most notably by discharging chlorine gas against Allied troops in 1915. This 'inhuman weapon' was something that 'no civilized people had hitherto employed in warfare.'[25] Gas, however, was more sinister than just a weapon to win battles: 'You see, this gas was a deadly poison which the cruel Germans had invented on purpose to kill the poor soldiers in awful agony.' But even their agony was not in vain: 'A battle won by our own boys! Doesn't this make you feel proud to know that they *are* our boys, and that we, too, are Canadians?'[26] The evil of gas, then, had a silver lining, for it allowed Canadian soldiers to show their mettle. This they did in convincing fashion. Even French-Canadian troops, 'quoique moins nombreux ne le cédèrent à personne pour leur bravoure et leur audace. Un de leurs régiments, le Vingt-Deuxième, se couvrit de gloire en plusieurs circonstances.'[27] The gallantry of Canadian soldiers had been so consistent and widespread that 'every battle they fought is a resplendent page of glory.'[28]

This unparalleled example had led to a rare sort of unity in wartime Canada. Indeed, 'a mighty united effort and the noble sacrifice of fifty thousand dead had deepened from coast to coast the sense of a common heritage.' This unity stemmed from the fact that both of the nation's founding races had an equal stake in the struggle. French Canadians realized that the future of France was at risk and, after all, Marshal Foch was 'un grand chrétien.'[29] The reason for Canada sending troops overseas was quite straightforward: 'Great Britain needed men, and Great Britain was the Motherland. France needed men, and many of Canada's earliest settlers had come from France.'[30] In this inspiring expression of amity that was the Great War, conscription was hardly mentioned as a source of discontent. On the contrary, it was a positive measure because, with it, 'Canada showed that she wished her men to be adequately supported on the firing line.'[31]

Of course, any text that departed from this line could find itself under attack. A Legion branch in Alberta discovered that *Medieval and Modern Times,* authorized by the province for use in Grade 12, had twice as many pages devoted to the American part in the Great War as the Canadian. Legion officials vowed to take the matter up with the provincial government with a view to having the text removed. In New Brunswick, veterans joined forces with the Saint John Council of Women to secure the withdrawal of *Myers' General History,* which they claimed gave an inaccurate picture of the empire's war effort. In Vancouver, the ever vigilant Cy Peck attacked the idea of dropping war history from the curriculum, insisting that the young have 'a right to know of the great record of endurance and sacrifice.' Legion members there received support from the provincial government in a campaign to change school history texts so that children were adequately exposed to the 'great efforts and splendid achievements' of Canadians in the Great War.[32]

The war was also deemed to be an excellent source of prose and verse selections for school readers, and, again, wartime utterances were used to their fullest. A typical collection was J.W. Wetherell's *The Great War in Verse and Prose* (1919), recommended as a reader for Ontario classrooms. If it was used as frequently as the education department desired, students would have learned the mythic version of the war backwards and forwards. Norah Holland's 'The Kaiser' and Borden's July 1915 speech at the London Guildhall ('we could not stand aside and see trampled in the dust a weak and unoffending people whose independence and liberties we had guaranteed') affirmed that the cause of the war had been just. Stead's 'We Are Men of the Furrow' revealed that the war had been forced on peace-loving nations by a militaristic enemy and depicted the Canadian soldier as a child of nature. Bliss Carman's 'The Man of the Marne' convinced students that the war had been a crusade, and Frederick George Scott's 'A Grave in Flanders' and Robert W. Service's 'Pilgrims' reassured youngsters that death in battle was a glorious and beautiful passing. Scott's 'On the Rue de Bois' linked the deaths of soldiers to the death of Christ, and Borden's Guildhall speech gave the war a sense of historic continuity by relating it to events from Canada's past ('beyond the Channel, in France or in Belgium, the grandson of a Durham and the grandson of a Papineau standing side by side in this struggle'). Add a smattering of Brooke, Grenfell, Seeger, and Binyon, and the student had a complete distillation of the received version of the war.

Even the standard readers provided a healthy dose of the traditional. J.E. Hodder-Williams's 'Jack Cornwall,' about the boy-hero of the Battle of Dogger Bank, Jesse Edgar Middleton's ultra-patriotic 'The Canadian,' Harold Peat's 'Canadians – Canadians – That's All!', a stirring passage from his wartime bestseller, and Stead's 'Kitchener of Khartoum' were all studied and memorized by Ontario students.[33] A reader used by thousands of Alberta students included Scott's 'In Memoriam,' McCrae's 'The Unconquered Dead' and 'In Flanders Fields,' Bernard Freeman Trotter's 'Ici Repose,' and prose selections from Borden's wartime speeches emphasizing concepts like self-sacrifice, patriotism, and devotion.[34] Even in the late 1930s, interest in traditional war writing as a vehicle for instruction was strong. Many of the old readers remained in use, and even new texts relied on the classics. *Life and Literature, Book 2,* published in 1938 for Grade 8 students, included only one poem that refers specifically to the Great War. It was not just any poem, however; it was Rupert Brooke's 'The Soldier,' the verse that had become the anthem of 1914.

Students visiting the school library after class would find little on the shelves to contradict the version of the war that appeared in their texts, for education departments encouraged schools to fill their libraries with books that subscribed to the traditional interpretation. In 1932 the Ontario Department of Education distributed a list of recommended books for school libraries that was dominated by nineteenth-century versions of this very twentieth-century war, including John Masefield's *Gallipoli,* Robert Borden's collected speeches *Canada in the Great War,* and poetry by Rupert Brooke, Laurence Binyon, Wilfred Wilson Gibson, and John McCrae. For good measure, the list also mentioned nineteen books by Sir Henry Newbolt, whose 'Play up! Play up! and play the game!' became a clarion call for the generation of 1914, and twenty-two by G.A. Henty, the great popularizer of the Boy's Own view of the British Empire. Schools in Prince Edward Island could avail themselves of a program in which a payment of $25, to be raised by the students or through donations, would secure a library worth $50. Significantly, the only L.M. Montgomery book offered in the homeland of Anne of Green Gables was *Rilla of Ingleside,* with its entirely traditional view of the war's impact on a small Canadian town.[35]

There were only a few attempts to challenge this use of the war as a constructive example. One of the only textbooks to present a more realistic account of the war was written by the principal of a Winnipeg high school. *Canada: Its History and Progress* was very frank in its discussion of things like conscription and profiteering and provided a view of the consequences of the war that few Canadian students would have received elsewhere in the school system: 'Men came back telling of the miseries, filth and horrors of trench life; of the death that came to their comrades in a thousand ghastly shapes; of men screaming with the agony of their wounds. The shell-shocked, the blinded and the maimed came back, and Canada began to realize the full meaning of modern warfare.' The Women's International League for Peace and Freedom probably approved of this text, because it mounted its own attack on the glorification of war and the military in school texts. The Toronto branch sponsored a survey of Canadian texts and found that as much as 30 per cent of their content was devoted to military history; there was no evidence, however, that a militaristic bias prevailed.[36] In Western Canada, Violet McNaughton's *Western Producer* carried on a similar campaign against the portrayal of war in texts. She did not object to the study of war per se but wanted school authorities to brand war as a primitive means of settling disputes. Professor Ira Dilworth of the University of British Columbia was less tolerant than McNaughton; he demanded an end to the teaching of history in schools, calling it one of the 'microbes of war.'[37]

Even if history had not been taught, however, students would have remained surrounded by the 'microbes of war.' Their school year was marked by a number of special days that, to a greater or lesser degree, served to inculcate the accepted version of the war. The most important of these was Armistice Day. Schoolchildren invariably played a leading role in the ceremonies, usually parading to the war memorial as a group (in many towns the parade itself originated at the local public school) and singing or laying wreathes at the monument. In this way, the youth of the nation paid public homage to the fallen, their tributes symbolizing both a respect for the war's sacrifices and a commitment to carry on the ideals for which those sacrifices were made. The eleventh of November was also an ideal opportunity to ensure that children were acquainted on a personal level with the significance of the war. The Amputations Association urged all Canadian children to spend time with veterans and war widows on Armistice Day, and the Canadian Legion advised teachers to invite local veterans to speak to classes in early November, a practice that continues to this day.[38] Presumably, mingling with the heroes they were honouring would give children a deeper appreciation of the war's legacy.

Other significant days, such as Empire Day, were used to achieve the same end.[39] In 1919 the Ontario Department of Education issued *Deeds of Valour,* a collection of Victoria Cross-winning exploits intended to stir the blood of schoolchildren and act as the focus of Empire Day observances. Manitoba's *Empire Day 1919,* also a series of Victoria Cross deeds, was issued with the same goal in mind: 'The lads [who died overseas] ... were lads who sat on the benches and played in the grounds of the Manitoba schools ... Their story should be an inspiration to every boy and girl in Manitoba.'[40] When interest in Empire Day waned, a casualty of growing Canadian national feeling, education ministries could adopt Flag Days for Canadians. The brainchild of W. Everard Edmonds, the head of the history department at Strathcona High School in Edmonton, Flag Days marked significant events in Canadian history; they included the Second Battle of Ypres, the date of the declaration of war, and Armistice Day. Edmonds provided a short explanatory essay, a list of selected poems, and a tentative program, and encouraged schools to mark two Flag Days each month to instil patriotism in schoolchildren.[41] The intent of these observances, and of the war as an Empire Day theme, was clear: to ensure that the sacrifice of Canadian soldiers remained a source of inspiration and instruction for schoolchildren.

It could hardly be otherwise, for the war was a constant presence in the lives of secondary and elementary students. Few schools failed to erect a memorial to the students and staff who had given their lives, and those memorials were avowedly didactic. Ridley College in St. Catharines, Ontario, erected a memorial chapel decorated with portraits of the dead, 'a fine type of the best young Canadian manhood ... [who] look out from their simple frames and pass on to their successors the call to service.' Memorial School in Hamilton, with its inscriptions of famous Canadian battles and its entrances named for war heroes, had the same potential to inspire the students and keep before them 'the splendid vision of the romantic, the heroic, the beautiful, the glorious!'[42] Even a simple honour roll, like the one put up in Magnetawan, Ontario, had the power to inspire children who 'glance at that illustrious scroll, find there new inspiration for their task, and, turning back to the dull pages of their text-book, will find them illumined by a light reflected thence.'[43]

In other locations, the town's entire commemorative activity was centred around the school. More than a few schools were commemorations in their own right, and institutions named after Kitchener, Haig, Byng, Allenby, and Currie are scattered across the country. Education officials in Scarborough township in Ontario renamed Chester Avenue School after the Battle of Courcelette; the school sits on Courcelette Road, not far from Haig Avenue. The Toronto board named a school after General Malcolm Mercer, who had been killed in action at Mount Sorrel in 1916, Saskatoon used the name of Hugh Cairns, a local winner of the Victoria Cross, and Brantford, Ontario, named a school after Major P.P. Ballachey, a local worthy and one of the first to fall from Brant County. It was also common to find the civic war memorial erected on the grounds of the elementary or secondary school, occasionally with a captured German artillery piece added for emphasis. This meant that a symbol of the war's sacrifice was the children's first sight at the beginning of the school day and their last sight at the end of it. The field piece would affirm the pacific Canada's victory over a militaristic enemy, while the memorial, be it a monument or the school itself, reminded the younger generation 'of the important duties they owe to their forefathers to carry on.'[44]

One of the more interesting attempts to keep the war before the eyes of youth was a scheme by the Imperial Order of the Daughters of the Empire to circulate reproductions of CWMF paintings to Canadian schools. As part of the IODE's broader war memorial scheme, each of its 800 branches agreed to pay for one set of eighteen prints to be given to a local school. The prints chosen for the collection were entirely traditional; they included Frederick Challener's *Canada's Grand Armada, 1914,* Edgar Bundy's *The Landing of the First Canadian Division at Saint-Nazaire, 1915,* James Kerr-Lawson's *The Cloth Hall, Ypres, Canada's Answer* by Norman Wilkinson, and *Canadians Arriving on the Rhine* by Inglis Sheldon-Williams. The scheme was openly didactic and was intended to ensure that the young were conscious of their place in the nation and the responsibilities of citizenship. The prints would give each child, especially one who lived in an outlying area, 'an opportunity to visualize Canada's part in this great war, and have his mind opened to the past and future of this great Empire.' They would remind the children of 'the glory and valour of the Canadian men ... [and] the magnitude of the sacrifice of the sons and daughters of the Empire' and were to be presented on an occasion called Memorial Day, which 'might afterwards be kept to reiterate the story to the children of the future.'[45]

There was some resistance to the plan. Lucy Woodsworth lodged a protest, as did a Vancouver parents' group and school officials in Winnipeg and Calgary. A.Y. Jackson suggested that copies of Varley's work should hang in schools beside the 'death and glory' genre in the IODE collection.[46] Many other people, however, heartily approved of the prints that were chosen. The *Canadian Annual Review* spoke of Challener's 'wonderful conception of Canada's Armada sailing out to the aid of the Motherland' and Kenneth Forbes's 'vivid portraiture of the PPCLI.' A Windsor, Ontario, chapter of the IODE encountered no problems when it presented the collection to schools in Walkerville and Sandwich, nor did the Dominion Chapter when it sent a collection to Bathurst Grammar School in New Brunswick.[47]

Resistance to the IODE scheme could only have been token in any case, for the collection merely illustrated the view of the war that was already deeply ingrained in the education system. The prints would have told students nothing they had not already read in their texts, seen on their school memorials, or heard on Armistice or Empire Day. It was this version of the war, not Varley's, that could be a force for good in Canadian schools. Only it could impress upon children the necessity of holding the same high ideals of service to the nation and to their fellow Canadians that characterized the memory of the Great War. Only it could ensure that the youth of Canada matured with a well-developed sense of civic duty and the responsibility that went along with citizenship. In the minds of many Canadians, these simple facts were enough to overcome all objections.

III

'THE TRUEST MEMORIAL to the sleeping victors of the struggle,' observed W.G. Smith in 1922, 'is a nation homogeneous in character, united in purpose, incessantly solicitous in its care of the living and exquisitely tender in its memory of the dead.'[48] By impressing the memory of the Great War frequently and forcefully upon the minds of Canadian schoolchildren, people of Smith's stripe felt sure they could create a generation that approximated his ideal. But there was another figure who was even more needful of the transformation that Smith envisioned: the new Canadian. There had been considerable emphasis on the problem of Canadianizing immigrants before 1914, and the war appeared to provide the ideal agent to complete the process and encourage immigrants 'to be more like us.' Canada's war exploits could be used to instil the patriotism and loyalty to the nation and empire that were deemed to be essential in turning immigrants into Canadians.[49] Used carefully, the memory of the war could create a nation homogeneous in character and, therefore, destined for greatness.

Even as it was providing a means by which to Canadianize immigrants, the war also made that process more essential than ever. 'We must keep the faith with those who sleep,' warned the Reverend J.E. Hughson. 'The things for which they died must be the things for which we live ... [W]e must write it over the portals of this great country, in letters that "the strangers within our gates" cannot fail to read as they come to take their place among us.' According to J. Murray Gibbon, the question of 'the foreign born' had been 'accentuated by the increased spirit of nationality which has grown out of the war – a spirit which demands that the foreign born shall either accept the ideals and obligations of Canadian citizenship or get out.'[50] Too many immigrants, thought some observers, had done neither. J.T.M. Anderson, the inspector of schools in Yorkton, Saskatchewan, and later a provincial education minister, observed that the war had demonstrated without a shadow of a doubt 'that Canada is a country full of unassimilated groups, with varying social ideals, varying languages, and varying ideas of Canadian citizenship and loyalty to the British Empire.' In light of this fact, enlistment rates became the easiest way to determine which ethnic groups had been fully assimilated. No other factors were allowed to impinge on this simple equation; an immigrant who had not joined up was an immigrant who had not yet been assimilated and, consequently, had not yet gained a sufficient appreciation of the duties of Canadian citizenship and the need for loyalty to the empire.[51]

Assimilation of the foreign born, then, came to be interpreted as one of the torches that the dead had passed on. Cenotaphs and memorial halls were beautiful, thought W.G. Smith, but a better memorial would be for young men and women to give a few years of their time to the educational life of the nation. They should fan out into the settlements of the foreign born in order to 'hold the frontiers of our national life.' 'What is needed is a new crusade of young Canadians in whom the fires of patriotism will burn, who will man the outposts of Canadian nationality,' he declared. Hundreds of thousands of Canadians had offered themselves to fight Germany; 'in times of peace can there not be a brigade or two of equally ardent spirits who will engage in the work of construction?' This work would be the only true memorial to the fallen: 'A thousand new teachers in as many teacherages would mean the beginning of a new day. Let not any of us refuse because perchance it might mean five or ten years of our life devoted to the cultivation of a national spirit – 50 thousand of our superiors laid down their ALL in Europe that a national spirit might be possible.'[52]

Any idealistic young Canadian could fill the role of teacher and mentor, but the returned soldier was the ideal incumbent. When the Masonic Order of Saskatchewan formulated its war memorial plans in 1921, it decided to create a series of scholarships that would be awarded to selected teachers willing to spend at least a year teaching 'in the more backward non-English speaking districts.' Of the first thirty-one teachers chosen, many were married veterans whose wives had served as nurses during the war. One such individual, the social scientist and decorated ex-infantryman Robert England, spent three years in a non-English-speaking district in Saskatchewan.[53] Another might have been the ex-soldier strategically placed in a newly created school district in Mennonite Saskatchewan, or the Irish-

Canadian war hero turned teacher who used his tales of glory on the battlefields of France to instil in his Ruthenian students a love of their new homeland.[54]

This hopeful scenario typified the way that the memory of the war should be used. It should not have to be force-fed to new Canadians, nor should it cast assimilation in such a negative light as Gibbon's 'believe or leave' dogmatism. J.T.M. Anderson may have favoured drilling new Canadians in the principles of the war by having them repeat certain leading phrases (like 'the British Empire ... [is] fighting for the freedom of the world against Germany') as part of their night-school training in English, but in general the myth did not deem such compulsion necessary.[55] On the contrary, the war experience was interpreted as a magnet that would draw immigrants to it. New Canadians would all be like Colonel Pete Anderson, the transplanted Dane whose memoirs were lauded for showing an 'enduring faith in his adopted country for which he has so firmly proved his love,' or the Syrian immigrant in Gibbon's *Drums Afar* who donated $1,000 at a Montreal patriotic fund-raiser because Canada had been good to him since he arrived there penniless twenty years earlier.[56] It was not a question of 'the foreign born' being forced to accept Canadianization; rather, the war myth was such an epic that immigrants would flock to it, clamouring to subsume themselves in the new national consciousness that had been forged in Flanders.

A clear example of the impact that the war could have on immigrants can be found in *The Viking Heart,* the critically acclaimed 1923 novel by Laura Goodman Salverson. Born in Winnipeg in 1890 of Icelandic parents, Salverson was a woman who appreciated the immigrant's feeling of dislocation. In her childhood, she had moved with her family between Manitoba, North Dakota, Minnesota, and Mississippi, an experience that imprinted her novels with a deep desire to lay down roots in the soil. *The Viking Heart* (originally entitled *The Pride of Country*) described the quest for belonging through the experience of a family of Icelandic settlers in Western Canada. The novel's final chapters are set during the war years. Borga Lindal, the matriarch of the family, is at first incensed that her son Thor is going to war but changes her mind upon seeing his battalion marching away: 'For the first time in her life she thought of Canada as a dear and precious possession – these soldiers had somehow made it so.' When Thor is killed in action, however, Borga has a crisis of faith and begins to curse the country that took her son. Her apostasy is only temporary, though. Looking out of the window of her farmhouse, her faith is restored when she realizes that Thor had died for everything she sees. Borga recalls the minister's words at the memorial service for Thor: 'your son is dead yet liveth, he lives in the life of his country.'

In a final affirmation of her conversion from Icelander to Canadian, she whispers to herself 'In the life of *my* country.'[57]

An even more explicit statement of the Canadianizing potential of the war myth appeared that same year. *The Translation of John Snaith*, by a young playwright named Britton Cooke, was first produced at Hart House Theatre in March 1923.[58] Set in Indian Point, a stagnating lumber town in northern Ontario, the play is full of characters who have little interest in the town beyond the accumulation of wealth. Even the mayor, emigrant Briton Hugh Treleaven, has no respect for Canada and only intends to remain there until he makes enough money to retire in England.

Literally overnight, however, the town is transformed by the news that John Snaith, the local malefactor-turned-soldier, has covered himself with glory and won the Victoria Cross. Even the cynical Treleaven is moved by this news: '[Snaith] died with his back to a mud wall pitching bombs, coolly, into the very – in the damned dirty, ugly mug of Death – while seventy wounded crawled back to the safety he bought for 'em with his life! But it was a man from Indian Point! It was one of us! It was a man out of this dirty, God-forsaken hole who did that little thing!' The mayor experiences an immediate conversion and alters his views of Canada and Indian Point: 'I think perhaps I was wrong. The spirit's here too – in the dirt under our feet! And Snaith has made it speak! ... He's lifted us all up!' Treleaven is not the only person affected by the news of Snaith's heroism; that night, Pavnick, Antoine, Teetom, Skovitz, Arnheim, Perkins, McPherson, Dobrovnik, and every other ethnic stereotype in the town flock to a huge patriotic meeting in celebration of the news.

But dark clouds loom on the horizon when the real John Snaith returns to Indian Point intending to reveal that he had deserted from his unit and sold his place in the ranks to an Englishman who could not join up because of kidney trouble. The Englishman was the real hero; Snaith's life remains a disgrace, but he is determined to redeem himself by confessing his misdeeds to the townsfolk. The truth, however, cannot be allowed to jeopardize the myth that has regenerated Indian Point and injected a new consciousness into its people. A Métis woman whom Snaith once wronged realizes this, and leads him away from the celebration to drown them both in a raging stream before he can reveal his secret.

The Translation of John Snaith is a fascinating glimpse at the operation of the myth in postwar Canada. The veracity of any portion of the myth was irrelevant; as long as its impact was positive, it did not matter how many falsehoods it contained. The tale of Snaith's gallantry had given Indian Point a new spirit, a new meaning; the fact that it was not true, and that Snaith remained a coward, could not be allowed to subvert that spirit. The truth, therefore, had to be suppressed, and Snaith had to die, taking his secret with him and leaving Indian Point to revel in the glory of his false heroism.

Borga Lindal and the residents of Indian Point were literary proof of the war's potential as an agent of Canadianization. The war story achieved what years of residence had failed to do: it transformed immigrants from 'the foreign born' into true Canadians who saw Canada, not their country of birth, as their real homeland. The same miracle could be worked on any ethnic group, not just easily assimilated Europeans. In 1929 the Canadian Legion Convention passed a resolution to exempt Japanese war veterans from quotas on fishing licences. Two years later, those veterans won the provincial franchise after a long campaign supported by Ian Mackenzie, one-time head of the Vancouver GWVA.[59] In both instances, there was a recognition of the same metamorphosis that Salverson and Cooke had described. War service had miraculously transformed immigrants into Canadians; more powerful than any other means of assimilation, the war had allowed Japanese veterans to rise above their ethnicity and join the imagined community that was postwar Canada.

IV

THE METAMORPHOSIS OF INDIAN POINT and its citizens pointed to a greater transformation that the war experience could bring on: the ultimate reconciliation of Canada's founding nations. The language, culture, and religion of immigrants gave them good reason for not assimilating immediately upon their arrival, but the case of aboriginals and French Canadians was rather different. Both groups had been present at the creation, so to speak, but the former had become wards of the government rather than full partners in the Canadian nation, while the latter had demonstrated a marked reluctance to subsume their identity into a pan-Canadian nationalism. Yet here too the Great War provided the solution. Native Canadians, and non-Natives who were sympathetic to their cause, pointed to the war as the ultimate proof of their dedication to Canada and their right to equal treatment in the new nation. At the same time, English Canadians confidently expected the war to be the basis for a final reconciliation with French Canada. The war's legacy would provide the impetus for both groups to become, not Native Canadians or French Canadians, but Canadians pure and simple.

There was no denying that the First Nations had responded enthusiastically to the call of 1914. They gave generously to the Canadian Patriotic Fund and other philanthropic causes and celebrated their response in poems that were every bit as conventionally patriotic as the most bullish English-

Canadian verse. Furthermore, aboriginals had one of the highest enlistment rates of any ethnic community in the country, English Canadians included. Some 3,500 Natives enlisted, from an eligible male population of just over 11,000, a response rate of over 30 per cent, or nearly twice the national average.[60]

In the memory of the war, these facts stood as indisputable proof that all Canadians could take immense pride in the First Nations' response to the crisis. Everard Edmonds wondered if any people who went to war did so 'from a higher or more disinterested motive than [Native Canadians].' No class of Canadians were more patriotic or loyal to British institutions than 'our Indian wards,' averred the Peterborough *Examiner*.[61] They were not subject to the Military Service Act, but this was irrelevant; as observers pointed out, by 1917 many bands had already sent every eligible male to war. Brant County, Ontario, the home of the Six Nations reserve, took special pride in the contribution of its Native citizens. 'The Six Nations stood by their ancient treaties with the British crown and proved their loyalty by the shedding of blood on the battlefields of Europe,' proclaimed the county's historian, while the local newspaper pointed out that Lieutenant Cameron Brant, a descendant of Joseph Brant (Thayendanegea), the great Mohawk chief who

A Japanese-Canadian soldier shaves in the trenches. Did his wartime service bring him greater emancipation within Canadian society? Probably not. (NAC PA3117)

had fought for England during the American Revolution, was the first man of the county to die in action. After Brant's death at Ypres in 1915, local elders predicted that 'such nobility of purpose and sacrifice of life will go far to further cement the many units of our citizenship into one great united front.'[62]

The prevalence of the Native as a stock character in accounts of the war recognized the First Nations' contribution and confirmed the unity of Canada's founding nations in battle. No factual account was complete without a salutary reference to the gallantry of Canada's 'braves at war,' and few fictional tales lacked the silent and determined Native volunteer who stood beside his countrymen of European stock, rough and uneducated but determined to fight the kaiser. In Theodore Goodridge Roberts's *The Fighting Starkleys,* he is Frank Sacobie, a Malaseet who joins up with the men from Beaver Dam. In Ralph Connor's *The Sky Pilot in No Man's Land,* he is a mysterious Métis woodsman who wonders 'if a fellow stood on one side while his country was fightin', where would he live when it's all over?' A short

Saskatchewan aboriginals display their patriotism, 1915. They, too, would find that the rhetoric of equality would bring them little of substance in the interwar period. (Ronald R. Mumford, NAC PA30224)

story by J.A. Holland tells the tale of Pierre Loiselle, a descendant of coureur de bois and Iroquois ancestors. Upon hearing of the Second Battle of Ypres, he leaves his lumber camp to enlist and is eventually killed in action at Mount Sorrel.[63]

Loiselle and characters like him were the epitome of the soldier as a child of nature, the figure that Canadians so idealized. The white trapper or prospector was inspiring, but he was still only a backwoodsman by vocation; the Native soldier was a true product of the wilderness. When an Ontario newspaper reported the death of a Cree veteran named Thomas Sutherland, the journalist noted that he and a party of other Cree had snowshoed hundreds of miles through the northland to enlist in Cochrane, Ontario. Everard Edmonds wrote of John Campbell, a Native living on the Arctic coast, who travelled some 3,000 miles by trail, canoe, and steamer to enlist in Vancouver.[64] In both stories, the journey of the intrepid volunteer was described with an almost palpable sense of awe.

The heroism of a legion of Sacobies and Campbells was proof that

The great Onandaga marathoner Tom Longboat buying a paper from a French boy at the front. The postwar years were not kind to Longboat, who battled alcoholism and unemployment. (NAC PA 1479)

Native Canadians had earned full partnership in the nation. At least, this was Frederick O. Loft's assumption. Loft, a Mohawk from the Six Nations reserve in Ontario, had gone overseas with the Canadian Forestry Corps and served in France for five months before being sent to Britain as unsuitable for further service. He had been struck by the tribulations of his people while trying to recruit them for the army and, before returning home in 1918, presented himself to the Privy Council in London to request a hearing on behalf of Canada's aboriginals. When the council instructed him to organize the Natives before presuming to act as their representative, he founded the League of Indians of Canada.[65] Loft was proud of his short service during the war, and of the contribution of other Natives, and assumed that the rest of Canada would want to recognize their sacrifices. 'Not in vain did our young men die in a strange land,' he proclaimed. 'The unseen tears of Indian mothers in many isolated Indian reserves have watered the seeds from which may spring those desires and efforts and aspirations which will enable us to reach the stage when we will take our place side by side with the white people, doing our share of productive work and gladly shouldering the responsibility of citizens in this, our country.' For Loft, this was only fair. 'We have the right,' he told chiefs, 'to claim and demand more justice and fair play as a recompense for we, too, have fought for the sacred rights of justice, freedom and liberty so dear to mankind.'[66]

The themes raised by Loft were taken up by others who supported his goals. Old Keyam, the voice created by Edward Ahenakew, mused about the heroics of Native soldiers and the generosity of many reserves. 'Is more proof needed of what we can do when we are roused?' he wondered. 'This should make the white people realize that we have made progress, that some of us have grown almost to the stature of manhood, that we have that in our nation which can be of value to this country ... The part that we took in the war proved that we had reached a stage of development that should allow us some freedom in the management of our own affairs.'[67] Many whites professed to agree with Loft and Keyam. 'That our Indians deserve full citizenship,' declared Everard Edmonds, 'can be doubted by no one who recalls the splendid part they played in the greatest struggle of all time.' For years Canada had treated the Native as a child, but 'it was no child's part he played in the War.' Having done 'a man's work, he will never again be content to stand aside, uttering no word in matters that directly concern him.' Aboriginals deserved full citizenship and a 'permanent share in the life and prosperity of our Dominion,' proclaimed an Edmonton radio station in 1930. Any other course, believed the GWVA, was illogical and unfair. While in uniform, the Native soldier received all of the privileges of his white comrades but 'when he returned to his own people he was once more treated as a man unworthy of his liberty.'[68] That state of affairs had to end.

It was Duncan Campbell Scott, the poet and deputy minister in the Department of Indian Affairs, who waxed most enthusiastic about the transformation that the war would bring for Native Canadians. No Native veterans would be content to return to 'their old Indian mode of life,' he predicted confidently. 'Each one of them will be a missionary of the spirit of progress, and their people cannot long fail to respond to their vigorous influence.' Because of the war, Canada would soon see the day, eagerly awaited in the Department of Indian Affairs, 'when all the quaint old customs, the weird and picturesque ceremonies, the sun dance and the potlatch and even the musical and poetic native languages shall be as obsolete as the buffalo and the tomahawk, and the last tepee of the Northern wilds give place to a model farmhouse.' On that day, the Native would become 'one with his neighbour in his speech, life and habits.'[69] Just as it would do for immigrants, the legacy of the war would allow Native Canadians to rise above their birth. After centuries of wardship, they could cast off the shackles of their heritage and become full citizens of the new Canada.

V

THE SITTING OF THE HOUSE OF COMMONS on Thursday 6 March 1919 started as a thousand other such sittings had done. There was the tabling of routine reports, on this day a list of people permitted to take intoxicating liquors into the Northwest Territories and a copy of correspondence relating to the gift of two submarines to Canada, and then a brief discussion of the operations of the government printing bureau. The members then embarked on the major business of the day, the replies to the governor general's speech from the throne. Michael Clark of Red Deer was first on the floor, and began by eulogizing the late Sir Wilfrid Laurier and offering his congratulations to 'every man in this House with French blood in his veins' for the fact that the Allied armies had been led to victory by a French marshal. He said nothing that could have been construed as controversial, insisting that 'there is little to be gained by fighting over past political battles.'

After Clark, other members stood to give the same basic speech. Ernest Lapointe, James McIsaac of King's on Prince Edward Island, A.B. McCoig of Kent in southwestern Ontario – all gave glowing praise of Canada's war effort with no hint of criticism. Shortly after nine o'clock, John Wesley Edwards, the fiery Orange MP from Frontenac in eastern Ontario, stood to address the House. He began innocuously enough, discussing the problems of repatriating ex-soldiers, but soon got to one of his pet themes. There were a few constituencies in Québec where rehabilitation would not be a problem, he remarked, simply because they had sent no soldiers. As a few members began sitting up in their seats, Edwards got into his stride. He produced a sheaf of figures, all of which proved that Québec's human contribution to the war had been shameful. However the statistics were manipulated, he insisted, the province trailed all others in enlistment. Edwards demanded that the government take this fact into account when allotting funds for reconstruction.

When Edwards had finished, Lucien Cannon, the member for Dorchester, rose slowly from his seat. 'Is it not time for the men of this country,' he sighed, 'to lay aside their provincial outlook, to lay aside their provincial prejudice and look at these questions from a national viewpoint?' Quebeckers had never asked if Ontario or the Maritimes had done its duty in all respects; they had been content to 'know that Canada has done nobly and we are proud of it.' Cannon ended his remarks with a plea:

> Let us be Canadians, let us according to the constitutional spirit of our institutions, represent not merely one county, not merely one province, but represent Canada from the Pacific to the Atlantic. Then on both sides of this House people will have understood their duty towards their common country. Ontario and Quebec will no more be separated, the provinces of Saskatchewan and Nova Scotia will no more be western and eastern provinces, but all the provinces will be component parts of a great whole and Canada will become a nation of free institutions and a nation proud of its Parliament.

Cannon's response corresponded entirely with the assumptions under which the myth took hold in 1919. Perhaps the war had given both English Canadians and French Canadians much to grumble about and, if they so desired, they could spend the next two decades pointing fingers at each other and refighting the battles of the war years. But what was the point of that? It served no more purpose than it did for the veteran to relive continually the worst day of his life in the trenches at Sanctuary Wood, or for the war widow to torture herself with the knowledge that her husband died in agony after an attack that should never have gone ahead in the first place. Such thoughts only kept the sores of war festering. Why dwell on them when the war's good was so manifest? So, while the veteran recalled the night in an *estaminet* before the attack, and the widow consoled herself that her husband had died with a smile on his face, so too did many Canadians desire to let bygones be bygones and embrace a view of the past that saw the war as the best opportunity to reconcile, finally and completely, Canada's founding European nations.

For people of this inclination, the war was tailor-made to achieve this object. All that was required was to utilize that combination of remembering and forgetting with which any society constructs its memory. It first had to be emphasized that French Canadians had as much stake in the war as anyone else. They, as much as English Canadians, had fought and died for their founding nation. In his 1919 popular history of the war, George Nasmith quoted a Paris newspaper on the arrival of the First Contingent in France: 'the blood of English-Canadians will flow for France; French-Canadians will shed blood for England.'[70] The fundamental difference between the two situations, that many English Canadians had been in born in Britain while only a fraction of French Canadians had ever seen France, was ignored. Regardless of how many generations of their families had lived in Canada, the memory of the war considered France to be the mother country of French Canada. Arthur Lapointe justified his enlistment by stressing the bond of affinity he had always felt for France, while Alfred Bienvenu emphasized that bond in a poem addressed 'à nos héros du 22e' [22nd Battalion]: 'Mais toi, vaillant soldat des grandes offensives, / Dont l'audace a prouvé qu'aux plus lointaines rives / Le vieux sang de Gaulois n'a pas dégénéré.'[71] Even in the man whose ancestors had left France for Canada 300 years earlier, the blood of Gaul was still presumed to course through his veins.

This image of the habitant fighting for the country that his ancestors had left centuries before was converted into a stock character in war literature. Typically, he is a crude, uneducated fellow who speaks with a caricatured French-Canadian accent, but his heart is always in the right place as he does his duty for king and country. In John Beames's *An Army without Banners,* the character is Pierre Normandin, who joins up despite being fifty-five years old and flat footed. 'Put me in front of one of them low, dirty, sausage-eatin' Germans with a bay'nit an' see,' he growls. Johnny Charbonneau, the hero of W.S. Atkinson's play *The Glory Hole,* is a French-Canadian backwoodsman who was 'never very sure whether he was fighting for the King of England or the Hudson's Bay Company ... now he's decided it's for Canada.' Like Normandin, Charbonneau is eventually killed in action, staying at his post for hours despite a gaping stomach wound.[72] V.V. Vinton's *To the Greater Glory* (1939), set in the village of St. Adèle, Québec, is another representative treatment. Though many villagers disagree with the war, many more are willing to enlist. Alphonse the dwarf proclaims pugnaciously that he would join up ('Me – if it wasn't for the way I was – I'd join up ... I'd help smash the Germans'), and Louis Vasseur and Henri Brossard both decide to enlist after the Military Service Act is passed; Vasseur even knocks down the local drunk for deriding those men who had joined up. At the end of the novel,

Brossard and another local soldier known only as the Joly Garçon receive a heroes' homecoming and conduct themselves as any English-Canadian veteran might have done, swaggering down the main street of St. Adèle with their bemedalled chests thrown out proudly.

In the myth, Brossard and Charbonneau were the real essence of French Canada; by considering all of the facts fairly and impartially, it would become clear that these characters were not mere literary artifice. Frederic Yorston, the editor of a souvenir booklet published by the *Montreal Standard,* insisted that, after a scientific and impartial examination of the facts, 'the judgement of posterity will in all likelihood be much more favourable than some who are now inclined to imagine.' The antiwar group had formed a small minority in Québec society, he claimed. 'The great majority of the people of Quebec are loyal and British in their attachments. This plain, solid and elementary fact is well known by every thinking man of whatever race in the Province of Quebec.' It saddened him that 'the true "voice of Quebec" … was smothered by the widespread publicity unfortunately given to the utterances of a small group of dissentients.'[73]

In 1919, J. Castell Hopkins made an attempt at the impartial examination Yorston had called for. He took a very conciliatory attitude towards the province of Québec, noting that the proportion of enlistments from Québec was not bad if all factors were taken into consideration. Many French-Canadian men were passive or indifferent to the war, but so were many men elsewhere in Canada; English-Canadian battalions were just as hard to fill in 1917 as French-Canadian battalions had been in 1916. Furthermore, more Ontarians than Quebeckers voted against conscription in 1917.[74] Later, historian William H.C. Wood agreed and ascribed a simple reason to Québec's apparently disappointing enlistment figures. The CEF was overwhelmingly single, at least when they enlisted, and Canada's British-born population had the highest proportion of single men of military age; the French-Canadian population had the highest proportion of married men of military age. Granted French Canadians did not enlist as enthusiastically as might have been hoped, concluded Frank Carrel, 'but if all conditions are fully weighed, their attitude is far from being as black as it has been painted.'[75]

Yorston's other contention, that the antiwar group within Québec did not represent the broader opinion of French Canada, was also taken up by other writers. Hopkins insisted that Henri Bourassa did not speak for the majority of French Canadians, however much he claimed to.[76] Such 'hot-headed extremists must not be allowed to prevail over the men of moderate views,' warned an English Quebecker in 1919. 'The guttersnipes and sweepings of the slums of Montreal,' boomed C.W. Peterson from his

Alberta fastness, 'even the ranting college professors, hysterical politicians and radical newspaper editors of the French element, do not represent French Canada.'[77] For people like Hopkins and Peterson, Talbot Papineau represented French Canadians. He and other war heroes like him – Rodolphe Lemieux, Joseph Kaeble, Jean Brillant – spoke with the true voice of French Canada.

It was through the example of men such as these – personifications of the essence of French Canada – that the war could serve as a basis for a new era of unity between Canada's two founding races. General R.E.W. Turner found the experience of the 14th Battalion instructive: 'From the outset it was composed of both English and French, and illustrated more than any other battalion of the 1st Canadian Division the spirit of unity between those two great races ... [B]y its union of French and English, the Royal Montreal Regiment helped to promote Canadian esprit de corps.' A commemorative booklet published for the tenth anniversary of the Armistice saw this same spirit in postwar Canada, declaring that the 'English and French speaking citizens of the Dominion were as one in reverence and feeling for Canada's sacrifices in the great war.'[78]

Many English- and French-Canadian observers used the unveiling of a war memorial to reaffirm the new spirit of understanding created by the war. At the dedication of a memorial at the Bank of Commerce in Lac-Mégantic, Québec, the local member of the legislative assembly observed that commemorating the men who had fought and died for Canada made the two founding races understand each other better through a common bond of suffering. A speaker at the unveiling of the Rimouski memorial put it in similar terms: 'une leçon aux générations futures auxquelles il rappellera la virilité, le grandeur d'âme et les vertus héroïques de ceux qu'il glorifie. Il leur rappellera aussi que les deux races qui habitent ce district et cette province savent vivre et mourir ensemble comme des héros.'[79] Charles Fitzpatrick, on laying the cornerstone for the memorial at Notre-Dame-de-Grâce in 1919, drew the same lesson: 'puisse notre beau Canada voir chacune des races qui l'habitent, développer dans l'harmonie ses qualités propres, apporter au service de la commune patrie le trésor varié de ses éléments de richesse et de ses aptitudes spéciales! Il y aura alors, entre tous, coopération, sans fusion, émulation sans empiêtement; il y aura véritablement bonne entente.'[80]

No memorial better expressed the opportunity for reconciliation offered by the myth than the Cross of Sacrifice erected in Montreal's municipal cemetery. Even its location is symbolic: it stands at the junction of the Roman Catholic Notre-Dame-des-Nièges cemetery and the Protestant

Mount Royal cemetery. In his speech at the unveiling in October 1922, G.P. Graham drew attention to the deeper meaning of the Cross. 'Ceux qui sonts morts,' he was quoted by *La Presse,* 'étaient unis dans une même pensée, un même but, un même idéal. Pourquoi ceux qui survivent ne seraient-ils pas unis par les liens d'une même et franche amité, d'une égale dévotion à l'achèvement de la prospérité nationale?' He wondered if the lesson of the dead would be in vain, their unity rejected, but decided that it could not be: 'Le monument qui se dresse maintenant, mitoyen entre nos deux champs des morts, nous prêche avec éloquence la doctrine d'unité nationale que nous devons tous écouter et pratiquer.' Just as unity had been imperative in wartime, Canada could not realize its national destiny without good relations between French and English. With this in mind, Graham ended with a plea: 'Allons souvent chercher au pied de la nouvelle croix qui se dresse aux cofins de nos deux cimitières le courage des concessions mutuelles et de la tolérance réciproque ... Les héros morts nous invitent à pratiquer, comme ils nous en ont d'abord donné l'exemple, les vertus nobles et fécondes qui, dans la guerre comme dans la paix, font les peuples puissants, riches et fortes.'[81]

Graham's address had its mate in literature, in the novel *Redemption* by the Nova Scotia-born writer Beckles Willson. Even during his tenure with the CWRO, Willson had been alive to the potential of the war in uniting French and English Canada, and in 1917 he suggested that the federal government investigate procuring the site of the Battle of Courcelette, where French- and English-Canadian troops had fought together. 'It might not be wholly without good political effect in Canada' if the field became a Canadian memorial park, he mused.[82] Willson's novel is an elaboration of that brief comment. The two protagonists, Gregory Vant and Emile Lanctot, represent Canada's European founders. Vant is the archetypal English Canadian, Oxford-educated but thanking God that he is a Canadian. When war breaks out, he is taken on as a minerals expert by the government but soon decides that his place is in the trenches; he resigns from the civil service, joins up, and is sent to France. Emile Lanctot, a member of Parliament from Vant's native Nova Scotia, was less impressed with the war and became a prominent *nationaliste* spokesman, frequently giving addresses denouncing the war. In time, those speeches gradually estrange Lanctot from his old friend Vant. Soon, though, Lanctot's attitude begins to change. He hears tales of the gallant deeds performed by French-Canadian soldiers from his constituency and is eventually convinced to become the judge advocate-general for the Montreal military district. From there, it is a short step into the front lines for Lanctot.

It is there that Vant and Lanctot meet again at the conclusion of the novel. Both lie wounded in a casualty clearing station, having performed conspicuous acts of gallantry in battle, and they ponder what the future holds for Canada. 'Is it to be the same old vulgar materialism, the same selfish scramble for wealth, the same old party politics, the same bigotry and crudity?' wonders Vant. Such a future is too terrible to contemplate, especially after Canada has gained new respect in the eyes of the world. He and Lanctot resolve to work together to heal their own differences and to mend the rifts in Canadian society. 'Somehow, back again in our own land,' Vant proclaims, 'we will find the way – to unity – and the beautiful things we have lost.'[83]

MANY CANADIANS AGREED with Gregory Vant and believed that the memory of the war could help them find the way – the true path through the divisive forces of class conflict, provincial jealousy, and racism, and towards unity, cooperation, and harmony between all citizens, be they Native, immigrant, English, or French. The myth could turn everyone into better Canadians and make them worthy of the country for which 60,000 men and women had given their lives. As Archibald MacMechan wrote, 'for four years Canada lived on the heights of heroism. The national spirit revealed in the fierce storm of war was alive, if latent, before the war; it is alive now. It has the power to shape a national ideal worthy of Canada's part in the great struggle and to lift our people to its height.'[84] The national spirit may have been temporarily obscured by the mists of materialism and sectionalism that beset postwar Canada, but the memory of the war could reveal it again, just as the war itself had done. That memory could sweep across the country like the north wind, purifying the nation's life, clarifying its true goals, and uniting the people in a common cause. In return for such gifts, the myth's proponents demanded only one thing: that it be embraced fully and faithfully. Considering what was at stake, it seemed little enough to ask.

Conclusion

In November 1928, a short poem by Hugh John Maclean, one of the legion of amateur Canadian poets whose identity has been lost to history, appeared in a number of newspapers. It was entitled simply 'Armistice Day, 1928':

> This is their day so reverently,
> > Bend ye the knee and bow the head,
> While memory parades them past,
> > The still battalions of the dead.
>
> They ask not any offering
> > Of kindred flame or wreathèd flowers,
> They only crave remembrance,
> > Through a few swiftly moving hours.
>
> Grant them their wish and let the thoughts,
> > Turn swiftly back to blood stained days,
> When common men with hero's hearts,
> > Lightly trod sacrificial ways.[1]

The poem is capable but nothing more, and it could easily have been missed in the slew of similar poems published that year. Yet in the last two lines, Maclean has distilled Canada's memory of the war into fewer than a dozen words. 'Common men' reminds us of the citizen-soldiers who dropped the tools of peace to don uniforms and rush to the defence of a principle. 'Hero's hearts' assures us that those common men rose above themselves in time of need; they revealed the strength that resided within, a strength that carried them through many a trying situation in the trenches. 'Lightly trod' conjures up images of the happy warrior, marching the roads of France and Flanders with a jolly whistle and a bright smile that would not desert him, even in death. And 'sacrificial ways' affirms the value of that death. The fallen did not lose their lives but gave them willingly so that their fellow Canadians could enjoy a better future, a future of greatness built on the sacrifices of the war years.

However, the dreams of a strong and vibrant pan-Canadian nationalism built on the memory of the Great War were dashed, and the belief that it could be an infinitely more powerful nation-building force than Confederation was proven over-optimistic. The myth's weakness lay, not in the fact that it had too little grounding in the realities of wartime, but in the fact that its rhetoric was too often contradicted by the realities of peacetime. The memory of the war might have been able to work its magic among immigrants, Natives, and French Canadians if it had been accompanied by some substantive steps towards the society it envisioned. As it was, the myth promised far more than it was able to deliver.

The memory of the war, for example, was unable to capture fully the hearts of the immigrant community. Some of its particulars undoubtedly took hold within many ethnic groups, and the Japanese-Canadian war memorial in Vancouver, a memorial volume published by the Icelandic community in Manitoba, and the Armistice Day address by a leader of Toronto's Italian community bear strong resemblance to the discourse of English Canadians.[2] Yet too often the high ideals of the myth stood in stark contrast to the realities of daily life. The war brought new Canadians no gradual emancipation, and their patriotism did little to convince their Anglo-Saxon compatriots that they should be admitted to full and equal partnership in the nation. Instead, exclusionary and racist rhetoric remained the order of the day. When Canadian Ku Klux Klan organizer J.H. Maloney rhapsodized about 'a Canada composed of those strong virile men of the north, the Nordic or Anglo-Saxon race ... whose sons died on Flanders field,' ex-soldiers of Greek, Japanese, Ukrainian, or African origin might well have wondered where they stood in the new Canada. They were certainly not considered equal to their comrades of British stock, despite the best efforts of the Canadian Legion to plead their case. Japanese-Canadian ex-soldiers may have won the provincial vote, but the franchise was extended very grudgingly by only a single vote in the British Columbia legislature. Those same veterans must have grumbled when Arthur E. Parker, the secretary of Win-nipeg's Board of Trade, declared during the tawdry controversy over the city's war memorial that naturalized Canadians could never achieve the same level of patriotism as the Canadian born of British stock.[3] For the newcomer of non-Nordic extraction, the signs were all around that Parker spoke the truth. Immigrants who had been fired in the postwar rush to hire ex-soldiers, who had been assaulted by marauding veterans in the years after the Armistice, or who had found that 1919 amendments to the Naturalization Act made it virtually impossible for aliens to become naturalized might well have realized that the war had done little to level the obstacles that stood in their way.

Native Canadians also found that reality failed to live up to the promise of the myth. Even had they been attracted by Duncan Campbell Scott's blatantly assimilationist vision, they would have found that it lacked even the advantage of sincerity. For Scott, enfranchisement was simply a strategy to eradicate all traces of Native heritage. He had little time for Loft or his rhetoric of the war as proof of Natives' right to full partnership in Canada, and he dismissed even Loft's military service. 'He volunteered for the war,' Scott wrote sourly of the League leader, 'but he was cunning enough to avoid any active service.'[4] Had Loft been less of a gentleman, he might have replied that Scott (the two were the same age) had not bothered to offer his services at all.

Not only was Native society as a whole disappointed by the legacy of the war, but even Native veterans found that their service did not put them on an equal footing with their white comrades. Of the 25,000 soldier-settlers who were given agricultural plots under the provisions of the Soldier Settlement Act, less than 1 per cent were Natives, and only a handful of those were granted free land off the reserves. Not until 1936 did Native veterans enjoy the same benefits as non-Natives under the War Veterans Allowance Act and the Last Post Fund, and even then the entitlement was given only under pressure from the Canadian Legion.[5] All too many Native ex-soldiers discovered that, despite their years of service at the front, they were no closer to enjoying the rights that they had ostensibly fought to defend. Ahenakew's Old Kayem told of a young Native veteran's encounter with a sanctimonious farm instructor who proclaimed that he had fought to defend the liberties guaranteed by the Union Jack. 'So did I,' shot back the Native, 'and I'm half-dead today because of it ... I sniped more of the enemy than you ever saw in the forestry corps. And I still don't know what liberty under the flag is. I've never known it.'[6]

For French Canada, the problem was not so much the disparity between the myth's rhetoric and postwar reality, but the unwillingness of French Canadians to concur in the proper combination of remembering and forgetting. Rather than laying the basis for a pan-Canadian nationalism, the memory of the Great War drove the two strains of nationalism apart. The events of 1914-18 became a stumbling block, not a bridge, and the adjurations made by the proponents of the myth were rebuffed. Few French Canadians were willing to forget conscription and the rancour that characterized the last years of the war, nor were they willing to be told exactly who represented the true soul of French Canada. Henri Bourassa, the *bête noire* of the myth, emerged as the dominant francophone voice of Québec, while figures such as Talbot Papineau, Jean Brillant, and Joseph Kaeble were soon all but forgotten, consigned to the roll of interesting but slightly misguided souls.

There is a final irony here that is striking. So often, the myth of the war had discarded unpalatable facts in favour of more appealing images. The soldier as a creature of the wilderness, the war as a human rather than a technological endeavour, military service as a cachet of inestimable value – all of these notions had caught on in spite of the fact that they had little basis in reality. The same process had occurred during the war. The statistical arguments made in defence of French Canada's human contribution to the war were entirely valid: the demographic characteristics of French-Canadian society, such as marriage age in the male population, and the ineptness with which recruiting was carried out in Québec, had as much or more to do with French Canada's enlistment rates than any imagined disloyalty or lack of attachment to Canada. Yet in the emotionally charged atmosphere of wartime, these facts were swamped by a wave of denunciations, recriminations, and accusations. It may have been true that ham-fisted recruiting practices acted as a brake on French-Canadian enlistment, but such an argument had little chance against sensational statements like the otherwise rational J.W. Dafoe's characterization of French Canadians as the only white race of quitters. For many French Canadians, the interpretation of the war that was popularized in the 1920s and 1930s could never sufficiently compensate for the interpretation of events that English Canadians had chosen to place upon the enlistment question. The acceptance of any version of memory is as much about forgetting as remembering; the spite that some English Canadians demonstrated during the conscription debate was simply too much for French Canada to forget.

There was more to the myth's failure than its constant contradiction by the realities of daily life in postwar Canada. The memory of the Great War never realized the high promise that its most vigorous proponents saw in it because it was so obviously assimilationist. It could indeed rejuvenate the country, but only if all citizens subsumed themselves in it. The nation it envisioned was a melting pot, in which all inhabitants would be rendered down into a single type. Natives would no longer be Natives, but Canadians; immigrants would no longer be immigrants, but Canadians; French Canadians would be content to be Canadians plain and simple. In each case, the myth of the war was to become a substitute for cultural diversity. It would give ethnic minorities the opportunity to surrender their own identities in exchange for membership in an imagined community that was homogeneous in belief and outlook.[7] For too many Canadians of non-British stock, it was a bad bargain at best.

Because the myth took on such strong patriotic and assimilationist overtones, it appears to be a typical example of an official memory that was created to secure the rule of the existent leadership by promoting a nationalistic, patriotic culture. Using John Bodnar's terms, one might suggest that a vernacular memory of the war as a wasteful and tragic episode that stemmed from the avarice of political and economic elites was driven to the ground by an elite memory of the war as a nation-building experience.[8] In light of the social and political unrest that plagued postwar Canada, elites may well have promoted such a version of the war as a thinly veiled way to control dissent by channelling energy and emotion into constructive, nonthreatening outlets.

Indeed, it is very clear that the myth, had it influenced Canada as its proponents hoped, would have served to solidify the nation's social and political status quo. Quite apart from its assimilationist overtones, the memory of the war looked forward to a day when social peace would prevail in Canada. However, it was a peace fashioned along Anglo-Canadian, middle-class ideals of social unity. When a Manitoba politician predicted in April 1919 that the postwar years would see greater unity between labour and capital, he meant that labour would remain in its proper place.[9] Rod Norquay's lumber camp may have been a paragon of cooperation, and Jack Maitland may have brought cooperation back to Blackwater, but in both cases it was cooperation based on paternalism rather than equality. And when Walter Blythe, in his last letter to Rilla before his death, wrote that he had 'helped to make Canada safe for the poets of the future – for the workers of the future ... for if no man dreams, there will be nothing for the workers to fulfill,' it was implicit that dreamers should not work and workers should not dream.[10] In short, the myth assumed that everyone would return to their proper places in the social hierarchy and proceed as if nothing had happened; any inconvenient questions about the justice of that hierarchy were to be deprecated. Instead of creating a less class-conscious society in Canada after the war, which would have been a more faithful rendition of the CEF experience, the myth would have created a society in which class divisions were reinforced but everyone was happy about it. The imagined community that the myth would forge was not a new Canada at all, but a Canada in which the old power structures were bolstered.

Nevertheless, the suggestion that the myth was simply a product of elite manipulation is profoundly unsatisfying. It robs countless Canadians of a sense of agency and prevents us from allowing that they might have embraced the myth, not to mention taken a hand in shaping it, because it spoke to their souls. Yet there is a very good reason why we must consider this possibility. At the core of the memory is not assimilation, or social peace, or even nation building; all of these were simply desired outcomes of the myth's operation. At the core of the memory were the fallen. They were the foundation upon which the entire edifice was constructed. Any attempt to forge an alternative vision of the war came up against the emotional needs of the hundreds of thousands of Canadians who had lost loved ones in those four years. As Adrian Gregory has argued, High Diction and all that it symbolized may have been a fatuous myth that deserved exploding, but to do so left a tragic vacuum for the bereaved.[11] For many Canadians, the prospect of that vacuum was a greater evil than even the war's losses. On the last Armistice Day of the interwar era, the *Globe* wondered if the myth still held in a post-Munich world: 'Can we say today, "They did not die in vain"? Can we chant this phrase in unison about the Cenotaph and mock their names with pious recitations of our faith? Can we go on hiding our shame behind sloppy platitudes to their glory? Or would it be better to bare the record and admit our failure? The fame of Canada's soldiers, the living and the dead, would be no less worthy on this account.' The editor's questions were quite justified, and modern readers would surely offer ready assent to his final assertion.

At the time, these were fighting words, and many people did believe that to say the soldiers had died in vain, to put to rest the pious recitations, and to admit the failure of the war generation would make the fame of Canada's soldiers less worthy. Such suggestions, by implying that the sacrifices of the war years had been wasted and that no good had come of the tragedy of 1914-18, were clearly intolerable. In the minds of many Canadians, rational and dispassionate enquiries like this were nothing less than insults to the fallen. Such reasoning comes out clearly in three incidents.

In April 1926, Canada's parliamentarians were debating the budget. It was an uninteresting debate, as many are, at least until G.B. Nicholson, the member for East Algoma in northern Ontario, commented that the sacrifice of Canada's war dead had been for high and noble motives. Immediately, Agnes Macphail jumped into the fray: 'Does the honourable member really believe that?' she demanded. 'If I did not believe it I should be the most desolate man in the world,' retorted Nicholson, but Macphail would not be put off. 'Will the honourable member admit,' she pressed, 'that the prime cause of the war was an economic one, and that the protection of women and children was not part of it?' Nicholson refused to admit anything of the kind, and replied with a restatement of the just war thesis. The war had been waged to rescue France and Belgium from German tyranny, 'but it was to save Canada as well. These men made the sacrifice in order to protect the homes of Canadians so that the mothers and wives, the sisters and sweethearts, the women of this country whom my honourable friend from southeast Grey represents, would never again be called upon to endure the tortures and to go through the hell of the experience which the women of North France and Belgium could not escape in those years.' The sympathy of the House evidently lay with Nicholson. After all, Macphail had questioned the meaning of the war; she had suggested that the dead had been sacrificed for something other than the high ideals that the memory of the war enshrined.[12] There may well have been some truth to what she said, but there was no room for her truth in Canada's myth. Her truth, as Nicholson pointed out, was a prescription for spiritual desolation.

A few months after this debate, the poet Thomas O'Hagan pondered the growth of Canadian nationalism in the pages of *Canadian Bookman*. In a very reasoned and dispassionate argument, he suggested that Canada did not yet have a national life because it had no flag, no national anthem, no distinct citizenship, and no final court of appeal. This might have passed without comment were it not for O'Hagan's next assertion: 'In vain shall we celebrate Vimy Ridge and Ypres, in recurring years, if we do not turn our eyes inward, and realize, indeed, the true significance of Canadian national life.'[13]

O'Hagan was as nationalist a poet as any, and his very valid argument reflects nothing more than a fervent hope that Canada would capitalize on the progress made during the Great War and achieve that national life. Yet it soon drew a blast from an irate reader. For Mrs. W. Garland Foster, it was not a rational consideration of Canadian nationalism but a vicious attack on the memory of her dead husband. 'Oh God, was it for this that my husband and thousands of others laid their bones in a foreign land?' she cried. 'Must they bear this insult to their faith?' She could see only one explanation for O'Hagan's essay: clearly, Henri Bourassa had poisoned his mind.[14] Naive though it may seem, Foster's reply did express a prevailing sentiment. In her eyes, O'Hagan had denied the assumption that a Canadian national life had sprung fully formed from the graves of Canadian soldiers in France and Flanders. By doing so, he had threatened to puncture the consolation that Foster and others had derived from the nation-building thesis. Whether there was any validity to O'Hagan's comments became irrelevant: all that mattered was that he, too, was articulating a recipe for spiritual desolation.

We move ahead seven years, to the Ottawa premier of Canada's official war film, *Lest We Forget*. Everyone who was anyone in the capital had turned out for what promised to be an important event on the year's social calendar: the governor general, Lord Tweedsmuir, who (as John Buchan) had written the most popular patriotic history of the war; Sir George Perley, Canada's long-time representative on the IWGC and now the elder statesman of Canadian politics; Cabinet ministers and members of Parliament; high-ranking officers of the Permanent Force and militia; the Legion executive – the audience was awash with dignitaries and 'aglitter with full dress uniforms and decorations.' The entire scene repelled the editor of the Ottawa *Citizen*. In an essay entitled 'Dress Up to See the Slaughter,' he sarcastically rejoiced that Ottawa's elite had the opportunity 'in comfortable seats, to see the glamor of the human slaughterhouse.' He predicted that the evening would be 'a stirring occasion, the narrative of the "war to end war" when 60,000 Canadian young men were done in to save the nation for this glorious day in Ottawa' when the pillars of state would parade in full dress with a pack of retainers.[15]

Relishing the evening as a gala social event rather than a remembrance of the war's losses was in rather poor taste, even by Ottawa's standards, and the editor was quite right to question the propriety of the entire affair. A.U.G. Bury, however, did not see it that way. He did not read the editorial as a scathing critique of transforming a sober commemorative film into a gay society ball; he read it as an outright attack on the war dead and, by extension, on the entire memory of the war. If the editor's assertions were correct, Bury wrote, then the fallen were either dupes or slaves who had died for nothing 'except their own folly or that of their country'; they were no better than the misguided and amoral drones who peopled the most lurid antiwar novel. If, on the other hand, 'they went, inspired by noble sentiment, and to noble service, and crowned both sentiment and service by the supreme self-sacrifice, then why should there be anything shameful or strange if ... we should keep their memories as fresh and as full of honour as ... we can.'[16] Here, Bury had employed the same reasoning as Nicholson and Foster. Unable to accept the editor's critique in the spirit in which it was intended, he could only see it as an attempt to undermine a memory of the war that offered real consolation to Canadians.

These three episodes reveal the complex process by which critiques of the myth actually contributed to its persistence. In the first place, any attempt to question the war or its aftermath raised the hackles of people who saw such questioning, not in the spirit of intellectual enquiry but as an attack on the fallen and their sacrifice. These defenders of the myth were then driven to restate its tenets in even stronger terms, a process that is evident in the remarks of Nicholson, Foster, and Bury. But critiques also fostered the myth in another way. If one intended to raise difficult questions about the war and its legacy, and at the same time avoid being contemptuously dismissed by a Foster or a Bury, one had to be doubly certain to praise the men and women who offered their lives for the cause. As J.B. Morton wrote, 'the more you insist upon the agonies and tortures and filth of modern warfare, the more honour you must pay to men who endured these things.'[17] This is precisely where Macphail, O'Hagan, and the editor of the *Citizen* had erred: they had not prefaced their remarks with a sufficient tribute to the men and women who had given their lives in the war.

Arthur Currie frequently spoke of the horrors of war and the fact that it brought out the very worst in humanity, yet he never drew the ire of the myth's most vociferous defenders. He got away with such comments not just because he was Arthur Currie, but because he always impressed upon his listeners the other half of the story: 'who can forget the example of untarnishable honour and flaming valour which shone amid the horror and the darkness of strife? Who can forget the deeds of kindliness and self-sacrifice which proved that the soul of man still held the divine spark?'[18] If critics of the war myth wished to be taken seriously by many contemporaries, they, like Currie, had to pay lip service to the very notions that they were trying to condemn. People like Agnes Macphail may well have found this exercise too intellectually distasteful to engage in, and even those people whose sympathy for the myth did not prevent them from being pragmatic found that their modest efforts at criticism were blunted in the attempt. 'I wrote *Rilla* not to "glorify war,"' maintained L.M. Montgomery in 1928, 'but to glorify the courage and patriotism and self-sacrifice it evoked.'[19] Modern readers might consider her remark to be curiously contradictory, but contemporaries would have understood her completely.

THE SANCTITY OF THE FALLEN, then, was paramount. No truth was so important to discover, no fiction so important to puncture, that it could justify calling into question the sacrifices of the dead. In this regard, we must take care not to underestimate the profound grief occasioned by the war. In studying Montreal's Anglo-Protestant elite, Margaret Westley interviewed a man who had lost his father and two uncles to the war. He recalled that a deep sense of sorrow pervaded his world, a feeling of sadness at promise missed and potential unrealized because of the war. His strongest memory was of the song 'Danny Boy,' which represented 'all the sadness of my childhood spent in the shadow of that war.'[20] This upper-class Montrealer can easily be transmuted into an immigrant Ukrainian farmer, a Toronto shop clerk, or a New Brunswick lumberworker. A family does not feel a loss any more keenly because it lives in comfortable circumstances. The Montrealer recalled that his friends and relatives dealt with their sorrow by believing that the fallen had willingly given their lives for principles that were important to them. There is no reason to suggest that people elsewhere in the social hierarchy did not embrace the myth for the same reasons.

It was not just the bereaved, however, who craved an explanation for the four years of agony that the country had endured. Anyone who lived through the war or its immediate aftermath looked for a way to give meaning to something that demanded explanation. To suggest that the four years of upheaval had meant nothing was, as G.B. Nicholson said, to surrender oneself to desolation. But it was also to turn one's back on a version of the past that could satisfy the craving for comprehension. One only had to accept the myth for the trials of 1914-18 to make sense. Canada's memory of the war conferred upon those four years a legacy, not of despair, aimlessness, and futility, but of promise, certainty, and goodness. It assured Canadians that the war had been a just one, fought to defend Christianity and Western civilization, and that Canada's sons and daughters had done well by their country and would not be forgotten for their sacrifices. To these great gifts, the myth added the nation-building thesis. By encouraging people to focus their thoughts on a time when the nation appeared to be united in a common cause, the memory of the war could prove that the twentieth century did indeed belong to Canada.

This is not to say that the myth, in and of itself, was an exercise in nostalgia; except in a few of its specifics, it did not gaze back longingly at an earlier era. It contained no explicit wish to return to the past, but instead looked to the past as a source of examples for the future. In this way, it affirmed the continuity of Canadian history. The war years did not mark a break with the past; they merely constituted another phase in Canada's evolution towards greatness. Painful and costly, the war had nevertheless conferred more than it wrenched away because it took Canada a few steps farther along the road to its destiny. If only everyone would realize this fact, the myth of the war could become a constructive force of unparalleled power. It would create a new nation, pure in its essence and secure from internal divisions. Like the adventure heroes examined by Graham Dawson, the war memory was 'ideally powerful and free from contradictions.' As such, it had the power to offer 'the psychic reassurance of triumph over the sources of threat.'[21] It could act as an antidote to both the disappointments of the present and the uncertainties of the future.

It is profoundly unsatisfying, then, to see the myth merely as a form of social control concocted by elites. As Raphael Samuel suggests, the invention of a certain view of the past is a process, not an event, and the memory that emerges is something that people create on their own, and for their own purposes.[22] Social control may have been a factor in the minds of some elites, but the memory of the war as a nation-building experience would not have caught on had it not been able to accommodate the widespread need to find meaning in the war. To dismiss the dominant memory as elite manipulation is to do a disservice to the uneducated veteran from northern Alberta who wistfully recalled the *estaminets* of France, the penurious spinster in Vancouver who sent a dollar to the war memorial fund, or the schoolgirl who marched proudly in a Nova Scotia Armistice Day parade. People like this embraced the myth, not because their social betters drilled it into their minds by sheer repetition, but because it answered a need, explained the past, or offered the promise of a better future. But they did more than simply embrace the myth: they helped to create it. By their very actions, each of these people played a role in nurturing the nation's memory of the war and giving it life within their consciousness as Canadians. That memory was not conferred on them from above; it sprouted from the grief, the hope, and the search for meaning of a thousand Canadian communities.

Notes

Abbreviations

AO   Archives of Ontario
CDC   Canadian Drama Collection, Mount Saint Vincent University
DFC   Dorothy Farquharson Collection of Canadian Sheet Music, McMaster University
HLRO House of Lords Record Office, London
HPL   Hamilton Public Library Special Collections
IWM   Imperial War Museum, London
JMH   John McCrae House, Guelph, Ontario
MTRL Metropolitan Toronto Reference Library
MU   Archives and Research Collections, McMaster University
NAC   National Archives of Canada
NBM   New Brunswick Museum
PANB   Public Archives of New Brunswick
PANS   Public Archives of Nova Scotia
PEIPA Prince Edward Island Public Archives and Records Office
QUA   Queen's University Archives
TFL   Thomas Fisher Rare Book Library, University of Toronto
UMA   University of Manitoba Archives

Introduction

1 Philip Child, *God's Sparrows* (London: Thornton Butterworth 1937; reprint, Toronto: McClelland and Stewart 1987), 146.
2 Lynn Hunt, 'History beyond Social Theory' in *The States of 'Theory': History, Art, and Critical Discourse,* ed. David Carroll (New York: Columbia University Press 1990), 103-4.
3 Mary Louise Roberts, *Civilization without Sexes: Reconstructing Gender in Postwar France, 1917-1927* (Chicago: University of Chicago Press 1994), 5-6; Raphael Samuel, *Theatres of Memory,* vol. 1, *Past and Present in Contemporary Life* (London: Verso 1994), 15.
4 Victor Huard, 'Armageddon Reconsidered: Shifting English-Canadian Attitudes to Peace Activism, 1936-1953' (paper presented to the Canadian Historical Association, 25 Aug. 1995, Montreal), 5.

5 Michiel Horn, *The League for Social Reconstruction: Intellectual Origins of the Democratic Left in Canada, 1930-1942* (Toronto: University of Toronto Press 1980), 144.

6 Russell Hann, introduction to *The Great War and Canadian Society: An Oral History,* ed. Daphne Read (Toronto: New Hogtown Press 1978), 25-6.

7 Lynne Hanley, *Writing War: Fiction, Gender, and Memory* (Amherst: University of Massachusetts Press 1991), 18-37; Paul Fussell, *The Great War and Modern Memory* (Oxford: Oxford University Press 1975); Rose Maria Bracco, *Merchants of Hope: British Middlebrow Writers and the First World War, 1919-39* (Oxford: Berg 1993); David Englander, 'Soldiering and Identity: Reflections on the Great War,' *War in History* 1, no. 3 (Nov. 1994): 300-18.

8 Marc Bloch, *Feudal Society,* trans. L.A. Manyon (Chicago: University of Chicago Press 1961), 102.

9 Roland Barthes, *Mythologies,* trans. Annette Lavers (New York: Hill and Wang 1972), 109, 143.

10 Christopher Shaw and Malcolm Chase, *The Imagined Past: History and Nostalgia* (Manchester: Manchester University Press 1989), 3-8.

11 Paul Connerton, *How Societies Remember* (Cambridge: Cambridge University Press 1989), 3; James Fentress and Chris Wickham, *Social Memory* (Oxford: Blackwell 1992), 25.

12 Michael Kammen, *Mystic Chords of Memory: The Transformation of Tradition in American Culture* (New York: Alfred A. Knopf 1991), esp. 9-13; 'Popular Memory: Theory, Politics, Method' in *Making Histories: Studies in History-Writing and Politics,* ed. Richard Johnson, Gregor McLennan, Bill Schwarz, and David Sutton (London: Hutchinson 1982), 207-8; John Bodnar, *Remaking America: Public Memory, Commemoration, and Patriotism in the Twentieth Century* (Princeton: Princeton University Press 1992), ch. 1.

13 Bloch, *Feudal Society,* 92.

14 Pierre Berton, *Vimy* (Toronto: McClelland and Stewart 1986); C.P. Stacey, 'Nationality: The Experience of Canada,' Canadian Historical Association *Historical Papers* (1967): 11; Desmond Morton and J.L. Granatstein, *Marching to Armageddon: Canadians and the Great War, 1914-1919* (Toronto: Lester and Orpen Dennys 1989).

15 Margaret E. Prang, 'Nationalism in Canada's First Century,' Canadian Historical Association *Historical Papers* (1968): 115; Stacey, 'Nationality,' 12.

16 A glance at virtually any university text bears this out. In C.M. Wallace, R.M. Bray, A.D. Gilbert, *Reappraisals in Canadian History: Post Confederation* (Scarborough, ON: Prentice-Hall 1996), the readings on the Second World War are confined to Dieppe. Chad Gaffield's *Constructing Modern Canada: Readings in Post-Confederation History* (Toronto: Copp Clark Longman 1994) has no readings on the military side of the war, while A.I. Silver, ed., *An Introduction to Canadian History* (Toronto: Canadian Scholars' Press 1991) includes only articles on foreign policy and the war. In Alvin Finkel, Margaret Conrad, with Veronica Strong-Boag, *History of the Canadian Peoples,* vol. 2, *1867 to the Present* (Toronto: Copp Clark Pitman 1993), the successful invasion of Sicily and the liberation of northwest Europe appear as mere afterthoughts to the disasters of Hong Kong and Dieppe.

Chapter 1

1 David Beatty, *Memories of the Forgotten War: The World War I Diary of Pte. V.E. Goodwin* (Port

Elgin, NB: Baie Verte Editions 1988), 199; NAC, H.C. Pullen Papers, Pullen to Ernestine Gilman, 14 Nov. 1918.

2 Gordon Reid, *Poor Bloody Murder: Personal Memoirs of the First World War* (Oakville, ON: Mosaic Press 1980), 239; Will Bird, *Thirteen Years After: The Story of the Old Front Revisited* (Toronto: Maclean 1932), 180.

3 *Daily Gleaner* (Fredericton), 10 Nov. 1932, 6; St. Stephen Public Library, Saint Croix Courier, *Journey Through Time,* 14 Nov. 1918; letter from M.N.W. Robertson, Burford, 10 Feb. 1994.

4 TFL, 'United Service of Thanksgiving and Prayer on the Occasion of the Signing of the Armistice by Germany Signifying her Unconditional Surrender held in St. James' Cathedral, Toronto, Tuesday, November 12th, 1918.'

5 *Guelph Evening Mercury,* 21 July 1919, 1; *Vancouver Daily Sun,* 21 July 1919, 3, and 20 July 1919, 1; *Phoenix* (Saskatoon), 21 July 1919, 3.

6 *Vancouver Daily Sun,* 19 July 1919, 7, 14; *Globe* (Toronto), 19 July 1919, 2.

7 Lorne Pierce Special Collections, Queen's University, 'Memorial Service held at Queen's University, Kingston, Canada, for Queen's Men who have given their Lives in the War, December 1st, 1918'; Edgar McInnis, 'Triumph' in *The Road to Arras* (Charlottetown: Irwin 1920), 27.

8 TFL, 'The Message from Mars, being a Christmas greeting from the Officers, NCOs and Men of the 4th Canadian Division to friends the wide world over. In the field – December 1918,' 55-6; Bernard McEvoy, 'When the Cenotaph Was Unveiled' in *Elvira and Fernando, and Other Selections* (Montreal: private 1927), 85.

9 *Saturday Night,* 18 Sept. 1920, 2.

10 Marina Warner, *Monuments and Maidens: The Allegory of the Female Form* (New York: Atheneum 1985), 140-2.

11 Pierre-Georges Roy, *Monuments commémoratifs de la province de Québec* (Quebec City: Commission des Monuments Historiques 1923), 2:121.

12 NAC, Arthur Currie Papers, vol. 10, f. 29, Hart to Currie, 13 Oct. 1925.

13 Quoted in John Ferguson, *The Arts in Britain in World War I* (London: Stainer and Bell 1980), 40.

14 Capt. W.H. Talbot in *Salute* 4, no. 6 (Oct. 1936):3; Stephen Leacock, 'The War Sacrifices of Mr. Spugg' and 'Some Just Complaints about the War,' in *The Hohenzollerns in America, with the Bolsheviks in Berlin and Other Impossibilities* (Toronto: S.B. Gundy 1919).

15 Theodore Goodridge Roberts, 'What Price Military Glory?' *Canadian Bookman* 15, no. 3 (March 1933):36; Leslie Roberts, *When the Gods Laughed* (Toronto: Musson n.d.), 202.

16 UMA, Charles W. Gordon Papers, box 30, f. 2, review of Owen McGillicuddy's *Sir Arthur Currie,* 16 Oct. 1925.

17 Erskine Church Archives, Ottawa, 'Erskine Church War Memorial,' n.d., 3.

18 Norah M. Holland, 'The Defeated' in *Spun Yarn and Spindrift* (London: J.M. Dent 1918), 94.

19 On the crucified soldier, see Maria Tippett, *Art at the Service of War: Canada, Art, and the Great War* (Toronto: University of Toronto Press 1984), 81-7.

20 Review of Nellie McClung's *Three Times and Out* in *Saturday Night,* 29 March 1919, 9.

21 Mark Blagrave, 'Garbo Talks ... Thespis Listens: The Impact of Cinema on Live Thea-

tre in Saint John, N.B. between the Wars' in *Myth and Milieu: Atlantic Literature and Culture, 1918-1939,* ed. Gwendolyn Davies (Fredericton: Acadiensis Press 1993), 37-8; Frank Carrel, *Impressions of War* (Québec: Telegraph 1919).

22 Frank Oliver Call, 'Rheims' in *Acanthus and Wild Grape* (Toronto: McClelland and Stewart 1920), 27; *Globe,* 26 July 1927, 4.

23 Kate Colquhoun, 'The Battle of St. Julien' in *The Battle of St. Julien and Other Poems* (Toronto: Ryerson Press 1928); Kim Beattie, 'The First Gas' in *'And You!'* (Toronto: Macmillan 1929), 8.

24 *A Brief Outline of the Story of the Canadian Grenadier Guards and the First Months of the Royal Montreal Regiment in the Great War* (Montreal: Gazette 1926), 21; W.C. Hancock, 'Fate,' *Acadia Athaneum* 61, no.7 (May 1936):26-9.

25 NAC, Department of National Defence Records, vol. 1819, f. GAQ 4-11, script for 'Lest We Forget'; Pierre van Paassen, *Days of Our Years* (Garden City, NJ: Garden City Publishing 1939), 62.

26 David Burns, 'The Devil Resigns to the Kaiser' in *Random Writings* (Brooklin, ON: private 1920), 2:100.

27 PANS, MG100, vol. 85 #66, J.E. Slocomb, 'Wanted – The Kaiser's Explanation,' 14 Dec. 1918; *Globe,* 19 July 1919, 4.

28 *Hamilton Spectator,* 21 July 1919, 5; *Guelph Evening Mercury,* 21 July 1919, 1.

29 'A Memorial Hall for OAC Guelph,' *OAC Review* 31, no. 10 (June 1919):459; foreword to *Canada in the Great War: An Illustrated Record of the Canadian Army in France and Flanders during the Years 1915 to 1918* (Ottawa: Heliotype 1919).

30 Rev. A. O'Malley, 'The Hun' in *Sonnets of a Recluse* (Barrie: Gazette n.d.), 2:36; Lieut.-Col. D. Donald, 'The War Memorial: An Appreciation,' *Caduceus* (Canadian Imperial Bank of Commerce) 1, no. 12 (March 1921):23; Rev. Wellington Bridgeman, *Breaking Prairie Sod: The Story of a Pioneer Preacher in the Eighties* (Toronto: Musson 1920), 158, 188.

31 Rev. Basil W. Thompson, in *Trinity War Book: A Recital of Service and Sacrifice in the Great War,* ed. Oliver Hezzelwood (Toronto: Ontario Press 1921), xiii.

32 *Globe,* 11 Nov. 1930, 4.

33 George G. Nasmith, *Canada's Sons and Great Britain in the World War* (Toronto: John C. Winston 1919), 82; Charles Stebbing, *Globe,* 6 June 1930, 4; NAC, Robert Manion Papers, vol. 67, f. s-300, G.E. Speight, Guelph to Manion, 20 Nov. 1938.

34 Leonard S. Klinck, introduction to *Record of Service 1914-1918: University of British Columbia, McGill British Columbia, Vancouver College* (Vancouver: Faculty Association Editorial Committee 1924); T.D.J. Farmer, 'Accomplishment Not Years' in *A History of the Parish of St. John's, Ancaster* (Guelph: Gummer Press 1924), 254.

35 Mary Kinley Ingraham, *Acadia* (Wolfville: Davidson Brothers 1920), act 4.

36 PANS, MG100, vol. 79 #25, Armistice Day supplement, 11 Nov. 1928; N. Willison, Lutheran College, Saskatoon, 'Remembrance Day,' *Kitchener Daily Record,* 11 Nov. 1938, 6; *Acta Victoriana* (Victoria University, Toronto), War Supplement (1919):6.

37 Address at the unveiling of the memorial tablet in Castle Memorial Hall, 9 Dec. 1921, in *McMaster University Monthly* 31, no. 4 (Jan. 1922):142; Lieut.-Col. H.V. Rorke, in D.J. Corrigall, *The History of the 20th Canadian Battalion* (Toronto: 20th Battalion Association 1935), ix.

38 DFC, #203.1 G.B. Castle, 'Canada on Parade / Le Canada en Parade' (Waterloo, ON: Waterloo Music 1931).

39 *Saturday Night,* 13 Nov. 1920, 5; 'Sculpture and the War,' *The Lamps* (Arts and Letters Club of Toronto), Dec. 1919, 84.

40 Antoine Prost, 'Les Monuments aux morts: Culte républicain? Culte civique? Culte patriotique?' in *Les Lieux de mémoire,* vol. 1, *La République,* ed. Pierre Nora (Paris: Gallimard 1984), 202.

41 Wilson Macdonald, 'War' in *A Flagon of Beauty* (Toronto: Pine Tree Publishing 1931), 131.

42 Thomas P. Socknat, *Witness against War: Pacifism in Canada, 1900-1945* (Toronto: University of Toronto Press 1987), 111, 128.

43 Review of Ernst Jünger's *Storm of Steel* in *Canadian Defence Quarterly* 7, no. 3 (April 1930):428.

44 Mabel Clint, *Our Bit: Memories of War Service by a Canadian Nursing Sister* (Montreal: Barwick 1934), 175-6; F.W. Bagnall, *Not Mentioned in Despatches* (Vancouver: North Shore Press 1933).

45 Richard E. Ruggle, 'Some Canadian Anglican Attitudes to War and Peace, 1890-1920,' *Journal of the Canadian Church Historical Society* 35, no. 2 (Oct. 1993):139; Canon W.J. Loucks, rector of Holy Trinity Church, *Globe,* 10 Nov. 1930, 1.

46 NAC, Sir Andrew Macphail Papers, vol. 6, f. 2, 'Armistice Address to Westmount Women's Club,' 10 Nov. 1933; University of Guelph Archives, Sir Charles G.D. Roberts Papers, XMI MS A003, letter and poem, Nov. 1938.

47 MU, Canadian Youth Congress Papers, box 12, f. 1, Owen to CYC, 22 Oct. 1937; Plumptre to CYC, 14 Oct. 1937; Ross to CYC, n.d. [Oct. 1937].

48 'Armistice Oratory,' *Saturday Night,* 16 Nov. 1935, 3.

49 'Sculpture and the War,' 85.

50 *Saturday Night,* 1 Aug. 1936, 1.

51 NAC, Royal Canadian Legion Papers, vol. 7, f. 8, circular #31/10, message from Conference of Presidents of Veterans Organizations, 3 Nov. 1931.

52 NAC, J.L. Ralston Papers, vol. 165, f. 1, speech at Pictou war memorial, 11 July 1935; Charles Stebbing, *Globe,* 6 June 1930, 4.

53 Quoted in *Toronto Daily Star,* 2 July 1929, 32; *Toronto Daily Star,* 10 Nov. 1928, 22.

54 Adrian Gregory argues this point very persuasively in *The Silence of Memory: Armistice Day, 1919-1946* (Oxford: Berg 1994), 122.

Chapter 2

1 J.M. Bliss, 'The Methodist Church and World War I,' *Canadian Historical Review* 49, no. 3 (Sept. 1968):213-33; quoted in J.T. Copp and T.D. Tait, eds., *The Canadian Response to the War, 1914-1917* (Toronto: Copp Clark 1971), 13-14.

2 UMA, Charles W. Gordon Papers, box 21, f. 16, 'Canada's Duty,' in *The Presbyterian,* 12 Nov. 1914, 438-9.

3 HPL, *Hamilton Herald* Scrapbooks, vol. c4.6, article, n.d., 24; United Church Archives, Samuel D. Chown Papers, f. 48, War Sermon 1915.

4 Michael Gauvreau, *The Evangelical Century: College and Creed in English Canada from the Great Revival to the Great Depression* (Montreal: McGill-Queen's University Press 1991),

258-60; David B. Marshall, *Secularizing the Faith: Canadian Protestant Clergy and the Crisis of Belief, 1850-1940* (Toronto: University of Toronto Press 1992), 160.

5 *Acta Victoriana* (Victoria University, Toronto), War Supplement (1919):6; Pte. R. Marshall Livingston, quoted in William Smith Duthie, ed., *Letters from the Front: Being a Record of the Part Played by Officers of the Bank in the Great War* (n.p.: Canadian Bank of Commerce 1920), 1:338.

6 *Caduceus* 2, no. 7 (Oct. 1921):37-8.

7 Grace Blackburn, *The Man Child* (Ottawa: Graphic 1930), 184.

8 Philip Child, *God's Sparrows* (London: Thornton Butterworth 1937; reprint, Toronto: McClelland and Stewart 1987), 134.

9 H.E.R. Steele, 'I Don't Want to Go Back,' *Canadian Magazine* 90 (Nov. 1938):17; PEIPA, T.E. MacNutt Papers, Accession 2825/462, military scrapbook, James Terry White, 'We Shall Remember Them,' from *Charlottetown Guardian,* 21 Jan. 1920.

10 Frank Oliver Call, 'Gone West' in *Acanthus and Wild Grape* (Toronto: McClelland and Stewart 1920), 29.

11 Theodore Goodridge Roberts, 'What Price Military Glory?' *Canadian Bookman* 15, no. 3 (March 1933):36; W.D. Lighthall, 'The Young Veteran (of the Great War)' in *Old Measures: Collected Verse* (Toronto: Musson 1922), 57; Archibald Macdonell, 'The Canadian Soldier – As I Knew Him at the Front,' *Queen's Quarterly* 28, no. 4 (April-June 1921):344.

12 Marjorie Pickthall, 'When It Is Finished' in *The Complete Poems of Marjorie Pickthall* (Toronto: McClelland and Stewart 1927), 195.

13 Crawford Kilian, 'The Great War and the Canadian Novel, 1915-1926' (MA thesis, Simon Fraser University, 1972), 86; George A.E. Parfitt, *Fiction of the First World War: A Study* (London: Faber 1990), 25, 82; Stanley Cooperman, *World War I and the American Novel* (Baltimore: Johns Hopkins University Press 1972).

14 John Oxenham, 'Christs All! – Our Boys Who Have Gone to the Front' in *'All's Well!':Some Helpful Verse for These Dark Days* (London: Methuen 1915), 15-16. The third stanza captures the tone of the poem: 'Yes, you are christs, if less at times your seeming, – / Christ walks the earth in many a simple guise. / We know you christs, when, in your souls' redeeming, / The christ-light blazes in your steadfast eyes.'

15 Acadia University Archives, J.D. Logan Papers, box 23, f. 269, William E. Marshall, 'In Memory of the Soldiers of Bridgewater, Nova Scotia who Gave their Lives in the Late World War of 1914-1919,' 19 April 1919.

16 Carmichael United Church Archives, Regina, Address by A.L. Maclean, 11 Nov. 1928.

17 Marjorie Pickthall, 'Marching Men' in *Complete Poems of Marjorie Pickthall,* 194.

18 Lorne Pierce, *Marjorie Pickthall: A Book of Remembrance* (Toronto: Ryerson Press 1925), 170.

19 Frederick George Scott, *The Great War as I Saw It* (Toronto: F.D. Goodchild 1922), 117.

20 George Godwin, *Why Stay We Here?* (London: Philip Allan 1930), 99, 209.

21 N.S., *Their Name Liveth: A Memoir of the Boys of Parkdale Collegiate Institute who Gave Their Lives in the Great War* (Toronto: Printers Guild n.d.), foreword; NAC, Royal Canadian Legion Papers, vol. 74, 'Report of the 5th Annual Dominion Convention, The Great War Veterans' Association of Canada, Port Arthur, Ontario, October 17-22, 1921,' 1.

22 Quoted in Marilyn Baker, 'To Honor and Remember: Remembrances of the Great

War. The Next-of-Kin Monument in Winnipeg,' *Manitoba History* 2 (1981):9; Arthur S. Bourinot, 'Immortality' in *The Collected Poems of Arthur S. Bourinot* (Toronto: Ryerson Press 1947), 8.

23 C.R.E., 'Two Easters: Vimy, 1917,' *Queen's Quarterly* 237, no. 1 (July-Sept. 1919):396; Lilian Leveridge, 'The Warriors' in *The Hero Songs of Canada* (private 1927).

24 NAC, W.L.M. King Papers, series J4, vol. 147, f. 1204, microfilm reel C-2731, minutes of meeting, 24 March 1926, 107352.

25 Knox United Church Archives, Calgary, 'Memorial Service on the occasion of the unveiling of the Window erected in memory of the men of Knox Church that fell in the Great War, Sunday, January 2nd, 1921'; Kate Reeves, '"By Its Beauty and Significance": The Memorial Window, Knox United Church, Calgary' (undergraduate essay, University of Alberta, 1993).

26 W.D. Lighthall, 'Deathless (October 30, 1917)' in *Old Measures,* 60.

27 John Bracher, 'A Living Memorial: The History of Coronation Park,' *Urban History Review* 19, no. 3 (Feb. 1991):214.

28 Paul Fussell, *The Great War and Modern Memory* (Oxford: Oxford University Press 1975), ch. 2.

29 Carmichael United Church Archives, Regina, 'A Unique National Memorial,' n.d.; Will Bird, *And We Go On* (Toronto: Hunter-Rose 1930), 101.

30 Toby A. Foshay, *J.D. Logan: Canadian Man of Letters* (Hantsport, NS: Lancelot Press 1982), 36-7.

31 Logan Papers, box 7, f. 54, preface in ms copy of *Insulters of Death,* 1916; the reviews are found in box 8, f. *New Apocalypse.*

32 Rev. R.G. MacBeth, *The Unreturning Brave: An Address in Memory of the Men Who Fell in the Great War* (Vancouver: R.P. Latta n.d.).

33 For example, of British Columbia war memorials, twelve inscriptions note that the fallen gave their lives; not a single one says they lost their lives. British Columbia Genealogical Society, *British Columbia War Memorials: An Index of Names* (Richmond: BCGS 1990).

34 Duncan Campbell Scott, 'To the Canadian Mothers, 1914-1918' in *Selected Poems of Duncan Campbell Scott,* ed. E.K. Brown (Toronto: Ryerson Press 1951), 170.

35 A.M. Stephen, 'The Cenotaph' in *The Land of Singing Waters* (Toronto: J.M. Dent 1927), 124; TFL, Sir Edmund Walker Papers, box 31, f. Canadian War Memorials 1919, Walker to Eric Brown, 18 Feb. 1919.

36 Isabel Ecclestone Mackay, 'Killed in Action' in *Fires of Driftwood* (Toronto: McClelland and Stewart 1922), 123.

37 Edgar McInnis, 'Requiem for a Dead Warrior' in *New Harvesting: Contemporary Canadian Poetry, 1918-38,* ed. Ethel Hume Bennett (Toronto: Macmillan 1938), 92-3; B.A. Ryan, 'April 1917,' *Canadian Bookman* 9, no. 4 (April 1927):103.

38 Sydney Arthur, *A Man's Worth: A Canadian College Romance* (Toronto: Hunter-Rose 1926), 293-4; William Lawson Grant, *In Memoriam: William George McIntyre* (private n.d.), 37.

39 Dedicatory poem, in Cyrus MacMillan, *McGill and Its Story* (Toronto: Oxford University Press 1921).

40 *Globe,* 10 Nov. 1928, 3; Harold Baldwin, *Pelicans in the Sky* (London: John Murray 1934), 24.

41 Eric J. Leed, *No Man's Land: Combat and Identity in World War I* (Cambridge: Cambridge University Press 1979), 190, 208.

42 CDC, #29.05 Sylvia M. Fletcher, 'Hedwig' (Banff 1937); Bird, *And We Go On,* 148; Dalhousie University Archives, Will Bird Papers, tearsheets from *Ypres Times.*

43 Mackay, 'The Returned Man' in *Fires of Driftwood,* 137.

44 Modris Eksteins, *Rites of Spring: The Great War and the Birth of the Modern Age* (Toronto: Lester and Orpen Dennys 1989), 190.

45 Quoted in Frank Field, *British and French Writers of the First World War: Comparative Studies in Cultural History* (Cambridge: Cambridge University Press 1991), 84.

46 Empire Club of Canada, *Addresses Delivered to the Members During the Sessions 1915-16 and 1916-17* (Toronto: J.M. Dent 1917), 45; NAC, Peregrine Acland Papers, f. 2, 'Thoughts of a Returned Soldier,' n.d.

47 Quoted in John F. Prescott, *In Flanders Fields: The Story of John McCrae* (Erin, ON: Boston Mills Press 1985), 134; Robert J.C. Stead, 'In the Wheat' in *The Empire-Builders* (Toronto: Musson 1923), 108.

48 Christopher Hussey, *Tait McKenzie: A Sculptor of Youth* (Philadelphia: J.B. Lippincott 1930), 4; Rebecca Sisler, *The Girls: A Biography of Frances Loring and Florence Wyle* (Toronto: Clarke, Irwin 1972), 36; Christine Boyanski, *Loring and Wyle: Sculptors' Legacy* (Toronto: Art Gallery of Ontario 1987), 35.

49 DFC, #445.3 Stanley Meredith and Keith Handyside, 'The World is Simply Mad on Uniform' (Toronto: W.R. Draper 1919); H.E. Amoss, 'Efficiency Jim,' *Canadian Magazine* 61, no. 4 (Aug. 1923):307-21.

50 NAC, J.L. Ralston Papers, vol. 165, f. 1, address at Pictou war memorial, 11 July 1935.

51 Janet Cox, 'The Coward,' in *Acadia Athenaeum* 59, no. 2 (Dec. 1935):46-50.

52 J.D. Logan and Donald G. French, *Highways of Canadian Literature: A Synoptic Introduction to the Literary History of Canada (English) from 1760 to 1924* (Toronto: McClelland and Stewart 1924), 352.

53 Scott, *The Great War As I Saw It,* 299.

54 J.W. Dafoe, *Over the Canadian Battlefields: Notes of a Little Journey in France, in March 1919* (Toronto: Thomas Allen 1919), 31; Glenbow Museum, Margaret K. Wallace Papers, f. 28, address by Reverend George Fallis, Vimy Ridge, 26 July 1936; *Spectator,* 7 June 1939, 32.

55 Mary MacLeod Moore, 'Corners of "A Foreign Field": The War Cemeteries of France and Belgium,' *Saturday Night,* 25 Sept. 1920, 25; Dafoe, *Over the Canadian Battlefields,* 13.

56 Diary for 11 Jan. 1916, in *Number 4 Canadian Hospital: The Letters of Professor J.J. Mackenzie from the Salonika Front* (Toronto: Macmillan 1933), 106; Bourinot, 'When Peace Has Come' in *Collected Poems of Arthur S. Bourinot,* 130.

57 NAC, Sir Robert Laird Borden Papers, series 1a, vol. 73, microfilm reel C-4316, minutes of IWGC 17th meeting, 18 Nov. 1919, 38141a.

58 *The Story of an Epic Pilgrimage: A Souvenir of the Battlefields Pilgrimage of 1928* (London: British Legion 1928); John J. Pershing, 'Our National War Memorials,' *National Geographic* 65, no. 1 (Jan. 1934):2; David Cannadine, 'War and Death, Grief and Mourning in Modern Britain' in *Mirrors of Mortality: Studies in the Social History of Death,* ed. Joachim Whaley (New York: St. Martin's Press 1981), 231.

59 I am using Victor Turner's definition, from 'Death and the Dead in the Pilgrimage Process' in *Blazing the Trail: Way Marks in the Exploration of Symbols,* ed. Edith Turner (Tucson: University of Arizona Press 1992), 35-8.

60 John Hundevad, 'The Origin' in *The Epic of Vimy,* ed. W.W. Murray (Ottawa: Legionary 1936), 6; John Pierce, 'Constructing Memory: The Idea of Vimy Ridge' (MA thesis, Wilfrid Laurier University, 1990), 57.

61 W.W. Murray, 'The Vimy Pilgrimage,' *Canadian Geographical Journal* 13, no. 8 (Dec. 1936):407; PANB, Milton F. Gregg Papers, vol. 2, f. 11, 'Memorandum respecting tentative arrangements for the visit of the Canadian Legion Pilgrimage to France in July 1936,' 5 May 1936; Stuart Armour, *A Pilgrim's Progress* (Cobourg, ON: Frank W. Lapp 1936), 32.

62 George Mosse, *Fallen Soldiers: Reshaping the Memory of the World Wars* (Oxford: Oxford University Press 1990), 32; Charles E. Royal, 'Canada' in *The Trail of a Sourdough: Rhymes and Ballads* (Toronto: McClelland and Stewart 1919), 116; T.C.L. Ketchum, 'The U.N.B. and Its Happy Warriors' in University of New Brunswick, *Memorial Magazine* (1919):138.

63 G. Kurt Piehler, 'The War Dead and the Gold Star: American Commemoration of the First World War' in *Commemorations: The Politics of National Identity,* ed. John R. Gillis (Princeton: Princeton University Press 1994), 173; Borden Papers, microfilm reel C-4316, Ware to Perley, 1 July 1920, 38007.

64 Thomas W. Laqueur, 'Memory and Naming in the Great War' in *Commemorations,* ed. Gillis, 156; Borden Papers, vol. 72, microfilm reel C-4316, report of Perley and Macready's visit to France, 7 May 1919, 37912; Ware to Perley, 1 July 1920, 38007.

65 Militia and Defence Records, series III A2, vol. 353, f. 61; NAC, Arthur Meighen Papers, vol. 54, microfilm reel C-3435, memo for Prime Minister, 14 Oct. 1921, 30656.

66 Meighen Papers, vol. 39, microfilm reel C-3428, Durie to Rev. J.C. Hodgins, 24 Jan. 1921, 23023; Guthrie to Meighen, 15 Feb. 1921, 23049; memo from #3 Area Superintendent, IWGC, n.d.

67 H.C. Osborne, 'The Gardens of the Dead' in *Guidebook of the Pilgrimage to Vimy and the Battlefields, July-August 1936* (Ottawa: Vimy Pilgrimage Committee 1936), 37; H.C. Osborne, 'Where the Empire's Heroes Sleep,' *Saturday Night,* 4 Dec. 1920, 29.

68 *Phoenix* (Saskatoon), 11 Sept. 1922, 7; David Beatty, *The Vimy Pilgrimage, July 1936 from the Diary of Florence Murdock, Amherst, Nova Scotia* (Amherst, NS: Acadian 1987), 23.

69 Allyson Booth, 'Figuring the Absent Corpse: Strategies of Representation in World War I,' *Mosaic* 26, no. 1 (Winter 1993):69-85.

70 Oliver Hezzelwood, 'Finding God' in *Poems and a Play* (Toronto: Ontario Press 1926), 71.

71 'The Glorious Dead' in Arthur Meighen, *Unrevised and Unrepented: Debating Speeches and Others* (Toronto: Clarke, Irwin 1949), 109-10; HPL, Brown-Hendrie Papers, Lily to William Hendrie, 3 July 1921, #H910.

72 CBMC, *Conditions of Competition in Design for Eight Memorial Monuments to be Erected in France and Belgium* (Ottawa: King's Printer 1920), 5.

73 CBMC, *Canadian Battlefield Memorials* (Ottawa: King's Printer 1929), 80-1; evidence of Currie, 4 May 1920, in annex C; foreword by S.C. Mewburn, 7.

74 King Papers, microfilm reel C-2729, King to Philippe Roy, 22 July 1922.

75 *Canadian Forum* 2, no. 18 (March 1922):559; M.O. Hammond, *Painting and Sculpture in Canada* (Toronto: Ryerson Press 1930), 60; CBMC, *Canadian Battlefield Memorials,* assessors' report, 10 Sept. 1921, 10.

76 HLRO, Lord Beaverbrook Papers, BBK A/236, Hughes to Beaverbrook, 17 July 1923; Hughes to Larkin, 17 July 1923; Hughes to Beaverbrook, 31 July 1923.

77 QUA, Walter S. Allward Papers, box 1, f. 9, Allward to André Ventre, 12 April 1926.

78 NAC, Ian Mackenzie Papers, vol. 33, f. B-6, text of Vimy speech; Department of External Affairs Records, vol. 1778, f. 184, pt. 2, transcript of Vimy broadcast; address by Rev. C.C. Owen, in Murray, *The Epic of Vimy,* 88; CBMC, *Canadian Battlefield Memorials,* annex B, 78; *Saturday Night,* 22 Aug. 1936, 3.

79 Borden Papers, vol. 73, reel C-4316, memorandum, 26 March 1920, 37959.

80 Harry Amoss, 'The Padre Who Was Born Again,' *Canadian Magazine* 58, no. 2 (Dec. 1921):127-38.

81 Duff Crerar, *Padres in No Man's Land: Canadian Chaplains and the Great War* (Montreal: McGill-Queen's University Press 1995), 165; quoted in John G. Reid, *Mount Allison University: A History, to 1963* (Toronto: University of Toronto Press 1984), 2:27; David B. Marshall, 'Methodism Embattled: A Reconsideration of the Methodist Church and World War I,' *Canadian Historical Review* 66, no. 1 (March 1985):48-64.

82 Theodore Goodridge Roberts, 'A Billet in Flanders (1915)' in *The Leather Bottle* (Toronto: Ryerson Press 1934), 81.

83 Marshall, 'Methodism Embattled'; Crerar, *Padres in No Man's Land,* 182; George Mosse, 'National Cemeteries and National Revival: The Cult of the Fallen Soldiers in Germany,' *Journal of Contemporary History* 14 (1979):4.

Chapter 3

1 George Mosse, *Fallen Soldiers: Reshaping the Memory of the World Wars* (Oxford: Oxford University Press 1990), 127.

2 *University of Toronto Monthly,* Jan. 1919, 60; *Vancouver Daily Sun,* 11 Nov. 1938, 8.

3 Modris Eksteins, *Rites of Spring: The Great War and the Birth of the Modern Age* (Toronto: Lester and Orpen Dennys 1989), 254.

4 Quoted in Marilyn Baker, 'To Honor and Remember: Remembrances of the Great War. The Next-of-Kin Monument in Winnipeg,' *Manitoba History* 2 (1981):8.

5 Brantford Public Library, f. War Memorial, *Brantford Expositor,* 14 Sept. 1992; 'Souvenir of the Dedication of the Brant War Memorial, Thursday May twenty-fifth 1933,' 2.

6 NAC, Sir Andrew Macphail Papers, vol. 7, f. 16, address 'In Retrospect: Armistice Day,' 11 Nov. 1936; Stephen Leacock, *The Unsolved Riddle of Social Justice* (London: John Lane 1920), 24.

7 QUA, C.G. Power Papers, box 88, address at Vimy Memorial unveiling, July 1936.

8 Gregory Clark, 'For Remembrance' in *So What?* (Toronto: Reginald Saunders 1937), 227; Robert J.C. Stead, *Dennison Grant: A Novel of To-Day* (Toronto: Musson 1920), 261; Kim Beattie, *'And You!'* (Toronto: Macmillan 1929), dedicatory poem.

9 Bernard Muddiman, 'The Man Who Went Back,' *Canadian Magazine* 57, no. 4 (Aug. 1921):273; Acadia University Archives, J.D. Logan Papers, box 9, f. 70, 'Lads' Laughter,' undated.

10 'Orderly Sergeant' [W.W. Murray], *Five-Nines and Whiz Bangs* (Ottawa: Legionary

1937), prologue; NAC, G.G.D. Kilpatrick Papers, 'The Canadian Corps,' address given at Sir Arthur Currie Branch, Canadian Legion, 1938.

11 *Caduceus* 12, no. 1 (April 1931):49; Kim Beattie, 'The Reunion' in *'And You!'* 89.

12 QUA, Sir Charles G.D. Roberts Papers, box 4, f. 107, James Norman Hall, 'The Return to Flanders'; W.W. Murray, 'The Vimy Pilgrimage,' *Canadian Geographical Journal* 13, no. 8 (Dec. 1936):409.

13 PANS, 85th Battalion Records, MG23 vol. 1, Ralston to Maj. Harvey Crowell, 20 Feb. 1930.

14 Will Bird, *Thirteen Years After: The Story of the Old Front Revisited* (Toronto: Maclean's 1932), 43, 114. Bird's articles, originally serialized in *Maclean's,* were immensely popular, drawing thousands of letters as well as invitations to speak at over a hundred public meetings in Central and Eastern Canada. Will Bird, *Ghosts Have Warm Hands* (Toronto: Clarke, Irwin 1968), 250.

15 Col. A.T. Hunter in *Saturday Night,* 24 Nov. 1928, 3; AO, playbill for *You're Lucky If You're Killed,* Grand Theatre, Fergus, 5 June 1933.

16 AO, Theatre Programs Collection, env. 3, program for The Dumbells in *Biff! Bing! Bang!,* opening 5 Sept. 1921 at the Grand Opera House, Toronto.

17 Advertisement for *Carry On,* in *Legionary* 3, no. 9 (Feb. 1929):11.

18 J.A. Caw, 'Journey's End,' *Caduceus* 11, no. 3 (Oct. 1930):89-90; *The Connecting File* (Royal Canadian Regiment) 11, no. 3 (July 1932):21.

19 *Globe,* 5 July 1930, 12; 9 Aug. 1930, 16.

20 *Globe,* 16 Aug. 1919, 2; *Saturday Night,* 28 Aug. 1926, 6; 25 Dec. 1926, 7; NBM, Printed Ephemera Collection F8-9, program for *Garrick* and *The Burgomaster of Stilemonde,* May 1921.

21 NAC, Arthur Currie Papers, vol. 8, f. 22, Garrette to Currie, 30 Oct. 1923; *Saturday Night,* 1 Sept. 1928, 6.

22 *Manitoba Free Press,* 21 April 1919, 5; *Toronto Daily Star,* 3 Aug. 1934, 4; *Manitoba Free Press,* 11 April 1919, 2; *Globe,* 4 Aug. 1934, 3.

23 *Canadian Baptist,* 22 May 1919, 11; Robert Shipley, *To Mark Our Place: A History of Canadian War Memorials* (Toronto: NC Press 1987), 122.

24 DFC, #445.3 Stanley Meredith and Keith Handyside, 'The World is Simply Mad on Uniform' (Toronto: W.R. Draper 1919); #947.6 J.B. Spurr, 'Cakes (The Dry Toast)' (Aurora, ON: J.B. Spurr 1919).

25 DFC, #961.6 J.B. Spurr, 'The Battle at the Gates of Love' (Aurora, ON: J.B. Spurr 1919); Stephen Leacock, 'Some Startling Side Effects of the War' in *The Hohenzollerns in America, with the Bolsheviks in Berlin and Other Impossibilities* (Toronto: S.B. Gundy 1919), 172-9.

26 *Manitoba Free Press,* 8 April 1919, 6; City of Toronto Archives, RG250, box 1, f. 7, advertisement by Ald. Fred Hamilton in Armistice Night Official Programme, 11 Nov. 1931; Alfred U. Russell, in *Canadian Baptist,* 6 Nov. 1930, 4.

27 Quoted in David Judd, Constance Wilson, Cathy Telfer, and Kathy Wilson, *Simcoe: County Town of Norfolk* (Simcoe, ON: Norfolk Historical Society 1985), 112; Joanne Hamilton, 'Dominion Day: A Mari Usque Ad Mare. A Study of the Dominion Day Celebrations from 1867 to 1972' (BA thesis, Waterloo Lutheran University, 1973), 24.

28 MTRL, 'Souvenir of the New Ontario Soldiers' Reunion and Discovery Week Cele-

bration, Sault Ste. Marie, Canada, August 4-8, 1923.'

29 Department of Soldiers' Civil Re-establishment, *Historical Tableau in Eight Scenes* (Ottawa: DSCR 1919); *Globe,* 25 Aug. 1919, 8.

30 Archie Gray, *The Towers of Mont St. Eloi* (Rodney, ON: Gray Printing 1933), preface; Theodore Goodridge Roberts, 'What Price Military Glory?' *Canadian Bookman* 15, no. 3 (March 1933):36.

31 Paul Fussell, *The Great War and Modern Memory* (Oxford: Oxford University Press 1975), 21-2.

32 John Cruickshank, *Variations on Catastrophe: Some French Responses to the Great War* (Oxford: Clarendon Press 1982), 28, 34, 118; Eksteins, *Rites of Spring,* 218.

33 L.R.H. Steward, 'A Canadian Perspective: The Fictional and Historical Portrayal of World War I' (MA thesis, University of Waterloo, 1983); Samuel Hynes, *A War Imagined: The First World War in English Culture* (New York: Atheneum 1987), 107.

34 George Godwin, *Why Stay We Here?* (London: Philip Allan 1930), 167.

35 Peregrine Acland, *All Else Is Folly: A Tale of War and Passion* (New York: Coward-McCann 1929), 343-4.

36 Roger Sarty, 'The Steel Helmet, or Two Pictures,' *Acadia Athenaeum* 61, no. 3 (Jan. 1936):12-13.

37 Theodore Goodridge Roberts, 'To the Unknown Soldier in Westminster Abbey,' *Canadian Bookman* 9, no. 12 (Dec. 1927):383; Theodore Goodridge Roberts, 'The Dreams of Glory,' *Canadian Bookman* 16, no. 1 (Jan. 1934):3-4.

38 Roberts's frequent suggestions can be found in QUA, Lorne Pierce Papers, section A, box 5, f. 10.

39 *Acta Victoriana* (Victoria University, Toronto) War Supplement (1919):5; Ontario Department of Education, *Annals of Valour* (Toronto 1919), 15.

40 House of Commons, *Debates* (supplement), 3 March 1924, 49; Rev. Frank Baird, 'Canada and the War,' University of New Brunswick, *Memorial Magazine 1914-1919* (Fredericton: n.p. 1919), 55.

41 University of New Brunswick, *Memorial Magazine,* foreword; J.W. Dafoe, *Over the Canadian Battlefields: Notes of a Little Journey in France* (Toronto: Thomas Allen 1919), 17.

42 'Message to the Boys and Girls of Canada,' New Brunswick Department of Education, *Canada War Book* (Fredericton 1918), 49; *Maclean's,* 1 Jan. 1932, 3.

43 J.A. MacDonald, *Gun-Fire: A Historical Narrative of the 4th Brigade, Canadian Field Artillery* (Toronto: Greenway 1929); Dundas Public Library, f. Dundas – Monuments, clipping dated 15 Dec. 1921.

44 Arthur Henry Chute, *The Real Front* (New York: Harper and Bros. 1918), introduction; J.F.B. Livesay, *Canada's Hundred Days* (Toronto: Thomas Allen 1919), ix.

45 Ontario Department of Education, *Annals of Valour,* 149; NAC, W.L.M. King Papers, series J5, vol. 10, f. 37, microfilm reel c-1988, speech of 11 Dec. 1921, 5854; Stuart Armour, *A Pilgrim's Progress* (Cobourg, ON: Frank W. Lapp 1936), 18.

46 R.H. Tupper, *Victor Gordon Tupper: A Brother's Tribute* (Toronto: Oxford University Press 1921), 53; 'A Sonnet to War' in *Major J.M. Langstaff, FIA, FAS, CA, Barrister-at-Law: A Memorial* (Toronto: Miln-Bingham n.d.).

47 Letter of 11 Dec. 1915, in Armine Norris, *Mainly for Mother* (Toronto: Ryerson Press 1919), 42.

48 Lorne Pierce Special Collections, Queen's University, 'Memorial Service at Queen's University, Kingston, Canada, for Queen's men who have given their lives in the War, December 1st, 1918,' 4, 8; Livesay, *Canada's Hundred Days,* 81.

49 George A.E. Parfitt, *Fiction of the First World War: A Study* (London: Faber 1988), 40.

50 Alfred Gordon, 'Play Ball!' in *Vimy Ridge and New Poems* (Toronto: J.M. Dent 1918), ix-xiii.

51 James Coyle, *Prince Edward Island Athletes in the Great War* (Charlottetown: King's Printer 1918), 3; Ralph Connor, *The Sky Pilot in No Man's Land* (New York: George H. Doran 1919), 275.

52 Mike Filey, *Toronto Sketches: 'The Way We Were'* (Toronto: Dundurn Press 1992), 32-3.

53 Jonas Crabtree, 'In Memoriam – November 11, 1937,' *Purple and White* (Assumption College, Windsor, ON) 12, no. 3 (12 Nov. 1937).

54 George Gibson, 'Seven Years Afterwards,' *Canadian Medical Association Journal* 16, no. 1 (Jan. 1926):85.

55 Quoted in *Hamilton Spectator,* 15 Dec. 1920; MU, 'The Victory Loan 1919: Its Message to Speakers,' 23.

56 Tupper, *Victor Gordon Tupper,* 62; obituary in *McMaster University Monthly* 27, no. 1 (Oct. 1917):6; Robert J.C. Stead, *The Cow Puncher* (Toronto: Musson 1918), 346.

57 Cecil Francis Lloyd, 'The Fighter' in *Landfall: The Collected Poems* (Toronto: Ryerson Press 1935), 38; *Expositor* (Brantford), 20 May 1933, 21.

58 Gray, *The Towers of Mont St. Eloi,* 253.

59 NAC, W.D. Lighthall Papers, vol. 6, f. 28, 'Canadian Poets of the Great War,' presidential address to the Royal Society of Canada, Dec. 1918.

60 James H. Pedley, *Only This: A War Retrospect* (Ottawa: Graphic 1927), 206; Daniel G. Dancocks, *Sir Arthur Currie: A Biography* (Toronto: Methuen 1985), 134.

61 S.J. Duncan-Clark and W.R. Plewman, *Pictorial History of the Great War* (Toronto: Hertel 1919), 21; UMA, Charles W. Gordon Papers, box 30, f. 2, review of Owen McGillicuddy's *Sir Arthur Currie,* 16 Oct. 1925. For Napoleon's message, see William Hazlitt, *The Life of Napoleon Bonaparte* (Boston: Dana Estes n.d.), 2:36-7.

62 Quoted in Maria Tippett, *Art at the Service of War: Canada, Art, and the Great War* (Toronto: University of Toronto Press 1984), 23.

63 King Papers, series J4, vol. 147, f. 1204, microfilm reel C-2731, memo by deputy minister, 11 April 1928, 107361; quoted in Tippett, *Art at the Service of War,* 77.

64 Dorothy M. Farr, *J.W. Beatty, 1869-1941* (Kingston: Agnes Etherington Art Centre 1981), 32; Dorothy Hoover, *J.W. Beatty* (Toronto: Ryerson Press 1948), 30.

65 IWM, E.H. Kennington Papers, Kennington to Yockney, 6 June 1918.

66 'Canada's War Pictures,' *Canadian Forum* 7, no. 74 (Nov. 1926):38; Arthur Lismer, 'The Canadian War Memorials,' *Rebel* (Toronto) 4, no. 1 (Oct. 1919):41; Barker Fairley, 'Canadian War Pictures,' *Canadian Magazine* 54, no. 1 (Nov. 1919):8.

67 A.Y. Jackson, 'The War Memorials: A Challenge,' *The Lamps* (Arts and Letters Club of Toronto), Dec. 1919, 76-7; A.Y. Jackson, 'War Pictures Again,' *Canadian Bookman* 8, no. 11 (Nov. 1926):340.

68 Hector Charlesworth, 'Reflections,' *Saturday Night,* 18 Sept. 1920, 2.

69 IWM, Paul Konody Papers, Roberts to Konody, 1 Jan. [1918]; Meirion and Susie Harris, *The War Artists: British Official War Art of the 20th Century* (London: Michael Joseph

1983), 105.

70 Michael Holroyd, *Augustus John: A Biography* (London: Heinemann 1975), 2:71; Konody Papers, Kennington to Konody, n.d.

71 Quoted in Maria Tippett, *Making Culture: English-Canadian Institutions and the Arts before the Massey Commission* (Toronto: University of Toronto Press 1990), 74.

72 AO, MU2057 (1919), program for the Canadian War Memorials Exhibition, New York, 1919.

73 IWM, William Orpen Papers, f.486/12, notes from CWMF, 7 March 1918.

74 Quoted in Tippett, *Art at the Service of War*, 38; *Globe*, 2 Oct. 1936, 15.

75 JMH, David McCrae scrapbook, letter from R.T. Sloan, Brantford, ON, 141; *Montreal Star*, 29 Oct. 1919, 9.

76 Eric J. Leed, *No Man's Land: Combat and Identity in World War I* (Cambridge: Cambridge University Press 1979), 104; Stuart Sillars, *Art and Survival in First World War Britain* (New York: St. Martin's Press 1987), 7.

77 J. Castell Hopkins, *Canadian Annual Review of 1919* (Toronto: Canadian Annual Review 1920), 30; W.B. Kerr, 'Historical Literature on Canada's Participation in the Great War,' *Canadian Historical Review* 14, no. 4 (Dec. 1933):430; *Globe*, 2 Sept. 1920, 9.

78 'Art and War Memorials,' *Canadian Bookman* 1, no. 4 (Oct. 1919):40; Tippett, *Art at the Service of War*, 91.

79 *Globe*, 29 Aug. 1919, 2; *Vancouver Daily Sun*, 6 Jan. 1919, 2.

Chapter 4

1 CDC, #24.13 Simon Jauvoich, 'Dawn in Heaven' (Winnipeg 1934).

2 Arthur G. Doughty, 'Canada's Record of the War,' *University Magazine* 15 (Dec. 1916):474; Douglas Durkin, *The Magpie* (Toronto: Hodder and Stoughton 1923; reprint, Toronto: University of Toronto Press 1974), 33.

3 Alfred Gordon, 'The Coward' in *Vimy Ridge and New Poems* (Toronto: J.M. Dent 1918), 19-20; Robert Stanley Weir, *After Ypres and Other Poems* (Toronto: Musson 1917).

4 Oliver Hezzelwood, 'Eat Christmas Dinner in Khaki' in *Poems and a Play* (Toronto: Ontario Press 1926), 66; Rev. A. O'Malley, 'The Slacker' in *Sonnets of a Recluse* (Barrie, ON: Gazette n.d.), 2:76.

5 Theodore Goodridge Roberts, *The Fighting Starkleys, or The Test of Courage* (Boston: Page 1922), 17.

6 Philip Child, *God's Sparrows* (London: Thornton Butterworth 1937; reprint, Toronto: McClelland and Stewart 1987), 118.

7 L.M. Montgomery, *Rilla of Ingleside* (Toronto: McClelland and Stewart 1920), 124; Harry Amoss, '1914' in *Prayer of the Good Trouper and Other Poems* (Toronto: Ryerson Press 1933), 53.

8 Walter Brindle, 'The Soldier's Story' in *France and Flanders: Four Years' Experience Told in Poem and Story* (Saint John: S.K. Smith 1919), 18.

9 Edgar McInnis, *The Road to Arras* (Charlottetown: Irwin 1920), 5; Ralf Sheldon-Williams, *The Canadian Front in France and Flanders* (Toronto: Macmillan 1920), 1.

10 William Howey, 'Blessings' in *Canadian Carols* (Toronto: Ryerson Press 1927), 61; L. Moore Cosgrove, *Afterthoughts of Armageddon: The Gamut of Emotions Produced by the War* (Toronto: S.B. Gundy 1919), 33.

11 Quoted in Daniel G. Dancocks, *Sir Arthur Currie: A Biography* (Toronto: Methuen 1985), 210.

12 See Edward M. Spiers, *The Army and Society, 1815-1914* (London: Longman 1980).

13 PANS, Horatio Crowell Papers, MG23 vol. 27, f. 10, Crowell to Antigonish *Casket,* 14 May 1920.

14 Law Society of Upper Canada (hereafter LSUC) Archives, Osgoode Hall, Toronto, f. 16-2-4 pt. 3, memo, 22 March 1927. This memo does not specify if the lieutenant's shooting was accidental; N.S., *Their Name Liveth: A Memoir of the Boys of Parkdale Collegiate Institute Who Gave Their Lives in the Great War* (Toronto: Printers Guild n.d.), foreword.

15 LSUC Archives, f. 16-2-4 pt. 1, Secretary, LSUC to Loring, 28 Nov. 1929.

16 MU, Macmillan of Canada Records, box 137, f. 12, Eayrs to H.M. Urquhart, 4 Nov. 1932; Macmillan to Urquhart, 7 March 1932, and reply, 11 March 1932.

17 Adrian Gregory, *The Silence of Memory: Armistice Day, 1919-1946* (Oxford: Berg 1994), 23.

18 MU, 'Programme souvenir publié à l'occasion du retour d'outre-mer du 22ème Battailon (Canadien-français), Quebec, May 1919'; Pierre-Georges Roy, *Les Monuments commémoratifs de la province de Québec* (Quebec City: Commission des Monuments Historiques 1923), 2:261.

19 Women's Section of the Brant War Memorial Association, *Brantford: The Telephone City* (Brantford: Hurley Printing 1924); L.M. Bruce, 'Waterloo County Great War Memorials,' *Waterloo Historical Society Report* 11 (1923):29; B.I. Scott, *Springhill: A Hilltop in Cumberland* (1926), quoted in Bertha Campbell, *Springhill: Our Godly Heritage* (Springhill, NS: Springhill Heritage Group 1989), 88.

20 M. Stuart Hunt, *Nova Scotia's Part in the Great War* (Halifax: Nova Scotia Veteran Publishing 1920), ix; T.D.J. Farmer, *A History of the Parish of St. John's, Ancaster* (Guelph: Gummer Press 1924), 255, 259.

21 James H. Gray, *The Roar of the Twenties* (Toronto: Macmillan 1975), 255.

22 PEIPA, R.L. Cotton Papers, Accession 2551/59, 'War Time Letters from England and France, together with lists of Some of the Prince Edward Islanders on Active Service for the Empire' (n.d.), 33-7.

23 Robert J.C. Stead, *The Cow Puncher* (Toronto: Musson 1918), 336-7.

24 David Carnegie, *The History of Munitions Supply in Canada 1914-1918* (Toronto: Longmans Green 1925), 250; Sir Llewellyn Woodward, *Great Britain and the War of 1914-1918* (London: Methuen 1967), 468ff.

25 Ralph Connor, *To Him That Hath: A Novel of the West of Today* (New York: George H. Doran 1921), 15; Harry Amoss, 'The Boy Who Came Home,' *Canadian Magazine* 58 (1921-2):422.

26 Grace Blackburn, *The Man Child* (Ottawa: Graphic 1930), 258.

27 Laurie Ricou, afterword to Robert J.C. Stead, *Grain* (New York: George H. Doran 1926; reprint, Toronto: McClelland and Stewart 1993), 249.

28 Lewis H. Thomas, *The Renaissance of Canadian History: A Biography of A.L. Burt* (Toronto: University of Toronto Press 1975), 27; Rose Potvin, ed., *Passion and Conviction: The Letters of Graham Spry* (Regina: Canadian Plains Research Center 1992), 19-20.

29 NAC, R.B. Bennett Papers, MG26 K, f.W-125, pt. 2, microfilm reel M-1463, J.A. Bar-

rett to Bennett, 16 Feb. 1934, 506029.

30 W.L.M. King Diary (transcript), fiche 42, 2 Oct. 1919; NAC, W.L.M. King Papers, series J5, vol. 7, f. 24, microfilm reel C-1987, D4079.

31 Quoted by King in House of Commons, *Debates,* 20 April 1920, 1406, 1416.

32 King Papers, series J5, vol. 10, f. 37, microfilm reel C-1988, cutting dated 3 Dec. 1921, 5849.

33 Owen McGillicuddy, *The Making of a Premier: An Outline of the Life Story of the Rt. Hon. W.L. Mackenzie King* (Toronto: Musson 1922), 63-8; letter from 'A Princess Pat,' *Globe,* 26 July 1930, 4.

34 R. MacGregor Dawson, *William Lyon Mackenzie King: A Political Biography, 1874-1923* (Toronto: University of Toronto Press 1958), 255.

35 House of Commons, *Debates,* 9 Feb. 1923, 182.

36 Stead, *Grain,* 134; Montgomery, *Rilla of Ingleside,* 57, 148.

37 NAC, Arthur Currie Papers, vol. 6, f. 19, W. Bullock to Currie, 24 April 1921.

38 MTRL, Dr. J.S. Freeborn quoted in J.H. Stevenson, 'Presentation Exercises: Unveiling of a Tablet to the Boys of the Magnetawan District Who took Part in the World War 1914-1918, August 12th 1919.'

39 Camilla Sanderson, 'I Envy You' in *Good Morning* (Toronto: William Briggs 1918), 40.

40 Modris Eksteins, *Rites of Spring: The Great War and the Birth of the Modern Age* (Toronto: Lester and Orpen Dennys 1989), 230; Robert Graves and Alan Hodge, *The Long Week-End: A Social History of Great Britain, 1918-1939* (London: Faber 1940), 14; Robert Weldon Whalen, *Bitter Wounds: German Victims of the Great War, 1914-1939* (Ithaca, NY: Cornell University Press 1984), 117.

41 Will Bird, *And We Go On* (Toronto: Hunter-Rose 1930), 342.

42 Rev. A.D. Robb, quoted in David B. Marshall, 'Methodism Embattled: A Reconsideration of the Methodist Church and World War I,' *Canadian Historical Review* 66, no. 1 (March 1985):48.

43 Theodore Goodridge Roberts, 'Under the Sun,' Saint John *Telegraph-Journal,* 14 June 1929; H.E.R. Steele, 'I Don't Want to Go Back,' *Canadian Magazine* 90 (Nov. 1938):16; Child, *God's Sparrows,* 117.

44 James Eayrs, *In Defence of Canada,* vol. 1, *From the Great War to the Great Depression* (Toronto: University of Toronto Press 1964), 44, 61.

45 UMA, Charles W. Gordon Papers, box 21, f. 3, 'The Cameron Highlanders of Canada,' 48; Bird, *And We Go On,* 100.

46 James H. Pedley, *Only This: A War Retrospect* (Ottawa: Graphic 1927), 16; Leslie Roberts, *These Be Your Gods* (Toronto: Musson 1929), 236.

47 *Proceedings of the 4th Convention of the Army and Navy Veterans in Canada, Toronto, Ontario, October 25th to 29th, 1921,* 102.

48 Hugh M. Urquhart, *The History of the 16th Battalion* (Toronto: Macmillan 1932), 346; J.N. Gunn and E.E. Dutton, *Historical Records of Number 8 Canadian Field Ambulance, 1915-1919* (Toronto: Ryerson Press 1920), 163.

49 Fred Bagley and Harvey Daniel Duncan, *A Legacy of Courage: 'Calgary's Own' 137th Overseas Battalion, C.E.F.* (Calgary: Plug Street Books 1993), 188-9. By comparison, membership in the British Legion was only 20 per cent of veterans at its peak, and usually fell below 10 per cent. Gregory, *The Silence of Memory,* 98.

50 Glenbow Museum, Israel Florence Papers, f. 8, '31st Battalion Association Yearbook, 1931-32,' 2; PANB, Milton F. Gregg Papers, vol. 2, f. 14, 'Notes relating to the Canadian Legion of the British Empire Service League,' n.d.

51 Wilkie GWVA statement of principles, in Wilkie Historical Society, *Wilkie, Saskatchewan: 1908-1988* (Wilkie, SK: WHS 1989), 2:735.

52 NAC, Victor W. Odlum Papers, vol. 22, Odlum to battalion commanders, 8 Feb. 1919; *Prestonian*, 19 April 1923, 16; NAC, Department of National Defence Records, vol. 4628, f. 7-1-1, pt. 1.

53 *Saturday Night*, 20 March 1920, 6.

54 Glenbow Museum, William Guthrie Papers, program for 10th Annual Reunion Dinner, Calgary, 16 Nov. 1928; Florence Papers, f. 7, program for 16th reunion dinner, Calgary, 10 Nov. 1934; program for dinner of 15th Battery, Toronto, 9 April 1926, in author's collection.

55 William S. Watson, 'Flanders Fields,' *McMaster University Monthly* 28, no. 7 (April 1919):301; R. Watkins-Pitchford, 'Memorial Arch,' *RMC Review* 15 (June 1934):31.

56 Kim Beattie, 'The Vision' in *'And You!'* (Toronto: Macmillan 1929), 90.

57 Frederick George Scott, 'The Unbroken Line' in *Collected Poems* (Vancouver: Clarke and Stuart 1934), 75; Eric J. Leed, *No Man's Land: Combat and Identity in World War I* (Cambridge: Cambridge University Press 1979), 3, 212.

58 Kent Fedorowich, *Unfit for Heroes: Reconstruction and Soldier Settlement in the Empire between the Wars* (Manchester: Manchester University Press 1995), 104.

Chapter 5

1 Archibald MacMechan, 'Minas to the Wotan Line' in *Late Harvest* (Toronto: Ryerson Press 1934), 19; Frederick George Scott, *The Great War As I Saw It* (Toronto: F.D. Goodchild 1922), 26.

2 Rupert Brooke, *Letters from America* (New York: Scribner's 1916; reprint, New York: Beaufort Books 1988), 168.

3 Quoted in Donald Read, *Edwardian England 1901-15: Politics and Society* (London: Harrap 1972), 12; quoted in Roland Stromberg, *Redemption by War: The Intellectuals and 1914* (Lawrence: University Press of Kansas 1982), 18.

4 Quoted in Charles V. Genthe, *American War Narratives, 1917-1918: A Study and Bibliography* (New York: D. Lewis 1969), 27; quoted in James G. Greenlee, *Sir Robert Falconer: A Biography* (Toronto: University of Toronto Press 1988), 216.

5 Loftus MacInnes, 'The Cynics' in *Canadian Poems of the Great War*, ed. J.W. Garvin (Toronto: McClelland and Stewart 1918), 131.

6 NAC, Department of National Defence Records, vol. 1819, f. GAQ 4-11, script for *Lest We Forget*.

7 John Herd Thompson, *The Harvests of War: The Prairie West, 1914-1918* (Toronto: McClelland and Stewart 1981), 12-13; H.V. Nelles, introduction to Grace Morris Craig, *But This Is Our War* (Toronto: University of Toronto Press 1981), ix.

8 Cecil Francis Lloyd, 'The Reason (August 4th, 1914)' in *Landfall: The Collected Poems* (Toronto: Ryerson Press 1935), 5.

9 Theodore Goodridge Roberts, *The Fighting Starkleys, or The Test of Courage* (Boston: Page 1922), 13; Harold Baldwin, *Pelicans in the Sky* (London: John Murray 1934), 19-20.

10 Peter McArthur, 'A Chant of War' in *Canadian Poems of the Great War,* ed. Garvin, 142-6.

11 AO, G.H. Perley Papers, MU4113, f. Speeches, Addresses, Reports, speech to Dudley and District Chamber of Commerce, n.d.

12 *Globe,* 6 June 1938.

13 Robert J.C. Stead, 'We Were Men of the Furrow' in *The Empire-Builders* (Toronto: Musson 1923), 103.

14 NAC, A. Fortescue Duguid Papers, vol. 2, f. 6, 'The Canadian as a Soldier,' typed ms, 14 July 1920. Such sentiments remain a feature of the discourse surrounding the Great War. The theme, for example, is explicit in Pierre Berton, *Vimy* (Toronto: McClelland and Stewart 1986).

15 Wayne Charles Miller, *An Armed America: Its Face in Fiction. A History of the American Military Novel* (New York: New York University Press 1970), 98; Peter Aichinger, *The American Soldier in Fiction, 1880-1963: A History of Attitudes toward Warfare and the Military Establishment* (Ames: Iowa University Press 1975), 18.

16 Maria Tippett, *Art at the Service of War: Canada, Art, and the Great War* (Toronto: University of Toronto Press 1984), 66-9; Robert F. Nielson, 'A Barely Perceptible Limp: The First World War in Canadian Fiction' (MA thesis, University of Guelph, 1971), 57.

17 J.A. MacDonald, *Gun-fire: A Historical Narrative of the 4th Brigade, Canadian Field Artillery* (Toronto: Greenway 1929), 197; QUA, C.G. Power Papers, box 88, speech at the unveiling of the Vimy Memorial, July 1936.

18 Donald Buchanan, 'The Artists See War,' *Interdependence* (League of Nations Society in Canada) 11, no. 4 (Dec. 1934):199.

19 Will Bird, *And We Go On* (Toronto: Hunter-Rose 1930), 221; Overseas Military Forces of Canada, *Report of the Ministry, Overseas Military Forces of Canada, 1918* (London 1918), 338.

20 Bertrand W. Sinclair, *Burned Bridges* (New York: Grosset and Dunlap 1919); Laura Goodman Salverson, *The Dark Weaver* (Toronto: Ryerson Press n.d.).

21 University of British Columbia Special Collections, 'A Short History of Captured Guns: The Great European War, 1914-1918' (Vancouver n.d. [1934?]), foreword; Jonathan F. Vance, 'Tangible Demonstrations of a Great Victory: War Trophies in Canada,' *Material History Review* 42 (Fall 1995):47-56.

22 Arthur Currie, 'The Canadian Corps and Its Part in the War,' address delivered to the Canadian Club of New York, 25 March 1920, 16; *Vancouver Sun,* 14 Nov. 1928, 2; Dr. A.R. Perry, quoted in Arthur Wright, ed., *Memories of Mount Forest and Surrounding Townships* (Mount Forest, ON: Confederate 1928), 75; JMH, David McCrae scrapbook, undated cutting, 3.

23 W.D. Lighthall, 'The Young Veteran (of the Great War)' in *Old Measures: Collected Verse* (Toronto: Musson 1918), 57.

24 Jean Blewett, 'Bugler Jim' in *Jean Blewett's Poems* (Toronto: McClelland and Stewart 1922), 111; NAC, Department of National Defence Records, vol. 6562, f. HQ899-120, Hanna J. McLaren, Lancaster, ON, to DND, 18 Aug. 1936; J.E.B. Seely, *Adventure* (London: Heinemann 1932), 267.

25 A.C. Macdonell, 'The Canadian Soldier – As I Knew Him on the Western Front,'

Queen's Quarterly 28, no. 4 (April-June 1921):349.

26 Jean Blewett, 'The Woman Patriot' in *Jean Blewett's Poems,* 108; letter of 9 Aug. 1916, in Armine Norris, *Mainly for Mother* (Toronto: Ryerson Press 1919), 91.

27 Kitchener Public Library, f. War Memorials, unidentified article, 6 Jan. 1928; MTRL, 'Yarmouth Town and County War Memorial, Official Program for the Unveiling Ceremony, Saturday Morning, June 9th, 1923.'

28 St. Catharines Public Library, 'Unveiling of the Township of Niagara Soldiers' Monument, Thursday November 11, 1926.'

29 Graham Dawson, *Soldier Heroes: British Adventure, Empire and the Imaginings of Masculinities* (London: Routledge 1994), 2-3; Mary Louise Roberts, *Civilization without Sexes: Reconstructing Gender in Postwar France, 1917-1927* (Chicago: University of Chicago Press 1994), 10.

30 George Godwin, *Why Stay We Here?* (London: Philip Allan 1930), 166.

31 Paul Fussell, *The Great War and Modern Memory* (Oxford: Oxford University Press 1975), 21.

32 Stuart Sillars, *Art and Survival in First World War Britain* (New York: St. Martin's Press 1987), 8; Rosa Maria Bracco, *Merchants of Hope: British Middlebrow Writers and the First World War, 1919-1939* (Oxford: Berg 1993), 15.

33 Katherine Hale, *Canada's Peace Tower and Memorial Chamber* (Toronto: n.p. 1935); W.W. Murray, 'In Remembrance,' *Maclean's,* 15 April 1929, 6; NAC, J.H. MacBrien Papers, vol. 3, f. 3, 'The Royal Military College of Canada,' undated ms.

34 For the full story, see George O. Fallis, *A Padre's Pilgrimage* (Toronto: Ryerson Press 1953).

35 *Gold Stripe* 2 (1919), frontispiece; NAC, Royal Canadian Legion Records, vol. 1, fiche 4, minute book vol. 1, minutes of GWVA Dominion Executive meeting, Ottawa, 7 March 1922, 254.

36 Sir Edmund Walker, quoted in Tippett, *Art at the Service of War,* 45.

37 HLRO, Lord Beaverbrook Papers, BBK E/1/10, Borden to Beaverbrook, 18 April 1918; BBK A/241, King to Beaverbrook, 22 June 1928 and reply, 24 June 1928.

38 Arthur Stringer, *The Stranger* (Ottawa: Dominion Victory Loan Publicity Committee 1919).

39 W. Eric Harris, *Stand to Your Work: A Summons to Canadians Everywhere* (Toronto: Musson 1927), 14; A.H. Chute, 'How Sleep the Brave,' *Gold Stripe* 1 (Dec. 1918):93.

40 *St. Catharines Standard,* 12 Nov. 1926, 1; *Hamilton Herald,* 16 Oct. 1920; Nathaniel A. Benson, 'Ode for Dominion Day,' *Queen's Quarterly* 10 (1930-1):145-6.

41 MTRL, 'Souvenir of the New Ontario Soldiers' Reunion and Discovery Week Celebration, Sault Ste. Marie, Canada, August 4-8, 1923.'

42 Pierre-Georges Roy, *Monuments commémoratifs de la province de Québec,* vol. 2 (Quebec City: Commission des Monuments Historiques 1923), 333.

43 *Le Livre d'or des Canadiens,* vol. 10 (Montreal: La compagnie de publication Mont-Royal 1918); C. Courneloup, *L'Épopée du Vingt-deuxième* (Montreal: La Presse 1919), 5.

44 K.S. Inglis, 'The Anzac Tradition,' *Meanjin Quarterly* 24, no. 1 (March 1965):26; George L. Mosse, *Fallen Soldiers: Reshaping the Memory of the World Wars* (Oxford: Oxford University Press 1990), 63-4.

45 Nellie Spence, 'The Schoolboy in the War,' *Canadian Magazine* 52, no. 3 (Jan.

1919):755; Mary Josephine Benson, 'The Intercepting Spark' in *My Pocket Beryl* (Toronto: McClelland and Stewart 1921), 82; Canadian War Records Office, *Souvenir: New Exhibition of Canadian Official War Photographs in Colour* (London: CWRO 1919), 8.

46 *Hamilton Spectator*, 15 Dec. 1920; PANB, MC80/1186, 'An Address by D.R. Moore, Delivered at the Unveiling of the Soldiers' Memorial Tablet at Stanley, New Brunswick. Labor Day, September 5th, 1921.'

47 J. Castell Hopkins, *Canada at War, 1914-1918* (Toronto: Canadian Annual Review 1919), 440.

48 Genthe, *American War Narratives,* 86; Desmond Morton, *When Your Number's Up: The Canadian Soldier in the First World War* (Toronto: Random House 1993), 277.

49 Sir Robert Falconer, *The German Tragedy and Its Meaning for Canada* (Toronto: University of Toronto Press 1915), 3.

50 William Lawson Grant, *In Memoriam: William George McIntyre* (private n.d.), 19; *Caduceus* 2, no. 2 (May 1921):6; 2, no. 6 (Sept. 1921):35.

51 Currie, *The Canadian Corps and its Part in the War,* 9; Duguid Papers, 'The Canadian as a Soldier.'

52 Esther Kerry, 'He Is A Canadian' in *He Is A Canadian and Other Poems* (Montreal: Regal Press 1919), 3-4.

53 Theodore Goodridge Roberts, 'Private North' and 'A Cook-house at Reveille' in *The Leather Bottle* (Toronto: Ryerson Press 1934), 83, 86.

54 Merrill Dennison, *Brothers in Arms* in *The Unheroic North: Four Canadian Plays* (Toronto: McClelland and Stewart 1923), 26. By 1929, this had become the most popular play in Canada with over 500 known performances. *Canadian Forum* 9, no. 106 (July 1929):365.

55 Godwin, *Why Stay We Here?,* 45.

56 Morton, *When Your Number's Up,* 278.

57 Robin Gerster, *Big-Noting: The Heroic Theme in Australian War Writing* (Melbourne: Melbourne University Press 1987), 75; Sillars, *Art and Survival,* 138.

Chapter 6

1 HLRO, Lord Beaverbrook Papers, BBK E/1/10, Beaverbrook to Borden, 1 Jan. 1916; NAC, Sir Edward Kemp Papers, vol. 133, f. C-27, pt. 2, memo, 10 Dec. 1918.

2 NAC, A.G. Doughty Papers, vol. 8, diary, 3 May 1916; Beaverbrook Papers, BBK E/1/10 Beaverbrook to Borden, 25 Aug. 1916.

3 Beaverbrook Papers, BBK E/1/39, 'History in the Making: Romance of CWRO in London,' n.d.; BBK E/3/30, 'Canadian War Records 1915 to 1916,' n.d.

4 Ibid., BBK E/1/29, 'Reports Submitted by the Rt. Hon. Lord Beaverbrook to the Rt. Hon. Sir Robert Laird Borden,' 11 Jan. 1917; BBK E/1/42, memo by Aitken, 'The Censor and Volume II, *Canada in Flanders,*' n.d., 2.

5 Ibid., BBK E/3/39, Currie to Beaverbrook, 3 July 1918; quoted in Daniel Dancocks, *Sir Arthur Currie: A Biography* (Toronto: Methuen 1985), 232; W.S. Wallace, 'Clio in Canada, 1918,' *Canadian Bookman* 1, no. 1 (Jan. 1919):46.

6 W.B. Kerr, 'Historical Literature on Canada's Participation in the Great War,' *Canadian Historical Review* 14, no. 4 (Dec. 1933):431.

7 W.H.C. Wood, 'Behind the Scenes of Canadian War History,' *Argosy* (Mount Allison

University) 4, no. 1 (1926):45; AO, M.O. Hammond Papers, series 10-K, W.H.C. Wood, 'The Canadian Record and Commemoration of the War'; Kerr, 'Historical Literature,' 427-8.

8 NAC, R.B. Bennett Papers, microfilm reel M-1463, f. W-125, Roper to Bennett, 17 Feb. 1932, 506009; resolution from Summerside Branch, 6 April 1932, 506012.

9 Will Bird, *The Communication Trench* (Montreal: Perreault 1932), preface.

10 PC 1652, 27 May 1921; NAC, Department of National Defence Records, vol. 2732, f. HQS 5393, Deputy-Minister to Canadian Legion, 28 Oct. 1929.

11 Ibid., memo by Duguid, 5 Jan. 1928; memo to Minister, 3 March 1928.

12 Ibid., report of Special Committee, 2 Jan. 1929; Bovey to McNaughton, 24 Jan. 1929.

13 NAC, A.G.L. McNaughton Papers, series II vol. 9, f. 39, memo, 18 May 1932; DND Records, vol. 2732, f. HQS 5393, memo by Duguid, 6 April 1932.

14 W.B. Kerr, in *Canadian Historical Review* 20, no. 1 (March 1939):64.

15 National Defence Records, vol. 1506, f. HQ 683-1-30-18, review by W.J. Gorman, in *Northern Miner,* 18 Aug. 1936; *Canadian Historical Review* 20, no. 1 (March 1939):65.

16 NAC, A.E. Kemp Papers, vol. 133, f. C-27, pt. 2, note regarding official films, n.d.

17 Bennett Papers, microfilm reel M-1105, f. M-750-W, Photo-Sound Corporation to Bennett, 20 Aug. 1934, 287006; Columbia Pictures of Canada to GWMPC, 16 Aug. 1934, 287008.

18 Ibid., Sutherland to Bennett, 5 Nov. 1934, 287018; NAC, Royal Canadian Legion Records, vol. 1, fiche 5, minute book vol. 2, minutes of Canadian Legion Dominion Executive Council meeting, Ottawa, 27 Nov. 1934.

19 *Toronto Telegram,* 5 April 1935; *Mail and Empire,* 26 March 1935.

20 Royal Canadian Legion Papers, vol. 75, 'Report of the Dominion President, 7th Dominion Convention, January 31st-February 3rd, Fort William, Ontario,' 32.

21 University of Guelph Archives, Norman M. Blaney Papers, clipping dated 7 Oct. 1926.

22 Oliver Hezzelwood, *Trinity War Book: A Recital of Service and Sacrifice in the Great War* (Toronto: Ontario Press 1921), 116; R.F. MacLeod, *Canada's National Railways: Their Part in the War* (Toronto: Canadian National Railway 1921), 19.

23 See, for example, the account of the disastrous attack on Regina Trench in October 1916, in S.G. Bennett, *The 4th Canadian Mounted Rifles, 1914-1919* (Toronto: Murray 1926), 40; R.C. Fetherstonhaugh, *The Royal Montreal Regiment, 14th Battalion, C.E.F., 1914-1925* (Montreal: RMR 1927), 239.

24 NAC, R.B. Viets Papers, Warren to Viets, 23 Dec. 1927.

25 J.D. Logan and Donald G. French, *Highways of Canadian Literature: A Synoptic Introduction to the Literary History of Canada (English) from 1760 to 1924* (Toronto: McClelland and Stewart 1924), 344-5.

26 John Cruickshank, *Variations on Catastrophe: Some French Responses to the Great War* (Oxford: Clarendon Press 1982), 41; Modris Eksteins, *Rites of Spring: The Great War and the Birth of the Modern Age* (Toronto: Lester and Orpen Dennys 1989), 218.

27 JMH, Matthews Family scrapbook, unidentified article, 26; Roger Sarty, 'Canadian Verse,' *Acadia Atheneum* 61, no. 6 (April 1936):21; *Canadian Bookman* 1, no. 1 (Jan. 1919):54.

28 JMH, Matthews Family scrapbook, unidentified article 'Canadian Poetry Written during the War,' 15.

29 University of Guelph Archives, L.M. Montgomery Collection, scrapbook of book reviews, 1911-36, pp. 183-91.

30 Mary Vipond, 'Best Sellers in English Canada, 1899-1918: An Overview,' *Journal of Canadian Fiction* 24 (June 1979):107.

31 J. Castell Hopkins, *Canadian Annual Review of Public Affairs for 1919* (Toronto: Canadian Annual Review 1919), 64ff; AO, MU2131 1919 #1, William T. Gregory, 'Who Won the War?'

32 Writers Club of Toronto, *Canadian Writer's Market Survey* (Ottawa: Graphic 1931), 162; NAC, Arthur Currie Papers, vol. 10, f. 32, LaMarsh to Currie, 11 Feb. 1929.

33 G.H. Stokes and A. Johnson, in *Canadian War Stories* 2, no. 2 (15 Sept. 1929):64; W.D. Stovel, 'National Publicity,' *Canadian Forum* 9, no. 101 (Feb. 1929):160.

34 *Vancouver Sun,* 12 Nov. 1929, 9; Victor Lauriston, *Romantic Kent: The Story of a County, 1626-1952* (private 1952), 725-6.

35 *Ottawa Journal,* 10 June 1927; Bird, *The Communication Trench,* 55; *Globe,* 22 Feb. 1928, 2.

36 *Legionary* 3, no. 11 (April 1929):22; 4, no. 5 (Oct. 1929):25.

37 Currie Papers, vol. 12, f. 35a, Moore to Currie, 12 Sept. 1928; Col. A.T. Hunter, 'The Modesty of Canada: Address delivered to the Canadian Legion at Cobourg on Armistice Day, 1928,' *Saturday Night,* 24 Nov. 1928, 3.

38 Fred Griffin, *Variety Show: Twenty Years of Watching the News Parade* (Toronto: Macmillan 1936), 53-4; Hugh M. Urquhart, *Arthur Currie: The Biography of a Great Canadian* (Toronto: J.M. Dent 1950), 279-80.

39 Leslie Roberts, *These Be Your Gods* (Toronto: Musson 1929), 237; R.T.L. [Charles Vining], 'Sir Arthur Currie,' *Maclean's,* 1 June 1933, 12; 'Certainly a Great Man,' *Saturday Night,* 9 Dec. 1933, 1.

40 Dancocks, *Sir Arthur Currie,* 280-3; *Canadian Defence Quarterly* 11, no. 2 (Jan. 1934); Henry Borden, ed., *Letters to Limbo by the Right Honourable Sir Robert Laird Borden* (Toronto: University of Toronto Press 1971), 63.

41 'The Third Battle of Mons' (editorial), in *The Legionary* 2, no. 1 (May 1928):11; H.M. Urquhart, *The History of the 16th Battalion* (Toronto: Macmillan 1932), 340; Urquhart, *Arthur Currie,* 276.

42 Robert J. Sharpe, *The Last Day, the Last Hour: The Currie Libel Trial* (Toronto: Carswell 1988), 52; *Toronto Daily Star,* 5 March 1919, 1; 6 March 1919, 6.

43 *Globe,* 6 March 1919; J.F.B. Livesay, *The Making of a Canadian* (Toronto: Ryerson Press 1947), 96.

44 Quoted in Sharpe, *The Last Day,* 10-11.

45 *Free Press* (London), 2 May 1928, 6; *Evening Telegram* (Toronto), 2 May 1928, 26; Sharpe, *The Last Day,* 226.

46 *Expositor* (Brantford), 2 May 1928, 4; *Calgary Albertan,* 2 May 1928, 4; *Halifax Herald,* 3 May 1928, 6.

47 Canadian War Museum, R.E.W. Turner Papers, classification 58A-1-9.3, Currie to Turner, 8 May 1928; Sharpe, *The Last Day,* 125.

48 *Toronto Daily Star,* 4 May 1928, 6; Roberts, *These Be Your Gods,* 235.

49 *Free Press* (London), 2 May 1929, 6; Royal Canadian Legion Records, vol. 7, f. 4, circular #16, 4 May 1928; PANB, Milton F. Gregg Papers, vol. 2, f. 9, Currie to Gregg, 7 May 1928.

50 AO, Archibald Macdonell Letters, MU2050 1914 #18, Macdonell to Hugh Cameron, 27 Oct. 1934; 'The Third Battle of Mons,' 11.

51 Review by Thomas Murtha, *Saturday Night,* 26 April 1930, 9; MU, Macmillan of Canada Records, box 78, f. 3, Pratt to Eayrs, 24 Feb. 1934; Eayrs to E.K. Broadus, 28 Feb. and 12 March 1934.

52 *The Book Review Digest: Books of 1930* (New York: H.W. Wilson 1931), 277; *Army Quarterly* 21, no. 1 (Oct. 1930):183; Macmillan of Canada Records, box 91, f. 12, sales figures, 7 July 1930 to 31 Dec. 1931.

53 'Preferences,' *Canadian Forum* 10, no. 119 (Aug. 1930):410.

54 Stanley Cooperman, *World War I and the American Novel* (Baltimore: Johns Hopkins University Press 1967), 198-9.

55 Quoted in *Free Press* (London), 9 Nov. 1928, 4.

56 *Saturday Night,* 19 Nov. 1927, 8; review in *Canadian Bookman* 10, no. 1 (Jan. 1928):20.

57 *Moose Jaw Times,* 27 May 1930; review of *Goodbye to All That, Farewell to Arms, All Else Is Folly,* in *Canadian Forum* 10, no. 113 (Feb. 1930):171.

58 Urquhart, *The History of the 16th Battalion,* 342.

59 Review of *Soldier of Quebec,* in *Canadian Defence Quarterly* 9, no. 2 (Jan. 1932):282; NAC, Sir Andrew Macphail Papers, vol. 6, f. 2, address 'In Retrospect: Armistice Day,' 11 Nov. 1936.

60 Mabel Clint, *Our Bit: Memories of War Service by a Canadian Nursing Sister* (Montreal: Barwick 1934), 175; *Legionary* 3, no. 12 (May 1929):22; Clifford H. Bowering, *Service: The Story of the Canadian Legion, 1925-1960* (Ottawa: Canadian Legion 1960), 61; *Legionary* 3, no. 9 (Feb. 1929):23.

61 Lieut.-Col. F.C. Curry, 'The Trend of the War Novel,' *Canadian Defence Quarterly* 7, no. 4 (July 1930):519-20.

62 Macmillan of Canada Records, box 137, f. 12, Col. C.W. Peck, 'Modern War Books,' *The Brazier* 18 (Dec. 1930):7.

63 F.W. Bagnall, *Not Mentioned in Despatches* (Vancouver: North Shore Press 1933), 54, 70.

64 NAC, G.G.D. Kilpatrick Papers, 'The Canadian Corps,' address given at Sir Arthur Currie Branch, Canadian Legion, 1938; Frederick George Scott, *The Great War As I Saw It* (Toronto: F.D. Goodchild 1922), 117.

65 Lloyd Roberts, 'Tom, Dick and Harry' in *Along the Ottawa: A Book of Lyrics* (Toronto: J.M. Dent 1927), 24; *Canadian Bookman* 12, no. 3 (March 1930):61.

66 Kerr, 'Historical Literature,' 432; *Saturday Night,* 9 Aug. 1930, 9; *Globe,* 12 Nov. 1930, 12; *Gazette* (Montreal), 21 June 1930, 13.

67 Peck, 'Modern War Books,' 7; Currie Papers, vol. 12, f. 37, Oliver to Currie, 4 June 1930.

68 House of Commons, *Debates,* 19 May 1930, 2267; Currie Papers, vol. 11, f. 33, Macdonell to Currie, 26 June 1930.

69 Currie Papers, vol. 11, f. 33, Currie to Macdonell, 25 June 1930; quoted in Sharpe, *The Last Day,* 76.

70 Will Bird, *And We Go On* (Toronto: Hunter-Rose 1930), preface.

71 *The Canadian Who's Who* (Toronto: Trans-Canada Press 1939), 3:60; review in *Saturday Night,* 25 July 1931, 7. The rest of the reviews are in Dalhousie University Archives,

Will Bird Papers, black scrapbook, unpaginated.
72 Bird, *And We Go On,* 342-3.
73 Urquhart, *History of the 16th Battalion,* 340-6.
74 Gregg Papers, vol. 1, f. 1, review of *Five-Nines and Whiz Bangs,* in *Legionary* (1938).

Chapter 7

1 There are various versions of the writing of the poem, but all share the same essentials. See John F. Prescott, *In Flanders Fields: The Story of John McCrae* (Erin, ON: Boston Mills Press 1985).
2 JMH, letter to the editor [*Canadian Churchman?*], in David McCrae scrapbook; Archibald MacMechan, *Head-waters of Canadian Literature* (Toronto: McClelland and Stewart 1924), 238.
3 Eugene Standerwick, 'The Future of Canadian Literature,' *Canadian Bookman* 17, no. 1 (Jan. 1935):3; *Globe,* 8 Nov. 1930, 4.
4 *Canadian Bookman* 1, no. 2 (April 1919):85; *Manitoba Free Press,* 9 April 1919, 11; *The Torch* (John McCrae Branch, Canadian Legion) 5 (1938):29.
5 James Harold Manning, *Courcelette and Other Poems* (Saint John: J. and A. McMillan 1925), 18; James Ferres, in *University Magazine* 18 (Feb. 1919):16.
6 Eric J. Leed, *No Man's Land: Combat and Identity in World War I* (Cambridge: Cambridge University Press 1979), 212.
7 Windsor Municipal Archives, RG2 A4, box 158, minutes of council meetings, 22 Dec. 1924 and 24 Aug. 1925.
8 Duncan Campbell Scott, 'To a Canadian Lad Killed in the War' in *Selected Poems of Duncan Campbell Scott,* ed. E.K. Brown (Toronto: Ryerson Press 1951), 78.
9 *Saturday Night,* 19 April 1919, 4; Christine Boyanski, *Loring and Wyle: Sculptors' Legacy* (Toronto: Art Gallery of Ontario 1987), 31-3.
10 *Free Press* (London), 15 June 1927, 6.
11 Michel Ragon, *The Space of Death: A Study of Funerary Architecture, Decoration, and Urbanism,* trans. Alan Sheridan (Charlottesville: University Press of Virginia 1983), 109.
12 Quoted in Robert Shipley, *To Mark Our Place: A History of Canadian War Memorials* (Toronto: NC Press 1987), 62.
13 Acadia University Archives, minutes of the meeting of the board of governors, 27 May 1919.
14 'A Memorial Art Gallery,' *Canadian Bookman* 9, no. 4 (April 1927):109.
15 Kitchener Public Library, f. War Memorials, clipping dated 6 Jan. 1928; Judge A.G. Boles to H.L. Staebler, 11 Jan. 1928; Arthur Thurston, *A Cenotaph Rises: The Missing Heroes, 1914-1919* (private 1991), 3-4.
16 *Journal of the Royal Architectural Institute of Canada* 4, no. 12 (Dec. 1927):423; James H. Gray, *The Roar of the Twenties* (Toronto: Macmillan 1975), ch. 12.
17 NBM, notes on Saint John war memorial, 5 Nov. 1962; NAC, R.B. Bennett Papers, microfilm reel M-1463, f. W-150, 506747, Perley, Stewart, and Manion to Bennett, n.d.; NAC, Arthur Meighen Papers, vol. 115, microfilm reel C-3463, 67359, resolution from PPCLI Club, Ottawa, 14 Jan. 1925.
18 *OAC Review* 34, no. 4 (Dec. 1921):132; John Rose, *The History of Shelburne* (private 1972), 494-501.

19 *Border Cities Star,* 25 June 1919, 1; 8 Sept. 1920, 13; 6 April 1921, 3.

20 Shipley, *To Mark Our Place,* 67, 79.

21 *University of Toronto Monthly,* Jan. 1919, 64.

22 *Border Cities Star,* 6 April 1921, 3.

23 NAC, W.L.M. King Papers, series J4, vol. 225, f. 2153, 153298-99, 'Notes regarding Resolution of Thanks to the Canadian Battlefields Memorials Commission,' 11 June 1936.

24 *Municipal Review* (War Memorials Souvenir Issue) 21, no. 11 (Nov. 1925):7; William John Shaw, *St. Paul's Church (Presbyterian), Hamilton, Ontario: A Century of Service* (private 1933), 83.

25 *Globe,* 11 Nov. 1930, 1.

26 'The Fallen and the Politicians,' *Saturday Night,* 21 Nov. 1931, 1.

27 NAC, Royal Canadian Legion Papers, vol. 7, f. 9, circular letter #32/2, 3 Feb. 1932.

28 PEIPA, T.E. MacNutt Papers, Accession 2825/462, S. Sivwright Maxner, 'One Single Day,' 27 Sept. 1932, in scrapbook, unpaginated; City of Toronto Archives, RG250, box 3, f. 12, memo from RDC, n.d.

29 NAC, Brooke Claxton Papers, vol. 1, f. Armistice Day 1933, uncited article, 16 Nov. 1933; *Globe,* 10 Nov. 1930, 14.

30 *Globe,* 10 Nov. 1930, 2, 14; and 12 Nov. 1930, 1-2; Bennett Papers, microfilm reel M-1463, f. W-126, 506229, J.W. Russell, Calgary Legion to Bennett, 29 Feb. 1932; 506352, Bergeron to Bennett, 17 Nov. 1932.

31 *Globe,* 12 Nov. 1935, 9-11; *Star-Phoenix* (Saskatoon), 12 Nov. 1936, 5; *Edmonton Journal,* 11 Nov. 1938, 10; *Vancouver Sun,* 11 Nov. 1938, 1; *Halifax Herald,* 11 Nov. 1938, 8.

32 Ronald Coppin, 'Remembrance Sunday,' *Theology* 68, no. 54 (Oct. 1965):525-30.

33 King Papers, series J4, vol. 205, f. 1963, microfilm reel C-4279, 141754, speech notes, 11 Nov. 1936; 141769, memo to King, 3 Oct. 1938.

34 Glenbow Museum, Noel Adair Farrow Papers, f. 128, article 'Splendor and Gaiety Characterize Annual Military Ball in Calgary,' n.d.

35 *Vancouver Sun,* 11 Nov. 1938, 6; *Edmonton Journal,* 12 Nov. 1937, 21.

36 King Papers, series J4, vol. 205, f. 1963, microfilm reel C-4279, 141720, file note, 31 Oct. 1935.

37 *Vancouver Sun,* 12 Nov. 1929, 24; *Kitchener Daily Record,* 11 Nov. 1938, 16.

38 UMA, Charles W. Gordon Papers, box 21, f. 14, 'The Falling Torch'; *Globe,* 10 Nov. 1930, 14.

39 JMH, Matthews Family Scrapbook, 'Veteran Leader Unveils Tablet to 43rd Battery,' n.d.; *Halifax Herald,* 11 Nov. 1937, 1.

40 W.R. Riddell, 'Canada' in *Addresses delivered before the Canadian Club of Toronto, 1925-26* (Toronto: Canadian Club 1926), 324; Bennett Papers, microfilm reel M-1463, f. W-126, 506091, Armistice Day message, 10 Nov. 1930.

41 R.G. Macbeth, *The Unreturning Brave: An Address in Memory of the Men who Fell in the Great War* (Vancouver: R.P. Latta n.d.), 95; PANB, Capt. W.F. Parker at Trinity Church, Sussex, NB, 26 June 1934, quoted in MC80/969, Lieut.-Col. George Machum, 'The Story of the 64th Battalion, c.e.f., 1915-1916,' 45.

42 Oliver Hezzelwood, *Trinity War Book: A Recital of Service and Sacrifice in the Great War* (Toronto: Ontario Press 1921), 4.

43 J.C. Cochrane, 'Confession' in *Priceville and its Roots (Routes)*, ed. Katie Harrison (Owen Sound: Priceville and Area Historical Society 1992), 176.

44 PANS, MG100 vol. 79 #12, unidentified Halifax newspaper editorial, 10 Nov. 1928.

45 Dalhousie University Archives, Will Bird Papers, column 'Lest We Forget,' in black scrapbook, unpaginated; Will Bird, *The Communication Trench* (Montreal: Perrault 1933), 264.

46 T. Finley McWilliams, 'Who Were These Men?' *McMaster University Monthly* 29, no. 7 (April 1920):298; 'Al Pat' [A.C. Joseph], 'Query' in *Rhymes of an Old War Horse* (private 1938), 4.

47 Edgar McInnis, 'Requiem for a Dead Warrior' in *New Harvesting: Contemporary Canadian Poetry, 1918-1938,* ed. Ethel Hume Bennett (Toronto: Macmillan 1938), 92-3.

48 Robert T. Anderson, 'Comrades of the War Years' in *Troopers in France* (Edmonton: Coles 1932), 121-3.

49 Quoted in *Maclean's,* 15 Dec. 1933, 22-4.

50 NAC, Sir Andrew Macphail Papers, vol. 7, f. 16, address 'In Retrospect: Armistice Day,' 11 Nov. 1936; Acadia University Archives, J.D. Logan Papers, box 8, f. E.R. Goulding Poems, Goulding to Logan, 18 Dec. 1919; Leslie Roberts, *So This Is Ottawa* (Toronto: Macmillan 1933), ix.

51 William Irvine, *The Farmers in Politics* (Toronto: McClelland and Stewart 1920); W.C. Good, *Production and Taxation in Canada from the Farmers' Standpoint* (Toronto: J.M. Dent 1919).

52 C.W. Peterson, *Wake Up, Canada! Reflections on Vital National Issues* (Toronto: Macmillan 1919); Stephen Leacock, *The Unsolved Riddle of Social Justice* (London: John Lane 1920).

53 J.O. Miller, *The New Era in Canada: Essays Dealing with the Upbringing of the Canadian Commonwealth* (Toronto: J.M. Dent 1917), 5.

54 L. Moore Cosgrove, *Afterthoughts of Armageddon: The Gamut of Emotions Produced by the War* (Toronto: S.B. Gundy 1919), 34; T.C.L. Ketchum, 'The U.N.B. on Active Service' in University of New Brunswick, *Memorial Magazine 1914-1919* (1919):32; Peterson, *Wake Up, Canada!* 337.

55 Ethel Stilwell, 'All Honour to our Men,' *Toronto Daily Star,* 11 Nov. 1927, 6; Hezzelwood, *Trinity War Book,* 328.

56 Walter Brindle, *France and Flanders: Four Years' Experience Told in Poem and Story* (Saint John: S.K. Smith 1919), 83; *Listening Post* 33 (March 1919):15.

57 J.A. MacDonald, *Gun-Fire: A Historical Narrative of the 4th Brigade, Canadian Field Artillery* (Toronto: Greenway 1929), 198; NAC, Arthur Currie Papers, vol. 6, f. 18, Bellew to Currie, 11 Nov. 1933.

58 PANB, Milton F. Gregg Papers, vol. 2, f. 14, review of *I, That's Me,* 3 Dec. 1937.

Chapter 8

1 Entry of 27 Aug. 1919, in Mary Rubio and Elizabeth Waterston eds., *The Selected Journals of L.M. Montgomery* (Toronto: Oxford University Press 1987), 2:339-40.

2 NAC, W.D. Lighthall Papers, vol. 6, f. 28, 'Canadian Poets of the Great War,' presidential address to the Royal Society of Canada, Dec. 1918.

3 Quoted in George H. Locke, *Builders of the Canadian Commonwealth* (Toronto: Ryer-

son Press 1923), 251; *Canada at War: Speeches Delivered by Rt. Hon. Sir Robert Laird Borden before Canadian Clubs* (Ottawa 1915), 29.

4 Sir Robert Falconer, *The German Tragedy and its Meaning for Canada* (Toronto: University of Toronto Press 1915), 69; Lintern Sibley, 'Canada's Mighty Gains from the War,' *Canadian Magazine* 46, no. 2 (Dec. 1915):163-9; quoted in Joseph Levitt, *A Vision beyond Reach: A Century of Images of Canadian Destiny* (Ottawa: Deneau 1982), 66.

5 Frederic Yorston, *Canada's Aid to the Allies and Peace Memorial* (Montreal: Standard 1919), 52.

6 *Le Canada* (Montreal), 29 June 1938; QUA, C.G. Power Papers, box 88, address to Montreal Rotary Club, 10 Nov. 1937.

7 W. Burton Hurd, 'Is There a Canadian Race,' *Queen's Quarterly* 35, no. 5 (Autumn 1928):615; *Halifax Herald*, 2 July 1929, 4.

8 F.H. Underhill, 'The Canadian Forces in the War' in *The Empire at War,* ed. Sir Charles Lucas (Toronto: Oxford University Press 1923), 2:286.

9 Walter Brindle, *France and Flanders: Four Years' Experience Told in Poem and Story* (Saint John: S.K. Smith 1919), 83; Violet Alice Clarke, 'Our Fallen Heroes' in *The Vision of Democracy and Other Poems* (Toronto: Ryerson Press 1919), 79; Kitchener Daily Telegraph, *Peace Souvenir: Activities of Waterloo County in the Great War, 1914-1918* (Kitchener, ON: Daily Telegraph 1919), 13.

10 Calgary Branch GWVA, *Southern Alberta Yearbook* 3 (1919); quoted in Donald Avery, *Dangerous Foreigners: European Immigrant Workers and Labour Radicalism in Canada, 1896-1932* (Toronto: McClelland and Stewart 1979), 82; quoted in J.E. Rea, *The Winnipeg General Strike* (Toronto: Holt, Rinehart and Winston 1973), 84.

11 NAC, R.B. Bennett Papers, microfilm reel M-1463, f. W-126, Amputations Association to Arthur Sauve, Postmaster General, 1 Nov. 1932, 506333; quoted in John Bracher, 'A Living Memorial: The History of Coronation Park,' *Urban History Review* 19, no. 3 (Feb. 1991):214.

12 Ralph Connor, *To Him That Hath: A Novel of the West of Today* (New York: George H. Doran 1921), 197.

13 House of Commons, *Debates,* 2 June 1919, 3019; Norman Penner, ed., *Winnipeg 1919: The Strikers' Own History of the Winnipeg General Strike* (Toronto: James Lewis and Samuel 1973), 127; Chad Reimer, 'War, Nationhood and Working-Class Entitlement: The Counterhegemonic Challenge of the 1919 Winnipeg General Strike,' *Prairie Forum* 18, no. 2 (Fall 1993):224.

14 Reimer, 'War, Nationhood and Working-Class Entitlement.'

15 This argument is implicit in Penner, ed., *Winnipeg 1919,* 46.

16 Quoted in L. McLeod Gould, *From B.C. to Baisieux* (Victoria: Thomas R. Cusack 1919), 131.

17 *Municipal Review* (War Memorials Souvenir Number), 21, no. 11 (Nov. 1925):7; quoted in Daniel Dancocks, *Sir Arthur Currie* (Toronto: Methuen 1985), 227.

18 Quoted in review of 'Lucky 7,' *Saturday Night,* 5 Sept. 1925, 6.

19 House of Commons, *Debates,* 12 April 1926, 2355; NAC, W.L.M. King Papers, series J4, vol. 154, microfilm reel C-4255, 110906, 'National Unity and International Cooperation,' notes for cenotaph service, Canadian Corps reunion, 1938.

20 New Brunswick Department of Education, *The Canadian War Book, January 1919* (Fred-

ericton 1919), 1; quoted in Violet Elizabeth Parvin, *Authorization of Textbooks for the Schools of Ontario, 1846-1950* (Toronto: Canadian Textbook Publishers Institute 1965), 97.

21 Quoted in Parvin, *Authorization of Textbooks,* 97; foreword to Joseph Hayes, *The 85th in France and Flanders* (Halifax: Royal 1920).

22 New Brunswick Department of Education, *The Canadian War Book,* lvii; AO, 'The Thrift Campaign in the Schools of Ontario' (1919), 7.

23 PEIPA, T.E. MacNutt Papers, Accession 2825/335e, address at Spring Park School, 9 Nov. 1938.

24 Emily P. Weaver, *The Book of Canada for Young People* (Garden City, NJ: Doubleday, Doran 1928), 252.

25 W.J. Karr, *Explorers, Soldiers and Statesmen: A History of Canada Through Biography* (Toronto: J.M. Dent 1938); W.S. Wallace, *A History of the Canadian People* (Toronto: Copp Clark 1930), 326. This text, authorized for Ontario schools, went through twelve editions between 1930 and 1939.

26 'The Canadians at St. Julien' in *Famous Canadian Stories Re-told for Children,* ed. Leslie Horner and Donald G. French (Toronto: McClelland and Stewart 1924), 294-5.

27 Jean Bruchési, *L'Épopée Canadienne* (Montreal: Libraire Granger Frères 1934), 188. This text, authorized for use in Manitoba, went through four editions between 1934 and 1939.

28 W.S. Wallace, *With Sword and Trowel: Select Documents Illustrating 'A First Book of Canadian History'* (Toronto: Macmillan 1930), 186.

29 Kathleen Moore and Jessie McEwen, *A Picture History of Canada* (Toronto: Thomas Nelson n.d.), 99; Bruchési, *L'Épopée Canadienne,* 188.

30 D.J. Dickie and Helen Palk, *Pages from Canada's Story* (Toronto: J.M. Dent 1936), 424. This text for nine-year-olds went through ten editions between 1928 and 1939.

31 Karr, *Explorers, Soldiers and Statesmen,* 337.

32 *Legionary* 3, no. 5 (Oct. 1928):28; 4, no. 6 (Nov. 1929):25; 3, no. 12 (May 1929):30; 4, no. 11 (April 1930):30.

33 *Ontario Teachers' Manuals: Notes on the Ontario Readers* (Toronto: Ryerson Press 1926), ix-xiii.

34 Edmund Kemper Broadus and Eleanor Hammond Broadus, *A Book of Canadian Prose and Verse* (Toronto: Macmillan 1926). This text was authorized by the Alberta Department of Education. According to publisher's figures, over 16,000 copies were shipped to Alberta schools between 1923 and 1928. MU, Macmillan of Canada Records, production card file.

35 Details of the program can be found in PEIPA, Department of Education Records, vol. 26.

36 G.J. Reeve, *Canada: Its History and Progress, 1000-1925* (Toronto: Oxford University Press 1926), 351; Thomas P. Socknat, *Witness Against War: Pacifism in Canada, 1900-1945* (Toronto: University of Toronto Press 1987), 112.

37 Donald M. Page, 'The Development of a Western Canadian Peace Movement' in *The Twenties in Western Canada,* ed. S.M. Trofimenkoff (Ottawa: National Museum of Man 1972), 93; *Vancouver Daily Sun,* 11 Nov. 1937, 3.

38 Bennett Papers, microfilm reel M-1463, f. W-126, 506310, resolution from Amputations Association of the Great War, undated [1932]; MacNutt Papers, Accession

2825 / 336d, circular letter to schools in Charlottetown *Patriot,* 5 Nov. 1938.

39 Robert M. Stamp, 'Empire Day in the Schools of Ontario: The Training of Young Imperialists,' *Journal of Canadian Studies* 8, no. 3 (Aug. 1973):40.

40 Ontario Department of Education, *Annals of Valour: Empire Day, Friday, May 23rd, 1919* (Toronto 1919), 7; Manitoba Department of Education, *Empire Day, 1919* (Winnipeg 1919).

41 Edmonds's *Canadian Flag Day Book* remained a recommended book for teachers past September 1939. Ontario Department of Education, *Courses of Study, Grades IX and X: Social Studies – History* (Toronto 1939), 25.

42 'Canadian Educational Institutions in the Great War: V. Ridley College, St. Catharines, Ontario,' *Canadian Defence Quarterly* 4, no. 3 (April 1927):352; *Hamilton Spectator,* 23 Sept. 1925, 19.

43 MTRL, J.H. Stevenson, 'Presentation Exercises: Unveiling of a Tablet to the Boys of the Magnetawan District Who Took Part in the World War 1914-1918, August 12th 1919.'

44 George P. Graham at unveiling of Amherstburg, Ontario, memorial, quoted in *Border Cities Star,* 12 Nov. 1924, 2.

45 *Saturday Night,* 2 Aug. 1919, 32; Glenbow Museum, Inglis Sheldon-Williams Papers, box 1, f. 7, Harry McCurry to Sheldon-Williams, 8 June 1923; NAC, IODE Records, vol. 23, f. 8, 'Resolution regarding Educational Work,' 16 Jan. 1919.

46 Maria Tippett, *Art at the Service of War: Canada, Art, and the Great War* (Toronto: University of Toronto Press 1984), 102; A.Y. Jackson, 'War Pictures Again,' *Canadian Bookman* 8, no. 11 (Nov. 1926):340.

47 J. Castell Hopkins, *The Canadian Annual Review for 1922* (Toronto: Canadian Annual Review 1923), 322; Windsor Municipal Archives, Hon. James Baby Chapter IODE Papers, box 1, f. 4, minutes of meeting, 11 March 1924; *Daily Gleaner* (Fredericton), 10 Nov. 1923, 3.

48 W.G. Smith, *Building the Nation: A Study of Some Problems Concerning the Churches' Relation to the Immigrants* (Toronto: Canadian Council of the Missionary Education Movement 1922), 178.

49 Marilyn Barber, 'Canadianization Through the Schools of the Prairie Provinces Before World War I: The Attitudes and Aims of the English-Speaking Majority' in *Ethnic Canadians: Culture and Education,* ed. Martin L. Kovacs (Regina: Canadian Plains Research Center 1978), 283.

50 Introduction to Rev. Wellington Bridgeman, *Breaking Prairie Sod: The Story of a Pioneer Preacher in the Eighties* (Toronto: Musson 1920), xv; J. Murray Gibbon, 'The Foreign Born,' *Queen's Quarterly* 27, no. 4 (April-June 1920):331.

51 J.T.M. Anderson, *The Education of the New-Canadian: A Treatise on Canada's Greatest Educational Problem* (Toronto: J.M. Dent 1918), 229; J. Murray Gibbon, *Canadian Mosaic: The Making of a Northern Nation* (Toronto: McClelland and Stewart 1938), 315.

52 Smith, *Building the Nation,* 178; W.G. Smith, *A Study in Canadian Immigration* (Toronto: Ryerson Press 1920), 397, 399.

53 Robert England, *The Central European Immigrant in Canada* (Toronto: Macmillan 1929), preface.

54 Adolf Ens, 'The Public School Crisis Among Saskatchewan Mennonites, 1916-1925'

in *Mennonite Images: Historical, Cultural, and Literary Essays Dealing With Mennonite Issues,* ed. Harry Loewen (Winnipeg: Hyperion Press 1980), 78; J.M. Anderson, 'A True Story of Nation-Building,' *Educational Review* (Saint John) 35, no. 9 (April 1921):264-5.

55 Anderson, *The Education of the New-Canadian,* 256.

56 PANB, Milton F. Gregg Papers, vol. 2, f. 14, review of *I, That's Me,* 3 Dec. 1937; J. Murray Gibbon, *Drums Afar: An International Romance* (Toronto: S.B. Gundy 1918), 308-10.

57 Laura Goodman Salverson, *The Viking Heart* (Toronto: McClelland and Stewart 1947), 305, 325.

58 Britton Cooke, *The Translation of John Snaith* in *Canadian Plays from Hart House Theatre,* ed. Vincent Massey (Toronto: Macmillan 1926), 1:175-213.

59 NAC, Royal Canadian Legion Records, '3rd Dominion Convention, Regina, Saskatchewan, November 25th-28th 1929: Record of Proceedings,' 136; Patricia E. Roy, 'The Soldiers Canada Didn't Want: Her Chinese and Japanese Citizens,' *Canadian Historical Review* 59, no. 3 (1978):341-58.

60 James Dempsey, 'Problems of Western Canadian Indian War Veterans After World War I,' *Native Studies Review* 5, no. 2 (1989):1; Robert Craig Brown and Donald Loveridge, 'Unrequited Faith: Recruiting the CEF, 1914-1918,' *Revue internationale d'histoire militaire* 51 (1982):78.

61 W. Everard Edmonds, 'Canada's Red Army,' *Canadian Magazine* 56, no. 4 (Feb. 1921):341; NAC, Department of Indian Affairs Records, vol. 3211, f. 520,486, pt. 1, *Examiner* (Peterborough), n.d.

62 F. Douglas Reville, *History of the County of Brant,* (Brantford, ON: Hurley Printing 1920), 2:614; NAC, Cameron Brant Papers, letter to chiefs of Six Nations, 1 May 1915.

63 Ralph Connor, *The Sky Pilot in No Man's Land* (New York: George H. Doran 1919), 93; J.A. Holland, '"Adieu, Pierre,"' *Canada in Khaki* 3 (1919):41-3.

64 Indian Affairs Records, vol. 3211, f. 520,486, pt. 1, Belleville *Intelligencer,* 22 Nov. 1919; Edmonds, 'Canada's Red Army,' 341.

65 Stan Cuthand, 'The Native Peoples of the Prairie Provinces in the 1920s and 1930s' in *One Century Later: Western Canadian Reserve Indians since Treaty 7,* ed. Ian A.L. Getty and Donald B. Smith (Vancouver: University of British Columbia Press 1978); Peter Kulchyski, '"A Considerable Unrest": F.O. Loft and the League of Indians,' *Native Studies Review* 4, nos. 1&2 (1988):95-117.

66 Quoted in Edmonds, 'Canada's Red Army,' 342; Indian Affairs Records, vol. 3211, f. 527,787, pt. 1, circular letter from Loft to Native chiefs, 14 Nov. 1919.

67 Edward Ahenakew, *Voices of the Plains Cree,* ed. Ruth M. Buck (Toronto: McClelland and Stewart 1973; reprint, Regina: Canadian Plains Research Center 1995), 83-4. Ahenakew, from the Sandy Lake Reserve in Saskatchewan, created Old Keyam in the early 1920s to articulate his concerns for the future of Native Canadians.

68 Edmonds, 'Canada's Red Army,' 340-2; Indian Affairs Records, vol. 3211, f. 520,486, pt. 1, broadcast on Government Radio Station, Edmonton, 12 April 1930; GWVA to Scott, 8 March 1922, quoted in Dempsey, 'Problems of Western Canadian Indian War Veterans,' 10.

69 Duncan Campbell Scott, 'The Canadian Indians and the Great World War' in *Canada and the Great World War,* vol. 3, *Guarding the Channel Ports* (Toronto: United Publishers 1919), 327-8.

70 George G. Nasmith, *Canada's Sons and Great Britain in the World War* (Toronto: John C. Winston 1919), 111.

71 Arthur J. Lapointe, *Soldier of Quebec 1916-1919* (Montreal: Éditions Edouard Garand 1931), preface; TFL, Alfred Bienvenu, 'L'Oublié: à nos héros du 22e' (Montreal 1919).

72 John Beames, *An Army without Banners* (Toronto: McClelland and Stewart 1930), 243; CDC, #19.13, W.S. Atkinson, 'The Glory Hole: A Play of the Great War of 1914-1919' (Vernon, BC, 1930).

73 Yorston, *Canada's Aid to the Allies,* 52, 56.

74 J. Castell Hopkins, *Canada at War, 1914-1918* (Toronto: Canadian Annual Review 1919), 269, 294.

75 W.H.C. Wood, 'Behind the Scenes of Canadian War History,' *Argosy* 4, no. 1 (1926):42; Frank Carrel, *Our French Canadian Friends: Address delivered before the Canadian Society of New York, February 1920* (Québec: Telegraph 1920), 9.

76 Hopkins, *Canada at War,* 288, 302; W. Eric Harris, *Stand to Your Work: A Summons to Canadians Everywhere* (Toronto: Musson 1927), 10.

77 J. Squair, introduction to Lieut.-Col. L.G. Desjardins, *L'harmonie dans l'union* (Québec: Le Soleil 1919); C.W. Peterson, *Wake Up, Canada! Reflections on Vital National Issues* (Toronto: Macmillan 1919), 18.

78 Quoted in R.C. Fetherstonhaugh, *The Royal Montreal Regiment* (Montreal: Gazette 1927), ix-x; Armistice Ceremonial Committee of Canada, *Armistice Day Ceremonial* (Toronto: ACCC 1928), 3.

79 Dr. G.S. Gregoire, MPP, quoted in *Caduceus* 2, no. 6 (Sept. 1921):36; Canadian Pamphlet Collection, York University, 'Programme officiel du dévoilement du monument aux soldats du district de Rimouski morts à la guerre, le 24 septembre 1920.'

80 Pierre-Georges Roy, *Monuments commémoratifs de la province de Québec* (Quebec City: Commission des Monuments Historiques 1923), 1:313.

81 Quoted in ibid., 1:341.

82 NAC, Department of Militia and Defence Records, series III A1, vol. 99, f. 10-14-27, Willson to Perley, 8 Dec. 1917.

83 Beckles Willson, *Redemption: A Novel* (New York: G.P. Putnam's Sons 1924), 398-9.

84 Archibald MacMechan, 'Canada as a Vassal State,' *Canadian Historical Review* 1, no. 4 (Dec. 1920):352-3.

Conclusion

1 HPL, Clippings File, f. Armistice Day, Hugh John Maclean, 'Armistice Day, 1928,' undated.

2 *Minningarrit Islenzkra hermanne* (Memorial Book of Icelandic Servicemen) (Winnipeg: Jan Sigurdsson Chapter IODE 1923); *Toronto Daily Star,* 5 Nov. 1927, 5.

3 Quoted in Donald Avery, *Dangerous Foreigners: European Immigrant Workers and Labour Radicalism in Canada, 1896-1932* (Toronto: McClelland and Stewart 1979), 108; James H. Gray, *The Roar of the Twenties* (Toronto: Macmillan 1975), 258.

4 NAC, Department of Indian Affairs Records, vol. 3211, f. 527,787, pt. 1, Scott to Sir James Lougheed, 21 Feb. 1921.

5 Fred Gaffen, *Forgotten Soldiers* (Penticton, BC: Theytus Books 1985), 36-8.

6 Edward Ahenakew, *Voices of the Plains Cree,* ed. Ruth M. Buck (Toronto: McClelland

and Stewart 1973; reprint, Regina: Canadian Plains Research Center 1995), 103.

7 Benedict Anderson, *Imagined Communities: Reflections on the Origins and Spread of Nationalism,* rev. ed. (London: Verso 1991), esp. 145.

8 John Bodnar, *Remaking America: Public Memory, Commemoration, and Patriotism in the Twentieth Century* (Princeton, NJ: Princeton University Press 1992), ch. 1.

9 Crawford Kilian, 'The Great War and the Canadian Novel, 1915-1926' (MA thesis, Simon Fraser University, 1972), 13; Capt. J.W. Wilton, MLA, quoted in *Manitoba Free Press,* 9 April 1919, 5.

10 L.M. Montgomery, *Rilla of Ingleside* (Toronto: McClelland and Stewart 1920; reprint, 1973), 199.

11 Adrian Gregory, *The Silence of Memory: Armistice Day, 1919-1946* (Oxford: Berg 1994), 120-1.

12 House of Commons, *Debates,* 23 April 1926, 2757; John Pierce, 'Constructing Memory: The Idea of Vimy Ridge' (MA thesis, Wilfrid Laurier University, 1990), 30.

13 Thomas O'Hagan, 'Some Memories – Literary and Dramatic,' *Canadian Bookman* 8, no. 6 (June 1926):176-7.

14 Letter to *Canadian Bookman* 8, no. 9 (Sept. 1926):286.

15 *Evening Journal* (Ottawa), 8 March 1935; *Citizen* (Ottawa), 7 March 1935.

16 Letter to *Citizen* (Ottawa), 9 March 1935.

17 John Onions, *English Fiction and Drama of the Great War* (London: Macmillan 1990), 52.

18 Foreword to Lieut.-Col. D.S. Tamblyn, *The Horse in War and Famous Canadian War Horses* (Kingston, ON: Jackson Press n.d.).

19 Quoted in Alan Young, 'L.M. Montgomery's *Rilla of Ingleside* (1920): Romance and the Experience of War' in *Myth and Milieu: Atlantic Literature and Culture, 1918-1939,* ed. Gwendolyn Davies (Fredericton: Acadiensis Press 1993), 112.

20 Margaret W. Westley, *Remembrances of Grandeur: The Anglo-Protestant Elite of Montreal, 1900-1950* (Montreal: Libre Expression 1990), 126-7.

21 Graham Dawson, *Soldier Heroes: British Adventure, Empire and the Imaginings of Masculinities* (London: Routledge 1994), 282.

22 Raphael Samuel, *Theatres of Memory,* vol. 1, *Past and Present in Contemporary Life* (London: Verso 1994), 17.

Bibliographical Essay

S OCIAL MEMORY is a burgeoning field of historical enquiry at present, thanks in part to a number of fine theoretical studies that have appeared in recent years. On a general level, Paul Connerton's *How Societies Remember* (Cambridge: Cambridge University Press 1989) and James Fentress and Chris Wickham's *Social Memory* (Oxford: Blackwell 1992) are both handy for the specialist and accessible to the general reader. Similarly useful is Christopher Shaw and Malcolm Chase's *The Imagined Past: History and Nostalgia* (Manchester: Manchester University Press 1989), which raises important questions about the idealization of the past. Though they deal with a specific country, Michael Kammen's *Mystic Chords of Memory: The Transformation of Tradition in American Culture* (New York: Alfred A. Knopf 1991) and John Bodnar's *Remaking America: Public Memory, Commemoration, and Patriotism in the Twentieth Century* (Princeton: Princeton University Press 1992) are essential in grasping the essence of the struggle between private and dominant memory. Another important study is Jacques Le Goff, *History and Memory,* trans. Steven Rendall and Elizabeth Clamon (New York: Columbia University Press 1992).

Anyone interested in delving more deeply into the social memory of the First World War would do well to begin with the work of scholars of European history and literature who have raised issues and concepts that might be tested in any of the belligerent nations. Paul Fussell's *The Great War and Modern Memory* (Oxford: Oxford University Press 1975), which found in the First World War the source of many features of modern culture and literature, is indispensable and still a delight to read. Subsequent works that have followed in his footsteps include John Cruickshank's *Variations on Catastrophe: Some French Responses to the Great War* (Oxford: Clarendon Press 1982) and George Parfitt's *Fiction of the First World War: A Study* (London: Faber 1990). The critique of Fussell by Robin Prior and Trevor Wilson ('Paul Fussell at War,' *War in History* 1, no. 1 [March 1994]:63-80) should also be read.

Three other books have been particularly influential on my own research. A wonderful study that stresses the forces of newness and innovation unleashed by the war is Modris Ekstein's *Rites of Spring: The Great War and the Birth of the Modern Age* (Toronto: Lester and Orpen Dennys 1989). Samuel Hynes's *A War Imagined: The First World War in English Culture* (New York: Atheneum 1987) is an engaging account of the tension between modernism and traditionalism in Britain, while George Mosse's *Fallen Soldiers: Reshaping the Memory of the World Wars* (Oxford: Oxford University Press 1990) examines the drive to find a higher meaning in the war experience and to turn that experience into something positive and uplifting. All three books will repay the readers with concepts that can be applied to any nation's experience. Certain to be as influential in coming years is Jay Winter's *Sites of Memory, Sites of Mourning: The Great War in European Cultural History* (Cambridge: Cambridge University Press 1995), which argues that traditional frames of reference persisted in European society in the postwar era.

The interested reader can find many excellent studies on specific subjects I have touched upon. In each case, Canadians are beginning to address questions that have been raised by European and American scholars. By the same token, younger writers are beginning to question the conclusions of Fussell and his intellectual heirs, emphasizing the resilience of the old order to the change ushered in by the Great War. Regarding the war's impact on art, for example, Maria Tippett's *Art at the Service of War: Canada, Art, and the Great War* (Toronto: University of Toronto Press 1984) is a fine study of the Canadian War Memorials Fund, while Stuart Sillars's *Art and Survival in First World War Britain* (New York: St. Martin's Press 1987) examines attempts to make sense of the war using both modernist and traditional artistic vocabularies. Nigel Viney's *Images of Wartime: British Art and Artists of World War I* (Newton Abbot: David and Charles 1991) is a beautifully illustrated account of Britain's equivalent to the CWMF. Biographies of many of the war artists who worked for Canada are also available, either as monographs or in exhibit guides: Sylvia Antoniou, *Maurice Cullen, 1866-1934* (Kingston: Agnes Etherington Art Centre 1982); *James Kerr-Lawson: A Canadian Abroad* (Windsor, ON: Art Gallery of Windsor 1983); Dorothy M. Farr, *J. W. Beatty, 1869-1941* (Kingston: Agnes Etherington Art Centre 1981); Christine Boyanski, *Loring and Wyle: Sculptors' Legacy* (Toronto: Art Gallery of Ontario 1987); Rebecca Sisler, *The Girls: A Biography of Frances Loring and Florence Wyle* (Toronto: Clarke, Irwin 1972); Michael Holroyd, *Augustus John: A Biography* (London: Heinemann 1974).

There are also a number of excellent studies of war memorials. Robert Shipley's *To Mark Our Place: A History of Canadian War Memorials* (Toronto: NC

Press 1987) is a useful survey, while Alan R. Young's '"We throw the torch": Canadian Memorials of the Great War and the Mythology of Heroic Sacrifice,' *Journal of Canadian Studies* 24, no. 4 (Winter 1989-90):5-28 examines the use of a traditional artistic vocabulary in war memorials. Marilyn Baker has written a good case study in 'To Honor and Remember: Remembrances of the Great War: The Next-of-Kin Monument in Winnipeg,' *Manitoba History* 2 (1981):8-11. For the details of two failed memorial schemes in Canada, readers should consult the articles by Donald E. Graves ('The Proposed Saskatchewan War Memorial Museum, 1919-26') and R.F. Wodehouse ('Lord Beaverbrook's Plan for a Suitable Building to House the Canadian War Memorials) in *Organization of Military Museums of Canada Journal* 7 (1978-79). From European historians, perhaps the best is Pierre Nora's *Les Lieux de mémoire* (Paris: Gallimard 1984), a first-class collection of essays on French memorials of various eras; interested individuals should read Antoine Prost's superb essay 'Les Monuments aux morts: Culte républicain? Culte civique? Culte patriotique?' in Nora's first volume. The essays by Thomas Laqueur ('Memory and Naming in the Great War'), Kurt Piehler ('The War Dead and the Gold Star: American Commemoration of the First World War'), and Daniel Sherman ('Art, Commerce, and the Production of Memory in France after World War I') in John R. Gillis, ed., *Commemorations: The Politics of National Identity* (Princeton: Princeton University Press 1994) are also excellent. Another fascinating article by Daniel Sherman, 'The Nation: In What Community? The Politics of Commemoration in Postwar France' in *Ideas and Ideals: Essays on Politics in Honour of Stanley Hoffmann,* ed. Linda B. Miller and Michael Joseph Smith (Boulder, CO: Westview Press 1993), 277-95, discusses the ways in which memorials allowed local communities to express an identification with the nation. Marina Warner's *Monuments and Maidens: The Allegory of the Female Form* (New York: Atheneum 1985) is essential to interpreting sculptural symbolism, as are the essays in Ann Compton, *Charles Sargeant Jagger: War and Peace Sculpture* (London: Imperial War Museum 1985). Arnold Whittick, *War Memorials* (London: Country Life 1946) is a valuable discussion of the theories of commemoration, written at a time when Britain had another war to memorialize, and K.S. Inglis provides a fascinating case study in 'The Homecoming: The War Memorial Movement in Cambridge, England,' *Journal of Contemporary History* 27 (1992):584-605. In *War Memorials as Political Landscape: The American Experience and Beyond* (New York: Praeger 1988), James M. Mayo discusses the degree to which American memorials perpetuated traditional and nationalistic ideals. It is a somewhat different story than the one told by Jane Leonard, 'Lest We Forget' in *Ireland and the First World War,* ed.

David Fitzpatrick (Mullingar, Ireland: Lilliput Press 1988), 59-67, which recounts the sorry tale of the failure to complete Ireland's national war memorial.

For overseas burials and memorials, readers might start with Philip Longworth's *The Unending Vigil: A History of the Commonwealth War Graves Commission, 1917-1967* (London: Constable 1967) and T.A. Edwin Gibson and G. Kingsley Ward's *Courage Remembered* (London: HMSO 1989). Both are excellent summaries. Herbert Fairlie Wood and John Swettenham's *Silent Witnesses* (Toronto: Hakkert 1974) is a guide to Canadian war cemeteries, still useful but now superseded by Terry Copp's *A Canadian's Guide to the Battlefields of North-west Europe* (Waterloo, ON: Laurier Centre for Military, Strategic and Disarmament Studies 1995). Master's theses by John Pierce ('Constructing Memory: The Idea of Vimy Ridge' [Wilfrid Laurier University 1993]) and Dave Inglis ('Vimy Ridge, 1917-1992: A Canadian Myth over Seventy-Five Years' [Simon Fraser University 1995]) look at the evolution of Vimy Ridge into a national symbol. For a more scholarly examination, see George Mosse, 'National Cemeteries and National Revival: The Cult of the Fallen Soldiers in Germany,' *Journal of Contemporary History* 14, no. 1 (Jan. 1979):1-20. There are a number of excellent essays on the equivalents to Vimy Ridge. Antoine Prost's 'Verdun' in the third volume of Pierre Nora's *Les Lieux de mémoire* (Paris: Gallimard 1986), part 2, 111-41 outlines the transformation of Verdun from an event into a national symbol, while the chapter entitled 'The Myth of Langemarck' in Jay Baird's *To Die for Germany: Heroes in the Nazi Pantheon* (Bloomington: Indiana University Press 1990) looks at the same process in a different setting.

Armistice Day has also been the subject of a number of fine studies recently. Adrian Gregory's *The Silence of Memory: Armistice Day, 1919-1946* (Oxford: Berg 1994) examines the evolution of the day through the interwar period and a second world war, while two articles provide interesting insights from a theological viewpoint: Owen Chadwick, 'Armistice Day,' *Theology* 79, no. 671 (Sept. 1976):322-9, and Ronald Coppin, 'Remembrance Sunday,' *Theology* 68, no. 544 (Oct. 1965):525-30. Maureen Sharpe's 'Anzac Day in New Zealand, 1916 to 1939,' *New Zealand Journal of History* 15, no. 2 (Oct. 1981):97-114 argues that Anzac Day, like Armistice Day in Canada, was strengthened by criticism of it. Bob Bushaway's 'Name Upon Name: The Great War and Remembrance' in *Myths of the English,* ed. Roy Porter (Cambridge: Polity Press 1992), 136-67 contends that the language of remembrance pre-empted a political critique of the Great War, while David Cannadine's fine essay 'War and Death, Grief and Mourning in Modern Britain' in *Mirrors of Mortality: Studies in the Social History of Death,* ed. Joachim Whaley (New York: St. Martin's Press 1981), 187-242 looks at various responses, including Armistice Day and spiritualism, to the losses of the war.

Not enough work has been done on Canadian veterans. Clifford Bowering's *Service: The Story of the Canadian Legion, 1925-1960* (Ottawa: Canadian Legion 1960) is dated and uncritical, while Desmond Morton and Glenn Wright's *Winning the Second Battle: Canadian Veterans and the Return to Civilian Life, 1915-1939* (Toronto: University of Toronto Press 1987), though an excellent political and administrative history, is less helpful on the character and culture of the veteran movement. John Scott, '"Three Cheers for Earl Haig": Canadian Veterans and the Visit of Field Marshal Sir Douglas Haig to Canada in the Summer of 1925,' *Canadian Military History* 5, no. 1 (Spring 1996):35-40 disputes the antipathy that veterans supposedly held towards their former commander. My own article '"Today they were alive again": The Canadian Corps Reunion of 1934,' *Ontario History* 87, 4 (Dec. 1995):327-44 is similar in tone, stressing the veterans' positive recollections of their war experience. The best work has been done by European historians: Robert Weldon Whelan's *Bitter Wounds: German Victims of the Great War, 1914-39* (Ithaca: Cornell University Press 1984), and another superb study by Antoine Prost, *Les anciens combattants et la société française, 1914-39* (Paris: Gallimard 1977), 3 volumes. An abridged English version is available: *In the Wake of War: 'Les Anciens Combattants' and French Society, 1914-39* (Oxford: Berg 1992).

The best study of the impact of the war on those who experienced it at the front is Eric J. Leed, *No Man's Land: Combat and Identity in World War I* (Cambridge: Cambridge University Press 1979), a wide-ranging book that emphasizes the degree to which the war imprinted itself upon the soldier. In 'Soldiering and Identity: Reflections on the Great War,' *War in History* 1, no. 3 (Nov. 1994):300-19, David Englander takes issue with Leed and questions the degree to which the trench experience irrevocably altered the personalities of those who endured it. Desmond Morton's *When Your Number's Up: The Canadian Soldier in the First World War* (Toronto: Random House 1993) is an entertaining and well-researched account, while David Englander's 'The French Soldier,' *French History* 1 (1987):49-67 and Richard White, 'The Soldier as Tourist: The Australian Experience of the Great War,' *War and Society* 5, no. 1 (May 1987):63-77 are useful case studies with wider relevance than their titles suggest. An important study that appeared too late to be considered for my research is Jeffrey A. Keshen, *Propaganda and Censorship during Canada's Great War* (Edmonton: University of Alberta Press 1996).

A fascinating account of the writing of the official history is Timothy H.E. Travers's 'Allies in Conflict: The British and Canadian Historians and the Real Story of Second Ypres (1915),' *Journal of Contemporary History* 24 (1989):301-25. It can be usefully compared to Alistair Thomson's '"The Vilest Libel of the War": Imperial Politics and the Official History of Gallipoli,' *Australian Historical Studies* 25, no. 101 (Oct. 1993):628-36 and E.M. Andrews's 'Bean and Bullecourt: Weaknesses and Strengths of the Official History of Australia in the First World War,' *Revue internationale d'histoire militaire* 72 (1990):25-47. By the same token, D.A. Kent's '*The Anzac Book* and the Anzac Legend: C.E.W. Bean as Editor and Image-Maker,' *Historical Studies* 21, no. 84 (April 1985):376-90 characterizes Bean as less an official historian and more a myth maker. There is little to choose between the interwar histories of Canadian units. The best are Kim Beattie's *The 48th Highlanders of Canada* (Toronto: Southam Press 1932), E.A. Russenholt's *Six Thousand Canadian Men* (Winnipeg: 44th Battalion Association 1932), and H.M. Urquhart's *The Sixteenth: The History of the 16th Battalion (Canadian Scottish) in the Great War* (Toronto: Macmillan 1932). For a different glimpse at the writing of history, see Charles W. Humphries's 'The Banning of a Book in British Columbia,' *BC Studies* 1 (Winter 1968-69):1-12, a fascinating tale of how one textbook became a casualty of the war, falling victim to an outcry that accused it of being anti-British.

Readers interested in literary views of the war will find material in virtually any poetry or short story collection published in the interwar period. Of the memoirs, easily the best are Will Bird's *And We Go On* (Toronto: Hunter-Rose 1930) and James H. Pedley's *Only This: A War Retrospect* (Ottawa: Graphic Publishers 1927), but any of the others cited in the notes will provide an entertaining diversion. There are also many excellent studies by literary scholars. Peter Buitenhuis's *The Great War of Words: British, American and Canadian Propaganda and Fiction, 1914-33* (Vancouver: UBC Press 1987) is a useful examination that stresses disillusion as a literary theme, while theses by L.R.H. Steward ('A Canadian Perspective: The Fictional and Historical Portrayal of World War I' [MA, University of Waterloo 1983]) and Crawford Kilian ('The Great War and the Canadian Novel, 1915-1926' [MA, Simon Fraser University 1990]) survey the survival of traditional literary devices in the postwar years. Two of the more interesting critical studies are John Onions's *English Fiction and Drama of the Great War* (London: Macmillan 1990), which examines the curious ambivalence of war literature and its tendency to attempt both heroic approbation and moral denunciation, and Frank Field's *British and French Writers of the First World War: Comparative Studies in Cultural History* (Cambridge: Cambridge University Press 1991), which considers such matters as the lost generation thesis and the war as a rite of purification. Sharon Ouditt's *Fighting Forces, Writing Women: Identity and*

Ideology in the First World War (London: Routledge 1994) is an excellent study of the strict demarcation of the literary war into home and front, and Stanley Cooperman's *World War I and the American Novel* (Baltimore: Johns Hopkins University Press 1967), though dated, is still a valuable study. Robin Gerster's *Big-Noting: The Heroic Myth in Australian War Writing* (Melbourne: Melbourne University Press 1987), which argues that Australian war writers have been more interested in creating heroes than writing objectively about war, should be read in conjunction with K.S. Inglis, 'The Anzac Tradition,' *Meanjin Quarterly* 24, no. 1 (March 1965):25-44, which also examines the creation of 'the myth of the Digger.' One of the most provocative of the recent works is Rosa Maria Bracco's *Merchants of Hope: British Middlebrow Writers and the First World War, 1919-1939* (Oxford: Berg 1993), which examines the popularity of traditional views of the war in middlebrow (as opposed to Fussell's highbrow) fiction.

Readers interested in the churches' response to the war will find a number of books useful. Duff Crerar's *Padres in No Man's Land: Canadian Chaplains and the Great War* (Montreal: McGill-Queen's University Press 1995) examines the impact of war on the men who ministered to the troops, while Michael Gauvreau's *The Evangelical Century: College and Creed in English Canada from the Great Revival to the Great Depression* (Montreal: McGill-Queen's University Press 1991) and David B. Marshall's *Secularizing the Faith: Canadian Protestant Clergy and the Crisis of Belief, 1850-1940* (Toronto: University of Toronto Press 1992) are both useful overviews. For a comparative perspective, Albert Marrin's *The Last Crusade: The Church of England in the First World War* (Durham: Duke University Press 1974) is excellent.

Finally, a number of works on disparate topics deserve mention. Thomas P. Socknat's *Witness against War: Pacifism in Canada, 1900-1945* (Toronto: University of Toronto Press 1987), an impressive account of the pacifist critique of the war, is essential to understanding the Canadian context. David Lenarcic's doctoral thesis 'Where Angels Fear to Tread: Neutralist and Non-interventionist Sentiment in Interwar English-Canada' (York University 1991) surveys the views of one group of intellectuals who resisted the blandishments of the war myth. Terry Copp's 'Ontario 1939: The Decision for War,' *Ontario History* 86, no. 3 (Sept. 1994):269-78 is a useful counterpoint that considers the persistence of the just war theory on the eve of the Second World War. My own article, 'Tangible Demonstrations of a Great Victory: War Trophies in Canada,' *Material History Review* 42 (fall 1995):47-56, examines the way in which captured artillery pieces expressed contemporary views of the war. Douglas How's *One Village, One War, 1914-1945: A Thinking about the Literature of Stone* (Hantsport, NS: Lancelot Press

1995) is an idiosyncratic yet fascinating reflection on many of the questions I have considered, written by a man whose curiosity was piqued by the names on the war memorial in Dorchester, New Brunswick.

I have only been able to scratch the surface of the primary source material available for studying the memory of the First World War. The National Archives in Ottawa and the provincial archives all hold a broad range of relevant material, but university and local archives also yielded valuable sources. Some of the richer collections are the Will Bird Papers at Dalhousie University, the L.M. Montgomery Papers at the University of Guelph, the University of British Columbia Library's Special Collections, various collections in the Glenbow Museum in Calgary, the John McCrae Museum in Guelph, Ontario, (which has a particularly good collection of ephemera), the Canadian Drama Collection at Mount Saint Vincent University, and the J.D. Logan Papers at Acadia University. Local collections also proved to be very rich repositories, for most municipal museums and libraries have documents relating to local war memorials, Armistice Day observances, veterans organizations, and other manifestations of the memory of the war. Many of these collections constitute untapped resources for the historian.

In the interests of space, I have kept this essay (and the notes that precede it) as brief as possible. For more detailed notes and suggestions for further reading, I hope readers will consult the UBC Press website, http://www.ubcpress.ubc.ca.

Index

Set in Perpetua by George Vaitkunas

Printed and bound in Canada by Friesens

Copy-editor: Barbara Tessman

Proofreader: Gail Copeland

Designer: George Vaitkunas